Studies in the Industrial Revolution

Studies in the Industrial Revolution

PRESENTED TO

T. S. ASHTON

FELLOW OF THE BRITISH ACADEMY
EMERITUS PROFESSOR OF ECONOMIC HISTORY
IN THE UNIVERSITY OF LONDON

EDITED BY
L. S. PRESSNELL

UNIVERSITY OF LONDON
THE ATHLONE PRESS

First published by
THE ATHLONE PRESS
UNIVERSITY OF LONDON
at 2 *Gower Street, London* WC1
Distributed by Constable & Co Ltd
12 *Orange Street, London* WC2

Canada
Oxford University Press
Toronto

U.S.A.
Oxford University Press Inc
New York

© *Contributors* 1960

First printed in Great Britain, 1960, *by*
WESTERN PRINTING SERVICES LTD
BRISTOL
Reprinted by offset-litho, 1964, *by*
JOHN DICKENS & CO LTD
NORTHAMPTON

Preface

For the greater part of his academic life, Professor T. S. Ashton has combined the writing of economic history with the teaching of currency and public finance. Not until 1944 was he formally translated to economic history to enter into what Professor H. J. Habakkuk[1] has described as his 'extremely fruitful tenure of the London chair'. If this conjuncture has been happy, indeed fundamental to his unique impact upon the study of economic history, it has imposed restrictions upon a volume designed as a tribute both to Professor Ashton and to his work in this field. Inevitably, in seeking to produce a compact group of essays, we have had to exclude many who would have liked to honour him as friend, as counsellor, and as scholar; the one omission that it is fitting to record is that of the late A. P. Wadsworth, who had been warm in his encouragement of the project, but who died before he could turn to his own contribution.

In bringing together these studies to celebrate Professor Ashton's seventieth birthday, we have sought to encompass as far as possible the main topics which he has illuminated. These form something of a unity on the theme of the industrial revolution. The one exception is in all other respects the most appropriate essay, in view of Professor Ashton's earlier service in currency and public finance; this is the re-appraisal by Professor R. S. Sayers of the return to gold in 1925.

Much help has been freely given by the contributors and by others in the shaping of this book. Professor F. J. Fisher, Professor R. S. Sayers and Dr A. H. John have given advice on various points. Professor A. Redford gave encouragement at an early stage. Mr G. Woledge, Librarian to the British Library of Political and Economic Science (The London School of Economics), secured the essential collaboration of Professor Ashton

---

[1] 'The Eighteenth Century', *Ec.H.R.*, 2nd. ser., viii (1956), 434.

himself in checking the bibliography. As editor, I have been able to draw freely on the help of the officers of the Athlone Press. Finally, I owe thanks to my wife for her support in bearing the crosses which are an editor's lot.

January 1959   L.S.P.

Contributors

T. C. BARKER
Lecturer in Economic History, London School of Economics

W. H. CHALONER
Senior Lecturer in Economic History, University of Manchester

E. F. SÖDERLUND
Professor of Economic History, University of Stockholm

J. DE L. MANN
Formerly Principal of St. Hilda's College, Oxford

J. D. CHAMBERS
Professor of Economic History, University of Nottingham

A. H. JOHN
Reader in Economic History in the University of London, London School of Economics

D. M. JOSLIN
Lecturer in History in the University of Cambridge, Fellow of Pembroke College

L. S. PRESSNELL
Lecturer in Political Economy, University College, London

A. J. TAYLOR
Lecturer in History, University College, London

J. POTTER
Lecturer in Economic History, London School of Economics

H. HEATON
Formerly Professor of Economic History in the University of Minnesota

R. S. SAYERS
Sir Ernest Cassel Professor of Economics (with special reference to Money and Banking) in the University of London, London School of Economics

Contents

Contents

ILLUSTRATIONS

Abbreviations

Ashton, *Eighteenth Century*	T. S. Ashton, *An Economic History of England: The Eighteenth Century* (1955).
BMAM	British Museum, Additional Manuscripts.
BPP	British Parliamentary Papers. The references are given in the form adopted in the official catalogues. The number of the paper is inserted in parentheses between the year and the volume number. Thus, *BPP*, 1850 (1248), xxiii refers to paper no. 1248 of the parliamentary session of 1850, volume xxiii. The pagination cited is that of the original paper, *not* that of the volume, which may contain a number of separate papers.
CRO	County Record Office.
Ec.H.R.	*Economic History Review.*
E.H.	*Economic History*, supplement to the *Economic Journal.*
E.J.	*Economic Journal.*
J.E.H.	*Journal of Economic History.*
JHC	*Journals of the House of Commons.*
JHC(I)	*Journals of the House of Commons of Ireland.*
M.S.	*Manchester School.*
NBR	*Nottingham Borough Records.*
PL	Birmingham Public Library, Boulton and Watt Collection.
PRO	Public Record Office.

The Beginnings of the Canal Age in the British Isles

OUR knowledge of the early history of British canal building continues to be derived chiefly from the fascinating—even hypnotizing—pages of Samuel Smiles. The first volume of his *Lives of the Engineers*, containing what a most discerning historian has aptly termed 'the romance . . . woven round the career of James Brindley and his ducal patron',[1] is a classic in its own right, and is unlikely to be superseded as the most readable account of Brindley's career. But the care which Smiles lavished upon the description of Brindley himself[2] was not matched by an equally careful investigation of earlier developments in waterway engineering, during the years before his hero is made to burst so dramatically upon the scene. One would never guess from the pages of Smiles either that river improvement was far advanced technically by the middle of the eighteenth century, or that, in the quarter of a century before the opening of the waterway from Worsley to Manchester, two canals had already been built in the British Isles. 'Very little had as yet been done', he wrote, 'to open up the inland navigation of England, beyond dredging and clearing out in a very imperfect manner the channels of some of the larger rivers, so as to admit of the passage of small barges.'[3] It is true that he alluded, with an air of authority, to 'the usual contrivance of wears, locks and flushes' which formed part of some northern improvement schemes,[4] but this vague reference gives no indication of

---

[1] Alfred P. Wadsworth in Alfred P. Wadsworth and Julia de Lacy Mann, *The Cotton Trade and Industrial Lancashire, 1600–1780* (1931), p. 221.

[2] For a discussion of Smiles's sources and other available material, see W. H. Chaloner, 'Francis Egerton, Third Duke of Bridgewater (1736–1803): A Bibliographical Note', *Explorations in Entrepreneurial History*, v, no. 3, 15 March 1953.

[3] *Lives of the Engineers* (3 vols., 1861), i, 334.

[4] ibid., i, 304.

the extent of these improvements. The general effect of Smiles's writing is to leave the reader under the impression that the first part of the Bridgewater Canal, opened from Worsley to a point beyond Barton in 1761 and (we now know) not completed to Manchester until a few years later,[1] was something quite new to the country. Despite clear assertions to the contrary, published both before and after Smiles wrote[2]—in certain cases in books which he himself cites—his misleading account continues to be faithfully repeated. Smiles's story, in fact, lacks an historical introduction. The present contribution is an attempt to indicate some of the points which such an introduction might include.

I

Dr. Willan has shown, in his valuable work on English river navigations,[3] how superficial were Smiles's backward glances. As economic activity quickened from the later sixteenth century onwards, so the need for water communication became more widely felt. Many places, fortunate enough to stand upon stretches of navigable river, already had access by water to the coast and to all similarly situated parts of the British Isles. As trade grew—and particularly as the traffic in heavy and bulky goods grew—inhabitants of other areas, less favourably situated, began to agitate for water communication so that they, too, could enjoy the same advantages. Before 1750, all those places in England where such agitations were successful were situated upstream on rivers; their needs could be met by improving existing waterways. Such improvements sometimes involved

---

[1] In 1762 the canal was two miles from Manchester. On 30 September 1763, according to a Manchester correspondent of the *St. James's Chronicle*, the coal wharf was still a mile from the town; but when he wrote to that paper again, on 1 July 1765, the canal was completed to Castlefield. *The History of Inland Navigations, Particularly those of the Duke of Bridgewater* (2 vols., 1766), i, 38–41; Herbert Clegg, 'The Third Duke of Bridgewater's Canal Works in Manchester', *Transactions of the Lancashire and Cheshire Antiquarian Society*, lxv (1955), 94–95.

[2] For example, *History of Inland Navigations*, ii (1766), 33; R. Dodd, *A Short Account of the Greater Part of the Principal Canals in the Known World* (1795), p. 17; John Holt, *General View of the Agriculture of the County of Lancaster* (1795), p. 93; Edwin A. Pratt, *History of Inland Transport and Communication in England* (1912), pp. 166–7.

[3] T. S. Willan, *River Navigation in England, 1600–1750* (1936).

considerable feats of engineering. Pound locks had to be built to maintain water levels[1] and artificial channels dug to cut out awkward meanders. Admittedly, the problem of water loss was not so important in river navigations as in the later canals; and the river improver had not to grapple with the same problems of water supply and flood prevention as had the canal builder. Nevertheless, the river improvement phase did produce several skilled engineers[2] and their achievements deserve notice. The canal was not such a novel departure as is often supposed.

Outside the British Isles, in those countries not so well endowed with natural waterways, deadwater navigations were already functioning most satisfactorily long before 1750.[3] In particular, the Languedoc Canal, built in the later seventeenth century to link the Mediterranean with Toulouse, and, via the Garonne, with the Bay of Biscay, was a well-known object of pilgrimage, familiar to numbers of British travellers.[4] When, in the early eighteenth century, Defoe was urging the merits of a canal to join the Forth and Clyde, he referred the sceptical to 'those Gentlemen who have seen the Royal Canal of Languedoc from Narbon to Thoulouse, as many in Scotland have'.[5] The Scottish gentlemen, however, did not take up the challenge. The first canals in the British Isles were, in fact, to be built by

---

[1] The first use of the pound lock in England was on the Exeter Navigation, built about 1564. The shortness of this waterway limited its effectiveness, and some of the claims that have been made for it as an important forerunner of the canals of the eighteenth century seem rather extravagant. As De la Garde pointed out in his *Memoir* (*Proceedings of the Institution of Civil Engineers*, iv (1845), 90–114), it was impossible for a waterway a mere three or four miles long to compete satisfactorily with land carriage because of the cost of the double transfer of goods. Dr. W. B. Stephens in his article on 'The Exeter Lighter Canal, 1566–1698' (*Journal of Transport History*, May 1957, pp. 1–9) has confirmed this view, but makes the point that traffic grew very considerably after the canal's reconstruction in 1676. A later, and more important, improvement scheme, carried out at the turn of the century, resulted in a further increase in traffic, nearly 500 craft using the canal in the year 1750–1. (Charles Hadfield, *The Canals of Southern England* (1955), pp. 34–35).

[2] A. W. Skempton, 'The Engineers of the English River Navigations, 1620–1760', *Transactions of the Newcomen Society*, xxix (1953–4 and 1954–5), 25–54.

[3] For a useful account of these, see A. W. Skempton, 'Canals and River Navigations Before 1750' in Charles Singer and others (eds.), *A History of Technology*, iii (1957), 438–70.

[4] See, for instance, John Lough (ed.), *Locke's Travels in France 1675–1679* (1953), pp. 116, 128–30, 134, 138.

[5] Daniel Defoe, *A Tour Thro' the Whole Island of Great Britain*, ed. G. D. H. Cole (2 vols., 1927), ii, 755.

3

Thomas Steers, Liverpool's first dock engineer, and by his successor, Henry Berry.

II

The merchants of Liverpool in the eighteenth century were a forward-looking group of men, very much alive to the importance of constantly improving the communications and harbour facilities of their port. Liverpool's trade, which had started to show definite signs of growth in the later seventeenth century as its vessels reached out across the Atlantic, increased very much more rapidly during the wars of William and Anne. Important natural disadvantages, however, had to be overcome if this rate of development was to be sustained. The harbour was exposed to strong westerly gales, and these, together with the extremely strong tidal currents, often caused vessels to be torn from their moorings and wrecked.[1] Such dangers led the Liverpool merchants to consider the possibility of building a dock to shelter their shipping. At the beginning of 1708, Sir Thomas Johnson, a leading merchant at the port, sought the advice of George Sorocold, the most eminent British engineer of his day.[2] By October 1709 Sorocold had made the necessary survey, and estimates of expected costs had been worked out and approved by the Corporation.[3] An Act of Parliament was secured in 1710[4] and the Council decided to 'proceed to the makeing of the said Dock . . . in and upon the ground . . . as now sett out by Mr. Steers of the City of London, who is brought down on purpose . . .'.[5]

Most of the known facts about Thomas Steers have been published in a useful paper, based to some extent upon documents

---

[1] Thomas Baines, *History of the Commerce and Town of Liverpool* (1852), pp. 344–5.
[2] *The Norris Papers* (ed. Thomas Heywood), Chetham Society, ix (1846), 165. Much information about Sorocold's life and work will be found in F. Williamson, 'George Sorocold of Derby, a Pioneer of Water Supply', *Journal of the Derbyshire Archaeological and Natural History Society*, lvii (1936), 43–93, and in F. Williamson and W. B. Crump, 'Sorocold's Waterworks at Leeds, 1695', *Publications of the Thoresby Society*, xxxvii (1945), 166–82. Sorocold is a much neglected figure whose life and influence deserve closer study.
[3] Liverpool Record Office, Town Books, 7 March 1708/9, 5 October 1709.
[4] 8 Anne c. 12.
[5] Liverpool Town Books, 17 May 1710.

in the possession of one of Steers's descendants.[1] Little is known about his life prior to his arrival in Liverpool, but his marriage to a Rotherhithe woman and the birth of their first child at Rotherhithe in November 1699 have led to the inference that he may have gained engineering experience at the Howland Dock, the first commercial venture of its kind in the kingdom. There are subsequent indications that this may well have been the case.[2] Unfortunately, the records of the Duke of Bedford, upon whose land the dock at Rotherhithe was built, while making it clear that the man chiefly responsible for the dock's design and construction was John Wells, described in the records as a shipwright of Rotherhithe, make no mention of Steers which would enable his connexion to be definitely established.[3] What is beyond dispute, however, is that Steers built the dock at Liverpool and that he subsequently settled in the town, secured the post of dockmaster, speculated shrewdly in land in the neighbourhood, and soon found himself a prominent member of the Common Council. Liverpool thus had an experienced engineer living on the spot to whom it could turn for advice and assistance on technical matters.

It soon became evident that the continued growth of Liverpool's trade depended upon the opening up of its hinterland as well as the development of its harbour facilities, and Steers was called upon to suggest schemes for improving the rivers of south Lancashire and Cheshire. In 1712 he carried out a survey of the Mersey and Irwell on behalf of 'the gentlemen of Manchester', as he described them on the plan he produced. This plan included 'an Account of the rising of the water, and how many locks it will require to make it navigable'.[4] When an Act of Parliament was passed, in 1721, to authorize the Mersey-Irwell Navigation, Steers was named as one of the undertakers.[5]

---

[1] Henry Peet, 'Thomas Steers, the Engineer of Liverpool's First Dock. A Memoir', *Transactions of the Historic Society of Lancashire and Cheshire*, lxxxii (1930), 163–242, and reprinted as a pamphlet in 1932.

[2] S. A. Harris, 'Paradise Street, Liverpool: the Derivation of the Name', *Transactions of the Historic Society of Lancashire and Cheshire*, civ (1953), 143–4.

[3] I am indebted to Mr. D. Swann, of the University of Leeds, for this information. For the Bedford connexion with the Rotherhithe Dock, see Owen Manning and William Bray, *The History and Antiquities of the County of Surrey* (3 vols., 1804–14), i, 227.

[4] Baines, op. cit., p. 39.   [5] Wadsworth and Mann, op. cit., pp. 214, 219.

He was actively engaged in another project of the Bubble period, the scheme for making the river Douglas navigable from its mouth on the Ribble estuary up to the coalfield at Wigan, and had completed a lock and a bridge at Rufford before the collapse of the boom halted operations.[1] Liverpool interests were also concerned in plans to make the river Weaver navigable from Frodsham Bridge up to the saltfield at Winsford. Steers was one of the witnesses examined by the committee of the House of Commons which considered the Bill.[2] He again testified before a parliamentary committee in 1734, when further powers were obtained to extend the Navigation from Winsford (to which point it had just been opened) as far as Nantwich.[3] Apart from his work on the Douglas, we do not know to what extent Steers was involved, either actively or in a consultative capacity, in the eventual building of these navigations within Liverpool's sphere of influence. But this sphere of influence also extended westwards: Liverpool's trade lay across the sea, and particularly in Ireland. It was in Ireland that Liverpool's dock engineer was to spend much of his time between 1737 and 1742, actively engaged in a canal-building venture which deserves to be recognized as a significant forerunner of the Canal Age in Britain.

III

The Irish, and particularly the inhabitants of Dublin, were anxious to develop their own coal resources in order to reduce their dependence on British imports. This was especially true of the coal measures around Drumglass, County Tyrone, and near the north-west tip of the Irish coast, at Ballycastle, County Antrim. The development of coalmining at Drumglass at the end of the seventeenth century[4] was soon followed by demands for water communication between the nearby Lough Neagh and the coast at Newry so that this coal could be marketed at a competitive price in Dublin. The Irish House of Commons discussed

[1] ibid., p. 215.
[2] T. S. Willan, *The Navigation of the River Weaver in the Eighteenth Century* (1951), p. 18.
[3] Liverpool Town Books, 16 June 1737.
[4] W. R. Hutchison, *Tyrone Precinct* (Belfast, 1951), pp. 131–2.

the possibility of such a waterway in 1703. A certain Captain Francis Nevill had carried out a survey and it was estimated that a canal, suitable for twenty-ton vessels, could be built for £20,000.[1] The scheme, however, did not become practicable for

another quarter of a century, by which time coal imports from Britain had increased to an annual figure of 60,000 to 70,000 tons.[2]

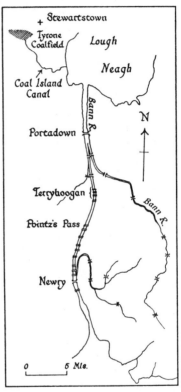

Legislation had been passed by the Irish Parliament in 1715 with the aim of encouraging land reclamation and inland navigation;[3] but its application depended upon the initiative of local M.P.s and magistrates, and, as no public funds were available to them, it is hardly surprising that little was achieved. In 1729, however, a measure was passed which replaced the unsubsidized and uncoordinated groups of local worthies by a much more businesslike central body of commissioners, empowered to spend the income from taxes specially earmarked for improvement purposes.[4] According to the commissioners, the annual yield of this taxation was £6,000 by mid-century. For the first nineteen years this income was devoted solely 'to the Works on the

The Newry Canal, opened
in 1742

[1] *JHC(I)*, ii, 388, 26 November 1703.

[2] *A List of the Absentees of Ireland . . . with Observations on the Present State and Condition of that Kingdom* (Dublin, 1729), p. 74. A committee of the Irish House of Commons investigated the high price of coal in Dublin in 1717 (*JHC(I)*, iii, 155, 160, 165, 170).

[3] 2 Geo. I c. 12 (Ireland), ineffectively amended by 8 Geo. I c. 6 (Ireland).

[4] 3 Geo. II c. 3 (Ireland).

great Canal from Newry to the Tyrone Collieries, during which time there was usually Savings upon it'.[1] Grants from other sources went towards constructing a harbour to serve the colliery at Ballycastle.

Work on the Newry Canal is said to have been begun in 1730.[2] From 1734 to 1736 it was under the direction of Richard Cassell, the leading architect in Dublin at that time and the writer of a paper on Artificial Navigation;[3] but apart from the fact that a stone lock was built, nothing is known of the amount of progress made before 1736 when Steers was called in to carry out a survey, for which he received fifty guineas. In the following year he entered into a contract to superintend the building of the canal for three summers, agreeing to spend four months in Ireland in 1737, and two months in 1738 and again in 1739. For these eight months' work he was to receive the handsome fee of eight hundred guineas.[4]

Towards the end of August 1737, a Dublin newspaper reported:

> By the last Letters from England, we have an Account that Mr. Steers, an Engineer of considerable Note, is set out for this Kingdom to finish the Canal at Newry, which it's reckon'd will be a very great Advantage to this Kingdom, with regard to furnishing this City with Coals, which we have hitherto had from Whitehaven etc. . . .[5]

A task more difficult than he had bargained for awaited Steers; he was away for seven months instead of four, and, at the end of the year, Liverpool Corporation was obliged to make a temporary appointment in his place, 'till Mr. Steers Return from Ireland'.[6] He came back early in 1738 to find a vast amount of work awaiting him. The existing dock accommodation at Liverpool was rapidly becoming inadequate and, while Steers had been away, Liverpool Corporation had approved a scheme,

---

[1] *JHC(I)*, vi, 93. Petition of 28 February 1758/9.

[2] *The Ancient and Present State of the County Down . . . with a Survey of the New Canal*, (Dublin, 1744), p. 113.

[3] *JHC(I)*, viii, appendix, p. ccxlix; M. B. Mullins, 'Historical Sketch of Engineering in Ireland', *Transactions of the Institution of Civil Engineers of Ireland*, vi (1859–1861); Maurice Craig, *Dublin 1660–1860* (1952), pp. 129–35. I owe these references to Dr. E. R. R. Green.

[4] Peet, op. cit., p. 184. [5] *Dublin Evening Post*, 20–23 August 1737.

[6] Peet, op. cit., p. 184; Liverpool Town Books, 30 December 1737.

which he himself had earlier proposed, to develop more land adjoining the existing dock and to build a pier to protect vessels as they lay at anchor. Now, on his return, Steers found he had to hurry off to London to support the Bill in parliamentary committee.[1] Then, on 7 June, just under three weeks after the Bill had become law, he was given charge of the whole undertaking at 'the same sallary as he . . . was allowed before on his makeing the present Wett Dock'.[2]

By the beginning of July, however, he was in Ireland again, and, in addition to supervising operations at Newry, gave general advice about the harbour works at Ballycastle, for which a public grant of £10,000 had been made towards the end of the previous year, after he himself had carried out a survey.[3] Again, Steers overstaycd his stipulated period in Ireland by three months, spending five months there instead of two. The same was true in the following year, 1739.[4] In October of that year further duties fell to him: he was elected Mayor of Liverpool. Although he contrived to be present for his election, the numerous adjournments of the Council between 18 October and 10 December tell their own story. The Newry Canal was still not finished, and he was obliged to spend a further two months in Ireland in 1740 and yet another four months in 1741.[5] Its completion was delayed by legal disputes. The *Dublin Journal* reported in its issue of 18–22 August 1741 that, although work had been stopped for two months because of the opposition of landowners, a settlement had just been reached—an event which 'occasioned a large Bonfire in Newry and great Rejoicing in all Parts of the Country'. The canal was open for traffic a few

---

[1] Liverpool Town Books, 7 June 1738. Evidence was heard on the Petition on 6 March. Several amendments were made in the committee stage and the Bill became law on 20 May. *JHC*, xxiii, 41–42, 59, 88, 105, 136, 140, 149, 163, 203; 1, 6, 14, 20 March, 7, 10, 14, 25 April, 20 May.

[2] Liverpool Town Books, 7 June 1738.

[3] *Dublin Evening Post*, 15–19 November 1737; 15–18 July 1738; 28–31 October 1738; *JHC(I)*, iv, 241–2, 244, 245; 10, 15, 16 November 1737 and appendix, pp. clxxxiii–cxcviii. For other information about the harbour and colliery at Ballycastle, see *A Letter from Hugh Boyd, Esq., of Ballycastle to a Member of Parliament on the Late Scarcity of Coals in the City of Dublin* (Dublin, 1750), and *JHC(I)*, v, appendix, p. xxviii (31 March 1750).   [4] Peet, op. cit., p. 184.

[5] ibid. Steers charged an additional £457. 10s over and above the eight hundred guineas for these extra months of work in Ireland. He also carried out a survey of the river Boyne, and received £30 in out-of-pocket expenses.

months later and, at the end of March 1742, the *Dublin News-Letter* announced:

> On Sunday last [28 March] the Cope of Loughneagh, William Simple Commander, came into this Harbour loaden with Coals, and being the first vessel that has come through the Canal, had a Flag at her Topmast Head, and fired Guns as she came up the Channel.[1]

Painted on the stern of the vessel was the motto: *Vincet Amor Patriae.*[2]

From the engineering point of view, the Newry Canal was a considerable undertaking.[3] It started from a lock to the south of Newry 'contrived to receive and shut out the Tide as Occasion may require' and ran for fourteen Irish miles (just under eighteen English miles by modern reckoning) up through nine other locks, reaching its highest level in a stretch between Poyntzpass and Terryhoogan. It then fell through five locks to Portadown where it joined the river Bann, which was navigable from there to Lough Neagh. At its northern limit the canal was 42 feet wide, but it was said to be 'something less' in other parts. Most of the locks were 15½ feet wide, 44 feet long and about 12 feet deep, and were built of hard stone brought from Benburb, County Armagh. Lough Shark, which lay just to the east of the canal on the high-level stretch, served as the main reservoir, though other streams also acted as feeders. Weirs were built at various points to dispose of any floodwater.

It is not to be wondered at that a canal, built on such a scale through gravel, blue clay, bog and marl, should soon have shown defects of construction. Winter floods breached the banks at places where the soil was loose and boggy. Part of the high-level stretch was so narrow—no doubt to conserve water—that two boats could not pass each other. Two of the locks, 'built from a French Plan . . . with Pipes in the Walls', often gave trouble when the pipes burst, and parts of these locks, built of brick, allowed water to seep through. A third lock had been made of common rough stone and it, like the two others, soon needed rebuilding. The reclamation of the bogs and marshes which fed

---

[1] Issue of 27–30 March 1742.   [2] *State of . . . Down*, p. 118.

[3] This description of the canal is based on *State of . . . Down*, pp. 115–19 and map; and Report from the Committee appointed by the Irish House of Commons, dated 31 March 1750 (*JHC(I)*, v, appendix, pp. xxvi, xxvii).

into Lough Shark resulted in 'a visible Decrease every Year' in the streams feeding that reservoir. By the summer of 1749 the canal was acutely short of water for several months.

Acheson Johnston, who described himself as Undertaker and Manager of the canal, told a committee of the Irish House of Commons in 1750 that £2,000 would be needed to remedy all its imperfections; but another witness went on to emphasize the great stimulus that its opening had given to coalmining in County Tyrone.[1] 'An English Gentleman of great experience in Coalmines', named John Fletcher, had joined a partnership with the Bishop of Down and others to work the collieries at Stewart's Town and Drumglass and had sent over colliers from Derbyshire to work there. He was confident that cheap water communication to Dublin justified this investment of capital. All in all, Thomas Steers, as he spent his last years working on the harbour improvements at Liverpool, must have been not dissatisfied with the results of his five seasons' work in Ireland.

He died in 1750, leaving behind a worthy successor who, like him, was to engage in canal building as well as harbour work. On 7 November 1750, Liverpool Corporation

Ordered that whereas Mr. Ald^n Steers is lately dead—that Henry Berey late Clerk to him who in the life time of the said Mr. Steers hath for some time past Overlooked the Work at the Docks be Continued to Oversee the said Works till further Order and the Dock Committee are to Agree with him for his pay.

Steers built the first large-scale canal in the British Isles: Berry was to build the first large-scale canal in England.

---

[1] *JHC(I)*, v, appendix, p. xxvii. Johnston was responsible for linking the Tyrone collieries with Lough Neagh. He was employed by the Commissioners to build a three-mile canal, rising through three locks, from the river Blackwater (ibid.). For an account of subsequent improvement of the waterway from Newry to the Carlingford Lough, see Sir John Rennie, 'On the Improvement of the Navigation of the River Newry', *Minutes of Proceedings of the Institution of Civil Engineers*, x (1850–1851), 277–93. In the course of this paper Rennie mentions the canal from Newry to the Bann (p. 281) but is under the impression that it was not built until the 1760s. See also Anthony Marmion, *The Ancient and Modern History of the Maritime Ports of Ireland* (4th ed., 1860), p. 124, the Second Report of the Commissioners on a General System of Railways for Ireland, *BPP*, 1837–8 (145) xxxv, appendix A, p. 74, appendix B, p. 60, and the report from Messrs. Henry, Mullins and M'Mahon printed in J. R. McCulloch, *A Statistical Account of the British Empire* (2nd ed., 1839), ii, 63.

IV

Henry Berry was born, in 1719 or 1720, some twelve miles to the east of Liverpool in the township of Parr.[1] His family's property lay near the southern perimeter of the coalfield in a district where a few small land-sale collieries were already yielding precarious profits, and, in addition to their farming interests, various members of the family were certainly connected with the mining and sale of coal by the middle of the eighteenth century.[2] The Berrys were Dissenters and the little we know about them is derived from the records of the local Independent chapel at St. Helens. Henry Berry himself became one of its trustees in 1742, soon after he had attained his majority, and his name appears again in later trust deeds drawn up in 1753 and 1788.[3] In a codicil to his will, added in 1808, he instructed his executors to see that after his death his body should be carried to St. Helens and laid to rest 'not in the Chapel where my parents are buried but in the Chapel Yard, as I would not have their graves opened'.[4]

Unfortunately, apart from one not very informative letter,[5] Berry's will is the only surviving shred of evidence about him written in his own hand or to his dictation. None of his memoranda books has yet come to light, though we know he left several of these at his death.[6] Nor, apart from a solitary obituary, was anything of a biographical nature published by any contemporary. It is out of the question, therefore, even to begin to

[1] Much information about Berry has been collected by Mr. S. A. Harris in his paper, 'Henry Berry (1720–1812): Liverpool's Second Dock Engineer', *Transactions of the Historic Society of Lancashire and Cheshire*, vol. lxxxix (1937) and in an additional note in vol. xc (1938).

[2] In 1758 John Berry was selling St. Helens coals in Liverpool and in 1759 and 1761 Peter Berry advertised the sale of a coalmine in the St. Helens neighbourhood (*Williamson's Liverpool Advertiser*, 5 May 1758, 29 June 1759, 26 June 1761). Peter and John Berry are the other two members of the family whose names appear in the records of the St. Helens Independent chapel. I owe the newspaper references to Dr. J. R. Harris.

[3] Records at the Congregational Church, St. Helens.

[4] Second codicil, dated 13 July 1807, to will proved at Chester, 5 August 1812, and now at the Lancashire Record Office.

[5] Willan, *Navigation of the River Weaver*, pp. 166–7.

[6] Liverpool Record Office, Todd Collection, K. 13024. Henry Berry, *post mortem* inventory and executorship accounts. I am grateful to Mr. H. A. Taylor, the Archivist, and Mr. S. A. Harris for drawing my attention to this source.

see him as a living person. We can only regard him as a mere name which appears in the records of the various activities in which he became involved.

The Parr township papers reveal that he was an overseer of the poor there in 1742 and surveyor of the highways in the following year.[1] His name continues to appear in these local records until 1747. By the end of 1750, as we have seen, he had established himself as Steers's right-hand man. How long he had served under Steers, it is impossible to deduce from the evidence at present available. It would seem unlikely that he was in Liverpool in 1742 and 1743; but the Parr Poor Law references to him after 1743, chiefly as an intermediary selling clothing to the overseers, might well indicate that he had by then removed to Liverpool. Of the reasons for his move or his early training, we know nothing.

Berry arrived in Liverpool at a time when the need to improve communications was attracting widespread interest in Lancashire. The early 'fifties of the eighteenth century, a period of cheap money, saw renewed interest in transport development.[2] Liverpool became particularly concerned with reducing the cost of bringing coal from the collieries in its hinterland, some ten miles away. Improved access to the nearest of these collieries had been obtained, during the 'twenties, by turnpiking the road to Prescot, and this turnpike had been extended to St. Helens under an Act passed in 1746.[3] In order to extend it still further, the Trust obtained a third Act, in 1753, permitting them to turnpike the roads from St. Helens to Ashton-in-Makerfield and from Prescot to Warrington. To meet the cost of these extensions, tolls were increased on the existing stretches, much to the disgruntlement of consumers of coal in Liverpool. Their annoyance was increased still further by the decision of the proprietors of Prescot Hall Colliery, the nearest colliery to Liverpool, to advance their pithead prices by 20 per cent in order to pay for

[1] These papers are in the St. Helens Reference Library.

[2] Wadsworth and Mann, op. cit., p. 220.

[3] For this turnpike, see the late F. A. Bailey's valuable paper on 'The Minutes of the Trustees of the Turnpike Roads from Liverpool to Prescot, St. Helens, Warrington and Ashton-in-Makerfield, 1726–89', *Transactions of the Historic Society of Lancashire and Cheshire*, vols. lxxxviii and lxxxix (1937 and 1938). The rest of the paragraph is based on this source.

an atmospheric pump they had just installed.[1] Liverpool had endured the irregular and unsatisfactory supply of coal for long enough. When the price was advanced without any improvement in deliveries, what had been an irritating hardship became an intolerable imposition.

It so happened that, at this juncture, the needs of the inhabitants and industrial users of the port of Liverpool coincided with the needs of the powerful salt interest. Salt was a most valuable cargo for freighting outgoing vessels and, from its rise at the close of the seventeenth century, Liverpool had been very much concerned with securing a constantly expanding output of Cheshire salt.[2] It was the relentless pressure from Liverpool that had led in the 'thirties to the improvement of the river Weaver, a tributary of the Mersey, in order to secure direct water communication between the saltfield and the port. More and more salt was carried down this river, but the increase in output called for ever-increasing supplies of coal, and these had to be brought mainly from south Lancashire. These loads had to be carried overland from the collieries to the Mersey, some five miles or so, before being put on to sailing barges bound for the saltworks. By the early 'fifties nearly 10,000 tons made this costly journey every year—almost four times as much as had been carried twenty years earlier.[3] As most of it went by packhorse on the overland stretch, it is not difficult to imagine the kind of fuel crisis that was threatening the continued expansion of the salt trade. The Liverpool salt interests, like the rest of the town's inhabitants, were seeking an alternative form of transport to replace the existing arrangements for carrying coal. If, at the same time, access could be had to those parts of the coalfield which still awaited development, thereby breaking the virtual monopoly of the existing pits, this would be an additional advantage.

The improvement of the Weaver had served its purpose very

---

[1] Letter from the Vicar of Prescot to the Provost of King's College, Cambridge, 7 April 1759. The late F.A. Bailey drew my attention to this source and lent me a transcript.

[2] T. C. Barker, 'Lancashire Coal, Cheshire Salt and the Rise of Liverpool', *Transactions of the Historic Society of Lancashire and Cheshire*, vol. ciii (1951).

[3] This figure is based upon shipments of coal up the Weaver (Willan, *Navigation of the River Weaver*, pp. 39–40).

effectively. It was quite natural, therefore, that when the Liverpool interests turned their attention to cutting out overland transport on the Lancashire side of the Mersey, they should consider the possibility of extending their existing Mersey-Weaver waterway up to the coalfield. Sailing barges could then carry coal direct from the collieries to the saltworks, take a cargo of salt to Liverpool, and then return to the coalfield once more. It was natural, too, that when the Liverpool interests decided to investigate the possibilities of such a waterway, they should turn to their Dock Engineer, who had himself grown up on precisely that part of the coalfield which it was proposed to open up.[1] There was a stream flowing from there to the Mersey, which was called the Sankey Brook or, at its southerly end, the Dalham Brook. The first step was to explore the possibility of making this brook navigable, as had been done with the river Weaver.

On 5 June 1754, Liverpool Corporation decided that 'the Brooke commonly called Dalham Brooke which emptys itself near Sankey Bridges' should be surveyed, at the Corporation's expense, by two 'able and skilful' men, they 'having first obtained the Licence of the principal Gentlemen or Land owners of the ground on each side of the . . . Brooke'.[2] The survey, which Henry Berry carried out with William Taylor,[3] must have convinced the Corporation that a waterway up to the coalfield was a practical possibility for, on 25 October 1754, the

---

[1] In the *post mortem* inventory of Berry's papers (at the Liverpool Record Office) are references to the Boyne Navigation, though no date is given. The Irish navigation commissioners turned their attention to the Boyne in the early 1750s and, by 1759, work—chiefly, and perhaps wholly, river improvement—was completed for most of the way from Drogheda to Trim (*JHC(I)*, vi, 134, petition from Drogheda, 6 April 1759). If Berry was concerned in this, he had river improvement experience before he built the Sankey. This would also be true if he had assisted Steers with the improvement of the Boyne from Drogheda to the sea, which Steers had surveyed in 1736 and supervised 'about the year 1740 and at different Times since' (ibid.). On the other hand, Berry's connexion with the Boyne could have been with the later improvements of the river (*JHC(I)*, xix, appendix, pp. mxxxi, mxxxiii). The Liverpool Town Books make no reference to Berry's being given leave of absence to go to Ireland during the 1750s.

[2] Liverpool Town Books.

[3] *JHC*, xxvii, 102, 17 January 1755. This was probably the 'Mr. Taylor' who surveyed the Salford-Wigan project prior to February 1754 (ibid., xxvi, 944, 4 February 1754). He may also be identified with the 'Messrs. Taylors of Manchester' who carried out a survey between the Trent and Mersey in the following year (*The History of Inland Navigations*, i (1766), 55).

Corporation decided to lend £300 towards securing the necessary Act of Parliament, to be refunded if the Act was secured but not otherwise. An advertisement appeared in *Whitworth's Manchester Magazine* on 29 October (Liverpool not yet possessing a paper of its own) giving notice that subscriptions for the 120 shares in the proposed navigation would be accepted at the Mayor's office in the Liverpool Exchange between 11 o'clock in the morning and 1 o'clock in the afternoon on 14 November and subsequent days. Subscribers were to contribute to John Ashton and John Blackburne an initial £5 per share towards securing the Act.

The official support of Liverpool Corporation for this venture—by sponsoring the survey, backing the application to Parliament, and placing the Mayor's office at the disposal of the promoters—reflected its domination by the merchants. Of the five merchants who first petitioned Parliament for permission to introduce the Bill, James Crosbie was Mayor, Charles Goore was to be Mayor, and Richard Trafford was to be Mayor's Bailiff, in the following year, while John Ashton had been Town Bailiff in 1749. The fifth petitioner, John Blackburne, was to join the Council in the following year and to be Mayor in 1761. Of the five, Ashton and Blackburne were the leading promoters. Both of them owned salt refineries on the Mersey, Ashton at Dungeon, near Hale,[1] and Blackburne in Liverpool itself. Ashton was undoubtedly the leading spirit. He advanced the money for the original survey,[2] and a few days before his death in August 1759 he was able to bequeath to his children 51 of the 120 Sankey Canal shares.[3] He was financer-in-chief of the undertaking, and, as we shall see presently, its successful completion owed much to his support of Berry's decision to depart from the traditional method of river improvement and to embark upon a deadwater navigation.

[1] Lancashire Record Office, will of John Ashton dated 22 November 1753 and proved at Chester, 29 July 1760. He had almost certainly acquired these saltworks when they were put up for auction in 1746 (*Adams Weekly Courant*, 9 December 1746, quoted by Arthur C. Wardle in 'Some Glimpses of Liverpool During the First Half of the Eighteenth Century', *Transactions of the Historic Society of Lancashire and Cheshire*, xcvii (1945), 150).

[2] Liverpool Town Books, 2 March 1757. The Corporation subsequently honoured its promise to pay for the survey.

[3] Lancashire *CRO*, codicil to will of John Ashton proved 29 July 1760.

The Beginnings of the Canal Age in the British Isles

The promoters' petition to Parliament pointed out that the Sankey Brook was already navigable for half a mile or so from its mouth to Sankey Bridges on the Prescot–Warrington road. If the navigation could be continued upstream so far as the coalfield, this 'would contribute greatly to the supplying of the towns of Liverpool . . . and Northwich . . . and parts adjacent with coal for carrying on the trade, manufactories and other necessary occasions of the inhabitants . . .'.[1] On the following day a favourable petition was presented from the merchants, industrial users and inhabitants of Liverpool, and, a little later, an equally enthusiastic petition arrived from the landowners and coal proprietors on the upper stretches of the Sankey.[2] Berry and Taylor testified before a committee that the venture was practicable[3] and there were no hostile petitions. The Bill became law on 20 March 1755[4] and on 7 May Liverpool Corporation resolved:

That liberty be given to Mr Berry for Two days a week to Attend the making Sankey Brooke Navigable—he providing and paying a skilfull person to superintend the works of the docks in his absence—to be approved by the Council.

There would seem to be little doubt that the Bill would not have had such a smooth passage through Parliament had Berry's real intentions been generally known. The Sankey was only a meandering brook. It could never have been made navigable. But to have stated this before work began would have placed the whole scheme in peril, for many who would support a river improvement scheme along traditional lines would have held back at the prospect of a deadwater navigation. A scheme for such a canal, from Salford to Leigh and Wigan, intended to provide Manchester and Salford with a better supply of coal, had, in fact, been thrown out by Parliament during the previous session.[5] There were good reasons, therefore, for the Sankey

[1] *JHC*, xxvii, 53, 16 December 1754.
[2] ibid., 55–56, 144; 17 December 1754, 7 February 1755.
[3] ibid., 102, 17 January 1755.
[4] 28 Geo. II c. 8.
[5] *JHC*, xxvi, 905, 944, 960, 969, 972–3, 977; 18 January, 4, 18, 25, 28 February, 5 March 1754. See also V. I. Tomlinson, 'Salford Activities connected with the Bridgewater Navigation', *Transactions of the Lancashire and Cheshire Antiquarian Society*, lxvi (1956), 57–58.

scheme to appear as just another river improvement. The Bill, of course, included the usual clause which permitted the under-takers to 'make such new cuts . . . as they shall think proper and requisite'; and this clause allowed them to make the whole waterway as one long cut. As a writer was to explain later:

after an attentive survey, he [Berry] found the measure [making the Brook navigable] impracticable and, knowing that the object they had in view could be answered by a canal, he communicated his sentiments to one of the proprietors [John Ashton] who, approving the plan, the work was commenced on 5 September 1755, but the project was carefully concealed from the other proprietors, it being apprehended that so novel an undertaking would be met with their opposition.[1]

It is difficult to know how much reliance should be placed on this later statement, though the wording of the petitions to Parliament, and the Act itself, all support the idea of a subterfuge. Contemporaries may have been deceived for a time. Subsequent historians, however, depending on parliamentary evidence rather than local records, have been permanently misled.

Although details survive of arrangements for providing compensation to landowners,[2] there is no known account of the actual building of the canal, nor any references to its building in any contemporary newspaper. We know no more of the problems which confronted Berry as he directed operations on the Sankey than we do about Steers's difficulties near Newry. The canal had no formal opening, but on November 1757—just over two years after work had begun—the *Liverpool Chronicle* carried the news that 'Sankey Brook Navigation is now open for the passage of flats [barges with sails] to the Haydock and Parr collierys'. The canal, from Sankey Bridges northwards, was then about seven miles long and rose some sixty feet through eight locks. A further three miles and a ninth lock remained to be built to serve other collieries in the St. Helens area. A plan of 1763, based on a survey made in 1759, shows that the northern end of the canal was completed by 1759 and a branch off this

---

[1] Obituary of Henry Berry in the *Liverpool Mercury*, 7 August 1812.
[2] Estate Manager's Office, Euston Station, London, Articles of Arbitration between the landowners of Parr, etc. and the proprietors of the Sankey Navigation, dated 9 December 1756.

northern stretch was half way to completion.[1] In all, £155 was called up on each of the 120 shares, making a total investment of £18,600.[2]

The canal provided a waterway five feet in depth and was navigated by sailing barges of about 35 tons.[3] The streams feeding into the Sankey Brook were tapped to supply the canal, which was built at a higher level than the brook so that floodwater could be taken off by weirs and sluice gates. The brook thus fulfilled a twofold function of water supply and flood prevention.

Although this stretch of canal from Sankey Bridges northwards later gave rise to criticism,[4] this was chiefly on grounds of inadequate maintenance and did not reflect upon Berry's engineering ability in any way. From the economic point of view, the new waterway was an outstanding success. By the spring of 1758, coal, loaded on flats in the canal at 4s 2d per ton of 30 cwt., was sold in Liverpool at 7s to vessels in the river and 7s 6d to householders.[5] By 1770, the total tonnage carried down the canal—chiefly coal—was nearing the 100,000 mark,[6] and important new industries were about to be attracted to the coalfield.[7] Shareholders appear to have reaped a rich return on their investment. It was later estimated that the annual dividend during the first eighty years of its existence averaged 33⅓ per cent.[8]

In 1762, when a second Act was secured to cut out the remaining navigable portion of the brook, by extending the canal south-westwards from Sankey Bridges to the Mersey,[9] Berry

---

[1] Estate Manager's Office, Euston Station, London, 'A Plan of the Sankey Navigation from the River Mersey into the Townships of Parr and Windle in the County of Lancaster. Survey in April and May 1759 by John Eyes and Thomas Gaskell and Plan by John Eyes in July 1763.'

[2] *PRO*, P.L.6.84/3. Dispute over shares bought by Edmund Rigby.

[3] T. Pennant, *A Tour from Downing to Alston Moor* (made in 1773), (1801), p. 19.

[4] J. R. Harris, 'Liverpool Canal Controversies, 1769–1772', *Journal of Transport History*, May 1956, pp. 158–72.

[5] *Williamson's Liverpool Advertiser*, 16 December 1757; *Liverpool Chronicle*, 6 January 1758, 17 April 1758.   [6] Parliamentary Return, 1771.

[7] T. C. Barker and J. R. Harris, *A Merseyside Town in the Industrial Revolution* (1954), pp. 23 ff.

[8] House of Lords Record Office, evidence given by Thomas Case to a Parliamentary Committee in 1829, quoted by L. W. Evans to a Select Committee on the St. Helens Railway (Transfer) Bill, 1864.   [9] 2 Geo. III c. 56.

was replaced by another engineer, John Eyes. By that date his outstanding achievement in Lancashire had been completely neutralized by accident and failure in Cheshire.

The Liverpool interests, in promoting the Sankey Canal, had always looked upon it as complementary to the Weaver Navigation. The new waterway was to make possible an internal

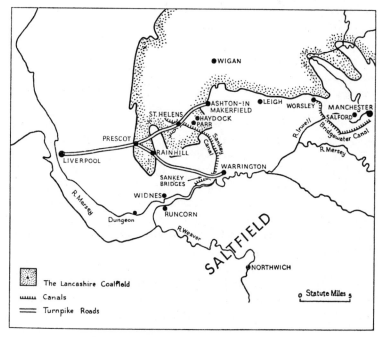

The Sankey and Bridgewater Canals in the early 1760s

triangular trade between Liverpool, the coalfield and the salt-field. When, in the summer of 1757, the canal was almost ready to carry traffic, Liverpool began to put pressure upon the trustees of the Weaver to undertake certain additional improvements to their river so as to bring it into conformity with the specifications of the Sankey Canal, which was a five-foot navigation.[1] This pressure was effective and the Liverpool

[1] Willan, *Navigation of the River Weaver*, p. 54; J. A. Picton, *City of Liverpool Municipal Archives and Records* (1886), ii, 145–6.

interests were soon able to instruct their Dock Engineer to take charge of the necessary alterations. Berry was looked upon in Cheshire as Liverpool's agent,[1] and the Cheshire men were only too glad to make the most of Berry's misfortunes when, in the spring of 1759, a freshet in the river breached a newly-made cut and the collapse of underground salt workings caused a lock to be destroyed.[2] Whether or not Berry could have been expected to take precautions against such eventualities, it is difficult to judge; but there are other indications that, while competent to deal with easy-flowing streams and brooks, he lacked experience in dealing with the problems to which river currents gave rise. After a weir for which he had been responsible had been entirely washed away, it was thought 'imprudent to employ him any longer'.[3] This decision appears to have been made just before the end of the year 1759. It may be relevant, therefore, to notice that in August of that year, with the death of John Ashton, Berry lost his staunchest and most influential supporter.[4] He returned to his job at the Liverpool docks, discredited as a canal engineer at precisely the time when Brindley's star was rising.

Berry nevertheless continued to command confidence as a dock engineer and was given charge of further extensions to Liverpool's dock system which were authorized in 1762, at the close of the Seven Years War. These included the construction of a third dock—the George's—which was completed in 1771.[5] Four years later, in 1775, he was called in as consultant by the promoters of a dock at Hull.[6] He was still in charge at Liverpool in 1785 when plans for the King's and Queen's docks were approved, and only resigned his office at the end of 1788, shortly after the King's dock had been opened.[7] He lived on in

[1] Willan, op. cit., p. 186.

[2] ibid., pp. 58–59.   [3] Ibid., p. 81.

[4] *Williamson's Liverpool Advertiser*, 10 August 1759.

[5] S. A. Harris, 'Henry Berry (1720–1812): Liverpool's Second Dock Engineer', *Transactions of the Historic Society of Lancashire and Cheshire*, lxxxix (1937), 98–101.

[6] Hull Dock Company, Letter Book A, 3 February, 20 August 1775; Sir William Wright, 'The Hull Docks', *Minutes of the Proceedings of the Institution of Civil Engineers*, xli (1875), 86. I owe the former reference to Mr. G. Jackson, of the University of Hull, and the latter to Professor A. W. Skempton.

[7] *Gore's General Advertiser*, 25 December 1788; Liverpool Town Books, 19 February 1789; Harris, op. cit., p. 103. In 1785 Berry had surveyed the Straits of Menai in connexion with a plan to build a bridge from the mainland to Anglesey (*Gore's General Advertiser*, 14 July 1785).

retirement to the good age of 92 and, at the time of his death, was enjoying an income of £1,000 a year. He left a personal estate worth £17,440 and a considerable amount of property.[1] Among his bequests was a silver cup which had been given to him by 'the Proprietors of the Sankey Brook Canal Navigation'.

V

The fact that two canals were built in the British Isles before 1761 in no way detracts from the achievement of Brindley's first waterway. His aqueduct at Barton and underground tunnel at Worsley deservedly caught the public imagination. Yet the previous deadwater navigations built by Steers and Berry, unspectacular though they may have been, ought not to be completely eclipsed by Brindley's outstanding achievement. They may, indeed, help to explain Brindley's success. How much did Brindley know about these earlier canals before he embarked upon his own? As Smiles has emphasized, one of Brindley's main characteristics was his inquiring mind. Is he likely to have planned his own undertaking without having first acquainted himself with the main features of Berry's recently-opened canal only a dozen miles away? Certain similarities between the two—such as the use of clay puddle and of sidelong ground—would suggest not. And did any of those employed in building the Sankey later serve Brindley and give him helpful advice? These are questions to which Brindley's own memoranda books give no answer.[2] It would seem remarkable, however, if there were no link at all between the achievements of the professional engineers and the early efforts of the gifted millwright who was so soon to outshine them all. The missing introduction to Smiles's account adds perspective to the early part of James Brindley's canal-building career and may, perhaps, make his sudden success the more comprehensible.[3]

[1] *Post mortem* inventory and executorship accounts.

[2] Of these, one is to be found in the Library of the Institution of Civil Engineers and the other in Birmingham Reference Library.

[3] Dr. W. H. Chaloner, Mr. Charles Hadfield, Dr. J. R. Harris, Mr. S. A. Harris, Mr. J. Potter, Dr. L. S. Pressnell, Dr. T. S. Willan, and Professor M. J. Wise kindly read this paper while it was in manuscript. I am grateful to them for their comments and suggestions, and to Dr. K. H. Connell and Dr. E. R. R. Green for helping me to grapple with the uncertainties of Irish history.

II

Isaac Wilkinson, Potfounder

MUCH has been written about the achievements and eccentricities of John Wilkinson, the eighteenth-century ironmaster whose friendship and co-operation with Boulton and Watt facilitated to an enormous degree the economic use of Watt's steam-engine patents. The exploits of John's brother William in France and Prussia are also fairly well known. Yet Isaac Wilkinson, the father of these two remarkable men, has remained a somewhat shadowy figure, although his famous sons obviously owed a great deal to his technical skill as a metallurgist and his persistence and ingenuity as an inventor.[1] In Isaac's early years the process of smelting iron ore with charcoal was still unchallenged by Darby's discovery of the secret of substituting coke as the fuel in the blast furnace (1709). As his life drew to a close the inventions of Henry Cort and Peter Onions were about to render obsolete the remaining British charcoal-fired blast furnaces. In this revolution Isaac Wilkinson had played, directly and indirectly, an important part.

Considerable obscurity surrounds both the birth and the last years of Isaac, the father of the famous eighteenth-century ironmaster, John Wilkinson. His place and date of birth are as yet unknown, but he was probably born about 1704, as he appears to have married and begotten at least two sons between 1724 and 1728.[2] Dr. H. W. Dickinson considered that he was not a

[1] The late A. Stanley Davies's short paper, 'Isaac Wilkinson (c. 1705–1784) of Bersham, ironmaster and inventor', *Trans. Newcomen Society*, xxvii, for 1949–50 and 1950–1 (1956), 69–72, is the only attempt at a connected study, and relies wholly on material already in print.

[2] The parish registers of Skelton in Cumberland, 6½ miles north-west of Penrith, contain two baptismal entries, the first dated 20 August 1724, for Joseph, son of Isaac and Ann Wilkinson, and the second on 20 January 1727, for John, the son of Isaac Wilkinson of Ellonby. This evidence must, however, be accepted with reserve, for although the Christian name Isaac was not common in early eighteenth-century Cumberland, the surname Wilkinson was. Unfortunately, we have no corroborative evidence of the Christian name of John's mother. It is always possible, too, that

23

Isaac Wilkinson, Potfounder

Cumberland man,[1] although he is first discovered in that county. Isaac was one of the many migratory ironmasters of the eighteenth century, and there is some evidence to suggest that he, or at least his family, belonged originally to a Shropshire family of small farmers. There is a tradition in that branch of the Wilkinson family which originated in the south Shropshire township of Eardiston in the parish of Ruyton-XI-Towns,[2] that the great John Wilkinson wished in his old age to adopt as an heir his infant relative, John Wilkinson of Eardiston (1801–61). The child's parents, however, would not agree to the proposal.[3]

Isaac is next heard of about 1728 at Clifton in Cumberland, three and a half miles south-east of Workington, where he was employed either as furnace keeper or foundry foreman at Cookson and Company's Brigfoot furnace, Little Clifton, established towards the end of 1723 on the banks of the river Marron 'to use Pitt coal in smelting the Iron Stone'.[4] The ironstone was obtained from Branthwaite and coal from the Company's own mines at Clifton and Greysouthen. There was a foundry in connexion with the works 'where light castings for the use of mill wrights and farmers were made, as well as those required at the proprietors' own colliery'.[5] It was at or near Howth Gill, Frizington, four miles east-south-east of Whitehaven in the same county that William Wood (1671–1730), of *The Drapier's*

the John baptized in 1727 may have died in early infancy and that the name John was given to another son born in 1728, a practice common at the time (*The Registers of the Parish Church of Skelton, Cumberland* (1918), pp. 43–44, ed. H. Brierley and R. M. Richardson).

[1] *John Wilkinson, Ironmaster* (1914), p. 10.

[2] The author was able to search the registers of Ruyton-XI-Towns through the kindness of the Rev. T. G. Pedlow.

[3] Information from Mr. Edward R. Wilkinson, of Clifton House, New Broughton, Wrexham; Ruyton-XI-Towns Parish Registers, 1801 (baptisms), 1861 (burials). It is unfortunate that the registers of Ruyton-XI-Towns are not extant before 1719, so that it is impossible to discover whether Isaac was related to the male Wilkinsons who were marrying and begetting children in the parish in the 1720s. The Bishop's transcripts for the parish in the Diocesan Registry of Lichfield yielded no trace of Isaac between 1688 and 1719.

[4] John Spedding to James Lowther, 30 August 1723. In his Ph.D. thesis, 'The development of the coal, iron and shipbuilding industries of West Cumberland, 1750–1914' (University of London, 1952), p. 9, Dr. Oliver Wood has proved conclusively that this furnace was set up in 1723, and not 'about 1750' as stated by H. A. Fletcher ('Archaeology of the West Cumberland iron trade', *Trans. Cumb. and West. Archaeol. and Archit. Soc.*, 1st ser., v, 1879–80 (1881), 9–10).

[5] Fletcher, op. cit., pp. 9–10.

24

Letters fame, was carrying out his unsuccessful experiments with the coke smelting of iron ore about the same time (1728–30), and this, coupled with Dr. Wood's new evidence, suggests that there was a general attempt by ironmasters in the area to discover the secret of Abraham Darby I's new process. It is clear from Gabriel Jars's description of Little Clifton furnace that its proprietors were smelting iron ore with coke in the early 1760s.[1]

Of Isaac's life at Clifton only a few details are known. Significantly enough, he is said to have combined his industrial occupation with the management of a small farm. According to another account, dating from 1838 only, but which seems to possess some measure of authenticity:

. . . Isaac Wilkinson wanted that firmness and constancy of purpose which distinguished his son, but was possessed of quick discernment and versatile talents, and was by them elevated from his originally low condition. 'I worked', said he, 'at a forge in the north. My masters gave me 12s. a week;—I was content. They raised me to 14s.— I did not ask them for it. They went on to 16s.—18s. I never asked them for the advances! They gave me *a guinea* a week. I said to myself, *if I am worth a guinea a week to you, I am worth more to myself!* I left them.[2]

If Isaac were ever a member of what would now be called 'the proletariat', he did not remain so for long. He must be thought of from the first as a highly skilled technician, probably with a certain amount of capital. Like the Darbys of Coalbrookdale, the Wilkinsons were a family of casters. But whereas the Darby brand of Nonconformity was Quakerism, the Wilkinsons were Presbyterians, becoming Unitarians in the latter part of the eighteenth century, under the influence of Dr. Joseph Priestley.

At some date between 1728 and 1738 Isaac left Little Clifton and became chief caster or 'potfounder' to the Backbarrow Iron Company in Furness, North Lancashire. This blast furnace had

---

[1] I. Fletcher, 'Archaeology of the West Cumberland coal trade', *Trans. C.W.A.A. Soc.*, 1st ser., iii, 1876–7 (1878), 266–313; H. A. Fletcher, op. cit., pp. 9–15; G. Jars, *Voyages métallurgiques*, i, 236 and MS. F14/4261 in Archives Nationales, Paris; *V.C.H. of Cumberland*, ii, 351, col. 2.

[2] W. Hawkes Smith, *Birmingham and South Staffordshire, or Illustrations of the History, Geology and Industrial Operations of a Mining District* (1838), p. 13 n. Smith's book appears to be the earliest source for this statement, which was copied, without acknowledgement, by Smiles and Randall.

been established in 1711 by a number of local landowners and made use of the charcoal-smelting process.[1] Dr. Stephen Fell, the Quaker apothecary of Ulverston, when writing to Benjamin Airey, agent of the Backbarrow Company, on 30 October 1738 to order '2 furness grates', sent his 'Kind Respects' to 'J. Wilkinson', which is almost certainly Barber's mistranscription of 'I. Wilkinson'.[2] On 8 July of the same year, Isaac, described as 'of the Parish of Coulton, High Furness', in which the village of Backbarrow lies, had taken out the first, No. 565, of his four patents, for 'a new sort of cast metallick boxes for the smoothing of linnen':

> My said cast metallick boxes, both top, sides and the barrs within them consist of one entire peice of any cast metall, either iron, brass, copper, bell metall, or any mixt metall, and are made or performed from a melted fluid of any of the said metalls cast into a mold invented for that purpose and then ground and finished in the same manner as other box irons now in use are.[3]

Another son, Henry, was born to him in 1730.[4] Neither the exact dates nor the places of birth and baptism of his daughter Mary and his son William are known, but it can be deduced that, unless there was a case of twins, Mary was almost certainly born in 1743 and William in 1744.[5] Even less is to be discovered about Isaac's other two children, Sarah and Margaret. Sarah (born 1745, died 1775) married Thomas Jones, surgeon, of Leeds in 1768; their son, also named Thomas, and born in 1773, was to play a sinister part in John Wilkinson's affairs after 1808.[6] To judge by the gap between the birth of Henry in 1730

[1] A. Fell, *The Early Iron Industry of Furness* (1908), pp. 207–8, 260.

[2] H. Barber, *Furness and Cartmel Notes* (1894), p. 30. *John* Wilkinson was at the most eleven years old at the time.

[3] Dickinson, op. cit., p. 56.

[4] A. N. Palmer, 'John Wilkinson and the old Bersham ironworks', *Trans. Cymmrodorion Soc. for 1897–8* (1899), 30.

[5] The deduction is as follows: Sarah was definitely born in 1745; William died in his sixty-fourth year in 1808 which places his year of birth as either 1744 or 1745. But it is hardly probable that he would be born in the same year as Sarah, so by elimination 1744 seems the likelier date. Similarly, Mary was eighteen when she married Dr. Joseph Priestley in 1762, which would place her year of birth as 1743 or 1744. As William was almost certainly born in 1744, Mary was very probably born in 1743.

[6] *Thoresby Society*, xxxiii (Miscellanea), 1935, p. 221, and xxxviii (Miscellanea), p. 147.

and that of Mary in 1743, Isaac must have married a second time. Margaret Wilkinson married Thomas Parkinson, who in 1771 was described as 'of Bush Lane, Cannon Street, London, glass seller'. On his death in 1803, he was resident at No. 1 Market Square, Bloomsbury, London. They had a daughter, Sarah Parkinson, who married a Mr. Stevenson and was alive in 1807, by which time her mother, Mrs. Parkinson, was dead.[1]

While in the employ of the Backbarrow Company, Isaac Wilkinson lived in a substantial, well-built house in Backbarrow village, called Bare Syke, about 150 yards to the south of the furnace. It is still standing and the initials I.W. and H.W. (John and Henry Wilkinson) and the date 1745 may still be seen carved in the rock behind the house. James Stockdale, in his *Annales Caermoelenses*, tells us that Isaac, being 'a man of a whimsical turn of mind, and full of strange projects, aided by his daring and clever son John . . . actually cut away the face of some high clay-slate-stone rocks behind the house, and formed them into fruit walls against which he planted peach, plum, pear, and other choice fruit trees; which, however, succeeded but indifferently'. In 1872 the irons for the trellis were still in position.[2]

Tradition has preserved some details of Isaac's industrial operations at Backbarrow. According to Stockdale, 'for a suitable consideration he obtained leave to take out of the iron furnace there . . . metal in a melted state, in large ladles, across the public highway to an adjoining low shed, where he had suitable moulds into which he poured the liquid and so made the common flat smoothing iron'.[3]

It is possible to fill out these semi-legendary accounts by reference to one of the Backbarrow Company's ledgers.[4] This ledger covers the years from 1747 to 1753 and originally contained ten pages of accounts (fols. 780-4) headed 'Isaac Wilkinson, Potfounder'. Of these pages two (fol. 780) are printed in facsimile on pages 242-3 of Fell's *Early Iron Industry of Furness*,

[1] Palmer, *John Wilkinson and the Old Bersham Ironworks*, p. 30; will of William Wilkinson, 15 September 1807 (Boulton and Watt Collection, Birmingham Public Library—hereafter referred to as *PL*).
[2] *Annales Caermoelenses* (1872), pp. 209-10.
[3] ibid., p. 209.
[4] Preserved in the Public Library, Barrow-in-Furness.

but are not preserved in the existing ledger, having presumably been torn out to make the illustration. From 25 February 1747 to 25 March 1748 Isaac was busy casting scale- and jack-weights for the Company at 10*s* per ton, open-sand plates, bars, balls and heaters at 20*s* per ton, open-sand boxes at 24*s* per ton, flask-stove backs, girdles and plates at 30*s* per ton, loom work at £4 per ton, and pots, pans and boilers at 47*s* 6*d* per ton, with a special tariff for saucepans. The figures are not easy to interpret, but other products of his art, including skillets, rollers, cylinders, ashgrates, sad irons, box irons, hatters' irons, flask moulds and boiler and pan patterns were apparently made for disposal on his own account, the Company selling him the iron at prices ranging from 10*s* 6*d* to 14*s* per cwt.[1] In the sixty-nine weeks ending 8 March 1748 Isaac worked up over 298 tons of Back-barrow iron. In the year 1744, according to Fell, who had access to a wider range of Backbarrow account books than those at present in existence, £770 was due to him from the Company for foundry work, 'of which about two-thirds were connected with Leighton Furnace,[2] and about one-third was returned as the value of the articles taken by him. In the same year as much as three hundred and twenty tons of pig iron was made into iron wares in the foundries at Backbarrow and Leighton . . . it is evident that his work was very lucrative.'[3]

Fortunately the prosaic details of the ledger can be sup-plemented from an unusual source, a graphic representation of local industrial operations. Built into the wall over the fireplace in one of the ground-floor rooms of Bare Syke there was for-merly an oil painting, by an unknown artist, showing the casting shop at Backbarrow furnace, with two figures in the centre fore-ground said to represent Isaac Wilkinson and his young son John. Casting is in progress and the molten metal is being carried in ladles to the moulds. 'Isaac' (the adult to the left of centre) is pouring or 'teeming', while 'John', the boy on his left, is skimming off the dross. To the right are two gentlemen in

[1] Fell says: '. . . he was in the Company's employ, but had the privilege of buying the iron wares, and of selling them, presumably in the immediate neighbourhood' (op. cit., p. 241).

[2] The Backbarrow Company had set Leighton furnace on blast for the first time in 1713 (ibid., pp. 209–10).

[3] ibid., p. 241.

opposite: Backbarrow furnace in the 1730s

cocked hats, said to be the proprietors of the furnace, William Rawlinson and John Machell.[1] Typical products of the furnaces are shown in the immediate foreground. The date of the painting has been placed in the 1730s; about 1872 it was removed to Penny Bridge Hall, near Greenodd, where it still hangs, and is reproduced in this book by kind permission of the present owner, Major J. U. Machell.

In 1747 Isaac Wilkinson of Backbarrow and three local gentlemen, William Crosfield of Cartmel, Job Rawlinson of Graythwaite and George Drinkall of Rusland, under the style of the Lowwood Company, acquired a fifty-one-year lease of land about one and a half miles from Backbarrow, together with certain water-rights over the River Leven, from George Bigland, on the site of the old Backbarrow bloomery forge, in order to erect a furnace and forge thereon. Fell considered that Isaac's interest in this unsuccessful project 'was not maintained longer than one or two years'. A phrase in the lease relating to the 'grinding and polishing' of iron suggests that the scheme was connected with the box iron business.[2]

There are no entries in the Backbarrow ledgers relating to Isaac of a later date than 25 March 1748, and it seems reasonable to assume that about this time he left Backbarrow to operate a furnace and forge on his own account at Wilson House on the river Winster near Lindale in Cartmel parish, about two miles north-east of Grange-over-Sands.[3] Whether he purchased an existing furnace or built a new one at Wilson House is not known. Stockdale considered that his object in settling there was to smelt iron ore with turbary or peat moss, large tracts of which surrounded the furnace on three sides. This assertion must be viewed with some caution, as it may be an echo of John Wilkinson's experiments there in the 1770s. We therefore know little with certainty of his activities at Wilson House but he was still living there on 24 January 1753, when describing himself as 'Gentleman' he took out his second patent, No. 675, for 'a New Sort of Cast Metallick Rolls for the Crushing, Flattening, Bruising, or Grinding of Malt, Oats, Beans or any Kind of

[1] Fell, op. cit., p. 268. [2] Ibid., pp. 219, 266.
[3] Stockdale, op. cit., p. 210. See also the critical remarks in *Trans. C.W.A.A.S.* (1914), N.S., xiv, 260.

Grain; and also for Crushing, Bruising, or Grinding of Sugar Canes'. He enrolled a specification but Dr. Dickinson observes 'the invention consisted simply in making the roll in a single piece in a mould invented and prepared for that purpose'. In fact it was a simple extension of the method of coring previously patented.[1] According to Richard Bennett and John Elton, Isaac Wilkinson's invention was one of the pioneer but unsuccessful attempts to develop the crude idea of roller milling.[2]

The manufacture of box irons appears to have been continued, for Stockdale notes that Isaac, helped by John, ground the bottoms of the irons smooth by means of a large grindstone, turned by a small water-wheel and dam, erected on Lindale Beck, at a place called Skinner Hill, 'about 150 yards above the higher public-house' at Lindale past which the beck runs till it reaches the river Winster at Castlehead. In 1914 this dam still provided the power for a flour mill.[3] Stockdale goes further. He insists that Isaac and John not only turned their attention to making bricks with the clay they obtained from underneath the peat moss at Wilson House,[4] but also constructed a canal and floated the first iron boat there.

The following passages from the *Annales Caermoelenses* relating to the activities of Isaac and John in the period immediately after 1748 have been the origin of much speculation and even of assertions, but unfortunately they are unsupported by any contemporary documentary evidence. It must be remembered that they were written down 120 years after the alleged events to which they relate:

The first operation after the purchase of the property [Wilson House] was to cut a canal into the midst of this large tract of turbary, sufficiently wide for the passage of a small boat, intended to be used in conveying the peat moss to the iron furnace; which boat, tradition says, was actually constructed, not of wood, but of *Iron*! . . . there are people still living (amongst others Mr. Nicholas Atkinson, of Cart Lane), who remembers having seen it about seventy years ago.[5]

---

[1] Dickinson, op. cit., p. 56.

[2] *History of Corn Milling* (4 vols., 1898–1904), iii, 297.

[3] op. cit., p. 212; Dickinson, op. cit., p. 15.

[4] op. cit., p. 211. Before this, all bricks used in the district had been imported. Stockdale added: 'Some of the bricks then made may now (1872) be seen in my fruit walls at Carke.' [5] op. cit., p. 210.

Isaac Wilkinson, Potfounder

. . . this small vessel . . . after being long disused in the canal John [*sic*] Wilkinson had cut for it into Witherslack Peatmoss, laid [*sic*] for years nearly covered with mud at the bottom of the River Winster, near to or in Helton Tarn. There are some few persons still living who remember having seen it lying there.[1]

Whatever substance there is in these assertions is more likely to relate to John Wilkinson's activities in this area after 1778 and not to Isaac's after 1748. Attempts have been made to salvage the remains of this vessel or to discover its exact whereabouts,[2] and one enthusiast claimed to have secured a piece of it.

Among the manuscripts used by Stockdale in compiling his book was the following contract note, with both signatures in 'excellent mercantile hands'. It indicates that fuel and water-power, rather than iron ore, formed the attraction of Wilson House as the site for a blast furnace:

Cartmel, Oct. 30th 1750.

Be it remembered that this day Robert Bare of Cartmel Church Town has sold to Isaac Wilkinson, of Wilson House, two hundred tons of Wettflatt [Thwaite Flat, on Lindal Moor] iron ore, to be put on board at Lousay [Lowsy or Louzey Point on the coast, west of Dalton-in-Furness], the said Isaac Wilkinson promising to pay for the same twelve shillings for each ton, but in case the said Isaac Wilkinson does not approve of the said ore, that then he is only to have fifty tons of the said ore, he giving the said Robert Bare notice in April next, that he will have no more than the said fifty tons. If no notice is given he to have the whole two hundred tons, the said Isaac Wilkinson paying for the same on the second day of February, 1751.

Robert Bare

Witness—Walter Cowperthwaite Isaac Wilkinson[3]

As late as 1914 there still existed at Wilson House a stone wharf where this ore could have been unloaded, as the river Winster was navigable up to this point in the eighteenth century. The Wilson House venture cannot have been a great success, and came to an obscure end in the mid-1750s. After his departure Isaac retained his property rights in the district until at least 1757. Stockdale quotes from a list of encroachments

[1] op. cit., p. 579.

[2] See *Foundry Trade Journal*, 26 August 1937, p. 154 (T. McIntire); *Edgar Allen News*, August 1948, p. 115.

[3] Stockdale, op. cit., p. 211.

made on Cartmel parish common lands bearing this date[1] and including the following presentment:

> Isaac Wilkinson, Bersham, for an incroachment at Wilson House, taken off the common to enlarge his fields, 10 perches at £21 per acre, £1. 6s. 3d. *Mem.*—Will pull down or pay before Easter.

Everything known at present of John Wilkinson, apart from the entry in the parish registers of Skelton, from his birth until 1750, rests upon an account given in the *Commercial and Agricultural Magazine* for November 1799, and on tradition written down at least thirty, and in some cases even sixty, years after his death. The account of 1799 runs as follows:

> This gentleman was born in the year 1728, at Clifton in Cumberland; from which he was removed to Kendal; and there in due process of time, put to school under the Rev. Mr. Rotheram. Having passed through the usual course of education, he at the age of 17 was apprenticed to a respectable merchant at Liverpool. With him he continued about five years; then returning to the place of his nativity, began those improvements in mineralogy and agriculture which are too well known to be insisted upon here.[2]

Doubt is cast on the statement that he was born at Clifton from the fact that no record of his birth has been discovered in that area. If tradition speaks truly, John Wilkinson's birth was quite as remarkable as his life and burial, for it is alleged that he was born in a common Cumberland market cart, either on the road between Ellonby and Penrith or between Workington and Little Clifton furnace. His mother had had occasion to attend the local market with butter and eggs from Isaac Wilkinson's farm, and was returning home when she unexpectedly gave birth to John, 'an event which, among the simple-minded people of the countryside, produced no little sensation, and more than one said prophetically in the Cumberland dialect: "John sum tyme wod bee a girt man." '[3]

Of his childhood we know nothing with complete certainty, except that he removed with his father to Backbarrow, in the parish of Coulton, in the Furness district of Lancashire, when he

[1] op. cit., pp. 212–13.
[2] *Commercial and Agricultural Magazine*, i, no. iv, 229–30 ('Memoir of John Wilkinson, Esq., Iron-Master, of Broseley', by Z.Z.).
[3] Stockdale, *Annales Caermoelenses*, 1872, pp. 209, 223.

was about ten years old. His father gave him the best education then available to Nonconformists, for in the early 1740s he was a pupil at a dissenting academy at Kendal, kept by the Unitarian divine Dr. Caleb Rotheram (1694–1752). Between 1733 and 1751 some 180 scholars passed through its walls, and a very general idea of the education young John Wilkinson received may be judged from the description of the academy as existing 'for the instruction of youth in various branches of useful literature; but principally with a view to qualify them for the ministerial office'.[1]

Stockdale's stories of a 'daring and clever son John' aiding his father's 'strange projects' at Backbarrow and on Lindal Beck must be heavily discounted, but his home surroundings were certainly such as to foster any interests he may have had in the direction of practical metallurgy.[2] In or about 1745 John was apprenticed to a merchant ironmonger in Liverpool, in whose shop or warehouse he remained for five years, i.e. until about 1750.

On coming out of his apprenticeship at Liverpool John set up on his own as a merchant ironmonger at Kendal in Westmorland; he had an account with the Backbarrow Company as early as October 1750, and between 13 October 1752 and 23 February 1753 he made purchases of iron from that source amounting to about £30 in value, in parcels which varied from as little as 6 stones to as much as 4 cwt.[3] The ledger of W. Latham of Sparke Forge in Furness shows some small purchases of iron in 1750–1 by a John Wilkinson, blacksmith, of Pennybridge, a small port near Greenodd, but there is no evidence to suggest that this man was the famous ironmaster.[4]

The 1750s marked the beginning of a rapid change in the Wilkinson family fortunes. As we have seen, Isaac Wilkinson

---

[1] *Monthly Repository*, 1810, p. 219; F. Nicholson and E. Axon, *The Older Nonconformity in Kendal* (1915), p. 634; *Dictionary of National Biography* (Rotheram).

[2] op. cit., pp. 209–12, 267–8.

[3] MS. Backbarrow ledger 1747–53 (Barrow-in-Furness Public Library). These purchases may not represent the whole of his dealings with the Company, as the next ledger is missing.

[4] DDX 192/1, fol. 45 (Lancs. *CRO*, Preston). Latham's cash book (DDX 192/2) contains entries for dealings with John Wilkinson of Pennybridge in 1755–7, 1760 and 1761 which show conclusively that there were two distinct John Wilkinsons. I am indebted to Dr. Alan Birch for calling my attention to these documents.

described himself as 'of Wilson House in the parish of Cartmel' as late as 24 January 1753, but in the course of that year[1] he migrated from the Furness district of Lancashire to the township of Bersham, a mile and a half from Wrexham in Denbighshire, and began to operate the iron furnace there, 'in company with one son [John] and some Liverpool gentlemen', according to a later account. This enterprise became known later as the Old Bersham Company.[2]

It is not surprising to find Isaac with important business connexions in Liverpool, for the bulk of the iron produced at Backbarrow was shipped down the coast to that port, to be used chiefly in the manufacture of anchors and chains.[3] Bersham Furnace was an old-established charcoal-smelting site, but had been the scene of early experiments in coke-smelting from 1721 onwards, recorded in John Kelsall's diary.[4] According to William Wilkinson, however, it was still a charcoal-smelting furnace when his father took it over in the 1750s.[5]

Isaac's wife, his sons William and Henry, and at least two daughters accompanied him to the new scene of operations and the family were soon installed in a country house, Plas Grono, in Esclusham Isaf, near the Oswestry–Wrexham turnpike road between the latter town and the Welsh hills. This seventeenth-century house, demolished in 1876, was 'of humble pretensions, consisting of four sitting-rooms, with other accommodations for a household of twenty'.[6] Isaac rented it from a local landowner, Squire Simon Yorke of Erddig Park, probably on a twenty-one-years' lease (1753–74), and it remained in the occupancy of the Wilkinsons until 1774, when it was let to Thomas Apperley, the father of 'Nimrod'. William Wilkinson lived there while manager at Bersham. Isaac and his wife became members of the Dissenting

---

[1] J. Wilkinson to Watt, 3 August 1779 (*PL*).

[2] J. Aikin, *A Description of the Country from Thirty to Forty miles round Manchester* (1795), p. 399. John was described as 'Ironmaster of Bersham' as early as 13 June 1757 (Forester MSS., Willey Park, Shropshire).

[3] Fell, op. cit., p. 253.

[4] For the earlier history of Bersham Furnace, see Palmer, op. cit., pp. 23–26, 60–63, and A. Raistrick, *Dynasty of Ironfounders* (1953), pp. 58–61.

[5] MS. 'A list of the different ironworks in England, Wales, Scotland and Ireland to the year 1794'. Copied from the papers of the late William Wilkinson, Esq. (*PL*).

[6] C. J. Apperley ('Nimrod'), *My Life and Times*, ed. E. D. Cuming, 1927, p. 4.

congregation (then of a Presbyterian persuasion) worshipping in the chapel in Chester Street, Wrexham.[1]

It seems likely that John was not actively associated in the Bersham concern at the beginning, for on 12 June 1755 he had married Ann, daughter of Mrs. Margaret Maudesley of Rigmaden Hall, a few miles north of Kirkby Lonsdale in Cumberland. Mrs. Maudesley was a member of the smaller gentry and in the Kirkby Lonsdale register John is described as 'merchant of Kirkby Lonsdale'. Whether he had actually left Kendal to carry on business in Kirkby Lonsdale or had merely taken up temporary residence during the calling of the banns remains undecided. His wife gave birth to a daughter who was baptized by the name of Mary at Kirkby Lonsdale on 12 April 1756. On this occasion the domicile of the family was given as Rigmaden,[2] but a move south occurred shortly afterwards, for by 1756 John, too, had definitely left the north of England and joined his father in Denbighshire. His first experience of married life was, however, of short duration, for the first Mrs. Wilkinson died before the year was out and lies buried in Wrexham parish church.

His marriage, and the sudden death of his wife, which gave John control of at least some part of an estate, may provide the answer to the oft-discussed question of how he began his career of capital accumulation. Certainly the period 1756–9 sees a remarkable expansion of his activities.

The connexions between the iron districts of north-west England and the furnaces of Denbighshire, Shropshire, and Cheshire were fairly close. Joshua Gee, merchant, of London, for example, took out a lease for raising iron ore in Frizington,

---

[1] Apperley, op. cit., pp. 219, 244; Palmer, op. cit., pp. 29–30; Dickinson, op. cit., p. 56; Henry Wilkinson (b. 1730), died at Plas Grono on 26 June 1756 and was buried in the Dissenters' graveyard at Wrexham.

[2] On 4 March 1781 Wilkinson wrote to Boulton and Watt from Castlehead: 'The sudden death of an old lady last week, grandmother to my daughter, has involved me in fresh business here. She has left us without a will and being an undivided manor and estate in which my daughter has one half, the active part in adjusting her affairs falls to my share' (*PL*). Two and a half years later he wrote to Boulton: 'On the 28th [October] I must attend a sale, at Kirkby Lonsdale, of Rigmaden estate, where my daughter is interested one moiety' (9 October 1784, *PL*). See also *Trans. C.W.A.A.C.*, N.S., v (1905), 237, 239. The date of Mrs. Maudesley's burial at Kirkby Lonsdale is wrongly given as 27 February 1782 on p. 239.

near Whitehaven, in Cumberland and much of the ore raised
there was shipped from Parton in small craft, carrying from
10 to about 60 tons, to Chester to be smelted eventually in a
furnace he operated at Upton-on-Tern in Shropshire.[1] And in
the 1760s it was calculated that every year 1,100 tons of Cumberland red ore was carted from Frodsham over Delamere forest
to Doddington furnace on the Cheshire–Staffordshire border.[2]
John Wilkinson is later found importing such ores into North
Wales.[3]

Of Isaac's operations at Bersham furnace only a few details
survive, but it was from this address that he took out the two
patents which form his main contribution to the development of
iron smelting and casting. According to Palmer, Isaac's output
consisted chiefly, if not entirely, of cast-iron objects—heaters,
water-pipes, and under the pressure of demand created by the
Seven Years War (1756–63) a beginning was made in the casting of cannon.[4] A large part of the ironstone used came from
Llwyn Enion in the township of Esclusham Uchaf, a mile and a
half from Bersham, and on 9 June 1757 Isaac leased for forty
years from John Hughes all the coal and ironstone to be found
under the Cae Glas estate in Esclusham Uchaf, near Llwyn
Enion. Wilkinson was to pay a basic rent of 24*s* per acre yearly
to Hughes, besides one-sixth of all the coal, cannel or slack
mined and 2*s* for every dozen strikes of ironstone raised. In
return Isaac was to have the right to lay a railway from the
king's highway to the pits across Hughes's land and over
Hughes's land from the colliery at the Ponkey (Welsh *poncau*: the
banks), which the Bersham Company rented from William
Higgons, paying him 1*s* 4*d* per 'score' of four 'piches'.[5] Palmer
lists succinctly the natural advantages of the site:

. . . the ore brought thence would be carried along roads which were
slightly down hill all the way. Next, it was always then thought

[1] H. A. Fletcher in *Trans. C.W.A.A.S.*, 1st ser., v (1880), 19–21; Ashton, op. cit.,
pp. 108, 214, 216.

[2] Richard Whitworth, *The Advantages of Inland Navigation*, 1st ed. (1766), p. 39;
2nd ed. (1776), p. 44.

[3] G. Nicholson, *Cambrian Travellers' Guide* (1813), pp. 551–2.

[4] *Williamson's Liverpool Advertiser*, 30 July 1756, p. 3, col. 3, and issues for
6–27 August.

[5] Palmer, op. cit., p. 32.

desirable to build a blast-furnace against the face of a low cliff, so that it could be charged from the cliff-top, and the molten metal be run off below at the level of the main road. Now there were at Pentre Debenni in Bersham many such sites, close to a main road, and near two water mills, with water-rights belonging to them, which mills could be used to work the bellows for supplying the necessary blast. And thirdly, charcoal was to be had in the neighbourhood.[1]

Such was the situation of the furnace at which Isaac failed but which his two gifted sons were to render world-famous.[2]

It has been stated that about 1761–2 the 'Old' Bersham Company (Isaac, John and some Liverpool merchants) was reconstructed and became the 'New' Bersham Company. This new partnership is said to have consisted not only of Isaac and John, but also of certain other unidentified persons who were later bought out.[3] There is some evidence to suggest that the changes of 1761–2 simply involved the exclusion of the non-active partners. For example, Isaac and John alone entered into the celebrated compact with the Coalbrookdale Company to charge uniform prices for cylinders, pipes and other articles in all markets other than those of London.[4] And on 10 May 1764 it was Isaac and John Wilkinson alone, as 'Ironmasters and Partners', who were described as having 'lately made and erected a new stone bridge' between the townships of Bersham and Esclusham.[5] By the 1770s, however, the New Bersham Company consisted solely of John and his brother William, who lived at Plas Grono and managed the iron-works, while his elder brother, from his headquarters at Broseley, directed the progress of his rapidly expanding industrial empire.[6]

The Wilkinsons gave up the tenancy of Plas Grono, which had been their North Wales headquarters since the 1750s, in 1774.[7]

[1] op. cit., pp. 24–25.

[2] It is not clear from whom Isaac and his associates rented Bersham furnace and the surrounding land in 1753, but on 20 August 1785 John Wilkinson obtained a lease for 100 years of the works and 68 acres of land adjoining from Richard Myddelton of Chirk Castle and his son Richard (Palmer, 'John Wilkinson and the Old Bersham Ironworks', p. 33).

[3] Aikin, op. cit., p. 399; Palmer, op. cit., p. 32. Palmer states that the first ledger of the New Bersham Company, which he once saw, began in 1762.

[4] V.C.H., Shropshire, i, 464.

[5] NLW, MS. Smallwood Notebook, p. 320.

[6] The date of William's entry into the partnership is unknown.

[7] Apperley, My Life and Times, pp. 219, 244.

Isaac Wilkinson, Potfounder

The New Bersham Company (the brothers John and William Wilkinson) thereupon took a preliminary six-year lease of the estate known as The Court, at £33 a year.[1] William Wilkinson appears to have lived there from 1774 until his second departure for France late in 1776 or early in 1777, and John stayed there on his frequent visits to Bersham, from at least 1779 onwards.[2] In February 1784, for example, he accommodated at The Court a party of six Frenchmen who were touring English industrial establishments,[3] and maintained a housekeeper, Molly, there.

Drs. Dickinson and Raistrick have pointed out that the only apparatus available to ironmasters for blowing blast furnaces at this time was simply a blacksmith's leathern bellows worked by a water-wheel, and that the pressing problem was to secure a stronger blast particularly as the use of coke in smelting was spreading. Coke carried a heavier burden of ore and limestone than charcoal and a higher pressure of blast was therefore necessary to melt the ore.

Isaac Wilkinson is reputed to have said:

I grew tired of my leathern bellows . . . and I determined to make *iron* ones. Every body laughed at me; but I did it, and then they all cried, Who could have thought it?[4]

Isaac Wilkinson is also credited by Aikin, quite wrongly, with having been the first to raise water by means of a Newcomen steam engine for the purpose of 'throwing it back into the mill-dam or reservoir'. According to Aikin this innovation took place at Bersham Furnace about 1756–8. Here Isaac erected 'an engine of great magnitude which brought up the contents of the river, as it were, at one stroke. This engine shook the buildings and ground for a considerable distance and required ten times more fuel than those at present constructed.'[5] While Isaac was

[1] Palmer, *History of the Town of Wrexham* (1893), pp. 202–3. From 1774 until 1800 Plas Grono was tenanted by Thomas Apperley, 'Nimrod's' father.

[2] J. Wilkinson, The Court, Wrexham, to James Watt, 16 July/12 September 1779. (*PL.*)

[3] J. Wilkinson, The Court, Wrexham, 10 February 1784 to B. and W. (*PL.*)

[4] W. H. Smith, op. cit., p. 13. De la Houlière wrote in 1775: 'It is impossible to make the bellows used in smelting furnaces too strong or of too great a capacity. . . . The tops and bottoms of these bellows are made of cast-iron plates.' (*Report to the French Government*, ed. Chaloner.)   [5] op. cit., p. 175 n.

not an innovator in this respect, the device must certainly have helped the Bersham Company to produce good coke-smelted iron.

From designing iron bellows and strengthening the blast by pumping back water, it was a natural step to experimenting with an entirely new blowing-machine. On 12 March 1757 Isaac Wilkinson of 'Barsham Furnace' took out patent no. 713 for a new type of bellows which he described as follows:

My said invention or machine for blowing furnaces or forges, lead works, copper works, or any other sort of works where a blast is required, is made in the manner following, viz: Vessels made square, round, oblong, octagon, or any other form, made of iron, wood, brass, copper, lead, or any other thing, or any compound thing, or things in number one, two, three, four, five, six, or more, and place one by the side of another, or one over another, and so contrived that when full of air, that the air is compressed by a pillar of water of a proper altitude, coming in and filling the place or space that the air took up before. And by means of valves, regulators, cocks, or siphons, opening and shutting alternately, the water is let out, and the air is taken in, and forced out by the water through a pipe at any distance required, so that a furnace, forge, or any other works may be blowed from any waterfall or falls, or from a fire engine or engines to several miles distance from the machine, by means of a pipe being fixed to the machine, to force or convey the wind through to the said work. When the wind is prest out of each vessel by the water, the water is again sent out by the motion of the machine opening the valves, regulators, cocks, or siphons, and filling them again with air to make a second blast. This machine is putt in motion by a water-wheel or wheels moving in any form, or a fire engine or engines, waterfall or falls, and siphons or valves, regulators and cocks, or by mixing the water and air together by the fall of water, so as the water shall compress the wind out of the vessels, as above, through a pipe to the said work.[1]

According to Dr. Dickinson, the description enrolled is not clear, 'for in one place it suggests a water pressure engine', while in another Isaac states that the machine needed water wheels or a steam engine to set and keep it in motion.[2] No drawing was enrolled with the patent, but a sketch of it is preserved in the

---

[1] *Patents of Invention: Abridgements of Specifications relating to Hydraulics* (1868), pp. 54–55.
[2] op. cit., p. 16.

Egerton MSS. in the British Museum.[1] This shows that the invention 'consisted simply of an iron cylinder reciprocating in a water-sealed wooden tub provided with suitable inlet and outlet valves. Equalization of blast was obtained by having three of these, side by side, actuated by levers, from a three-throw crank in a water-wheel shaft.'[2]

While engaged in developing the blowing-engine, Isaac was busy with his fourth and last patent, no. 723, which he took out on 21 April 1758, from Bersham. It was related to his earlier activities in the casting line, viz. to the preparation and manner of forming the moulds and cores applicable to the casting of tubular and other metallic objects. He described the invention as follows:

The outside or cope of the mould or moulds in which the guns, or cannon, fire engines, cylinders, pipes, and sugar rolls, or such like instruments, or any of them is or are intended to be cast must be made of sand, mixt with a little horse or cow dung or any other thing to make it porous. This sand is made wett and then rammed up, the pattern, being first put in iron boxes made for that purpose, or two, three, four, five, or any number of parts or pieces, as the nature of the instrument to be cast requires; then the boxes are to be taken asunder into pieces and the patern taken out; then the sand in the boxes is dried in a stove, and when dry it must be blacked or faced with some wett charcoal dust, or black lead, or any other mixture or thing to make the sand come off or part from the metal when cast. The insides or cores of all the different instruments above-mentioned are made with iron bars, either hollow and full of holes, or solid and traced or fluted, and if the bore is large it may be made of bricks walled, and the barrs of iron or bricks are to be wrapped round with ropes made of straw or hay, to take the air of, and must be then covered with a proper thickness of the said sand, and then dried and blacked, as before directed; and then the moulds are put together, and the instruments cast, and bored, and turned as required.[3]

No drawings were enrolled, but it can be said that it is

---

[1] *BMAM*, Egerton MSS. 1941, fols. 5–20. The sketch is of a 'Section of the Blowing Cylinder and one of the Regulating Bellies, used at Mr. Wilkinson's Iron furnace, at Willey near Broseley'. See also *Journal of Natural Philosophy . . .*, ed. Wm. Nicholson, i (1802), 219–20.

[2] Dickinson, op. cit., p. 16.

[3] *Abridgements of the Specifications relating to Metallic Pipes and Tubes, A.D. 1741–1866* (1874), p. 1.

apparently the first written description of dry-sand moulding in a flask or box, with bonding, venting and facing materials, in any language. It indicates that this particular branch of the moulder's art was then in its early stages of development: 'In fact, apart from its archaic wording, Isaac Wilkinson's patent might well be a description of the methods in use today.'[1]

Isaac's succession of attempts to develop the blowing-engine patent of 1757 appears to have been one of the major factors in his failure. Aikin gives what is perhaps the earliest evidence on this subject. He wrote in 1795 that Isaac Wilkinson's Old Bersham Company had

proved unsuccessful, partly in consequence of an expensive scheme to convey a blast by bellows from a considerable distance, to the works by means of tubes underground.[2]

Aikin added that after Isaac had relinquished control at Bersham, John Wilkinson 'by means of a very ingenious mechanism brought it to succeed in a wonderful manner'. By 1777 the New Bersham Company (John and William Wilkinson) had begun to achieve a considerable reputation as suppliers of blowing-engines to blast furnaces. The *Cumberland Pacquet* of 1 April 1777 contained the following puff, undoubtedly inspired by the vendors:

We hear that a pair of bellows are placing at Netherhall Furnace; they were cast at Birsham near Wrexham, and weigh, exclusive of the pistons, 146 cwt. The quantity of air discharged by these is astonishing. Every sink of the piston is calculated to produce 126,000 cube inches; one revolution of the wheel sinks the piston eight times and the wheel revolves five times a minute; so that the whole quantity of air produced in one minute is 5,040,000 cube inches.

Isaac also seems to have been much exercised by the problem of cooling and moistening the blast, and, although the subject is

---

[1] *The Engineer*, Modern Foundry Equipment supplement, 28 May 1937, article by J. E. Hurst on 'The Progress of Foundry Practice', p. i. See also Dickinson, op. cit., p. 17.

[2] Aikin, op. cit., p. 399. A. Stanley Davies (*Trans. Newcomen Soc.*, xxvii, for 1949–1950, 1950–1 (1956), suggested that by 1777 the machine had been improved by fitting the cylinders with pistons instead of water seal (p. 72).

not directly mentioned in his blowing-engine patent, the proposed long pipes may have suggested the idea.

An ironmaster writing in 1799 or 1800 stated:

> In the summer season we all know that the furnaces never work quite so well as at any other time . . . this has been applied [? ascribed] to the rarefaction which the air experiences by the heat it receives from the sun. The late Mr. [Isaac] Wilkinson, to prevent this, actually made a long subterraneous passage through which he caused all the air to go that went into his furnace, in hopes that by this contrivance it would be cooled, and thereby condensed before it entered the furnace pipe. How this experiment succeeded with him I cannot say.[1]

John Wilkinson developed this idea, too, for De la Houlière noted after a visit to his Shropshire furnace in 1775 that long underground vaults were being built at Broseley for use as air chambers 'from which to lead these torrents of air into the tuyères'.[2]

Isaac decided in 1757 to try out his blowing-engine in the rising iron district of South Wales, although it seems clear that his invention can hardly have been a success there. Between 1757 and 1771 his name is associated with the activities of no fewer than three 'companies' or partnerships for the purpose of carrying on iron-works in South Wales. Bristol and Glamorgan capital figured prominently in these ventures and the evidence suggests that Isaac's contribution to them consisted of technical skill rather than finance.

The first of the South Wales ventures was the Dowlais Iron Company of Merthyr Tydfil in Glamorgan. The genesis of this concern is to be found in the acquisition by Thomas Lewis of Newhouse in Llanishen, Glamorgan, together with some unspecified partners, of a ninety-nine-year lease from 1 November 1757, of 'all those mines and veins of ironstone and all quarry-stone and coal arising, growing, to be found in or upon, or out of the free common or waste called Pantywain; and after the decease of Thomas Williams in, upon or out of any other coal pits on the said common or waste called Tilla Dowlas and Toryvan'. This lease was granted by two yeomen of Merthyr, David John

---

[1] *Souvenir of Lowmoor Ironworks, 1791–1906* (1906), p. 151.
[2] *Report to the French Government*, ed. Chaloner.

and Thomas Rees.[1] Thomas Lewis and Company were to have full liberty to work these deposits in return for a yearly rent of £38 and engaged to erect a furnace or furnaces thereon.[2] Significantly enough, they were to be free to lead water across the estate 'to turn any wheels, and to erect or place pipes for carrying air or water through their lands'.[3]

According to Lloyd the building of 'Myrthy Furnace' began in 1757, but the new Dowlais Iron Company for the manufacture and sale of pig iron did not come into formal existence until 1 January 1760, as the result of articles of co-partnership executed on 19 September 1759. Towards the new Company's capital of £4,000 Thomas Lewis and Thomas Price of Watford, Glamorgan, contributed three-sixteenths (£750) and two-sixteenths (£500) respectively, while Thomas Harris, Esq., of Bristol contributed three-sixteenths (£750), John Curtis, Esq., of Bristol and Nathaniel Webb of Bristol two-sixteenths (£500) each, while Richard Jenkins, mercer of Cardiff, John Jones, ironmaster of Bristol, Edward Blakeway,[4] draper, of Shrewsbury, and Isaac Wilkinson of Plas Grono, Denbighshire, gentleman, were to contribute one-sixteenth (£250) each.[5] Blakeway later became a most intimate business associate of John Wilkinson in Shropshire.[6]

One clause of the articles read:

... the said Isaac Wilkinson hath obtained a patent for his new invented machine for blowing furnaces, forges and other iron works, by valves, cyphons, and other engine or engines for the term of 14 years,

[1] The indenture of lease is dated 20 September 1757. There had been a preliminary ninety-nine-year lease from David John on 29 July 1757 relating to a yearly rent of £6 for his moiety of mineral rights in Cefn Dowlais and Toryvan and to the buildings of the proposed furnace.

[2] John Lloyd, *The Early History of the Old South Wales Ironworks, 1760–1840* (1906), pp. 22–30.

[3] Lloyd, op. cit., p. 37.

[4] Blakeway 'never executed the same' (*PRO*, E.112/2096/135).

[5] From the record of legal proceedings in the Court of Exchequer in 1777 it appears that although Isaac Wilkinson never executed the co-partnership articles of 1759 he 'did pay and bring into the co-partnership stock the sum of two hundred and fifty pounds and thereby became entitled in equity to one sixteenth part or share' (ibid).

[6] When Blakeway declared his intention to withdraw from the projected Dowlais Company on 31 July 1759, John Wilkinson was one of the two witnesses to the document in which Blakeway surrendered his one-sixteenth share to Thomas Harris (Dowlais MSS., document 693).

and hath agreed to and with the said other partners that they shall have the benefit of the said patent in their said furnace and other iron works to be erected by them.

In return for this concession the remaining partners agreed that 'if any one furnace erected by the said co-partners should make on an average more than 20 tons of mettle per week during the first blast, that then the said I. Wilkinson should receive the sum of £50 for every ton of pig iron so exceeding the quantity of 20 ton'.[1] Nothing is known of the success attained by these experiments, save what can be deduced from the fact that Isaac sold his one-sixteenth share in the Dowlais Iron Company to Nathaniel Webb as from 25 March 1762.[2] Whatever may have been the fortunes of the furnace during 1757–62, by 1777 it was the basis of 'a very profitable and gainful trade', having been for the previous ten years under the control of John Guest[3] from Broseley in Shropshire, who had therefore been a close neighbour of Isaac's son John and was to be Isaac's partner in the latter's second venture in South Wales.[4]

Isaac next founded the Plymouth ironworks near Merthyr in Glamorgan. From an indenture dated 14 December 1763 it appears that Isaac Wilkinson, ironmaster of Plas Grono, in the parish of Wrexham, and John Guest, ironmaster of Broseley, in Shropshire, intended shortly to erect furnaces, forges, engines, mills, store-houses and pot-houses for making iron in the parishes of Merthyr Tydfil and Aberdare. To this end they made agreements with certain of the Earl of Plymouth's tenants in the area and as the Earl still held the mineral rights in these lands, the two ironmasters finally had to come to an agreement with

[1] Lloyd, op. cit., p. 30. If the partners put additional furnaces into blast, 'the said Wilkinson should receive the like gratuity for every additional furnace'.

[2] *PRO*, E.112/2096/135. Webb, who died in 1771, was in sole charge of Merthyr Furnace from December 1764 to July 1765, and in joint charge, with Price, from December 1765 to January 1767.

[3] John Guest died on 25 November 1787, possessed of six-sixteenths of the shares in the Dowlais Iron Company (Lloyd, op. cit., p. 33).

[4] According to later tradition Isaac Wilkinson first brought Guest from Broseley to South Wales. The obituary notice of Sir John Josiah Guest (1785–1852) in the *Gentleman's Magazine* for 1853 states that John Guest accompanied to South Wales 'a well-known cannon founder named Wilkinson, and the first furnace was raised under their joint superintendence, at Dowlais' (i, 91). This, however, may refer to the Plymouth furnace.

the Earl himself, which gave them, for the sole purpose of carrying on the iron-works, the right (any unexpired prior grants being excepted) 'to dig, raise or carry away any coal or iron ore which can or may be found in or under any of the lands, tenements or estate of the said Earl of Plymouth'.[1] The lease was for ninety-nine years, at a rent of £60 per annum, to date from 1 May 1765, but little is known as to the success of Guest's and Wilkinson's efforts. Charles Wilkins, not a particularly reliable source, states that Isaac Wilkinson and Guest built a furnace at Plymouth, 'the ruins of which were visible a few years ago, behind the old Vulcan Steps at Dowlais. . . . At a considerable distance from this furnace there was a water-wheel which acted as the motive power to a large bellows, supplying the furnace with blast. The blast again was conveyed through a long clay pipe of a very frail character. The whole thing soon collapsed and Wilkinson retired from both Dowlais and Plymouth.'[2]

Guest and Wilkinson found great difficulty in obtaining possession of the land held by the Earl's long-leasehold tenants, and the first successful Plymouth furnace was erected later by the celebrated Anthony Bacon, who held the lease in 1785.[3] Bacon certainly operated it with great profit.

Undeterred by the continuing unsatisfactory nature of his South Wales speculations Isaac next became sole owner of the Cyfarthfa iron-works in Glamorgan, probably in 1767,[4] and also leased on 9 July 1768 two houses and fields in Merthyr Canaid in the parish of Merthyr Tydfil from Rees Thomas of Aberdare at a yearly rent of £18.[5] Here at Cwm Canaid he opened a coal pit at a cost of over £200, contracting with a team of three local master-colliers, Lewis Edwards and William and Abraham Evan of Merthyr Tydfil (who could not sign their names), 'for driving levels and other preparatory work'. Hoping to obtain from this mine all the fuel necessary 'for the blast of Cyfartha [*sic*] furnace', Isaac unfortunately made a second contract with

[1] Lloyd, op. cit., pp. 72–73.
[2] *History of the Iron, Steel, Tinplate and Other Trades of Wales* (1903), p. 42.
[3] Lloyd, op. cit., pp. 72–73, 74.
[4] According to E.112/2094/75 (*PRO*), he was 'in the beginning of 1768 and for some time before that the owner of certain ironworks situate at Cyfartha [*sic*]'.
[5] Lloyd, op. cit., p. 50.

them on 2 December 1768,[1] 'being desirous of having the same brought and conducted by some persons well-skilled in works of that nature'. The contract, drawn up by Evan Jones, Wilkinson's clerk or agent, is a good example of the methods used in developing the coal resources of South Wales in the eighteenth century. The mine was let as a going concern. Isaac provided the requisite timber and maundrells, pickaxes, wedges and hammers (which were to become his property at the end of the blast), but no other equipment for coal-getting. The three colliers were to 'carry the said cole-work on' as directed by Wilkinson or his inspectors, and were to win all the coal necessary to supply 'the blast-furnace during the first blast and at the same time to supply the forge, air furnaces, etc., or whatever quantity Wilkinson should have occasion for. The fuel was to be delivered into the boats in raw cole' and to be measured on Cyfarthfa furnace bank 'when coaked, according to the measure of the tub they have at Dwylais furnace'. For each dozen tubs of coke the three colliers were to be paid 4*s*.[2] If they managed to get the works 'in the little vain and the big vain' ready before the beginning of the blast they were to discharge surplus labour, and in any case, as soon as the levels and heads were large enough for the task, with 'sufficient room for the rubitch in the job'. At the end of the blast Isaac was to receive the mine back in good repair. No mention was made of any payment beyond the 4*s* per dozen tubs of coke.

One Samuel Davis undertook the custody of this agreement, and soon after December 1768, the three colliers, who alleged that Isaac still owed them 'a considerable sum of money' for work done before 2 December 1768, contrived to secure possession of it from Davis. Isaac Wilkinson alleged that they did this, first, in order to charge him extra for driving the levels and opening heads and air-holes, and, secondly, in order to be in a position to ask for more than 4*s* per dozen tubs of coke. Isaac counter-claimed that they owed him money. About June 1769 he ordered the levels leading into the Cwm Canaid mine to be shut up and had the doors locked. The three colliers were

---

[1] In it he is described as 'gentleman, of the City of Bristol'.

[2] According to Isaac Wilkinson, this constituted ample recompense, 'and could be reckoned a good price'.

'warned off' the mine and 'turned off' from their work, which Isaac alleged had not been properly carried out (although the three colliers said he had 'at several times expressed his satisfaction and approbation' to them).

In June or July 1769, when the colliers applied for the £103 due to them, they were repeatedly told by Wilkinson's agent that for want of cash Isaac 'would be obliged to leave the said coal works, not having money or credit any longer to go on'. Meanwhile Isaac had 'sued out a bailable writ out of the Court of Great Sessions of the County of Glamorgan', thereby causing the arrest of the colliers. They were held to bail for the sum of £50 or thereabouts, at a time when they claimed that Isaac owed them over £100. According to the colliers' version, Isaac then offered them 'drafts or bills on his correspondent in London to the amount of £90', which they refused, having heard that the ironmaster's bills 'were often returned and not paid'.

The colliers then began a cross-action in self-defence,[1] for the recovery of the money they considered to be their due, and proposed to sue out a bailable writ against Isaac, returnable at the following Great Sessions of Glamorgan held at Cowbridge (July or August 1769). The ironmaster then proposed that the dispute should be referred to the arbitration of William Bassett of Miskin, 'a gentleman of property in the neighbourhood of the said works'. Bassett refused to arbitrate, but suggested orally that Isaac should give the contentious trio his promissory note for £60. According to the ironmaster Bassett had very improperly advised the colliers 'to try the cause at Cowbridge [on account of] the aversion the persons in that neighbourhood had to the said works and the partiality which they would be inclined to show' in favour of the colliers. Isaac's apprehension turned out to be well-founded, but he made out the required promissory note at Cowbridge on 8 August 1769, calculating that after this transaction the colliers would be in his debt to the extent of over £50 under the terms of the original agreement. In addition there was the damage to the mine at Cwm Canaid, owing to the colliers' failure to carry on the levels and heads in a workmanlike manner 'whereby divers large quantities of coals' had been

[1] Isaac's version of the affair gives the colliers as the aggressors with himself bringing the cross-action.

lost to the value of over £50. In fact the mine had been 'totally ruined'.

The affair was not, however, at an end. The colliers caused Isaac's promissory note to be put into suit against him in the Court of Exchequer, in order to recover £60 plus all the costs of the proceedings. No defence was made and the colliers proceeded to judgement. Phineas Cotes, of Banstead Place, Surrey, and Thomas Parkinson, of Bush Lane, Cannon Street, London, glass-seller (Isaac's son-in-law), thereupon went bail for the unfortunate ironmaster, but the colliers sued out a writ of *scire facias* against Cotes and Parkinson as well, and seem to have proceeded to judgement and execution.

Isaac and his friends thereupon made several attempts to come to 'a fair and just account', and, their efforts proving unavailing, also took the case into the Court of Exchequer as the injuries caused by the colliers were without remedy by the strict rules of the common law (February–November 1771). Wilkinson, Parkinson and Cotes believed that the colliers had confederates 'at present unknown'. These confederates, having the original agreement of 2 December 1768 in their possession, sometimes claimed that no such written document had been executed and refused to produce it in court.

According to the Court of Exchequer record, Isaac was no longer by 1771 the owner of iron-works and coalmines in the parish of Merthyr Tydfil. By this time, too, the claims of the colliers had expanded somewhat. They claimed not only arrears of payment from before 2 December 1768 but also extra recompense for 'digging a canall and making a damn' beside the mine at Cwm Canaid, among other things. They considered they had done work to the value of about £200 and had only received about £80 from Wilkinson.

Finally, however, the colliers appear to have abandoned the struggle. According to the last deposition on the Court of Exchequer file (8–11 November 1771) they decided to produce the agreement for inspection in court and admitted that 'their account with the complainant Isaac Wilkinson was fully closed and settled . . . on the 8th day of August, 1769'.[1]

[1] *PRO*, E.112/2094/75. In this document Isaac is described as 'of the City of Bristol, dealer in iron' (April 1771).

Of his last years little is known. His son-in-law Dr. Joseph Priestley characteristically lamented the fact that he had received 'little fortune' with his wife, Isaac's daughter Mary Wilkinson, whom he married in 1762, 'in consequence of her father becoming impoverished, and wholly dependent on his children, in the latter part of his life'.[1] He was resident at Plas Grono as late as 14 December 1763,[2] but between 1764 and 1766 he removed his headquarters to Bristol, where Priestley spent a considerable part of a long vacation in an unspecified year while on the staff of Warrington Academy (1761–7).[3]

In 1764 Isaac entered into partnership with two of the Dowlais Iron Company proprietors, Thomas Harris of Bristol and John Jones, ironmonger, also of Bristol, to carry on a 'manufactory' in Cheese Lane, Bristol, for the production of iron cylinders, pipes and cannon.[4] In 1766, however, Isaac expressed a desire to quit the concern and sell his shares to Harris and Jones, who in return were granted a licence to use his patent of 1758 for moulding and casting iron goods in dried sand on payment of 7*s* 6*d* a ton to the patentee for all cylinders and pipes so cast and 5*s* a ton for all guns.

Harris and Jones were to have a monopoly of the process within a fifty-mile radius of Bristol and in addition Isaac was not to grant anyone else a licence to use it in any part of South Wales. The agreement was signed on 24 December 1766, and came into full effect as from 1 January 1767. It was not followed by Isaac's departure from Bristol. He had now reached his sixties and decided to settle down in that city as a merchant ironmonger and ironfounder at no. 7 Hampton Court in the parish of St. Paul's.[5] No details are known of his business activities, except that they were not very successful.

Traces of a violent family quarrel can be observed during the last years of his life, a quarrel in which John Wilkinson and his

---

[1] *Memoirs of Joseph Priestley to the year 1795* (London, 1806), pp. 46–47. See also Palmer, *History of the Older Nonconformity of Wrexham* (1888), p. 135.

[2] Lloyd, op. cit., p. 72.   [3] *Memoirs . . . p.* 51.

[4] Wilkinson held two shares of one-sixteenth and Harris and Jones seven of one-sixteenth each (Dowlais MSS.).

[5] Sketchley's *Bristol Directory*, 1775, p. 105. In 1766 he had been described as 'of the parish of St. Philip and Jacob'.

E   49

sister Mary[1] found themselves ranged against Isaac and his younger son William. A curious and tantalizing glimpse of this quarrel is given in a letter from Matthew Boulton to James Watt dated 23 September 1781.

... I was prejudiced against W[alker] before I saw him, but that is now vanished and [I] don't think we shall have any cause of complaint. It was Le Founder [i.e. John Wilkinson] that grounded my prejudice, but as I learned from old W[alke]r[2] that he had been appointed an arbitrator between Le Founder and his Father and that after the award was made Jno. would not abide by it, but brought the affair into the King's Bench again, when Lord Mansfield confirmed the award ...[3]

There is some reason to believe that the dispute concerned the ownership and management of Bersham furnace.

W. Hawkes Smith preserved some typical anecdotes of Isaac's last years which indicate his fondness for bold speculation. He prophesied in his old age (1779) to a young friend, possibly John Harper of Wednesbury: '... *you* will live to see *waggons drawn by steam*. I would have made such a waggon for myself if I had had time.' According to the same writer Isaac was 'on the verge of an important discovery, for he distilled coals in order to extract the *tar*, as Lord Dundonald did some years afterwards, without being aware that the *gas* evolved might be retained and made highly useful as a combustible'.[4] In 1781 he was complaining that members of the Hornblower family of engineers had stolen from him some unspecified industrial secret, apparently connected with the steam engine.[5]

He died intestate on 31 January 1784, but although he was still 'of the City of Bristol', the event passed unnoticed in the

---

[1] When Priestley wrote to John Wilkinson on 19 September 1796, to inform the ironmaster of his sister's death, he stated: 'There could not be a better mother, and I will add, sister too. She always warmly took your part, and would never believe your father's account of your using him ill.' (Priestley-Wilkinson correspondence, Warrington Public Library.)

[2] i.e. Samuel Walker (1715–82), ironmaster, of Rotherham, Yorks. (*Minutes relating to Messrs. Samuel Walker & Co., Rotherham ...*, ed. A. H. John, 1951.)

[3] *PL*. I am indebted to Mr. Eric Robinson for noting and elucidating this cryptic passage.

[4] op. cit., p. 13.

[5] Watt to Boulton, 30 August 1781 (*PL*). For J. C. Hornblower's connexion with Isaac about 1760, see *Journal of Natural Philosophy*, i (1802), 219–20.

three Bristol newspapers of the day.[1] The sole evidence of his death comes from the laconic entry in the *Gentleman's Magazine* for 1784, where he is described as 'formerly an ironmaster at Bersham in Denbighshire'.[2] On 13 May 1786 letters of administration of his possessions were granted to Thomas Guest (d. 1808), the South Wales ironmaster, and son of John Guest, 'a creditor of the said deceased', while John and William Wilkinson, Mrs. Mary Priestley and Mrs. Margaret Parkinson, 'the natural and lawful and only children of the said deceased', renounced all interest in the estate.[3] Isaac Wilkinson's widow died in the summer of 1786.[4] Isaac's life was in many ways a failure, but out of his misfortunes in South Wales arose the gigantic prosperity of Anthony Bacon, the Guests, the Hills, the Homfrays and the Crawshays, while on the basis of Bersham furnace his son John was to erect a great industrial empire.

[1] *Bonner and Middleton's Bristol Journal, Felix Farley's Bristol Journal* and *Sarah Farley's Bristol Journal* have all been searched without result.

[2] Vol. liv, pt. i, p. 151. The obituary notices in the *Gentleman's Magazine* were culled mainly from newspaper reports.

[3] Principal Probate Registry, General Register Office, London.

[4] Journal de Pierre Toufaire, 15 July 1786 (MS. in possession of Mme Rondeau, Ligueil, France).

The Impact of the British Industrial Revolution on the Swedish Iron Industry

SWEDEN was exceptionally well-endowed with those natural resources most essential to the iron industry in the age of charcoal-smelting: pure and relatively easily reducible ores, water power in amounts that the technology of the time was well capable of harnessing, and extensive forests conveniently situated and yielding charcoal of low phosphoric content.[1] In the event of a rapid increase in total European demand for iron or a shift in this demand towards Swedish, as opposed to other types of iron, a considerable expansion of the Swedish iron industry could readily be achieved. Changes of both kinds did occur in the first half of the seventeenth century, and they stimulated a great interest—both within Sweden and abroad, especially in the Netherlands—in investment in Swedish iron production. The aim of this investment was to build up a productive apparatus which would be both technically up to date and organized in a manner well adapted to contemporary local conditions.[2] Among the implications of this was the need to organize and finance the supply of skilled and unskilled labour as well as of raw materials and fuel, and to guarantee a steady flow of victuals and other necessities. It was the manner in which these needs were met that largely determined the special character of the Swedish iron industry before the era of modern industrialization.[3]

[1] The phosphoric content of charcoal made from conifers is very low, 0·10–0·20 per cent; that of charcoal made from deciduous trees two or even three times as high. Cf. *Jernkontorets Annaler*, cxxii (Stockholm, 1938), 245.

[2] The most recent work on the history of the Swedish iron industry in the seventeenth and eighteenth centuries is K. G. Hildebrand, *Fagerstabrukens historia*, i (Uppsala, 1957), on which much of the following survey is based. Cf. E. F. Heckscher, *An Economic History of Sweden* (Harvard, 1954), pp. 92 ff., *Sveriges ekonomiska historia från Gustav Vasa*, i, 2, pp. 462 ff., and B. Boëthius, *Gruvornas, hyttornas och hamrarnas folk* (Stockholm, 1951), pp. 109 ff.

[3] Hildebrand, op. cit., pp. 253–349.

The Industrial Revolution and Swedish Iron

The deposits of iron ore most suitable for exploitation before the invention of the Thomas-Gilchrist process are mainly situated in a belt stretching east–west across Sweden 60–100 miles north of Stockholm. The majority of them lie in a coniferous forest region little suited to cultivation. This meant that the new or enlarged iron-works of the seventeenth century had to obtain additional supplies of foodstuffs from elsewhere though, at the same time, carrying with it the advantage that new cultivation made but little inroad upon the forest, which maintained itself by natural regrowth. The relatively slow growth, on the other hand, demanded that the iron-works should be widely scattered if the forest were to suffice for an enduring iron industry. The location of the works was therefore determined primarily by forest resources; water power was to be found virtually all over the region covered by the iron industry.

Before the expansion of the iron industry there had been little incentive to settle in this great tract of forest. Consequently, one of the chief tasks for many of the new enterprises was not merely the establishment of the iron-works themselves but also the organization of human settlement in the forests in order to secure a supply of labour for lumbering and charcoal-burning, as well as for transport, particularly of the charcoal. It therefore emerged as a characteristic feature of business policy in the new industry that entrepreneurs would seek not only to incorporate existing farms in their organization but also take the initiative in establishing new tenant farms in the forest—often indeed financing them. The occupiers of the farms paid their rents mainly or wholly in the form of charcoal burned in the forests owned by or at the disposal of the ironmaster. Because of the indifferent quality of the soil, grain crops were often insufficient to cover even a very modest *per capita* consumption; and in most of the iron-producing area the only way in which the necessary additional supplies could be secured was through the iron-works' truck shops. Here charcoal was bartered against barley, rye or other foodstuffs, and even the independent farmers, delivering charcoal to the works, could count on getting grain and other necessities on credit when their production of charcoal turned out to be insufficient to cover their purchases. The organization, in these and other ways, of a fairly uniform

53

supply of charcoal at fixed or only slightly varying prices constituted one of the most important entrepreneurial functions in the Swedish iron industry until as late as the 1860s and 1870s. It may be added that a thorough analysis of a great number of accounts very clearly demonstrates that only in exceptional cases did the truck system directly contribute to the works' profits; the accounts of the truck shops very often show a net loss even over comparatively long periods. The maintenance of a sufficient supply of grain was a *conditio sine qua non* of an enduring industry, and in years of crop failure it had to be achieved regardless of cost. The charcoal-burning farmers could not afford to pay high prices for the grain without a proportionate rise in the price paid for their charcoal, and there was thus no economic reason for the works to overcharge them for the goods bought at the shop.[1]

In most early Swedish iron-works it was the size of the charcoal supply that determined the level of production. Although ore represented a larger proportion than charcoal of the cost of production of pig iron, it does not seem that a rise in the consumption of ore generally increased marginal costs to any notable extent. In the manufacture of wrought iron at those iron-works that did not produce their own pig iron but bought it from blast furnaces situated in the vicinity of the mines, a similar relationship held between pig iron and charcoal. In both cases, the decisive factor was the marginal cost of charcoal. This was largely determined, not simply by the amounts delivered at comparatively low prices by the tenants and other farmers dependent of the works, but also by the length of the haul. Even with the favourable transport conditions afforded by the frozen lakes and snow-covered winter roads of Sweden, the cost of transporting charcoal increased rapidly with the distance involved. For those iron-works which were located within the central area of the industry the extent and quality of the forest resources at their disposal set a fairly rigid limit to the quantity

---

[1] The main characteristics of the entrepreneurial organization of the early Swedish iron industry have long been common knowledge among Swedish economic historians. To this has recently been added valuable detailed information published in Hildebrand, op. cit. The present author has also had the privilege of seeing the proofs of S. Montelius, *Fagerstabrukens historia*, v, 1, largely based on hitherto unknown material in private archives.

of charcoal which could be produced at relatively low cost under their own management. In this area the competition for the charcoal of independent farmers was often intense, which resulted in high prices for such charcoal even though the market was strictly regulated. Several iron-works certainly found themselves compelled to satisfy a large proportion of their requirements of charcoal in this manner, but in general the ironmasters did not willingly fill more than marginal needs by purchases on the open market.[1]

These circumstances played a decisive role in determining the entrepreneurial organization of the early Swedish iron industry: a large number of small units where the annual production of wrought iron rarely exceeded about two hundred tons. The fact that the internal economies of large-scale production attainable under the old technology were of small significance undoubtedly worked in the same direction. This division into many units appears to have had a great influence upon the iron industry's reaction to the new conditions that came into being as a result of the industrial revolution in Britain and the attendant technical innovations.[2]

The ultimate purpose of an iron-works is obviously to produce iron. But the entrepreneurial organization of the Swedish iron-works of this early period was much more concerned with the preliminary stages which made this production possible. The number of workers directly employed in the production of pig iron and wrought iron was far smaller than the number of those engaged in producing and transporting charcoal, foodstuffs and sundry raw materials. According to the accounts of the Horndal iron-works, which have been preserved from the mid-seventeenth century, the average number of skilled workers at the blast furnace and the forges amounted to eighteen (in the eighteenth century), while some 170 farmers and tenants were credited for charcoal deliveries, transport services, etc.[3] In this respect Horndal was a typical representative of the medium-sized eighteenth-century Swedish iron-works, which was a

[1] Cf. Hildebrand, op. cit., pp. 256 ff., 261 ff., 289 ff.

[2] The total number of Swedish ironworks seems to have changed very little from the late seventeenth to the early nineteenth century. According to Professor Boëthius (op. cit., p. 117), it was 324 in 1695, 352 in 1748 and 340 in 1803.

[3] Personal and general ledgers, Fagersta Bruks Arkiv, Fagersta, Sweden.

The Industrial Revolution and Swedish Iron

complex combination of forestry, agriculture, retail trade, iron production and, sometimes, ore mining. Even in the late nineteenth century the attention of the management was often devoted much more to the first two activities than to the last two. As late as 1908 a German industrialist with a thorough knowledge of the contemporary Swedish iron industry saw as one of its main characteristics the fact the owners and managers concentrated their interest on agriculture and forestry while the production of iron and steel took only second place or was virtually regarded as a side-line.[1]

This type of entrepreneurial organization continued for a considerable time under market conditions that were generally fairly favourable. About 90 per cent of the output seems normally to have been sold abroad, mainly to Holland until the later seventeenth century, and then, from the 1680s onwards, mainly to England. In the 1730s and 1740s, however, market conditions deteriorated and the expansive phase of the Swedish iron industry was succeeded by a long period of stagnation. This stagnation was largely voluntary and was maintained in spite of the considerable improvement in market conditions that occurred as early as the 1750s. Co-operation between the iron-masters and the Government secured the imposition of restrictions not only upon the annual output of each individual iron-works but also upon the entry of newcomers into the industry; the fact that such a large proportion of production was exported and thus had to pass through the customs, afforded an excellent means of ensuring that the maximum permitted output was not exceeded. The purpose of the restrictions was, of course, to stabilize both prices and costs of production at a level favourable to existing works. These twin objects seem, on the whole, to have been achieved during the second half of the eighteenth century in spite of the fact that the Swedish industry was far from enjoying a monopoly position in the export markets.[2]

As K. G. Hildebrand has shown in his recent account of the

[1] Letter from E. Possehl to A. Wahlberg, 1 August 1908, ibid.; quoted in A. Attman, *Fagerstabrukens historia*, ii (Uppsala, 1958), 538.
[2] Cf. Heckscher, *Econ. Hist. of Sweden*, pp. 93, 176 f., Boëthius, op. cit., pp. 281 f., B. Boëthius and A. Kromnow, *Jernkontorets historia*, i (Stockholm, 1947), 46 ff., 53 ff., Hildebrand, op. cit., pp. 40, 106 f., 161 ff.

Swedish iron industry in the seventeenth and eighteenth centuries, this had not been true even before the beginning of Russian competition in the early eighteenth century, though up to the 1760s Sweden remained the main source of British imports of wrought iron. During the period of economic expansion after the Seven Years War, there was, however, a rapid increase in imports from Russia and from the mid-1760s these normally exceeded imports from Sweden, in some years by more than 50 per cent. In the British market, which was by far the most important one in Europe, the Swedish industry thus obviously did not enjoy a monopoly position. But Swedish exports to Britain remained fairly stable all through the century, only in exceptional circumstances amounting to less than 15,000 or more than 20,000 tons a year. The increase of imports from Russia was due to an increase in total British imports of wrought iron, not to a decrease in imports from Sweden.[1]

This development was naturally not welcomed in Sweden, though it does not seem to have had any unfavourable consequences for the Swedish ironmasters. For the greater part of the period 1750–1800 total demand for Swedish iron was good. The sharp rise in marginal costs which, as has been said earlier, appeared when attempts were made to increase output in existing iron-works, provides a plausible explanation of why the producers generally preferred not to exceed their average output, despite the growing demand; the fact that only exceptionally were newcomers permitted to enter the industry explains why production did not expand through the construction of new works. There are certainly good grounds for assuming that —given the industry's existing structure—its volume of production was very nearly optimal, at any rate for already established enterprises. A large output, without any increase in the number of iron-works or any significant extension of them, would in all likelihood have brought about higher costs of production; and, moreover, the larger output would probably have had to be sold at lower prices. The volume of production for which the industry was built and organized could instead now be sold at

---

[1] K. G. Hildebrand, 'The Export Markets for Swedish Iron in the Eighteenth Century', *Scand. Econ. Hist. Rev.*, vi, 1 (1958), 1 ff., and *Fagerstabrukens historia*, i, 106 f.

prices which were on the whole favourable, despite the competition from the Russian iron industry.[1]

In the latter half of the eighteenth century this competition from Russia was almost wholly confined to England; in other markets, sales of Swedish iron were rising. There was an expecially marked growth in Swedish exports to the Latin markets, Portugal, Spain, France and the Mediterranean ports: about 10 per cent of total Swedish exports in the first half of the century, they rose to between 20 and 30 per cent from the 1770s onwards. This change was of more than passing significance. The Swedish iron industry became, thanks to this, less dependent on a single market than it had been at the beginning of the century, and moreover less dependent on that very market where technical developments first came to produce sweeping changes in demand.[2]

As is well known, these changes meant, *inter alia*, that British imports of wrought iron fell heavily. In the last quarter of the eighteenth century they had risen to an average of about 50,000 tons annually; for the period 1816–30 they were in the region of 15,000 tons or even less. Although the decline in imports primarily affected Russian bar iron, the new market situation emerging from the expansion of the puddling process in Britain also carried serious consequences for the Swedish iron industry. Its exports to Britain, even in the late eighteenth century, had comprised 40 per cent or more of total exports; after the Napoleonic wars they fell to 15–20 per cent.[3]

Adjustment to this new market situation was greatly facilitated by a remarkable temporary increase in direct exports from Sweden to the United States. This export had already begun during the period of the 'Continental System', when American ships were seeking return cargoes from Europe and thus, in part, made up for an earlier re-export of Swedish bar iron from England. But these direct exports soon reached much larger dimensions than the re-export trade had ever attained. Even

[1] On the market situation for Swedish iron in the second half of the eighteenth century, cf. Heckscher, op. cit., p. 177. Heckscher's interpretation of the situation resulting from the restrictions differs in various respects from the tentative interpretation given here. Cf. Heckscher, op. cit., pp. 179 f.

[2] Hildebrand, *Scand. Econ. Hist. Rev.*, vi, 39.

[3] cf. Attman, op. cit., p. 6.

before the end of the Napoleonic wars, direct exports went up to about 10,000 tons annually and reached over 20,000 tons in the 1820s. In the 1830s annual exports to the United States were normally between 20,000 and 30,000 tons per annum, thus exceeding even the highest eighteenth-century level of exports to England. An important cause contributing to this expansion of American iron imports from Sweden was the fact that import duties on hammered iron—and all Swedish bar iron at this time was hammered—were considerably lower than those on rolled iron, i.e. primarily British puddled iron.[1] Partly because of changes in the tariff but presumably mainly as a result of the rapid expansion of the American iron industry, this favourable situation came to an end in the 1840s. Meanwhile, however, the respite thus granted to Swedish iron was undoubtedly of vital importance to the Swedish industry.[2]

That the decline in British imports of Swedish bar iron was not still more drastic—imports from Russia fell by a good 80 per cent—was undoubtedly due to the existence of certain specialized uses for the Swedish product, uses in which the competition of puddled iron was less evident. For example, a significant proportion of British imports of Swedish bar iron went via Hull to Sheffield and other places, to be used as raw material in the production of steel. This manufacture was based very largely upon imported bar iron, mainly Swedish and, to only a small extent, Russian; the iron was converted into blister steel, and this in turn served as the raw material of crucible steel and shear steel. These types of steel were high-grade products, and the degree of success of the production process depended almost wholly upon the quality of the raw material. Output of blister steel increased fairly slowly up to the 1840s, but a rapid expansion then began and from 1846 to 1856 production in Sheffield seems to have almost doubled. As it was still based mainly upon imported iron, there followed a corresponding expansion in the demand for high-quality Swedish bar iron.[3]

Another important circumstance which eased the process of

[1] See below, pp. 270–1.
[2] E. W. Fleisher, 'The Beginning of the Transatlantic Market for Swedish Iron', *Scand. Econ. Hist. Rev.*, i (1953), 178–92; Attman, op. cit., pp. 6 ff., 18 f. and the works quoted ibid., p. 665, n. 2.
[3] Attman, op. cit., pp. 11 ff.

adjustment in the Swedish industry was the fact that British imports of Swedish iron were designed not only to satisfy English home requirements but also to supply a re-export trade. This re-export, mainly from London, was particularly directed towards markets where metallurgical technology was little developed, especially, in the early nineteenth-century, India. Bar iron manufactured with charcoal was far better suited than puddled iron to treatment by simple working-up techniques. Indeed, Swedish bar iron was not displaced from these markets until the advent of basic open-hearth steel. In more general terms, one may say that the Swedish iron industry, with its old-fashioned technical survivals, owed its continued existence partly to the fact that in many areas of the world technical progress, despite the industrial revolution, was very slow.[1]

The condition of the Swedish iron industry in the decades immediately following the Napoleonic wars may be broadly summarized as follows. A relatively small proportion—some 20 per cent—of its output was sold to the English steel industry; prices of this bar iron were two or three times higher than those of ordinary charcoal iron, but quality requirements were very exacting; there does not seem to have been any severe competition in this highly specialized market. A further relatively small proportion was exported—or re-exported—to regions that technically were comparatively little developed; competition there does not seem to have been keen either, but the demand remained fairly limited. The major proportion was exported to such countries as the United States, Germany, Denmark, France, Portugal, and to the Mediterranean. In several of these markets the prerequisites existed for technical developments of a sort which might well lead to the substitution of cheaper iron for the Swedish charcoal iron.

Sweden lacks coal deposits useful for iron production. In the circumstances then prevailing, therefore, the Swedish iron industry was forced to continue to depend upon charcoal for its survival. Before railway construction began in the 1850s, there

---

[1] From 1815 to 1850 total annual British exports of foreign iron in bars only rarely exceeded 5,000 tons. Most of these re-exports seem to have consisted of Swedish wrought iron (Attman, op. cit., p. 9). Cf. E. F. Söderlund and P. E. Wretblad, *Fagerstabrukens historia*, iii, 2 f.

had been no innovations in transport, despite some canal building, such as would significantly disturb the preconditions upon which the entrepreneurial organization of the iron industry had been founded. Technical modifications and internal economies designed to facilitate adaptation to changes in market conditions had therefore to be introduced within the framework of the old entrepreneurial structure, viz. a large number of relatively small works scattered over an extensive region of central Sweden. Adjustment had to embrace, firstly, an increase in the production of bar iron of the high and uniform quality demanded by the English steel industry; secondly, in order as far as possible to offset the risk of substitution, a reduction in the cost of production of ordinary charcoal bar iron without, however, any loss of those characteristics of quality which had made it so much in demand.

In the first half of the nineteenth century, the Swedish iron industry still employed methods that had remained unchanged in all important respects since they were introduced in the sixteenth and seventeenth centuries. Most of the steel-making iron was manufactured from ore from one mine, Dannemora, and by the so-called Walloon process. With quite minor modernizations, this process was able to produce an iron which, in its limited range of uses, was excellent both technically and economically; it survived in fact at a few works right through to the present century. The rest of the bar iron output—about 90 per cent at the beginning of the nineteenth century—was produced by a method introduced into Sweden in the sixteenth century and known there as the 'German process'. The pig iron was first refined in an open charcoal hearth, then hammered, next reheated in the same hearth and finally forged into bars of the desired dimensions. The process required much labour to yield a product of good quality, and the consumption of charcoal was heavy.[1] The technical problem to be solved was that of finding a more economical process which could be relied upon to produce iron that was consistent and homogeneous in quality—the quality of steel-making iron if so desired and if the necessary ores were available; such a process should also

---

[1] Excellent descriptions and illustrations in S. Rinman, *Bergwerks Lexicon* (Stockholm, 1788-9). Cf. Boëthius and Kromnow, op. cit., iii, 1, p. 57.

preferably allow the bars to be rolled instead of forged, as this would lower costs and make it easier to achieve exact dimensions.[1]

It was natural enough that a solution to these problems should have first been sought by way of the introduction of the most modern English technique, puddling, in a form modified to suit Swedish conditions. It soon became clear, however, that this was a blind alley. Several other solutions were tried, most of them involving modifications of methods already practised in Sweden, but these efforts also met with little success. The innovation by which success was at last achieved, although originating in England, owed nothing to the new English technique but derived from what may be called a survival from the pre-industrial era.[2]

In the first half of the nineteenth century in England there was still some production of malleable iron, unimportant in quantity but outstanding in quality, which used charcoal pig iron as its raw material. Swedish metallurgists went to study the process both in South Wales and at Ulverston in Lancashire. On the basis of these studies and partly with the assistance of imported English labour the new technique was introduced into Sweden and given there the name of 'the Lancashire process'.[3] The technical problems connected with the adaptation of this process of refining to the needs of the Swedish industry were solved as early as the beginning of the 1830s. It soon emerged, however, that the new process could not be applied economically until the refined iron could be reheated (before being hammered or rolled) to a higher temperature than could at that time be achieved with wood or charcoal. This problem was solved in 1845 by G. Ekman's invention of a gas generator functioning on charcoal or wood. The advantages of the combination of the Lancashire process with the gas-heated furnace were multiple: there was a considerable saving of charcoal—as early as the 1850s the consumption of charcoal per ton bar iron had been brought down by some 50 per cent; the iron produced by this method was of a more uniform quality; and the

---

[1] Cf. Boëthius and Kromnow, op. cit., pp. 471 f. and *passim*.
[2] ibid., pp. 370 ff., 457 ff., 461 ff.
[3] ibid., pp. 468 f., 475.

temperature of the iron heated in the furnace was high enough for the rolling technique to be used.[1]

The new method was adopted from about 1850 onwards. Lancashire iron soon became the chief product of the Swedish industry and kept this position right up to the 1890s; in 1887 for instance some 80 per cent of the total Swedish output of iron and steel was made in Lancashire furnaces.[2] Lancashire iron was of excellent quality, homogeneous and reliable, and also excellent for steel-making if suitable pig iron was used. For a number of reasons it was also cheaper than iron produced with the earlier methods, and demand was fairly satisfactory in spite of a comparatively rapid increase in total output of wrought iron which rose from less than 100,000 tons in 1844 to over 220,000 tons in 1887. The growth in production coincided with a new expansion of British imports from Sweden which doubled from the 1840s to the 1870s, mainly as a consequence of increasing re-exports to India and the U.S.A., and also to Turkey, Canada, China and Japan. Britain thus once again became the most important market for Swedish iron, and once again it became evident that iron manufactured with charcoal, for which Sweden still enjoyed exceptional facilities, was preferred in markets where quality requirements were exacting or where metallurgical technology was little developed.[3]

The Lancashire process not only made it possible to produce increasing quantities of better and cheaper iron. It was, up to the 1870s when a fairly adequate railway network became available to the Swedish iron industry, the main incentive to the first important structural change within this industry since the seventeenth century. The Ekman furnace and the rolling machinery made possible considerable internal economies by introducing larger-scale production; even before the advent of railways the lower consumption per ton of charcoal also tended to break the rigid limits imposed on optimal output by the rapid rise in the marginal cost of charcoal. The result was a gradual concentration of the production and the emergence of a Swedish iron

[1] ibid., pp. 402, 475, 485–92, 496 f., Attman, op. cit., p. 170.
[2] Kommerskoll. berättelse rörande bergshanteringen (Returns of the Swedish Board of Trade on Mining and Metallurgical Industries), 1887, cf. Attman, op. cit., p. 274.
[3] Cf. Attman, op. cit., pp. 245 f., 249.

industry on something approaching a modern industrial scale. Fairly obviously, and not least by furthering this adaptation to modern industrial production, it was the Lancashire process that made the largest contribution to enabling the Swedish iron industry to overcome the prolonged crisis caused by the revolutionary effects of the introduction of puddling. It also facilitated the transition from the mode of entrepreneurial organization peculiar to the early Swedish iron industry with its many scattered, often isolated works and its patriarchal relationship between ironmasters and their workers, to the present-day large-scale production based on the converter, and the open-hearth and electric furnaces.

The profound changes that have occurred within this industry have at no stage amounted to anything like an industrial revolution, rather to an industrial evolution though with long periods when capital yield was low and technical, economic and organizational problems seemed almost insoluble. That these difficulties could be overcome appears mainly to have been due to three easily discernible factors.

One of them is evidently the high degree of technical skill developed within an industry in which iron of comparatively high quality had been produced for more than two centuries. This skill would, however, have been of little avail if cheap puddled iron could have been substituted for charcoal iron for all purposes. But in fact there was a persistent demand for good quality charcoal iron as long as its price was not too high compared with that of puddled iron, and not only in technically underdeveloped countries. A growing proportion of the demand derived from technical and economic changes made possible by the introduction of the puddling process, from the needs created by the industrial revolution. Towards the end of the nineteenth century far more Swedish iron was used in the steel-works, machine shops and hardware industries of Great Britain, Germany and the United States than in all the underdeveloped areas put together. The industrial revolution did not rob the Swedish iron industry of its markets. Provided that it was capable of adapting itself to the new and ever-changing conditions, the same natural resources that had been the preconditions of Sweden's dominant position in the European iron export trade in the seventeenth and the early eighteenth centuries could give her a similar position in the world market for high-quality iron in the industrial era. By achieving this Sweden became the only country in the world without coal deposits where a virtually unprotected iron industry has been able not only to survive but to keep its position as one of the major export industries.

IV

Clothiers and Weavers in Wiltshire during the Eighteenth Century

AMONG the industrial riots of the eighteenth century few are better known than those which took place in the Wiltshire cloth industry in the winters of 1726 and 1738. In their own day they were widely thought of as symptoms of a declining industry—declining because of its rigidly capitalistic structure and its inability to compete with its more loosely organized rival in Yorkshire. Josiah Tucker pointed the contrast in a dramatic passage in which he suggested that master and workman in the west of England might be compared to planter and slave in the American colonies and that it was not surprising that the industry was migrating to the freer atmosphere of the north.[1] From his cure in Bristol, before he became Dean of Gloucester, Tucker was well placed to observe conditions in the three cloth-making counties of Wiltshire, Gloucestershire and Somerset; but it seems not improbable that his opinion of the western clothiers was formed partly as a result of his acquaintance with the Trowbridge clothier, William Temple.[2] Temple's attitude as expressed in *The Case as it now stands between the Clothiers and the Weavers*, written after the riots of 1738, strongly suggests the overbearing conduct attributed by Tucker to the masters; and the account of the workers, 'who think it no crime to get as much wages and to do as little for it as they possibly can, to lie and cheat and to do any bad thing provided it is only against their Master', might have been drawn from the *Case* itself. However this may be, Tucker must have

---

[1] J. Tucker, *Instructions to Travellers* (1758), pp. 38–39. It was privately printed in 1757 and must have been written before the Gloucestershire riots of that year. See R. L. Schuyler, *Josiah Tucker* (1931), p. 12.

[2] See below, p. 77. Tucker may have made Temple's acquaintance over the naturalization controversy on which Temple shared his opinions.

remembered these riots and the controversy which they provoked. A later commentator, Arthur Young, explicitly avowed that his view of the industry was coloured by this source;[1] and his poor opinion of its condition in Wiltshire is even further from the truth than Tucker's.[2]

For many centuries there had been large capitalists and a proletariat of landless workers in the woollen industry of all the western counties. The low wages paid and the starving condition of the work-people had been a theme for Government anxiety and parliamentary discussion during various depressions in the two previous centuries. But after 1660 the manufacture of fine medley broadcloth had gone ahead prosperously in west Wiltshire, and there was far less discontent among its makers than among other western manufacturers. This prosperity lasted over the turn of the century, but it is clear that the workers must have been suffering from various oppressive practices long before the first riot took place in 1726, for none of the grievances then complained of were new. In spite of this, there is no sign in the first quarter of the century of the workers' associations which were formed in Taunton and the Devonshire towns from 1700 onwards;[3] and there were no disturbances such as those which occurred further west and resulted in the Act of 1725 forbidding both combinations and truck.[4] Perhaps the fact that few woolcombers were employed deprived Wiltshire of the leadership which these men exerted in Devonshire, for woolcombing had always been a well-organized trade. When rioting did finally break out in Trowbridge, Bradford-on-Avon and Frome at the end of November 1726, it was after a bad harvest which had sent up the price of bread; but the main cause must have been the financial crisis arising from the declaration of war with Spain the previous October.[5] The shortage of cash and the general stagnation of trade which followed may be seen in the letter book of a firm of Trowbridge clothiers, Usher and Jeffries, which has been preserved by Messrs. J. and T. Clark of the same

[1] *Annals of Agriculture*, vii, 163.
[2] For a general account of the Wiltshire cloth industry see the article by the present writer in *V.C.H. Wilts.*, vol. iv, to be published in 1959.
[3] W. G. Hoskins, *Industry, Trade and People in Exeter, 1688–1800* (1935), pp. 58 ff.
[4] 12 Geo. I, c. 34.
[5] I owe information about this crisis to Professor Ashton.

place.[1] At the end of October they told both their London factors and a country customer that they were short of money and in the following month they were proposing to send no more cloth to London till there was some prospect of a sale for it. Their cloth book, which has also been preserved, shows that the practice of paying their weavers in instalments and sometimes by note of hand instead of in coin became more frequent that autumn. The notes were sometimes drawn on a man who supplied them with beef—a form of truck which put the recipients at his mercy. Usher and Jeffries did not lower wages, but other clothiers must have done so, since the weavers complained of a heavy fall. The crisis must also have intensified the older grievances. It is odd to find that truck was not mentioned among these, for other sources suggest that it was frequent. Those cited were the use of weights containing seventeen ounces to the pound and the lengthening of the warping bars which might oblige the weaver to weave three or four more yards for the same price. The first had been mentioned in 1714 by clothiers themselves, who said that they were being undersold by such practices;[2] while the second may be seen, from 1721 onwards, in the cloth book just mentioned, although from late in 1725 Usher and Jeffries were paying by the yard. The riots continued intermittently from 27 November until the beginning of January, the mob having been roused a second time by the arrest of two of their number.[3] They were ended at last by the intervention of dragoons combined with a promise by the Government through Giles Earle, M.P. for Malmesbury, who had been asked to investigate the situation, of redress for all grievances if peaceful application were made. Such Government intervention on the side of the workers sharply differentiates these riots from others in the century; but it was just as much due to fear of Jacobite influence as to concern for industrial relations. One of the observers, a Middlesex Justice named Vaughan who was staying at Bath, gave serious attention to the Jacobite danger, hearing that one of the people most trusted by the weavers was a wealthy

---

[1] The letter book runs from the beginning of 1726 to 1742 with several gaps; the cloth book from 1721 to 1726. Jeffries was related to the Clarks by marriage.

[2] *Bromley's Papers* (Bodl. Lib.), iv, no. 20.

[3] *PRO*, SP.35/63, nos. 72, 82, 94, 95 and SP.35/64, nos. 1–6, 9 and 10.

gentleman who was a 'Stickler among the Tories';[1] but he soon changed his mind and reported that the majority of the weavers were dissenters and, so far from having Jacobite sympathies, went about with K.W.G. in their caps, signifying that they were King George's weavers. The sympathy which the country gentry felt for them had given the clothiers an opportunity to exploit a situation which still seemed to have an element of danger.

In fact, some antagonism between gentry and clothiers can be traced throughout the century. It was fed from two sources, the burden of the poor rates and the prohibition of the export of wool. The latter only came to the fore in later years, but the poor rates were already an issue, for the landowners and farmers paid them and the clothiers did not, as was remarked both by Vaughan in 1727 and by the author of the 'Essay on Riots' in 1738. This was not strictly accurate, for it was the custom in the Wiltshire industrial districts to tax tradesmen on stock;[2] but the Trowbridge rate books show that it was assessed at an extremely low figure—no more than £50 for most of the clothiers living there in 1711.[3] It was resentment on this account which sharpened the pen of an anonymous writer from Westbury who sent a letter to Lord Harrington apropos of the trial of the rioters of 1738,[4] complaining of the hardships which the smaller gentry suffered from such taxes. The clothiers, he said, were not only the tyrants of the countryside but manifestly flourished on it, keeping their coaches and becoming Justices of the Peace even though their parents had been poor work-people. His account of the workers' sufferings from truck may well be true, but he was mistaken in the origin of the Justices he mentions[5] and it looks as if jealousy played some part in forming his opinions. Magistrates were particularly annoyed by the fact that clothiers often

[1] He was Webb of Monkton Farleigh whose house had been searched for arms in 1722 on very irresponsible information, *Wilts. Arch. Mag.*, xi, 215.

[2] Cf. E. Cannan, *History of Local Rates* (2nd edn., 1912), p. 96, for a case from Bradford-on-Avon in 1776.

[3] Wilts. *CRO*, 206. The series of rate books begins in 1761 but an isolated assessment for 1711 is in the poor book of that date.

[4] *PRO*, SP.36/47, no. 37.

[5] They were two brothers at Westbury Leigh, 'who are clothiers & Justices'. The only clothiers who answer this description are John and Thomas Phipps, but their father was Paul Phipps whose monument in Westbury church describes him as Esquire.

dealt summarily with their work-people instead of bringing cases to petty sessions;[1] and there was a distinct unwillingness among many of them to take action in the clothiers' favour. Even some who were clothiers did not always sympathize with their fellows in the trade; and the opinion of the Westbury writer that 'it would be more rational to make a shepherd of a wolf as [sic] a Justice of a clothier' is belied by the conduct of John Cooper of Trowbridge, a clothier in a large way of business who, as a Justice, first reported the riots of 1726. It may have been the fact that he suffered from unfair competition which influenced his opinion that the riots were solely due to oppression; but his efforts to get other clothiers to shorten their warping bars and to refrain from exacerbating the situation by arresting rioters caused much bitter feeling which persisted long afterwards. The gentry were also sceptical about trade depressions. Vaughan thought that it was not the weavers but the clothiers who were disaffected, since they (quite rightly) attributed the stagnation in trade to Government action. In 1738 it was admitted that trade was bad in general owing to foreign competition, but the suggestion that clothiers were experiencing any particular difficulties was dismissed on the ground that the price of cloth had not fallen.[2]

The upshot of the riots of 1726 was the summoning of representatives of both sides to London where the Privy Council recommended them to agree among themselves about the matters in dispute.[3] Articles of Agreement were drawn up ordaining the use of avoirdupois weights and of warping bars of a fixed length and providing that all disputes should be heard by two Justices, with the possibility of an appeal to Quarter Sessions but not further.[4] They were immediately embodied in a Bill which became law the same session.[5] The most important clause in it, as far as Wiltshire was concerned, was the clear recognition of the yard as the unit by which payment should be made. A rate per yard had, of course, always been stated in wage assessments by Justices at Quarter Sessions (although the

---

[1] 'James Montagu's Charge to the Grand Jury, 1720,' 55, in *Wiltshire Tracts*, xii (Wilts. Arch. Soc. Lib.).
[2] 'A Defence of the Essay on Riots': see Note, p. 96 below, item (g).
[3] *PRO*, PC.1, 4/22.
[4] ibid. There is a copy in *JHC*, xx, 747.   [5] 13 Geo. I, c. 23.

last year in which a rate for the cloth industry had been made in Wiltshire was 1655); but it is probable that the unit for payment was generally thought of as the piece, since the length of the white cloth which had formerly been the main production of the county was fixed by statute. There were no regulations for medleys and their length was apt to vary. After 1726 payment by the yard was an accepted principle in Wiltshire. It would be attributing too much influence to eighteenth-century legislation to suggest that this was the result of the act. Indeed it clearly was not, since the clause made no impression in Gloucestershire where, in 1756, clothiers were paying by the piece and lengthening it without extra payment.[1] The difference in Wiltshire was due to the fact that the issue had been fought out there.

In some other respects there was an attempt to make this act and that of 1725 effective. Convictions for truck and for non-payment of wages are found in the Order Books of Quarter Sessions for both counties between 1727 and 1733, but the result was not what the framers of the statutes intended. In Wiltshire, workers who showed any disposition to challenge their masters were paid what they asked and discharged;[2] and a man so discharged could get no more work. In this way the clothiers avoided the clause in the statute of 1727 which made the Justices' decision final. In Gloucestershire no notice seems to have been taken of this clause,[3] and even in Wiltshire it seems to have been forgotten by 1739 if we may trust the Westbury writer already referred to.

The next outbreak, in the late autumn of 1738, has some puzzling features, for this year was not one of scarcity or crisis. But the industry had for some years been feeling the impact of competition and changes in fashion[4] and it seems probable that the fall in orders for export in the autumn of 1738 proved the last straw. In that year, it is true, exports had been satisfactory, but goods were exported in the summer and it was orders for the following year which provided employment for autumn and

---

[1] W. E. Minchinton, 'Petitions of the Weavers & Clothiers of Gloucestershire in 1756', *Bristol and Glouc. Arch. Journ.*, lxxiii (1954), 219.

[2] See below, p. 75.

[3] *JHC*, xxvii (1756), 503.

[4] See below, p. 86. It was said that wages had dropped from about 1735, *The Miseries of the Miserable*, p. 6: see Note, p. 96 below, item (k).

winter. In 1739 exports dropped disastrously, largely owing to the fact that the Levant Company which, we know, bought goods in Trowbridge,[1] had heavy stocks unsold in Asia Minor.[2] It is probable that the apologist for the clothiers who said that there had been not less than sixty looms unemployed for several weeks before the riot[3] was pointing out one of its main causes. It was to one of these unemployed and not to one of his regular weavers that Coulthurst, the Melksham clothier whose premises were attacked, had given the warp at 1*s* 2*d* per yard which provoked the riot;[4] and this may explain why all the Melksham clothiers, among whom were several Quakers, said that they never paid more, while the weavers who rioted regarded it as a reduction. The mob which assembled on the first day of the riot came, in part at least, from the far side of Trowbridge; and it spent that day in destroying cloth in the looms round that town. It looks as if the riot may have been an attempt to prevent a fall in wages from spreading to areas which had been paying a higher rate.

This riot provoked a very different response from that of 1726. The 'thirties had seen a number of riots in the west, mainly over turnpikes; and the Melksham outbreak occurred just after one by the Kingswood colliers. The mob, which quickly got drunk, terrorized the inhabitants for three days and it was probably thought that an example should be made. In fact, the Government may even have used influence to secure a verdict against the rioters.[5] To the great satisfaction of the clothiers, all but one of the men arrested were found guilty and three of them were hanged. Nevertheless, the grievances of the weavers and the protests of the clothiers were far more widely publicized than in 1726, owing to the fact that the case on both sides was argued at length in the *Gloucester Journal* from which copious extracts were transferred to the *Gentleman's Magazine*. For this we have to thank the anonymous author of the 'Essay on Riots', who deserves a place among the pamphleteers of the eighteenth century if only for the note of real acquaintance with the lives of the poor

[1] *JHC*, xxvi (1753), 609.   [2] *PRO*, SP.36/48, no. 44.
[3] *Gents. Mag.*, ix (1739), 125.   [4] *Glouc. Journ.*, 26 December 1738.
[5] *PRO*, SP.36/47, no. 51. This letter from a Chippenham Justice to Lord Harrington, one of the Secretaries of State, thanks him 'for the kind part you have acted in this affair'.

which is sounded in his writings. He described himself as 'a Gentleman of Wiltshire' and he evidently lived in the neighbourhood of Trowbridge and Melksham; but it has not been possible to discover his identity, although it was known at the time. He had already written several pamphlets[1] and in 1738 he had begun to contribute papers to the *Gloucester Journal* under the pseudonym of 'Country Commonsense'. His writings reveal him as a Tory, a tolerant but devoted member of the established church and a social reformer of the paternal type whose attitude, both in his concern for his poorer neighbours and in his ignorance of the stresses of industry, foreshadows that of many a later critic of social conditions. A passage in which he combats the idea that truck was infrequent because there were few prosecutions for it shows how effectively he could put the case of the workers:[2]

When a Person goes into a Poor Manufacturer's House, sees Bread and Cloth upon the Table, is told by the Poor Man, that he is forced to take 'em of his Master for Work and on saying '*Tis your own Fault* in not prosecuting your Master, is answered, *I dare not, I shall starve if I do!* such a one did so, but could get no work afterwards:— When another offers Superfine Cloth of several Sorts, some shillings a yd cheaper than the common price and says, He took it of some Master he work'd for, but refuses to tell his Master's name. . . . When he heard a Master in publick blame Truck and in a few Days is accidentally told by a Workman to that same Master, that he keeps back a certain Sum out of such a Quantity of Work which he pays in Goods; when the Goods is shewn and when on asking the poor Man's Leave to speak to the Master about it, he is conjur'd to say *nothing* in these emphatical terms: *My Master trucks almost as little as anyone and is one of the best Masters in the Town he lives in* (where are many) *but if he was to hear I had complained wou'd turn me off, and I should never get Work more; as was such a One's case*; . . . When 'tis common in the mouths of the Poor, Such a Master trucks *so much*, such a one *so much* in a Piece . . . I say that when things are come to this pass, we may not only conclude that Truck is yet a common Trade with some . . . but also that the oppressed Poor are under their Masters' Power or Influence by some private ways or other. . . .

[1] They were: *An Enquiry into the Encrease and Miseries of the Poor of England* (1738); *A Dissuasive from Party and Religious Animosities* (1736); *A Dissertation on Patriotism* (1735) and *The Harmony of Reason and Christianity*.

[2] 'A Defence of the Essay on Riots': see Note, p. 96 below, item (g).

Clothiers and Weavers in 18th Century Wiltshire

The *Gloucester Journal* had been unable to print more than two numbers of 'Country Commonsense',[1] but it published not only the 'Essay on Riots' and two later articles but also the lengthy rejoinders which they provoked,[2] from which it may be inferred that widespread interest was aroused. Although the Essay contained the stereotyped complaints about the tippling in alehouses indulged in by the poor, its author was mainly concerned with the policies which had provoked them to riot; and no one, from the Government to the clothiers, escaped criticism. It is not surprising that the latter resented his charges of lowering wages, paying in truck and forcing work-people to deal at shops where weights were light and to live in high-rented houses, although he could, it is clear, have given instances for all of them. No body of employers would relish a proposal for an inquiry into their practices by 'a commission of gentlemen and employers of the best character', or welcome the suggestion that the public would benefit by learning what their profits really were. The three long essays in their defence all came from Trowbridge. The best known of them is Temple's, which was the last to appear. Of the others, an attack on the factors which first appeared in a London newspaper, 'Old Commonsense', admitted the weavers' distress but attributed it to the clothiers' difficulties caused by the long credit which they were forced to give to the factors. The third is signed 'A Manufacturer in Wilts.' The author denied all knowledge of truck or of combinations to keep down wages, but pointed out, in milder language than Temple's, that work-people, like their employers, must suffer when trade is dull. He did indeed stigmatize the Essayist's proposals as 'the product of some inhabitant of Bedlam', but these proposals were impracticable under eighteenth century conditions. They included one for fining any clothier who dismissed, in less than six months, a workman on whose evidence he had been convicted of truck, and any other clothier,

---

[1] *Glouc. Journ.*, 11 July 1738. Cf. *Gents. Mag.*, ix (1739), 9. The two numbers appeared on 13 and 27 June. In apologizing for being unable to print more, the editor undertook to publish them separately and the volume was advertised on 5 September with a second volume advertised on 20 February 1739. Neither seems to have survived.

[2] For a list of publications on the riots of 1738 see Note at the end of this essay, pp. 95–96 below.

up to the number of seven, who refused to employ a man so dismissed. Another was for regulating wages on a sliding scale according to the price of cloth, which was to be published weekly.[1] It is odd that a man who repeatedly refers to the non-execution of good laws, owing to the venality of those who should carry them out, should have thought that the first proposal had any chance of being successful; and the second offered the clothiers only too clear an instance that the writer did not understand the conditions of the trade.

It is Temple's reply which has seemed to many readers the final argument against the clothiers. His self-righteousness, his contempt for the workers and his attacks on all who sympathized with them, especially on Cooper whom he calls Tarquinius Superbus and accuses of always favouring the workman, form the strongest possible illustration of Tucker's opinion of the clothiers. Almost any quotation will show Temple at a disadvantage as compared with the Essayist. Maintaining that the Act of 1727 puts it out of the power of any clothier to defraud his workmen, he explains:[2]

> The Clothiers about *Trowbridge* have scarce ever a Summons from the Justices on such Occasions; being sensible of the Partiality of a *certain Person*, and unwilling to suffer the *Chagrin* and Mortification of seeing their Servants triumph in their Frauds and Abuses. Therefore they generally leave the Reparation they think in justice due to them to the Servant's own Conscience, or they pay him his full Wages and discharge him, *which last is always done by most Clothiers in the common course of their Trade.*

That this passage was a confirmation of what the Essayist alleged escaped Temple's normally acute logical powers, probably because anger blinded him to its implications; but to any reader who compares it with the passage on truck quoted above, Temple's remark 'The Cause of the Poor is popular and apt to bias many thinking and judicious Persons who have not much to do with them'[3] will seem justified for other reasons than those he gives. All the same, Temple did not hate the common

[1] 'Certain Measures . . .': see Note, p. 96 below, item (c).
[2] 'The Case . . .', p. 7: see Note, p. 96 below, item (j). The 'certain person' refers to Cooper.
[3] ibid., p. 5.

people however much he despised them. The people he hated were his critics, especially Cooper, whom he suspected of being the patron of the Essayist. Allowance must be made for his resentment at being stigmatized as an oppressor, for all his writings show that he took pride in himself as an upright and honest man. He too was acquainted with his work-people though in a different relationship from that of the Essayist. The following passage is not an answer to the latter's point that taxes raised the cost of living, but it gives a touch of reality to the argument:[1]

I believe 999 Poor out of 1,000 never think of any such thing. I have Opportunities of hearing many of their low humorous Dialogues, without their knowing it; And tho' I have conversed with and heard thousands of them utter their Sentiments freely drunk and sober, yet I have never heard a Complaint of that kind from them.

All Temple's experience led him to agree with the large body of opinion which maintained that high prices were necessary to induce the poor to work. This theory had appeared in the late seventeenth century during a period of low prices[2] and there can be no doubt but that it had a basis in fact. Even the Essayist had pointed out in one of his earlier pamphlets that the cheapness of provisions meant that working people could get their bread with half work.[3] In August 1760 the third George Wansey of Warminster appended the following note to his balance sheet:[4]

... We having been at war with France 4 years, have had this year a great Trade for all Sorts of Goods, and Cloth hath obtained some Advance. ... But Corn also being cheap Our Workfolks are grown Scarce, dear, Saucy and bad ... we can get but little Work done, and with difficulty and a great deal very bad, that I have made this year but 191 Clo⁵ whereas I have last year made 262 Cloths.

This confirms the belief that Temple was speaking from experience. The wages question occupied much of his mind in the

[1] ibid., p. 18.
[2] See D. Marshall, *The English Poor in the Eighteenth Century* (1926), pp. 30 ff., also E. S. Furniss, *The Position of the Labourer in a System of Nationalism* (1920), pp. 117 ff.
[3] *An Enquiry into the Encrease and Miseries of the Poor of England*, p. 4.
[4] Wilts. CRO, 314/2.

succeeding years and he must be identified with the clothier mentioned in a note to Tucker's *Brief Essay*:[1]

A certain very ingenious gentleman and himself a great manufacturer in the clothing way . . . is engaged in a scheme which he intends to exhibit to the publick of a very singular nature. . . . He has carefully observed that in exceeding dear years, when corn and provisions are at an extravagant price, then the work is best and cheapest done:—but that in cheap years, the manufacturers are idle, wages high and work ill done. He has carried these observations through many years back; and confirmed them by the testimony of several great writers upon trade. Therefore he infers, that the high duties, taxes and excises upon the necessaries of life, are so far from being a disadvantage to trade, as things are circumstanced among us, that they are eventually the chief support of it:—and ought to be higher still, in order to oblige the poor either to work or starve.

Tucker himself could hardly believe that such a policy was justified, and this may explain his remark that Temple 'understands the principles of commerce extremely well but pushes some of them too far'[2] when the latter published *A Vindication of Commerce and the Arts*[3] in 1758 in reply to Bell's *Essay on Populousness*. The proposals made in the *Vindication* answer Tucker's description in the note quoted above, but they were not so brutal as has sometimes been thought. They embodied, in fact, a form of insurance. Temple proposed to tax the necessaries of life when cheap and, from the fund so raised, to pay out a certain sum per head in time of sickness or unemployment. In other respects, the *Vindication* is an able defence of the contribution of trade and commerce to the growth of civilization, set out with much learning and some exaggeration.[4] Temple had had a good education which included the acquisition of a knowledge of French and Latin and of classical literature. The lesson which

---

[1] J. Tucker, *A Brief Essay on the Advantages and Disadvantages which respectively attend France and Great Britain with regard to Trade* (2nd edn., 1751), p. 55 n.

[2] A. F. Tytler (Lord Woodhouselee), *Memoirs of the Hon. H. Home of Kames*, iii, 161.

[3] It was published under the pseudonym 'J.B., M.D.' whom Tucker identified as Temple, see preceding note and *DNB*.

[4] McCulloch thought that 'the refutation [of Bell] left nothing to be desired' and he had a high opinion of Temple's ability, see J. R. McCulloch, *A Collection of Scarce and Valuable Tracts on Commerce* (1859), xii, and *Literature of Political Economy* (1845), p. 52.

he drew from history and his own observation was that, since the mass of mankind would only work to satisfy its wants, the multiplication of wants led to an increase in civilization; but he was unable to envisage the poor as capable of wanting anything above the lowest forms of satisfaction. He must, however, be acquitted of having written *Considerations on Taxes* published in 1764, or its expanded edition, *An Essay on Trade*, which appeared in 1770;[1] so that the penal workhouse system recommended by that author cannot be laid to his charge. He died in 1773 and his will included a legacy of £500 to Wilkes and one of £2,000, together with his library of 15,000 volumes, to Gresham College to found a professorship of Trade and Commerce, the holder of which was to insist on Temple's principles as displayed in the *Vindication* and other writings, which, it seems, may have been still unpublished.[2] Perhaps it is as well that, as Young added in reporting the bequest,[3] 'the will was litigated and no appointment was ever made'.

This long digression on Temple has seemed necessary because it is from the controversy in which he played so great a part that opinions about the west of England cloth industry have largely been derived. It is now time to abandon polemics and to try to discover from contemporary evidence of a more factual nature what the circumstances of the clothiers and their relations with their work-people really were. The records which have survived are too few to present a complete picture, but they may serve to show examples of people and relationships which were probably not uncommon.

---

[1] They are attributed to him by W. Cunningham, *Growth of English Industry and Commerce in Modern Times* (1907), ii, 704, n. 1, and, following him, by Furniss, op. cit., p. 97 n. 1. It is true that they contain Temple's opinions, often in his own words, but they also contain acknowledged quotations from the *Vindication* and the writer expresses admiration for its author. The conclusive evidence against Temple's authorship is that neither is mentioned in his will or obituary notice whereas the *Vindication* is. Higgs attributes both to J. Cunningham.

[2] According to J. Britton, *Beauties of Wiltshire*, iii (1825), 203, Temple left a manuscript Treatise on Commerce ready for publication. His will provides for the employment of a qualified person to publish a reasoned summary of his works.

[3] *Annals of Agriculture*, vii, 473-4. A copy of the will with part of a favourable Counsel's opinion on it is among the Gresham College MSS. in the City of London Records Office. I am indebted to the Clerk of the Mercers' Company for searching the minute book of the Gresham Trustees in the custody of the Company, but, after a record of the decision to take Counsel's opinion, there is no further information.

Clothiers and Weavers in 18th Century Wiltshire

There is much evidence which represents the clothiers in the light in which Tucker saw them. In 1726, those of Bradford-on-Avon, headed by one named Heylin, 'a very warm man, and apt to run into violent measures and more hated by the populace than ever I knew a man',[1] seem amply to have justified Earle's remark: 'Here are some angry and revengeful people, who think that all authority consists in punishment.'[2] He pointed out that if the weavers were to send up a petition somebody must be appointed to draw it up, for any person in the neighbourhood who could read and write would be 'unwilling to disoblige the clothiers for the sake of justice only'.[3] In 1739 the anonymous writer of the letter from Westbury said that if he signed his name the clothiers' resentment would be more than he could bear. The Essayist received numerous insulting messages.[4] In fact, the clothiers could not bear criticism. Above all they wished to be masters in their own businesses. On the report of a later riot in 1787, another clothier, John Clark, a man who had been deeply affected by Methodist preaching and had established his own chapel in Trowbridge, wrote in his diary, 'It is very difficult to know how to act. Surely the working poor should have every encouragement, but it cannot be right for them to dictate to their masters.'[5] Such an attitude could easily degenerate into tyranny, but clothiers were not alone in desiring the subordination of their work-people. Much eighteenth-century opinion, with some notable exceptions, considered it a virtue of which French workers had a far greater share than the English. If only the English would work as hard as the Dutch and behave in as docile a manner as the French, the difficulties of competing with those nations would, it was thought, be well on the way to solution.

To the country gentry, then, the work-people were oppressed and half-starved; to their employers they seemed, if opportunity were given, independent and insolent. We hear of them mainly during periods of bad trade when their sufferings were greatest, just as we hear of the most violent among the clothiers. When

[1] *PRO*, SP.35/64, no. 1.
[2] *PRO*, SP.35/63, no. 95 (1).   [3] ibid., no. 95 (3).
[4] *The Miseries of the Miserable*, p. 27: see Note, p. 96 below, item (k).
[5] W. Jay, *Memoir of the late Rev. John Clark* (1810), p. 62. Clark was called Reverend as an independent minister, but he was never ordained.

the workers' misfortunes came from causes for which the clothiers could not be blamed, the latter showed a good deal of sympathy. In the bitter winter of 1739–40, when frost caused unemployment for at least six weeks, collections were made in all the clothing towns. Melksham produced £100.[1] Cooper was particularly generous at Trowbridge, giving food and money freely; and a somewhat fulsome account of his generosity in the *Daily Gazetteer*[2] gave Temple occasion to point out that it only amounted to sixpence a head and that other people could be generous too.[3] The weavers showed their gratitude to Cooper by presenting him with a wagon-load of coals drawn by twenty-four of them 'with a carter to drive them' thirteen miles from the nearest coalmine in the Mendips.[4] In later periods of bad weather or exceptionally high prices there were similar collections and clothiers, like many other employers, bought flour to be sold at reduced prices. These instances of charity do not affect the main issue but they show that clothiers were not inhuman. Nor were they the only people to believe that charity was one thing and business another.

Clothiers, of course, had their own troubles. 'If things take not a different [turn] know not what we shall doe except we almost give off', wrote Jeffries in February 1727. In 1741, George Wansey, in recording his hopes of getting out of his difficulties, added, like the good and pious man he was:[5]

> Now if it please God to do this great Thing for me: To deliver me out of my present difficulties, to open for me a free and advantagious Vent for my Goods, and grant me a good Trade according to the desires of my Heart, I would never forget in prosperity What disappointments for Want of Sales, What Straits for Want of Money, I have went through. . . . I would be just and speedy in my payments, not taking long Credit from any, I would be charitable to the Poor, and would use myself to Acts of Charity and Kindness. I would be a kind Master to all my Servants, not be pressing to have my work done at the lowest Rates of anybody; but be glad to see the poor live comfortably by my Work.

To do him justice, there seems to be every probability that he

---

[1] *Glouc. Journ.*, 29 January 1740.   [2] *Daily Gazetteer*, 26 January 1740.
[3] *Glouc. Journ.*, 12 February 1740.   [4] ibid., 19 February 1740.
[5] Diary in the possession of the Rev. J. Wansey, entry of 10 September 1741.

abided by this resolution and it was not until 1760 when 'the Poor' had the upper hand in bargaining power that he began to complain. John Clark survived more than one crisis in his affairs.[1] In 1784–5 the fourth George Wansey gloomily considered his lack of prospects with a mounting number of cloths unsold.[2] Yet all these men made profits, some very soon after their moments of depression; in fact the younger Wansey, on making up his accounts three months later, found that he had added £250 to his stock that year.

In bad times the factors, sometimes supposed to have been the most hated men in the industry, were frequently blamed for the long credit they exacted. One of the apologists for the clothiers in 1739 repeated the accusations which had been made in the 1690s and gave an account of the way in which the factors had circumvented the Blackwell Hall Act of 1697 and were still making the clothier wait for his money.[3] The surviving correspondence, while fully substantiating the charge of long credit, suggests that in normal times relations were not so strained. A series of letters between Usher and Jeffries and their factors, Yerbury and Filkes in 1726–7 and Richard and William Yerbury in 1733, shows that, in the absence of banking facilities, the factor rendered valuable services to the clothier. In both years Usher and Jeffries raised money by drawing bills upon them which could not be met by the sums owing, so that, in advising that they had done so, they were careful to add that they would see that funds were provided by the time the bills became due.[4] Pamphleteers declared that factors charged exorbitant sums for such accommodation, but in normal times it seems to have been only the current rate of interest. In times of scarcity conditions naturally became more rigorous. Jeffries wrote on 4 December 1727:

I did not think you would have insisted on a remittance of £47.7.6 to answer our drawing tho' I allow 'tis about a month before 'tis our

[1] Jay, op. cit., pp. 23, 46.

[2] Diary of the fourth George Wansey, Wilts. *CRO*, 314/4/3. Entries of 10 October 1784 and 24 April 1785.

[3] See Note, p. 96 below, item (h). Defoe gives the other side of this controversy, *The Complete English Tradesman* (1728), ch. 25.

[4] This was possible because Usher and Jeffries sold much of their cloth to country customers.

right to draw soe I find we must expect noe favour from you. . . . [It] shall be remitted in Cash to answer in due time if I borrow it from 10 folks. As to the time of payment I find you are fixed tho you both consented when I was with you to pay in 8 months. In our oppinion the terms we have hither[to] gone on with is very Sufficient in the general course of trade (you tho[ught] so yourself once).

And in a later letter on 11 December, after having been unable to persuade the factors to alter their decision, he added:

I observe the huge sums you mention that you advanced for us but you do not mention the consideration that you have rec^d for it and I think there has been more Cash paid into your hands from us than we have had from you in the Course of two years' trade.

The new terms seem to have been an annual settlement, but the practice of making interim drawings and of raising money by bills, for which in due course cash had to be provided, continued as before, and without recrimination. The letters are full of requests to know what was sent out for inspection and what was sold; and the partners seem to have kept an estimate of what was due to them and to have drawn against it as necessary without meeting strong objections from the Yerburys, except in bad times. Fifty years later this seems to have been usual and factors, if one may judge from one case, only put a stop to such drawings if too much of the drawer's stock was lying unsold.[1] It does not look as if the average Wiltshire clothier was greatly injured by long credit, but his main market was at home where sales were normally fairly brisk. Those whose market was provided by the Levant and, still more, by the East India Companies (as was the case to some extent in Wiltshire and to a far greater one in Gloucestershire) had to wait much longer and complained far more loudly.

But if large and medium clothiers were comparatively unaffected by long credit, those who attacked the factors were probably correct in attributing to it the increasing difficulty found by weavers and other men of small means in maintaining themselves as clothiers,[2] for the credit extended by the factors was apt to be abruptly withdrawn when the demand was over.

---

[1] Wilts. *CRO*, 314/4/3, entry of 10 October 1784.
[2] *The Clothier's Complaint* (1692), p. 8.

This practice of giving credit to men with little capital was universally condemned by clothiers as leading to bad work, lowering of wages, oppression and bankruptcy; but it could not be denied that some men had managed to survive in their new capacity.[1] It was not impossible for a weaver, still less for a master clothworker or an overseer, to become a clothier, though it was probably easier in the villages than in the towns where fine cloth was made. One example may be seen in the history of the Little family of Biddestone in north Wiltshire. Richard Little, who described himself as a broadweaver and signed his will with a mark, died in 1737. He owned three tenements and some freehold land which he divided between his two sons. His pecuniary legacies amounted to £125. His elder son, James, died in 1766, describing himself as a clothier. He had acquired much more land and also a fulling mill which he left to his eldest son Aaron, together with all money due on bills, bonds and securities. His pecuniary legacies to his other children amounted to £1,050. Aaron married a wife whose father is described as 'Esquire'.[2] His will, made in 1805, described him as a gentleman and did not mention the cloth industry. His pecuniary legacies to five younger children totalled £5,000 and he left the remainder of the estate to his eldest son.[3]

Whether Richard Little had inherited his property we do not know. He may have been a survivor of the farmer-weavers of the seventeenth and earlier centuries. But a sober, hard-working and determined weaver might add loom to loom, take warps to put out to other weavers and then, by making a few pieces for himself to sell to individual buyers or at fairs and markets, turn himself into a clothier. He would be lucky if he survived depressions; but even in 1803 such men were not unknown.[4] In 1726 the possibility of becoming a clothier was one of the weaver's most valued privileges.[5] Stories circulated about weavers' sons who

[1] S. Rudder, *History of Gloucestershire* (1779), p. 63. He is speaking in particular of the East India trade which was larger in Gloucestershire than in Wiltshire, but not unknown in the latter county.

[2] *Bath Chron.*, 18 March 1773.

[3] Wilts. *CRO*, Arch. Wills L, 1737, Richard Little. Prerogative Court of Canterbury (Somerset House), Tyndal, fol. 108: James Little; Lushington, fol. 418: Aaron Little. I have to thank Mr. J. E. Little for bringing these wills to my notice.

[4] *BPP*, 1802–3 (95), vii, 4, 97, 205.

[5] *PRO*, SP.35/63, no. 95 (2).

had risen to wealth, but they seem to have started with more capital than a simple weaver's son would have been likely to possess. Thus Samuel Cam (grandfather of Byron's friend John Cam Hobhouse), who died in 1792 worth £80,000 or more, was said to have been a weaver's son, but the diarist who recorded this added that he started with four or five hundred pounds,[1] which was the patrimony of many clothiers' sons.

Those clothiers who have left records show no trace of having obtained their capital from any source other than their own families. Having begun with money obtained from relatives, they acquired a dowry with their wives and added to their stock year by year. But men were also drawn into the trade who knew nothing of its technical side and merely looked on it as an investment. In 1753 Francis Yerbury of Bradford, discussing with his factor the case of a Melksham clothier who had gone bankrupt and fled to Spain where he was supervising a cloth manufacture, thought that knowledge of the industry was not necessary to make cloth:[2]

Let a Spaniard be sent over to Bradford tho' ever so great a Dunce, if he have but money and wool he may in a few months probably make as good cloth as the eldest Tradesman in the town. This you know full well and that there are many instances of it; People never bred to the trade, and more, Boys have entered into it and have cut as good or better figure than many who have been regular bred to it, all which greatly depends upon the hands they employ.

The Essayist thought that, considering the risks and trouble entailed, it was not worth while to borrow to enter the trade unless the gross profits were nearly three times the current rate of interest.[3] How far this statement can be relied upon it is difficult to say, for the writer disclaimed any knowledge of the industry; but if it can be taken at its face value one may suppose that a gross profit of 12 to 15 per cent would satisfy the man who entered the trade as an investment, since interest was limited by the usury law to 5 per cent and was often lower. An apologist for the clothiers in 1739 said that net profits on four-fifths of the goods made in the past seven years did not exceed 3 per cent;[4]

[1] MS. Diary of George Sloper, fol. 197 (Wilts. Arch. Soc. Lib.).
[2] *PRO*, SP.36/118/72, no. 12.
[3] *Glouc. Journ.*, 9 January 1739.   [4] *Gents. Mag.*, ix (1739), 125.

but it looks as if he meant 'net profit' to include interest on capital. If he did we may suspect him of some exaggeration. Only one clothier, the third George Wansey, has left accounts from which profits can be calculated, and he was not typical of the superfine clothiers, since most of his production was in seconds at 13*s* a yard and under, down to cheap cloth for export at 5*s* and 6*s*. His inventories and balance sheets have been preserved, the former from 1753 to 1760, the latter from 1755 to 1761.[1] He kept his accounts with great care, estimating the cost of each cloth and noting what each was sold for. The following table summarizes his operations for the period:

Year ending 20 August	Capital	Cloths made since previous August		Gross profit[1]	Percentage on capital at previous August	Added to capital during year
		Number	Cost			
	£		£	£		£
1753	4037	209	2396			
1754	4322	235	2854			285
1755	4647	(Not entered)		575	13·3	325
1756	4612	230	2817	227[2]	4·9	−35
1757	4851	262	3417	533	11·5	239
1758	5220	245	3154	675	13·9	369
1759	5398	262	3684	521	10	178
1760	5706	191	(Not entered)	630	11·7	308
1761	6010			619	10·8	304

[1] Obtained by adding his household and schooling expenses to the sum which he added to his capital.

[2] Result of the Lisbon earthquake.

This result depended upon all his debts proving good, but he expected to lose at least £500 of them. His profits, especially if allowance is made for possible bad debts, do not seem high judged by the above standard. They were made in a period when trade was reviving and in 1760 and 1761 it was exceptionally brisk; but, as we have already seen, labour difficulties prevented him from exploiting this situation and his percentage profit was lower than in some earlier years. The superfine clothiers' profits were probably higher than Wansey's; but

[1] Wilts. *CRO*, 314/2.

it is questionable whether any large fortunes were made in the middle of the century. Two periods when profits were high can be distinguished in the history of the medley trade. The first was during the last quarter of the seventeenth and the early years of the eighteenth century when the French wars had devastated part of the Continental clothmaking area and the clothiers were able to exploit the new finishing methods taught them by the Dutch. The second was the period after 1760 when the production of new and lighter types of cloth, particularly the fine twilled cassimeres invented by a Bradford clothier in 1766, gave a renewed impetus to the trade, which lasted into the following century. There were, naturally, many bad years during both these periods, but there can be no doubt that in each of them the average profits of the superfine clothiers were higher than in the intervening one. This was a period of stress and change. Clothiers themselves were apt to attribute their difficulties partly to the number of competitors whom the hope of high profits had drawn into the trade. There were certainly many who had not served an apprenticeship (in 1706 they were estimated at one-third of the whole)[1] and efforts were made more than once to get legislation to remedy this situation.[2] In fact, competition did not come only from the shopkeepers and men with little capital whom the clothiers were anxious to exclude, but also from clothiers in other branches of the trade who were themselves hit by competition from Yorkshire. Yorkshire did not compete directly with the superfine clothiers, but much of the coarser material produced in Wiltshire was being superseded in the 'thirties. At least one Devizes manufacturer turned to cloth-making in 1740 when his trade in druggets fell off[3] and it is probable that his was not an isolated case. Thus a larger number of clothiers was competing for a share in a trade which was not, at that time, expanding fast enough to absorb them.

After 1760 the Wanseys again provide some material bearing on profits. George's eldest son, William, began trade in 1767 in partnership with his mother with a total capital of £1,000 of which £500 was his own. His wife brought him £2,600 and on

---

[1] J. Haynes, *A View of the present State of the Clothing Trade in England* (1706), p. 83.
[2] *JHC*, xxiii (1741), 657; xxiv (1742), 117. Cf. *PRO*, SP.35/63, no. 95 (2).
[3] R. Brooks, *Observations on Milling Broad and Narrow Cloth* (1740), p. 1.

the death of a brother he had £300 more. He died in 1805 worth about £50,000 so that, as a member of the family wrote, 'he gained by industry, management and the blessing of Providence £46,000 in under forty years of trade'.[1] On a very rough computation this represents an average addition to his capital of between 7 and 8 per cent per annum (as against his father's average of about 5 per cent); and he also lived on a more liberal scale. His youngest brother, the fourth George, also starting with £500 in 1777, had nearly doubled it by 1783. It may be surmised that profits were higher in the 'nineties, after carding and spinning machinery had been introduced, than they were earlier. In 1790 George was installing it, and for the year ending February 1791 he made over £1,000, but we do not know his capital at that date. He attributed this result 'to my early introduction of machinery of which I now partake the good effects, by which I have been able to make my cloth with credit and profit and extend my trade to double the former amount'.[2] It may be noted that another brother, Henry Wansey of Salisbury, in 1791, reckoned gross profit at 10 per cent of the price of the finished cloth, but if machinery were used he considered it would be more than half as much again.[3]

Mr. Charles Wilson has recently suggested that in the woollen industry the dispersed outwork system meant that entrepreneurial control was partial and uneven.[4] As far as the Wiltshire fine-cloth industry is concerned, such control was no more partial than it was in the cotton industry. There were, it is true, plenty of small clothiers who wanted no innovations, but throughout the seventeenth and eighteenth centuries, and earlier also, it contained numbers of men who possessed 'a sense of market opportunity combined with the capacity needed to exploit it'. This was fully shown in the developments which took place in the last three decades of the century, with the invention of new and finer types of cloth and the undertaking by many clothiers of their own marketing in foreign countries.[5] The

[1] Wilts. *CRO*, 314/3.
[2] ibid., 314/4/3, entry of 27 February 1791. He did even better in 1792.
[3] i.e., £120 in a price of £750. Even without machinery the profit is over 11 per cent on the outlay. *Wool Encouraged without Exportation*, by F.A.S. (1791), p. 68.
[4] *History*, xlii, no. 145 (June 1957), 101.
[5] Cf. *BPP*, 1802–3 (95), vii, 382.

capitals then employed were much larger than anything mentioned earlier in the century. John Anstie of Devizes, the inventor of cloth mixed with silk, did a large trade on the Continent of Europe, especially with Russia. He failed in 1793, probably owing to the war with France which interfered with his returns. What his capital was at this time we do not know, but he had over £92,000 due to him on debts for goods exceeding £1,000[1] and he owned ten separate factories or workshops, including fulling mills, in and round Devizes.[2] But his wages bill was only £250 per week; and although much of this would have been in small sums to pickers and spinners, the number of his employees must have been well under a thousand. It is probably owing to their production for a semi-luxury market that the Wiltshire entrepreneurs cannot rank among the really large capitalists of the age.

But although there were many entrepreneurs in the full sense of the word, it must be admitted that the 'dispersed outwork system' gave them trouble. Contrary to what is sometimes thought, the concentration of looms in shops was not a feature of the western woollen industry in the eighteenth century; but when fancy cloth came to the fore in the 'eighties it was necessary to have the pattern under the master's eye. Loomshops for weaving such cloth soon came to include looms for plain cassimeres as well, and when this development reached Trowbridge in 1787 it provoked a serious riot among the narrow weavers. The occasion is interesting from the fact that the Justices attempted conciliation, though unsuccessfully.[3] Much, but not all, narrow cloth continued to be woven in shops but broadcloth was not, apparently because the size of the building which would be needed for broad looms made the proposition uneconomic.[4]

It might be supposed that the worst oppressors among the clothiers were the men at the lower end of the scale, who were struggling to raise themselves to a secure position; and this, in fact, was what the clothiers alleged. But truck and other forms

---

[1] Wilts. *CRO*, 25.
[2] *Salisbury Journ.*, 10 and 17 March and 21 April 1794.
[3] *Bath Chron.*, 1, 22 and 28 February 1787.
[4] *BPP*, 1802–3 (95), vii, 299, 344.

of oppression were by no means the offences only of the poorer clothiers. Heylin of Bradford was a man of sufficient substance to consort with the smaller country gentry;[1] and Coulthurst, whose mill and shop were attacked in 1738, gave a dowry of £6,000 with his daughter.[2] Both in 1726 and 1738 there were those whom the weavers called 'good honest gentlemen' who paid in cash and were not the first to lower wages; but it is doubtful whether they were in the majority. The fact that, at the time of the riot in 1738, the Trowbridge clothiers were said to have ordered the town-crier to proclaim that 'full wages would be paid and no truck'[3] implies that it was a common element in wages and makes it difficult to believe the statement of thirty-five Bradford and Melksham clothiers that they never paid in it.[4] It was, of course, partly the result of the shortage of coin, which was perennial in the eighteenth century. It is also possible that capital may have been more fully employed than in earlier times so that less was kept in the form of cash to meet daily needs. Where the second George Wansey kept up to £1,000 by him in coin,[5] his grandson only once had £500 and generally only about £200 at his stocktaking, in coin and bills together. In 1754 he only had £129, and he was probably more careful to keep a balance in coin than many clothiers were.

For all their hardships, weavers might have been surprised at Tucker's comparison of their lot to that of slaves. They considered themselves as master workmen, free to work for whom they would and especially for more than one clothier at a time. They did not treat their employers' goods with too much respect and towards the end of the century they indulged in several new forms of embezzlement, perhaps driven to it by rising prices.[6] Earnings are notoriously difficult to estimate. In 1726 weavers were asking for a payment of 1s 4d a yard for superfine, 1s 2d for second and 1s for coarse broadcloth which Earle reported that

---

[1] *Wilts. Arch. Mag.*, xi, 207.

[2] *Gents. Mag.*, xxi (1751), 284.

[3] *Glouc. Journ.*, 5 December 1738.   [4] ibid., 20 January 1739.

[5] *Ec.H.R.*, 2nd ser., ix (1956), no. 2, p. 250. Although the grandfather may at one time have made ten cloths a week, the entries in his day book at the time when the amount of coin is recorded suggest that his trade was about the same size as his grandson's.

[6] *JHC*, xxxiv, 414, 451. Wiltshire joined in the petition but all the evidence came from Gloucestershire.

many clothiers paid but which he considered to be 'a bare sub-sistence with hard labour'.[1] It looks as if a top rate of 1s 4d and even 1s 6d was paid by some clothiers up to the 1730s; but lower rates were more common and, according to the Essayist, they fluctuated widely.[2] Usher and Jeffries made all the qualities mentioned, but from late in 1725 they paid 1s 3d for both super-fines and seconds and 1s for coarse. Some information about what weavers earned at these rates is available from their cloth book. It records the amount of wool sent to be spun for each cloth, the names of the spinners and, in most cases, the length of the warp, the number of hundreds in it and the name of the weaver. Where the price is not given it has been possible to calculate it, since every entry at this time shows that payment was being made by the yard. The table on the following page shows the earnings of four weavers between the late autumn of 1725 and early in 1727.

The men could also earn 1s 4d per fortnight for warping on the master's premises. They did not always come, but between 5 March and 13 August, the only period for which these details are recorded, Fricker earned 8s, Gaby 9s 4d, Lucas 5s 4d and Rose, who sometimes warped two and once three chains, 16s. It is clear that Rose must have had two or even three looms. Gaby once warped two chains and may have had two looms, but the dates at which he and the other two men took warps are con-sistent with their having only one each. All, however, may well have had a second, working for another clothier. The delay in making the last payments to Fricker and Rose reflects the stag-nation of trade in the winter of 1726–7; if the last two cloths are left out of account Fricker's earnings would have averaged 9s 8d per week. Temple's estimate that a weaver could finish a medley cloth in three weeks[3] was evidently not unfair, since all these weavers did so on some occasions; but the table does not support his contention that it was an average time. Two other weavers, who were paying off a debt for cloth in 1723–5, took an average of 4¾ and 5½ weeks respectively for each cloth. Whether this was due to unemployment, bad yarn or simply to idleness it

---

[1] *PRO*, SP.35/63, no. 95 (1).
[2] *The Miseries of the Miserable*, p. 14: see Note, p. 96 below, item (k).
[3] *The Case*, p. 15; see Note, p. 96 below, item (j).

Name	First and last dates when warps taken	Weeks	Number taken	Average time weeks[1]
J. Fricker	24/11/25 19/11/26	51	13	4¼
J. Gaby	3/12/25 25/ 9/26	42	14	3¼
J. Lucas	15/ 1/26 19/ 9/26	35	9	4
W. Rose	6/12/25 20/10/26		24	

Name	Last payment made	Earnings			Weeks covered[2]	Per week	
		£	s	d		s	d
J. Fricker	?/3/27	27	17	10½	c. 71	7	10
J. Gaby	31/11/26	30	1	3	48	12	6
J. Lucas	5/11/26	19	12	8	42	9	4
W. Rose	13/ 1/27	49	6	6	57	17	3

[1] Obtained by dividing the number of weeks by one cloth less than the number shown.

[2] Between date when the first warp was taken and the last payment.

is impossible to say; neither they nor any of those in the table seem to have gone to harvest, though weavers sometimes did so.

From these earnings deductions must be made for winding the bobbin, size, candles, bobbins and loom harness, though a weaver might have a child who could do the first. We have no estimate of what this might amount to until the end of the century, when a Gloucestershire clothier, in 1803, gave these costs as amounting to a little under one-sixth of the price paid for weaving and added that much more size had been needed with handspun yarn.[1] A man with three looms would probably have to keep a journeyman at a minimum rate of six or seven shillings a week; but a man with two could manage with his children or apprentices, provided that one of them was old enough to have had several years' experience. John Bezer, one of the men executed for the riot of 1738, had at one time two looms which he worked with three apprentices.[2] The advantage, indeed one might say the necessity, for a man with up to two looms of keeping apprentices rather than journeymen must have contributed to the constant overstocking of the trade.

Later in the century, earnings at 1s 3d a yard were higher, but only because working hours were longer. In 1803 an old Chippenham weaver, working with his niece, earned about 15s a week for both, while a young man at Bradford earned from 8s to 10s as a journeyman.[3] Against the increasing fineness of the cloth, they had the advantage of firmer machine-spun yarn and they may also have used the new method of winding the bobbin (the 'bobbing shuttle'), which had been adopted in Gloucestershire a few years before 1757 and was said to lead to a saving of one day in eight.[4] They managed to weave about two and a half yards a day,[5] where their predecessors in 1726 seldom did over two and generally much less; but their working day was fourteen to seventeen hours in summer. It is, perhaps, a confirmation of Temple's theory that his complaint about idleness is never heard when prices were high at the end of the century.

In addition to the weaver's earnings his wife and daughters could add to the family income by spinning. The Essayist denied

---

[1] *BPP*, 1802–3 (95), VII, p. 300. The only evidence from Wiltshire, however, gave a lower estimate, about 1s from 15s, probably not including bobbin winding. Ibid., p. 20.

[2] *Glouc. Journ.*, 10 April 1739.   [3] *BPP*, 1802–3 (95), VII, pp. 20, 77.

[4] *A State of the Case . . . relating to the late Commotions . . . in the County of Gloucester* (1757), p. 23. The 'bobbing shuttle' was not, as is often stated, the fly shuttle, see A. P. Wadsworth and J. de L. Mann, *The Cotton Trade and Industrial Lancashire, 1600–1780* (1931), pp. 452, 467.

[5] *BPP*, 1802–3 (95), VII, pp. 6, 19. This is the most usual figure; one witness said he had woven four yards a day, which seems almost incredible.

that they could make anything like the 2*s* 6*d* or 3*s* a week suggested by Temple;[1] but in 1739 spinning had fallen by over 40 per cent, so that his opinion is no guide to more prosperous times. His statement that superfine clothiers did not care that children should spin does not mean that they could earn nothing; much material besides superfine cloth was made in the county for which children's spinning would be adequate. Among all the textile occupations the price of spinning fluctuated most. That of warp spinning, which was a specialized occupation, was particularly apt to rise in good times; in 1760 Wansey complained that the cost of one sort had risen 36 per cent. On the other hand, the price of weaving settled down in the second half of the century at 1*s* 3*d* a yard for superfine broadcloth; and there is no indication that it fluctuated at all.[2] In Shepton Mallet, which was an extension of the Wiltshire clothing area, this price dated from an agreement of 1756, just after the making of fine cloth had been introduced there;[3] and it seems probable that it was settled in Wiltshire when trade revived in the 1750s. There were reports of riots in 1750 and 1752[4] which may have been due to wage disputes, but there is little information about them and in 1750 the report was denied by the *Bath Journal*.[5] In 1752 dragoons were sent and a number of weavers were arrested. Afterwards, it was only food prices, machinery, or the suspicion that they would be forced into loom shops which could provoke a riot. It is clear from their evidence in 1803 that the latter was the prospect which alarmed them most.

It is improbable that the weavers had any permanent society until the end of the century; but it looks as if the riots of 1726 and 1738 were not spontaneous outbreaks. In both years weavers were meeting in small groups of twenty or thirty before the riots took place and they seem to have been trying to put pressure on clothiers for some time beforehand. They were

[1] *The Miseries of the Miserable*, p. 13: see Note, p. 96 below, item (k). The estimate of earnings by weft spinners (6*s* 1*d* per week) given for 1781–96 in the Handloom Weavers' Report of 1840 seems much overrated. *BPP*, 1840 (43), XXIII, p. 439.
[2] *BPP*, 1802–3 (95), VII, pp. 19, 55.   [3] ibid., p. 62.
[4] *Gents. Mag.*, xx (1750), 187; xxii (1752), 237.
[5] *Bath. Journ.*, 15 and 23 April 1750.

certainly doing so in 1741, in order to make clothiers employ weavers in their own parishes; but this time the clothiers took fright and asked for dragoons to be sent.[1] It is difficult to understand why Usher and Jeffries began to pay by the yard in 1725 when they had not done so previously,[2] unless they were yielding to the demands of the weavers; and when the riot did take place, the rioters themselves impressed all the disinterested observers as a serious and reponsible body of men. In 1739 this was not the case, perhaps because there were no disinterested observers; but there is some, though rather doubtful, evidence that attempts had been made to negotiate with Coulthurst before the riot started.[3] Once it had begun, however, the behaviour of the mob was not such as to suggest that it could be treated with on a reasonable basis.

All the evidence, then, suggests that the heavy fall in weaving prices came in the 'twenties and 'thirties during the least prosperous period of the industry. The temptation to lower them must have been almost overwhelming, for clothiers had nothing but labour costs on which they could economize. The price of wool reacted only slowly to economic conditions and that of Spanish wool was subject to Continental as well as English demand. This also applied to soap, oil and dyestuffs; but these formed only a small proportion of the whole cost. Various estimates put the proportion of labour costs from a little under half up to 75 per cent of the total.[4] For superfine cloth it was probably less than half, owing to the high cost of the wool.[5]

Weavers' wages never rose again to the earlier level but the

---

[1] *PRO*, SP.36/56/82 (1741).

[2] The few prices entered before 1725 never represent a definite figure per yard. The nearest work out at about 1s 2d.

[3] A Bristol paper reported that he had received a message from the men saying that they would trust him no longer, but he denied this, *Daily Gazetteer*, 5 December 1738. There was also a report that an attorney had been brought to London in custody for abetting the rioters, *Glouc. Journ.*, 26 December 1738.

[4] *Bromley's Papers* (Bodl. Lib.), iv, no. 1 (1714); 'Essay on the Decline of the Foreign Trade' (1744) in J. R. McCulloch, *Collection of Scarce . . . Tracts* (1859), p. 209. For an interesting suggestion about costs by a modern woollen manufacturer, see K. G. Ponting, *The West of England Woollen Manufacture* (1957), pp. 107–8.

[5] An account in Usher and Jeffries's cloth book appears to give the cost of wool as 52 per cent and that of labour, apart from that involved in dyeing, as 41 per cent. This interpretation is not certain. Any other would give a higher percentage to labour.

extremely low prices cited by the Essayist did not continue in the latter part of the century. It seems that a weaver with a family of the right size and age must at times have done sufficiently well to support his feeling of superiority over the agricultural labourer even though his average annual wage may not have been much greater. The real trouble was the problem of numbers and the frequent periods of unemployment. These factors had secured to the clothiers by the 'eighties a considerable measure of the subordination they desired.[1] But there is also much evidence that they were not anxious to provoke the men too far. The rioters of 1787 were leniently dealt with, which, said the *Bath Chronicle*, 'they may attribute entirely to the bounty of their prosecutors'.[2] The fluctuation of spinning prices suggests that it was the totally unorganized and mainly feminine mass of spinners which felt the full force of depressions. Even here, a Chippenham clothier in 1750 found it necessary to deny in print that he had tried to persuade other clothiers to lower rates.[3] The weavers seem, at least, not to have been ground down to the lowest level. In the 'nineties a Union certainly existed, for the 'Company of broad and narrow weavers', said to be over 2,000 in number, was advertising in 1793 its refusal to take out warps without the usual allowance for spooling.[4] By 1801 a Committee of workers had been 'appointed by deed for putting the act [against truck] into action' and was employing a solicitor; and one committee member, a weaver, had no qualms about giving his name in print.[5] They had come far indeed since 1726.

NOTE

List of Publications on the Riots of 1738
(Dates given in new style)

(a) 'Essay on Riots', *Glouc. Journ.*, 19 December 1738; reprinted in full, *Gents. Mag.*, ix (1739), 7 ff.; extract in J. Smith, *Chronicon Rusticum Commerciale or Memoirs of Wool* (1747), ii, 301–2.

(b) Account of the riot by the Melksham clothiers, *Glouc. Journ.*, 26 December 1738.

[1] See *V.C.H. Wilts.*, iv, loc. cit.
[2] *Bath Chron.*, 22 March 1787. [3] *Bath Journ.*, 3 June 1750.
[4] *Bath Chron.*, 11 April 1793. [5] *Salisb. Journ.*, 4 March 1801.

(c) 'Certain Measures to put into practice for the Revival of Trade & for the effectual Relief of the Poor Manufacturers of England' (by the Essayist), *Glouc. Journ.*, 9 January 1739. Not reprinted.

(d) 'Remarks on the Essay on Riots by a Manufacturer in Wilts.', *Glouc. Journ.*, 30 January 1739; also in *Daily Gazetteer*, 10 and 12 March 1739, as 'A Reply to . . .'; reprinted in full in *Gents. Mag.*, ix (1739), 123 ff., and in part by Smith, op. cit., ii, 303–5.

(e) Manifesto by thirty-five clothiers of Bradford-on-Avon and Melksham offering a reward to anyone who secured a conviction for truck against any superfine clothier. *Glouc. Journ.*, 6 February 1739.

(f) Similar manifesto by William Temple. Ibid., 13 February 1739.

(g) 'A Defence of the Essay on Riots' (by the Essayist). Ibid., 13 February 1739. Not reprinted.

(h) A letter signed 'Trowbridge' to 'Old Commonsense', 24 February 1739, attacking the factors; reprinted (almost in full) in *Gents. Mag.*, ix (1739), 89–90 and 126, in *Glouc. Journ.*, 8 May 1739, and by Smith, op. cit., ii, 310–13, as if it were part of (j), which it is not.

(j) 'The Case as it now stands between the Clothiers and the Weavers' by Philalethes (W. Temple), *Glouc. Journ.*, 27 February–10 April 1739. Extracts (abridged) in *Gents. Mag.*, ix (1739), 205–6, 233–7 and (also abridged) in Smith, op. cit., ii, 305–10. Reprinted as a pamphlet (copy in Univ. of London Library).

(k) *The Miseries of the Miserable*, by the Essayist in reply to Temple, adv. in *Glouc. Journ.*, 27 March 1739 (copy in Wilts. Arch. Soc. Lib.).

V

Population Change in a Provincial Town
Nottingham 1700–1800

AMONG the distinguishing characteristics of the new industrial society that was coming to birth in England in the
eighteenth century was its capacity to support a vastly
larger population than before, and, more significantly, to permit its continuous growth. There had been earlier occasions
when population had taken a leap forward: there had never
been a time when the direct checks to population growth had
continuously receded until they virtually disappeared under
the influence of successive triumphs of man over his environment. Above all, the age-old balance between town and country
was being upset and the character of social life was on the eve of
transformation through the growth of industrial towns and the
problems of the quality of urban life to which it gave rise.

The economic processes involved in this break with the past
have been studied with a success to which this book is itself a
tribute; but the process of change from small-scale to large-scale
society, from provincial market town to populous industrial
centre with only vestigial connexions with the surrounding
countryside, has received less attention than it deserves.[1] One
reason is that the mechanics of population growth during the

---

[1] For the most detailed treatment of the demographic side of urban history at
this time, see F. Beckwith, 'The Population of Leeds during the Industrial Revolution', *Thoresby Society*, xli, Miscellany, vol. xii, pt. ii (1948), pt. iv (1953). For the
general development of urban history, see the important bibliographical studies of
S. G. Checkland, 'English Provincial Cities', *Ec.H.R.*, 2nd ser., vi (1953), 195–203,
and W. H. Chaloner, 'Writings on British Urban History', *Vierteljahrschrift für
Sozial- und Wirtschaftsgeschichte*, xlv, pt. i (1958), 76–87. In the former of these two
studies, Professor Checkland also discusses problems of method in the writing of
urban history, and suggests that 'it is time that the professional historian turned his
attention to the nature of cities as determinants of national life rather than as end
products' (op. cit., p. 202).

period are still under discussion.[1] How did the change from small-scale to large-scale community take place? To what extent was it the consequence; to what extent the cause of concurrent economic growth; and what is the answer to the paradox of population check during the period of unprecedented food surpluses, and population advance during the period when surplus gave way to shortage amounting, in the last years of the period, to near famine?

One way of approaching these problems is to examine them where they can be seen at close quarters and in the greatest detail; and such conditions can best be found in villages which experienced enclosure of common and commonfield and in those provincial towns and industrialized villages which were caught up in the swift advance of industry and population in the second half of the eighteenth century. The story of enclosure of village commons continues to be told and retold and never fails to throw fresh light on the infinitely varied nature of agrarian change;[2] but the experience of the semi-agricultural provincial town which was transformed into a populous industrial centre was an even more radical breach with the past and provides, to a greater extent than the village, the essential characteristics of the general situation with even richer sources of information on which to draw.

The problem of enclosure was present here, too, but it was

---

[1] For a discussion of the two sides of the theoretical aspect of this question, see H. J. Habakkuk, 'English Population in the Eighteenth Century', *Ec.H.R.*, 2nd ser., vi (1953), 117–33, and Professor Thomas McKeown and R. G. Brown, 'Medical Evidence related to English Population Changes in the Eighteenth Century', *Population Studies*, ix (1955–6), 119–41. Mr. D. E. C. Eversley in his article 'A Survey of Population in an Area of Worcestershire from 1660–1850 on the Basis of Parish Records', *Population Studies*, x (1956–7), 253–79, has provided data relating to population change in a rural area in the light of which these theoretical models can be considered. In this study of Nottingham I have followed Mr. Eversley's lead and have attempted to present a series of births, marriages, deaths and child deaths for the period 1700–1801. The employment of uniform ratios throughout the century for converting baptisms into births, and burials into deaths, in which I have followed Mr. Eversley, is open to obvious objections, but no satisfactory alternative ratios have been devised. For the most recent discussion of this problem, see J. T. Krause, 'Changes in English Fertility and Mortality, 1781–1850', *Ec.H.R.*, 2nd ser., xi, no. 1 (August 1958), 52–70.

[2] This is especially well brought out by the two most recent but contrasting studies, W. G. Hoskins, *The Midland Peasant* (1957), and Joan Thirsk, *English Peasant Farming* (1957).

98

incidental, not central to the process of transition. The form which it took, however, varied from town to town, and might exercise an important influence on subsequent economic development and social conditions. This is pre-eminently exemplified in the history of Nottingham. The fields and meadows surrounding it were separately owned while those who exercised common rights over them were burgesses with a limited municipal as well as a parliamentary franchise, and so the question became an issue in local politics. In 1787, a plan was presented to the Nottingham Corporation by a committee of gentlemen for 'Improvements of the Town' to be financed from the revenues which would arise from enclosure of the fields and meadows over which the Corporation possessed manorial rights. The plan was rejected, and when an advocate of enclosure presented himself for election as senior councilman, he was decisively defeated by a majority of 600 out of a total poll of 1,051, 'the largest number of electors who ever exercised their privilege in one day for the appointment of a senior council-man';[1] and the question was not raised again for twenty years.[2]

By this decision the town left itself no choice but to grow within its ancient manorial boundaries, and before the end of the century there were complaints that it was being overlaid with streets, courts, alleys, yards—'a resurrection of buildings generally without order, seated like clusters of mushrooms in a field cast up by chance'.[3] By turning its face against enclosure, it had condemned itself to a period of unparalleled overcrowding and squalor, and any advantage that later generations gained by the postponement of building on the common lands was bought at a heavy cost to those who had to suffer the immediate consequences. When at last enclosure came in 1845, a densely packed community of 53,000 people were contriving to live and multiply on a site which a century earlier had been occupied by slightly more than one-fifth of that number, and the economic growth of the town had been slowed down almost

[1] *Nottingham Borough Records* (hereafter *NBR*), vii, 223, and W. H. Wylie, *Old and New Nottingham* (1853), p. 331.
[2] *NBR*, viii, 48–49, October 1806; it was raised again in 1813 (ibid., 172–3); in 1822 (ibid., 293); and in 1833 (ibid., 410).
[3] F. C. Laird, *Topographical Description of Nottinghamshire* (1810), p. 102.

to the point of stagnation.[1] The study of enclosure in its urban as well as its rural setting has a contribution to make to the understanding of the processes of industrialization.[2]

One reason for the disparate share of attention received by the village and the town may be that the growth of the one has frequently been regarded as the counterpart and consequence of the decline of the other; the villages, it has been widely believed, were being emptied by enclosure to provide a labour force for the towns. This explanation fails to take into account the fact that, in the absence of technical changes which would effect economies in the use of labour, the numbers engaged in agriculture tended to rise rather than to fall, and except for those villages which were unsuitable for arable cultivation, enclosure appears to have had little effect on the movement of population.[3] The contribution of rural immigration to urban growth was of course enormous, but this was nothing new; the novelty lay in the fact that the towns no longer relied on the villages to keep them alive;[4] if Nottingham is any guide, they were able from the middle of the eighteenth century to expand with growing momentum through their own powers of natural increase; and though in actual volume the tide of immigration rose, the ratio of urban growth which came from this source substantially declined. That this upward improvement of urban

[1] See Wylie, op. cit., and J. D. Chambers, *Modern Nottingham in the Making* (1940).

[2] See also the valuable study by Phyllis M. Giles, 'The Enclosure of Common Lands in Stockport', *Transactions of the Lancashire and Cheshire Antiquarian Society* (1950–1), p. 73. I am indebted for this reference to Dr. J. D. Marshall. For the influence of urban landowners on the burst of enclosure activity in the late 1750s and 1760s, see H. G. Hunt, 'The Chronology of Parliamentary Enclosure in Leicestershire', *Ec.H.R.*, 2nd ser., x (1957), 265–72. In regard to the enclosure of the Leicester open fields, which began in 1764, Dr. W. G. Hoskins says that the houses generally had ample yards and often gardens, and there was 'nothing remotely resembling the horrors of Nottingham': *The Making of the English Landscape* (1955), p. 223.

[3] Even in Leicestershire, the classic county of enclosure for pasture, this appears to be true. See *V.C.H. Leics.*, iii (1955), 148: 'Over much of Leicestershire inclosure had no apparent effect on population. . . . The parishes in which numbers did fall after inclosure were those on the heavy clays. . . . Depopulation following parliamentary inclosure . . . was thus merely the last episode in a long history of the adjustment of farming methods to soils and relief which were essentially unfavourable for arable cultivation.'

[4] See Ashton, *Eighteenth Century*, p. 8, for destructive effects of town life on population.

population would have taken place without enclosure, few would now deny; whether it would have taken place without large-scale industrialization is a more difficult question. There is good reason for thinking that it was under way before the impact of the new mechanized industry was felt and in places where it was never felt at all. The role of industrialization seems to have been not to initiate population growth so much as to sustain it, to enable the expansive forces to retain their momentum and to prevent them from falling back, as they had so often done before, in face of the direct checks which had hitherto been generated when population growth outstripped the growth of productive forces.

The provincial town is a microcosm within which this unique alliance of industrial and demographic forces may be observed, and a brief report on one such town during the period of profound sociological change may not be out of place in a volume dedicated to one who has done so much to illuminate the economic context in which it took place.

In many ways, Nottingham in 1700 retained the classic characteristics of the village from which it had sprung. On three sides it had fields and meadows, an area of nearly 1,500 acres, mainly in the hands of private owners but subject to common rights by burgesses and by the inhabitants at large.[1] The fields— the Sand and Clay fields, an area of 654 acres—appear to have been in regular course of cultivation in the middle of the seventeenth century when 'some had to be annually sown with corn' or, according to another account, 'cultivated two years by the plough . . . and every third year enjoyed exclusively by the housekeeper burgesses', but before the opening of the eighteenth century, 'It was agreed that the proprietors should fence their respective lots, if they chose; that the land should be laid down for mowing and pasturage . . . and that two gaps in each fence should be made on or before the 12th August and which should continue open till the 12th November; during which time the production of the fields was to be the sole property of the burgess house-keepers.' Since many of the burgesses were said to be too

---

[1] See C. Deering, *Nottinghamia Vetus et Nova* (1751), p. 2, and J. Blackner, *History of Nottingham* (1815), p. 30.

poor to buy cattle, it was agreed that the non-burgesses should have the privilege of turning in three head of cattle each during the commonable time. As late as 1807 the non-burgesses were protected in this right as a result of legal action, with the proviso that the right should be enjoyed only by those who occupied toftsteads.

In addition there were the Meadows (283 acres), divided into East Croft and West Croft and commonable by the burgesses for various periods of the year. There was also a considerable area in the possession of the Corporation as lord of the manor consisting of the Forest (124 acres), Mapperley Hills common (54 acres) and the Coppice of the Hunger Hills which was open all the year round to the burgesses and inhabitants at large. Except on the east, where there was a narrow break in the green ring, the town was surrounded by its ancient fields, meadows and waste; and so it remained until the enclosure acts of 1839–1845.

The approaches to the town were as medieval as the fields and meadows through which they made their way. From the south, the road from the bridge which spanned the Trent was carried over the Meadows partly by means of the Leen Bridge, consisting of twenty-two arches, the repair of which was determined by an inquisition in the reign of Henry VIII which derived its authority 'from time immemorial'. It carried its passengers to Bridge End from which point they made their way through swampy ground to Hollowstone, a narrow precipitous cart-track up the face of the rock to St. Mary's Hill, Stoney Street, Broad Lane and the road to York. The western entrance was a deep cutting made by centuries of traffic over Lenton Sands, past the end of Butt Dyke—'where the townsmen used to exercise themselves, in shooting at a Mark with Bows and Arrows'—to Chapel Bar, 'the only Ancient Gate which had escaped the Injuries of Time, and was preserved entire until 1743'.[1] In that year it was pulled down in the course of widening the road at the cost of Lord Middleton and with the aid of his colliers, presumably in order to enable his coal-carts to make the journey more easily. At the same time Hollowstone was widened and the gradient reduced 'so that two or more carriages may conveniently pass

---

[1] Deering, op. cit., p. 3.

each other'; and it may be supposed the swamp at Bridge End was made good for wheeled traffic.

For more than half a century before this, however, the town had been growing in economic importance and still more in social significance. The economic advance was due to the expansion of the framework knitting industry which, from small beginnings in the seventeenth century, had developed rapidly in the early decades of the eighteenth century until, in 1750, it is said to have found employment for 1,200 frames working in wool and cotton, and for a considerable number of workers in the ancillary industries of needle-makers, sinker-makers, setters up of frames, etc. The growing social significance of the town derived from its position as a local capital to which the aristocracy and gentry of the region gravitated on important social occasions. Some of them also lived in the town and left an unmistakable tribute to the graciousness of their age and way of life in the houses which have survived the flood of industrial building and the zeal of twentieth-century townplanners.

The social pre-eminence of the town dated from 1674 when the Duke of Newcastle began the building of his palladian mansion on the site of the old castle with its 64 acres of deer park. His successors intended to make gardens of it—'the finest in all that part of England', as Defoe says—but unfortunately it remained only a reported intention not an accomplished fact. But Nottingham now possessed a ducal seat and became a centre of attraction to the people of quality in the neighbourhood. They thronged to the races—'Eleven or twelve noblemen, an infinite throng of gentlemen from all the countries round, nay even out of Scotland itself', and 'a train of coaches filled with the beauties from the north was not to be described'—a finer assembly than could be seen at Newmarket.[1] Eleven gentlemen including the Hon. Wm. Pierrepont, the Hon. Rothwell Willoughby, John Sherwin, Francis Thornhaugh, maintained coaches besides a considerable number who kept chaises or chariots, and several had handsome residences set about with beautiful formal gardens and orchards. Contemporaries spoke with admiration of Pierrepont House and Plumptree House and John Sherwin's house. The last had a close of grassland in Pilcher Gate and a

[1] D. Defoe, *Tour* (Everyman ed., 1928), ii, 148–9.

large cherry orchard and the site was remembered, a century later, in the densely packed areas of Cherry Street, Cherry Place and Sherwin Court. Other streets that carried into the nineteenth century the fragrance of those days were Currant Street, Garden Street and Orchard Street. Those houses of the period that survived, Newdigate House (1675), Willoughby House (1730–40), People's Hall (1740), Lord Howe's House (1752) and perhaps especially Bromley House, built for George Smith the banker in 1732, reflect the ideas of comfort and elegance of early Georgian England. But from the point of view of the conditions that determined its growth the buildings which failed to survive are of greater importance.

These may be easily located with the aid of Deering's list of streets and the accompanying map by Badder and Peet.[1] By far the greatest concentration was on Back Side, later called Parliament Street, where there were 214 houses and 1,313 inhabitants out of a total population of 10,720. The map shows several solid blocks of property separated by extremely narrow passages, with only one thoroughfare (Sheep Lane, now Market Street) wide enough to admit the passage of a farm-cart. There can be no doubt that the density of population in this area was approaching a nineteenth-century standard and the term 'Rookeries' by which this and other congested places came to be known, would not have been inappropriate a century earlier.

The next largest concentration was Narrow Marsh, along the foot of the rock on which the old Anglo-Danish burgh had been built. Here there were 535 inhabitants, but their houses were more dispersed and they had tree-lined avenues and gardens down to the banks of the Leen. This was no doubt an advantage to the tanners who congregated there in the seventeenth century, but it rendered the houses liable to flooding. In 1736, we are told, the parlours were two feet under water. In normal times the Leen meandered vaguely over the meadows, leaving semi-stagnant loops and wholly stagnant pools and collecting on its way to the Trent the surface drainage from the upper part of the town. It was highly esteemed, however, by the inhabitants of Nottingham who admired it for its sylvan beauties and gratefully used its waters for industrial and domestic purposes.

---

[1] Map printed in Deering, op. cit., between p. 12 and p. 13.

[*opposite:* Nottingham, c. 1751

Narrow Marsh and its continuation Broad Marsh were not the only areas liable to flooding. A similar problem existed in the neighbourhood of St. Peter's Church. This was the focal point of a number of busy thoroughfares—St. Peter's Gate, Pepper Street, Wheeler Gate, Hounds Gate, St. Peter's Lane— and it also received the water of the little brook or drain the 'Rowell'[1] which ran down Wheeler Gate from the upper part of the town towards the Leen. The area was so boggy that it could only be crossed 'not without danger' by the aid of a plank and a handrail from St. Peter's Church side to Castle Gate, and from this point through Lister Gate and to the Leen was 'one continued Swamp'.[2] In 1706 the immediate neighbourhood of St. Peter's Church was raised and paved and the sheep market moved there. In 1729 it was to be swept and kept clean, and the standard of cleanliness was laid down precisely in the order of 1748. 'The Dirt to be taken away from Peter's Church Wall twice in the winter and once in the summer if necessary.'[3] Not a high achievement as a measure of public health, but an improvement on the laconic entry of 1706: 'Twenty loads of mucke betweene Sheepe Penes and ye Hen Crosse 12/–.'[4] In accounting for the remarkable improvement in public health which took place in the middle of the century, the crude measures taken by obscure town officials cannot be ignored.

The margin of swamp was thus slowly being pushed back, and the process was assisted by the arrangements for the disposal of 'Rammell'; it was to be carried into Trent Lanes, the Swan Pool, Sheep Skin Pool, the 'Holloway at the west end of Castle Gate and Hunsgate to fill up the same'.[5] But this thoughtfulness on the part of the Corporation may have had its penalties as well as its advantages since the Leen which provided the main drainage for these areas was also the main water supply of the town. No misgivings seem to have been entertained, however, on this score. Deering, a doctor and leading scholar of the town, wrote as to the Leen: 'it lies at the foot of the Town, and tho' it is slower than the Trent, yet are not the Vapours thence arising capable of becoming hurtful, not only on Account of the Great

---

[1] See *NBR*, ii, 445, and vii, xiv.
[2] Deering, op. cit., p. 17.
[3] *NBR*, vi, 221.
[4] ibid., 32.
[5] ibid., 28, 68, 91, 172.

height the town stands above it, likewise because of the Openness of the Ground below, which readily admits the Ventilation of the Wind to disperse all noxious Particles, and the few boggy Enclosures between the River and its backwater, are by the prudent Care of the Corporation raised and made good Land'.[1]

The presence of hurtful vapours was evidently a matter of some concern. The water supply, however, was felt to be above suspicion. The town had formerly been supplied from its numerous wells and by water-carts bringing a supply from the river, but in the last decade of the seventeenth century a company had been formed to supply the town with water from the Leen by means of 'an engine', one of the many joint-stock pumping enterprises undertaken at that time. 'The original sharers,' writes Deering, 'as in all new Projects, met with many difficulties and found it very expensive for some Years, before they could rightly bring it to bear, but of late is brought to a competent Perfection, so that they are in condition of supplying any part of Nottingham; the East part of the Town has Water immediately from the Engine, whilst the West part receives it from a large reservoir made in Butt Dyke . . . besides this, least any time, there should be want of water on account of the River Leen being low, the Company rent of his Grace the Duke of Newcastle, a large Pond in the Park, lying close by the River, to which they have fixed Flood-Gates, serving in Time of Floods to let water in, and in Time of Scarcity, to furnish water enough to set the Engine to Work.'

The historian of 1740 could look back with pride on what had been accomplished 'during these forty years last past. It is plain', he says, 'that the Improvement of the Town, by mending Roads and raising and paving Streets as well as beautifying it with Sightly Buildings, was a Task left to later Generations . . . and no Stranger who has taken the Pains to consider the situation and present Buildings, the State of Trade and Manufacture, the plenty of Provisions brought to Market, the excellent Malt Liquor brew'd at Nottingham, but will gladly subscribe to what is said of them in the following lines:

> Fair Nottingham with brilliant Beauty graced,
> In ancient *Shirwood's* South West Angle placed

[1] Deering, op. cit., p. 85.

> Where Northern Hills her tender Neck protect,
> With dainty Flocks of golden Fleeces deckt. . . .'

The geographical situation here delicately alluded to moved Deering to ecstasy: 'Were a Naturalist in Quest of an exquisite Spot to build a Town or City upon, could he meet with one that would better Answer his Wishes?' At that time the town consisted of about 2,000 houses containing between 10,000 and 11,000 people, arrayed along the southern face of a sandstone outcrop stretching from Hollowstone along High Pavement, Back Side, Butt Dyke, to the Castle Rock; to the north, west and south of this sandstone crescent lay the open fields and meadows, the famous crocus meadows which in early spring spread a purple hem to the skirts of the old town. No town in England, it was said, had so fine an approach as 'the most beautiful mile' which lay through the crocus meadows between Trent Bridge and Hollowstone; and from the last quarter of the seventeenth century when it was described by Thomas Baskerville as a 'paradise restored'[1] and by Celia Fiennes as one of the neatest-built towns she had seen, to the last quarter of the eighteenth century when the German tourist Moritz said it was the best he had seen outside London, and certainly the cleanest, there was a chorus of praise. It echoed somewhat sadly down the years to the beginning of the present century when in 1901 Ann Gilbert looked back with touching nostalgia to the time when the fields lay open and the streets laid out by the enclosure commissioners were no more than field paths bordered with blackberry brambles and the Meadows were a playground, the very mention of which called up idyllic memories. 'I cannot hope to give you an adequate idea of that fair expanse. Often in my dreams I find myself and companions wandering by its streamlets watching the fish in the clear water, or the dragon flies skimming along the surface, or gathering the flowers that grew

---

[1] 'Paradise restored, for here you find large streets, fair built houses, fine women, and many coaches rattling about, and their shops full of all merchantable riches. . . . It is divided into the upper and lower towns, for when you have a mind to leave the large and more spacious parts of this town . . . you must descend right many stairs ere you get to the bottom and here you find . . . another town full of shops and people, who have a convenience to cut in the rock warehouses, stables, and what rooms they please': 'Thomas Baskerville's Journeys in England, temp. Car. II', *Hist. MSS. Comm.*, 13th Rep., Appendix, pt. ii, Portland Papers, ii, 308–9.

along the banks. . . . But the most interesting and beautiful custom of all was the yearly visit in March to our crocus covered meadows, young and old turning out . . . to revel among them.'[1]

According to eighteenth-century standards, Nottingham was a clean and well-appointed town; it was also reputed by Deering to be a healthy one, owing to the fact that it stood on a well-drained sandstone site above the flood plains of the Trent and was free from the evil vapours and stinking fogs to which medical opinion attached so much importance. His criteria of healthfulness may not be ours; and, as will be shown later, he was more complacent than the facts warranted, even on his own showing. On another aspect of the well-being of the town, however, he is completely convincing; he leaves us in no doubt that it was well supplied as to quantity, quality and variety of food, and that the level of prices was such that the poorest members of the community could share both in the abundance and the variety.

There was ample room in the Market Place, one of the biggest in England, for the display of every kind of merchandise: corn, malt, oatmeal, and stalls and booths for bakers, gardeners, milliners, pedlars, turners, braziers, tinners, chandlers, collar-makers along Long Row on the northern side; a horse market, formerly separated by a wall, on the southern side; a beast and swine market on the west, and at the east end there were the shambles for no fewer than sixty butchers, capable, says Deering, of supplying five times as much meat as the town required. There was also a poultry market round the Hen Cross, where the country folk sold geese and turkeys and pigs on Saturdays and a market at Week Day Cross for butter, poultry, fruit, fish on Wednesdays and Fridays and still more butchers' shambles.

The town had a further advantage 'hardly to be matched by any other of the Kingdom, to wit: not only good Barley to turn into Malt and Ale (for which the Town is famed all over England) but the best, coolest and deepest Rock Cellars to stow their Liquor in'; and the inhabitants equipped themselves with 147 licensed houses, one to every eighty or so, in which to consume it.[2]

[1] Mrs. A. Gilbert, *Recollections of Old Nottingham* (2nd ed., 1904), pp. 18, 28.
[2] The names and locations are given in *NBR*, vii, 552.

He divides the supplies of food available into 'immediate necessaries' and 'less necessaries', and in the former he includes carrots, turnips, parsnips, cabbages, savoys, potatoes as well as meat, bread, butter, cheese, eggs, beans and peas and, of course, beer, small ($1\frac{1}{2}d$ a gallon), middling ($2d$ a gallon) and stong ale ($4d$ a quart). The 'less necessaries' include all forms of poultry, rabbits, a long list of freshwater and sea fish, and also 'Broccoli till within six or seven Years was only to be met in Gentlemen's Gardens, but now are sold in the Market, cauliflowers, asparagus . . . Sugars, Spices and all sorts of Grocers Goods almost as cheap as in London', wine and cider 'as about London'. Tea, coffee, chocolate were also available and the use of the first had spread 'so that almost every Seamer, Sizer and Winder will have her Tea and will enjoy herself over it in a Morning, not forgetting their Snuff . . . and even a common Washerwoman thinks she has not had a proper Breakfast without tea and hot buttered white Bread'.

As to prices, he says that nothing was so cheap as to be contemptible, nor anything requisite to a comfortable way of living so dear but that 'middling People' may have a share, but the fact that tea was beginning to compete with beer among the poorest classes suggests that the standard even for them included something more than the bare necessities of life.

At the same time, all forms of meat could be bought at a low price, beef, veal, mutton and pork being sold at about $2\frac{1}{2}d$ per lb.; eggs were three or four a penny; fowls could be bought for $1s$ $4d$ a couple; a pig or Christmas goose cost less than half a crown and rabbits were $3d$ each. William Felkin, writing of his grandfather at this time, states that during his apprenticeship he paid $5s$ a week for his board and lodging and had $2s$ $6d$ for himself, and 'when he got out of his apprenticeship he could earn $12s$ a week; thus he could save $5s$ to $7s$ a week'. Food, he says, was cheap, but clothing and furniture were dear.[1] Since employment opportunities were expanding, especially for skilled men, owing to the development of framework knitting and its

[1] I am indebted to Mr. S. D. Chapman for this extract from the newly discovered memoir, 'Progenitors of the Felkin Family as ascertained by William Felkin III and summarised in a Memo. dated 1872', p. 53. William Felkin I was born in 1745 and died in 1838, so that the extract above would refer to the last phase of the cheap period, i.e., 1750–65.

dependent industries, and to the important discovery in 1730 that cotton yarn could be used in the frame, the conditions of life of the artisan class were probably as good as in any provincial town in England, and better, as far as Nottingham was concerned, than they were to be again for a hundred years.

In spite of those favourable circumstances, the town was scarcely able to maintain itself by its own powers of natural increase. The century started relatively well with a balance of births over deaths in each of the first two decades but there followed a period of high death rates; between 1720–30 the death rate (i.e. church burials inflated by 1·10) never seems to have fallen below 40 per thousand and three times was over 50; in 1736 it was over 70 and in the year March 1741 to March 1742 it was nearly 80 and one in thirteen of the people died.[1] But in the five years centring on 1745 it fell to slightly under 30 and remained within three or four points of that figure for twenty years. As far as Nottingham is concerned, the age of massacre by epidemic was over; the age of continuous growth by natural increase had begun; and whereas between 1700 and 1740 there was an excess of deaths over births, between 1740 and 1780 about 40 per cent of the town's growth came by natural increase and somewhat over 40 per cent between 1780–1801.[2] From the fifth decade of the century, it can no longer be said that this town—whatever may be said of others—destroyed life almost as fast as the countryside replenished it.

[1] The 'unconverted' March to March burials for 1736 and 1741 were 747 and 818 respectively. The population according to Deering, corrected by Sir John Sutton, was 10,720 in 1739. The immigration was probably between 75 and 100 per annum. Cf. the worst known death rates of the nineteenth century: Byron Ward, 30·9 between 1840 and 1843. See my *Modern Nottingham in the Making* (1940), p. 12. The month of maximum burials, July 1736, coincided with the high point of the flood of that year, when the water rose three feet in the houses of Narrow Marsh. Other years of high floods and high mortality are February 1683; midsummer 1728; May 1787; February 1795.

[2] These figures have been obtained by calculating the difference between births and deaths (i.e., baptisms and burials inflated by 1·15 and 1·10 respectively), and working back from the figures of population given by local historians in 1739 and 1779, and forward from the Hearth Tax Return of 1674. This gives a different result from that obtained by using the Dissenters' registers. See J. D. Chambers, *The Vale of Trent* (1957), pp. 19–21. Owing to inconsistencies in the records of the Dissenters, the present method appears to be more satisfactory for comparative purposes until improved ratios have been devised. I am grateful to Mr. G. A. Yewdall for enabling me to see the results of his researches on this problem.

It is not easy to associate this new demographic pattern with corresponding changes in the town's economy, and still less with an improvement of its food supply. It was a period of rising prices and it was marked, for the first time since 1701, by food riots sufficiently serious to have left some local record. In 1754 the quartern loaf was 4*d*; in 1757 it was 10*d*; and miners and their wives expressed their disapproval at the expense of unfortunate millers who were using efficient but newfangled French equipment, and corn dealers who had adopted the enlightened practice of selling by sample. The episode gave rise to a remarkable pamphlet by an anonymous writer who showed that the results of the riots were the opposite to those intended since selling by sample brought more not less grain to market and the use of French grinding-stones and bolting mills had the effect of raising the efficiency of milling, not as the miners believed, of adulterating the flour with gypsum and bones.[1] In 1762 the Corporation forwarded a petition to Parliament on the distresses of the people and in 1766 occurred the famous cheese riots when cheeses were rolled down Wheeler Gate and Peck Lane and flung about with such energy that the Mayor who was struck with one as he was on the point of reading the Riot Act had to be carried insensible into the Exchange.[2]

On the side of industrial expansion there were numerous innovations devised by the ingenious Nottingham mechanics beginning in 1756 with the tuck-presser which enabled the stockinger to produce a variety of shades in a vertical line and so give the appearance of coloured ribs. In 1759 Jedediah Strutt established his Derby Rib workshop at Derby for the production of ribbed hose, and in 1763 it was adapted by a Nottingham workman to the making of eyelet holes, the first step towards the making of machine-made lace. In 1767 velvet was made on the stocking frame; in 1768 brocade, 'the most beautiful article ever wrought thereon. Here all the variegated colours of the rainbow were cast into captivating shades, all the tints of the full blown carnation were displayed in diversifying splendour; the twigs

---

[1] *Seasonable Considerations upon the Corn Trade, as it respects Landowner, the Tenant, the Miller and Baker, and the labouring parts of the population.* . . . By a true-born Englishman (Nottingham, 1757). Not in the Nottingham Library or in the British Museum, but quoted extensively by T. Bailey, *Annals of Nottinghamshire* (1852–5), iii, 1231 ff.

[2] ibid.

and branches of trees were represented in all their intertwining forms';[1] in 1776 knotted work, 'the most beautiful and durable stockings ever made by human hands'; and the warp machine which 'united the stitch of the stocking frame with the warp of the loom' and made the cloth for the jackets worn by the sailors at Trafalgar and the earliest form of net for window curtains.

Brilliantly skilful and ingenious as the Nottingham mechanics were, they provided only a supporting chorus for the two principals of world-wide fame who had recently settled in their midst. In 1768 James Hargreaves and Richard Arkwright were both in Nottingham with their epoch-making innovations in the spinning of cotton. Besides Hargreaves's own mill in Mill Street, by 1777 Nottingham had its jenny mills containing the machines of Hargreaves's own make. One of these was described as having three carding engines worked by horses, about fifty 'Spinning wheels' of twenty-six spindles each, with slubbing wheels, doubling jacks and 'every necessary implement for finishing cotton yarn for hosiery'.[2] Arkwright's cotton mill in Hockley was a large establishment; on 3 September 1772 'upwards of three hundred persons employed in Mr. Arkwright's mill built in Hockley walked in a procession through the town, with streamers flying, preceded by the head workman, who was clothed from head to foot in white cotton. After parading the streets, they marched to the Marshall-hills[3] to gather nuts, and on their return in the evening, were regaled with a plentiful supper.'[4] Mr. Arkwright was already practising the gentle art of personnel management at which he later proved himself so adept.

These events cannot be said to have initiated but only to have reinforced and sustained the upward trend of population growth. It was already well under way before they took place and, in its early stages, has more claim to be regarded as a cause than an

---

[1] Blackner, *History of Nottingham*, pp. 223–4.

[2] A. P. Wadsworth and J. de L. Mann, *The Cotton Trade and Industrial Lancashire* (1931), p. 494. Hargreaves's mill was a three-storey building 40 feet by 30 feet situated at the north end of a passage leading from Chapel Bar to Back Lane (now Wollaton Street); see Bailey, *Annals*, iv, 6.

[3] Between the Coppice and Carlton.

[4] John F. Sutton, *The Date Book of . . . Nottingham and its Neighbourhood, 1750–1850* (1852), p. 95 (3 September 1772).

effect of industrial expansion. There is more reason to relate the change to non-economic causes, such as the greater immunity of a population that had been savagely thinned by successive attacks of disease during the previous twenty years, or perhaps to the reduced virulence of the organism which carried the infection. Contemporaries themselves had little light to throw on this subject. Deering, himself a doctor, was content to say that 'Once in five years a Distemperature in the Air, either brings with it some Epidemical Fever (tho' seldom very Mortal) or renders Small Pox more dangerous than at other Times, of this last, the year 1736 was a fatal Instance for from the latter end of May to the beginning of September, the Distemper swept away a great number of Souls (but mostly Children). . . .' Apart from this reference the subject excited no contemporary comment, private or corporate, and even the visitation of 1741–2, when one out of thirteen of the townspeople died, gave rise to nothing more than a collection of examples of those who had exceeded 'the ultimate Term of the Psalmist or even were outliving 93 the Age of St. John the Evangelist'.

The stolid indifference with which these epidemic years were met contrasts strongly with the activity amounting sometimes to panic to which the visitations of the plague had given rise a century before. On those occasions the borough authorities made arrangements to isolate the sick in huts built for the purpose, appointed 'visitors' and provided them with funds, presumably for the benefit of the victims; they also ordered the slaughter of cats and dogs, and the confinement of swine, advised against large gatherings at funerals and unnecessary visitings, and forbade the holding of Goose Fair.[1] In 1667 we are told that the plague made 'a cruel Desolation in the higher part of Nottingham, for very few died in the lower, especially in the street called Narrow Marsh, it was observed that the Infection had no Power, and that during the whole Time the Plague raged, not one who lived in that street died of it, which induced many of the richer sort of People to crowd thither and hire lodgings at any Price, the preservation of the People was attributed to the Effluvia of the Tanners Ouse (for there were 47 Tanners in that Place) besides which they caused a Smoak to be made by burning moist

[1] *NBR*, v, 184 (20 June 1637); 247 (27 February 1645/6); 253 (August 1647).

Tanners Knobs'.[1] That men should choose these dire alternatives is perhaps itself a sufficient tribute to the terror which the plague inspired.

The greater attention that was paid to plague was probably due to the fact that it is reputed to have been a disease of adults rather than of children and to that extent represented a greater threat to the family as a whole through the death of the breadwinner. Since the parish registers distinguished between the burials of children and adults by referring to the former as 'son of' or 'daughter of', and to adults as wife, widow, spinster or, in the case of a man, by name, it is possible to test this by comparing the proportions of the categories so distinguished at the two periods. Deering seems to have used this method when he states that out of 2,331 burials between 1732–9 (excepting the year 1736) there were 1,072 'infants'. Such a total would give a ratio of 46 per cent of child[2] burials for those years. A more satisfactory basis of comparison with the plague years would be 1736 when the ratio was 72·9 per cent. This is the highest of the century, but lesser peaks were reached in 1708 (56·1 per cent), 1717 (66·5 per cent),[3] 1725 (55·2 per cent), 1730 (62·1 per cent), 1739 (57·1 per cent). The ratios of child deaths in the plague years 1637–8 are 35·3 per cent and 39 per cent; 1645–6, 38·8 per cent and 38·6 per cent; 1647–8, 48·5 per cent and 56·3 per cent. In 1649 it goes down to 34·9 per cent. (The figures of 1667 are useless as the distinction between adult and non-adult burials was largely ignored.)

An interesting confirmation of the view that plague was feared because of its differential impact upon adult lives is provided by the panic that suddenly arose and as suddenly

---

[1] Deering, op. cit., pp. 82–83. See also L. F. Hirst, *Conquest of Plague* (1953), p. 44.

[2] Since a number of registers in the latter part of the century give the age at death, it becomes possible to define 'child' deaths more clearly. Mansfield, a growing frame-work knitting centre, had 51·8 per cent of its burials under 20 between 1779 and 1799; I am indebted to Mr. Yewdall for the information that between 1779 and 1788 the proportion of burials at Leeds (township only) under 10 was 51·7, and between 0 and 20 was 57·1; six Bedfordshire parishes between 1780 and 1789 give a ratio of 48·9 per cent under 10 and 55·2 per cent under 20; Mr. Eversley defines 'child' burials as 20 years or under: see 'A Survey of Population in an Area of Worcestershire', *Pop. Studies*, x (1956–7), 261.

[3] St. Mary's and St. Nicholas's only.

subsided in 1781. The outbreak of that year evidently gave rise to the fear that plague had returned; on 26 June 'a thousand handbills on fine paper about the Plague reported' were printed at the cost of the Corporation, but within four days the report was contradicted.[1] Instead of plague the town was probably suffering from an attack of influenza.[2] It is interesting to note that though the death rate rose to over forty per thousand, the proportion of child deaths was only 38 per cent, the lowest of the century.

On the assumption of unbroken consistency in the differentiation of child deaths, a comparison of the two periods shows that the ratio of child deaths tended to rise in the last quarter of the seventeenth century.[3] The passing of the plague era brought relief, apparently, only to the adult death rate; and what is more surprising, this differentiation in favour of adult lives seems to have been more pronounced in the second half of the century than the first. Thus, between 1701 and 1750 the ratio of child deaths in five-year periods never fell below 46 per cent (1711–1715) nor rose above 56·2 per cent (1736–40). But in the second half of the century it never fell below 52·1 per cent (1781–5) and it rose in 1791–5 to 61·7 per cent. It would appear, therefore, that in so far as there was a fall of the death rate of the town population in the second half of the century, it did not operate to the special advantage of the lower age groups (except in so far as the particularly severe child epidemics such as occurred in 1708, 1717, 1725, 1730, 1736 and 1739 were somewhat less frequent) and that it implied the saving of adult lives to at least the

---

[1] *NBR*, vii, 128. Unfortunately none of these handbills has survived.

[2] See C. Creighton, *History of Epidemics* (1891), ii, 364. The attack of 1782 'affected ⅔ to ⅘ of the adults everywhere, but the children not so much'.

[3] The large parish of St. Mary's gives the following percentages of 'child' deaths for the century (years of defective registration omitted):

1601–10	*1611–20*	*1621–30*	*1631–4*	*1645–55*
55·8	31·9	36·7	37·2	43·6

1658–65	*1671–80*	*1681–90*	*1691–1700*	
36	42	46·5	50·8	

In regard to the period 1601–10 there is evidence of plague in the town in 1603, 1604–5, 1609–10; *NBR*, iv, 267–99. It may also have been accompanied by smallpox, which was receiving widespread notice at the end of the sixteenth and beginning of the seventeenth century, including its first mention in literature in 1602: Creighton, op. cit., i, 463.

same extent as of the lives of children.[1] In regard to the behaviour of the crude death rate, it will be seen from the table
given at the end of this chapter that it fell from a very high level
between 1725–40 to a low level between 1745–60; it returned to
a level slightly below that of the first two decades of the century
until the last quinquennium of the period, when it took a sharp
turn downwards. It is not a question, therefore, of a steady
decline under the influence of ameliorating factors of diet and
environment, but rather of a sudden and temporary plunge
downwards as a result of the absence of a factor which had made
the preceding period one of exceptionally high mortality, followed by a return almost to the death rates of the pre-epidemic
period. It has been suggested above that the fall from 1745 may
have been due to the greater immunity enjoyed by the surviving
population after the severe thinning process endured by the
previous generation; but it is of equal significance that, though
there was a return to the moderate death rates of the early
decades of the century and a rise of the child death rates above
them, there was no return, in spite of rising prices and increasing
urban congestion, to the high plateau of 1725–40. The death
rate stayed in the foothills until it took its descent into the valley
at the end of the century.

It would not be true to say that in this period the town experienced an industrial revolution since the expansion consisted
of the proliferation of the types of small units that already
existed; only two steam factories were established in these years
—a worsted mill in 1788 (burnt down in 1791 and not replaced)
and a cotton mill in 1792; but the immense impetus given to the
hand-frame industry by the innovations mentioned earlier and
by the successive steps in the mastery of machine-made lace,
together with the stimulus given to machine building and
maintenance and to the housing industry, provided employment opportunities for a growing volume from outside as well as
for the increasing supply of the native-born labour from within.
Between 1779 and 1801 the population grew by 11,000 of
which nearly 60 per cent were immigrants. In these circumstances a rise in the marriage and birth rates is to be expected,

---

[1] See also Eversley, op. cit., 265, for an interesting discussion of this question in
relation to the village populations studied.

an expectation that, as the figures show, is more than amply realized.

The very high birth rates from 1770 must themselves be included among the factors accounting for the higher child death rate: there were more children in the community and they provided a relatively higher proportion of the deaths. The surprising thing is that the crude death rate remained steady and in the last period centring on 1801 took a turn downwards when conditions of life might have been expected to lead to the opposite trend. It was a period of acute social tension arising partly from industrial fluctuations—accentuated by the vagaries of fashion and technological change and the incidental casualties of fire and flood—but especially from the effects of food shortage and famine prices. In 1792 a mob of hungry men and women made a bonfire of the doors, shutters and implements of the butchers as a protest against the price of meat; in 1795 a subscription was raised to provide bread tickets for the relief of the poor suffering from 'deficiency of employment and the extraordinary rigour of the season'; it was the year of the six-week frost from 24 December to 9 February when the Trent was frozen over as low as Gainsborough, and the thaw which followed flooded the houses of Narrow Marsh to a depth of three feet and the Trent 'bearing down in its mighty stream horses and sheep, haystacks and trees . . . was amply sufficient to show the unprecedented extent of the calamity'. Conditions in the following year were if anything worse; wheat rose to 100s a quarter; bakers' shops were looted by hungry mobs and again in the following year. In 1800 prices were higher still, and 'bread was an article of great scarcity this year'; fierce food riots broke out in April and again in August; the Corporation opened a subscription to assist the poor but the most effective measures were taken by two local mill owners, Messrs. Davison and Hawksley, who supplied 'an immense quantity of corn, considerably below the price they had given for it' to their own work-people and sent flour which had been ground by their own steam engine to be sold at a reduced price in Nottingham. In the same year a local surgeon, Mr. Attenburrow, began to vaccinate free of charge, and a first step was taken to tame this 'disease of fearful malignity, committing extensive and frightful

117

ravages'.[1] That the death rate should fall to the second-lowest figure of the century is a tribute to the efficacy of vaccination in stemming the rising tide of epidemic disease, and to the humane impulse of a single man.[2]

Environmental factors also contributed to this result. The new houses in which the working population lived may have been better and, at this time, even less crowded than those of their forebears half a century earlier, but they were innocent of the elementary decencies of life and lacked a regular water supply.

'The gathered filth within doors is scattered daily, in the dirty passages without . . . and many of these streets and lanes, if so they may be called, are without any sort of pavement, consequently without regulated water courses.'[3] Until 1830, when Thomas Hawksley inaugurated one of the greatest civic innovations of the age—filtered water under pressure supplied in standpipes for the use of the working population—the inhabitants had to buy their water in pails from water-carriers. The Leen, however, was no longer the main water supply. In the last quarter of the century, nine pumps had been erected by the Corporation, but the water was 'hard and curdling', so that many householders continued to use the Leen water for culinary purposes although it constituted the main sewer of the town.[4] During the same period a society was formed by the Quakers for relieving distress 'by the aid of medicines, by the distribution of apparel, by temporary loans', by arranging visits in time of sickness and

[1] Sutton, op. cit., p. 233.

[2] On 25 March 1799 the doctors of the town, moved 'by the great mortality amongst the children of the poor from Small-pox', gave their consent to a plan for free inoculation at the General Hospital. This was a doubtful expedient owing to the difficulty of arranging the isolation of those affected. In the following year Mr. John Attenburrow began free vaccinations in his surgery on Bestmarket Hill. His example was followed by the other doctors and in 1805 a public subscription was opened to provide the services of a surgeon for this purpose and in 1813 the service was taken by St. Mary's Workhouse and in 1814 a 'fever house' was also established there. See F. H. Jacob, *A History of the General Hospital Nottingham* (1951), pp. 102–3.

[3] Laird, *Topographical Description of Nottinghamshire*, pp. 102–3.

[4] Blackner, op. cit., p. 26. For the work of Hawksley, see my *Modern Nottingham in the Making* (1940). For erection of new pumps see *NBR*, vii, 196 (in 1779); 193 (in 1782); 196 (three in 1793); 234 (in 1788); 251 (1790 and 1791); 284 (in 1793). In 1804 one of them had to be removed because 'the ordure had so far penetrated the rock . . . which rendered the water . . . at times . . . quite nauseous to the taste and altogether unfit for culinary purposes'. Blackner, op. cit., p. 26.

lying-in. In September 1782 the General Hospital was opened and by 1814 it claimed to have treated 10,913 in-patients and 28,954 out-patients, of whom a total of 27,300 were said to have been 'cured'.[1] The cumulative effect of these changes cannot be measured but it should not be overlooked. The initiating impulse in the new pattern of population growth must, however, be looked for in the long series of substantial balances of births over deaths between 1743 and 1763, a change which took place independently of contemporary economic factors, and may, perhaps, be described as an example of the autonomous action of the death rate. It followed a period when the death rate had behaved with almost equal independence of external circumstances but in the reverse direction. The epidemics between 1720–30 were no doubt reinforced by the weather and harvest ✔ conditions and again in 1741–2; but the demographic effects were disproportionately severe. In terms of subsistence none of these years was as critical as 1709–10 but all were overwhelmingly more critical in terms of mortality; and the crisis of 1736 was entirely a crisis of public health not of subsistence. During the period of low death rates which followed the fearful visitation of 1741–2 the child population was recruited as fast as but, it would appear, no faster than the adult population; whether there was an increased expectation of life is unknown; we can only say that the adult population—perhaps the group from fifteen to fifty-five—was being rapidly reinforced both by natural increase and by immigration, and the effect was reflected in the rising marriage rate and birth rate. Here was the new industrial army in full spate of self-recruitment; marrying and competing for jobs and houses; stimulating the local economy by their production and consumption; creating new markets for their products by their own inventive genius (all the inventions in the stocking industry were the work of ordinary mechanics including the inventions of Strutt in the first instance); hoping to make a fortune—which they never did—but determined to fight for the standards which they had

---

[1] See also Jacob, *A History of the General Hospital Nottingham*, pp. 54 ff., on methods and treatment. He notes that treatment had altered little by 1854, which suggests that Nottingham medical practice had reached a mid-nineteenth-century standard by the end of the eighteenth century.

enjoyed in the good years when prices were low and reliable work-men in short supply; organizing the Framework Knitters' Union of the Midland Counties during the slump of the American war and rioting fiercely when they were denied parliamentary help in the attempt to regulate wages;[1] looting the bakers and terrorizing the butchers in times of famine; ducking the 'Jacobin democrats' in their midst with savage delight while the Cor-poration looked on in complacent apathy, and taking a condign revenge on the troops—with equal disregard of decency and fear of reprisals—when they carried out their duties of keeping order with excessive zeal;[2] but above all, marrying and beget-ting children and filling up the vacant spaces within the boundaries of the old town. From 1770–80 the emphasis shifted from the death rate to the birth rate; for the first time since the epidemic years it topped forty per thousand and reached a climax in 1790 of more than forty-six per thousand from which it fell in 1801 to forty-one—an explosion of population brought about by the changing age structure supported by—and sup-porting—an expanding industrial economy.

If 1770 marked the beginning of the explosive birth rate, it also marked the return of the higher death rates, especially of children. While the general death rate remained at about the level of the first twenty years of the century, the child death rate definitely rose above it. Factors making for the greater chances of life for children—cheaper and more suitable clothes, more plentiful supply of soap and domestic utensils, a more enligh-tened attitude to nursing and child care, better facilities for the provision of food supplies, a better water supply—were not equal to the pressure exerted by larger families and the in-creasingly severe struggle of a lowly paid labour force to meet

[1] I have described these riots in *Nottinghamshire in the Eighteenth Century* (1932), pp. 40–44.
[2] On the occasion of a dispute between the stockingers and a hosier in 1791 the Oxford Blues, after the Riot Act had been read, charged a meeting of the men with drawn swords and 'the Troopers ensured to themselves the hatred and contempt of the working men . . . the consequence of which they felt most severely during the winter for it was customary to see them with their faces as dark coloured as their coats. At length an order came for their removal; and, as they had to go down Hollowstone which was very narrow, the people planted themselves on the top of the rock, well provided with night soil in vessels from their privies . . . with which they plentifully supplied the Troopers as they passed below.' Sutton, op. cit., p. 178.

the difficulties of rising prices and cyclical unemployment. In view of the severities of the time, it is remarkable that the rise was not higher; but it came within striking distance of the bad years from 1720–40. The general death rate, however, kept well below it, and since vaccination had so far made no impact on the ravages of smallpox, something must be allowed to the influence of environmental factors for the restraint upon the death rate. By 1800, thanks to the charitable impulse of a local doctor, vaccination was in full swing; and this more than anything else accounted for the fall of the death rate at the end of the period. The power of epidemic disease was now definitely tamed; the death rate might rise under the influence of overcrowding and falling health standards; but it could never again run amok; the town had broken through the demographic barrier that had formerly kept its population in check, and it was now launched on the uncharted path of continuous growth.

APPENDIX

1. The basis for the rates which follow consists of the baptisms, burials and marriages of the three parishes of St. Mary's, St. Peter's and St. Nicholas's taken from January to December and quinquennial population estimates calculated from the difference between births and deaths and counting back from the enumeration made of Deering in 1739 and Sutton in 1779 and forward from the Hearth Tax of 1674. The births and deaths have been arrived at by inflating baptisms by 1·15 and burials by 1·10. The use of these inflation ratios for the whole period is open to serious objection. For this reason the uninflated raw figures are also presented in five-yearly averages.

2. The marriages have been inflated by 1·10 (until 1754) after deducting those marriages in which both partners came from outside. These marriages are very numerous: between 1700 and 1754 (inclusive) they numbered 1,918 compared with 5,149 marriages in which at least one partner was a native. It may be presumed that some of the marriages from outside would be contracted by immigrants who would settle in the town after marriage and these, together with the unrecorded marriages of Quakers, Roman Catholics and others (e.g. in parishes outside the town) make some inflation necessary though the particular ratio chosen may be open to question.

3. The registration of child deaths between 1703 and 1719 (inclusive) in St. Peter's Parish was defective and a correction by inflating by 1·3 was made to bring them into line with the preceding and [*continued* p. 124]

Population Change in Nottingham 1700–1800

	Population	Natural increase	Immigration	Birth rate per thou	General death rate per thou	Child death rate per thou	Marriage rate per thou
1700	7,000			35·55	33·13	17·91	10·81
		+102	98				
1705	7,200			34·31	31·93	16·37	9·56
		− 55	80				
1710	7,225			31·61	35·26	19·95	7·52
		− 49	824				
1715	8,000			35·33	34·35	19·41	10·07
		+157	843				
1720	9,000			35·29	37·23	17·91	10·36
		−271	1071				
1725	9,800			39·73	43·93	23·17	10·93
		−614	814				
1730	10,000			36·25	44·40	22·68	11·48
		+333	267				
1735	10,600			39·06	40·06	23·83	11·17
		− 193	363				
1740	10,770			38·35	48·33	23·10	11·62
		−350	500				
1745	10,920			38·75	31·17	15·17	11·68
		+343	787				
1750	12,050			37·96	34·27	17·45	10·50
		+187	613				
1755	12,850			38·46	32·00	16·64	10·83
		+444	506				
1760	13,800			36·22	31·25	15·93	10·10
		+ 38	482				
1765	14,320			38·63	36·32	17·10	11·49
		+423	597				
1770	15,340			40·32	38·54	21·44	11·06
		+400	770				
1775	16,510			43·03	34·27	18·67	12·22
		+557	883				
1780	17,950			40·67	35·64	17·45	10·72
		+687	1393				
1785	20,030			42·92	35·85	20·13	12·30
		+952	1818				
1790	22,800			46·29	33·94	19·11	12·51
		+1239	1311				
1795	25,350			45·38	35·16	21·76	12·01
		+1739	1772				
1801	28,861			41·07	30·79	17·25	13·42

Population Change in Nottingham 1700–1800

	Baptisms	Burials	Child burials	Marriages
	Uninflated five-yearly averages of:			
1698–1701	216·4	210·8	114·0	68·8
1702–7	214·8	209·0	107·1	62·6
1708–12	198·6	231·6	131·0	49·4
1713–17	245·8	249·8	141·2	73·2
1718–22	276·2	304·6	146·6	84·8
1723–27	338·6	391·4	206·4	97·4
1728–32	315·2	403·6	206·2	104·4
1733–37	360·0	386·0	229·6	107·6
1738–42	359·2	473·2	226·2	113·8
1743–47	368·0	309·4	150·6	116·0
1748–52	397·8	375·4	191·2	115·0
1753–57	429·8	373·8	194·4	139·2
1758–62	434·6	392·0	199·8	139·4
1763–67	481·0	472·8	222·6	164·6
1768–72	537·8	537·4	299·0	169·6
1773–77	617·8	514·4	280·2	201·8
1778–82	634·8	581·6	284·8	192·4
1783–87	747·6	652·8	366·6	249·6
1788–92	917·8	703·4	396·2	285·2
1793–97	1000·4	810·2	501·4	304·4
1798–1802	1030·6	807·8	452·6	387·2

succeeding years. I a mgrateful to Mr. C. W. J. Granger, M.A., for his advice on this and on other matters relating to the statistical aspect of this study.

4. A comparison of the data provided by the register and the 'Abstract of the Answers', etc., published in connection with the Census Returns of 1801 and 1811 shows some disturbing discrepancies. On nine occasions between 1760 and 1800 the totals of baptisms and burials given in the Abstract differ by 15 per cent to 33 per cent from those provided by the registers, whether taken from March to March or January to December, and for each year between 1807–10 the baptism totals of the Abstract compared with those of the registers are short by 425 (33·8 per cent), 499 (41·0 per cent), 467 (39·4 per cent), 590 (49·2 per cent) respectively. There are also discrepancies in the marriage record but not on this scale. The printed registers, edited by W. P. W. Phillimore, T. M. Blagg and J. Ward (1898–1902) have been used throughout. The case for a large-scale re-examination of the registers becomes more urgent in view of these difficulties regarding the printed Abstract.

5. The quinquennial totals of population and quotas for immigration are necessarily very speculative, and are in the nature of guesswork in the light of the only known facts, i.e. the entries in the registers and the enumeration of population in 1739 (10,720), 1779 (17,711) and 1801 (28,861). Any change in the ratios of inflation would, of course, alter these totals and the rates associated with them. They are presented for what they are worth as a basis of comparison throughout the century.

6. The effect of the 'famine' of 1709–10 seems to be reflected in the marked fall of the marriage and birth rates rather than the death rate. It should be noted, however, that the fall in the number of marriages began in 1708, which was also the year of the highest mortality, much higher than 1709. The figures (uninflated) for this obscure period are as follows:

	1707	1708	1709	1710	1711	1712
Baptisms	241	221	193	188	177	214
Burials	241	287	200	217	265	189
Marriages	56	42	50	45	50	60

7. The fall in the general death rate in 1745 was proportionately greater than that of the child death rate and the rise in 1770 was entirely confined to the child death rate; but in 1780 there was a rise in the general death rate and a fall in the child death rate probably connected with the peculiar incidence of the influenza epidemic of 1780–1 on adults (see above, p. 115). Possibly this also helps to explain the fall in the marriage rate and birth rate at this time. The relatively low marriage rates of the period 1750–60 would probably be a reflection of the very high child mortality rates of 1725–40, though the effect would be largely neutralized by heavy immigration.

8. The lower general death rate between 1775–95 compared with that of 1765 and 1770 implies considerable saving of adult lives since the child death rate shows a substantial rise, but the fall in 1801 (1798–1803) is entirely confined to child deaths and is almost certainly due to the introduction of free vaccination in 1800.

The Course of Agricultural Change
1660–1760

I

HISTORICAL studies in agriculture have traditionally centred on land. Its ownership and tenure were much discussed during the last century, while enclosure was the subject of a great debate in the opening decades of this. Yet the ownership and organization of land, important although they are, do not exhaust the economic content of agriculture: and, indeed, were themselves often the consequences of more fundamental factors. Our knowledge of markets, for example, of changes in prices and rents or even of the adoption of new techniques remains imperfect. And without such additional evidence, it is almost impossible to form an accurate picture of the fortunes of agriculture.

Even if the historian were better informed the task would still be no easy one. Difficulties would arise, in the first place, from the variety of farming practice. Agriculture from the economic point of view, it has been said, 'should be regarded as a generic term covering a complex of industries producing wealth by the growth of crops and the rearing of livestock'.[1] Climate, altitude and soils, for example, have imposed a degree of specialization from time immemorial. Long before the eighteenth century, the wet uplands of the north and west were associated with the breeding of cattle and with the predominance of spring-sown cereal crops: the clay lands of central England with wheat growing: and the thin soils of the south-east with sheep and barley. When Defoe published his *Tour through England and Wales* this pattern had already been greatly elaborated. The environs of London, as of Norwich and Bristol, were devoted to

[1] Edgar Thomas, *An Introduction to Agricultural Economics* (1949), p. 12.

market gardens, to grazing grounds, and to farms which produced fodder for the cows and horses of those cities. Cheshire, High Suffolk, parts of the upper Thames valley, and a large region comprising north Wiltshire, east Somerset and south Gloucestershire, were all primarily engaged in dairy farming, often associated with the keeping of pigs. In the Vale of Aylesbury, 'all the gentlemen hereabouts are graziers, tho' all the graziers are not gentlemen'.[1] Much the same was true of the counties of Leicester and Northampton, and of parts of the East Riding and Somerset. Farmers on the downlands of southern England were also graziers, but were concerned more with the sale of wool and lambs than with fatstock. 'There were orchards and hop fields in east Kent and Worcestershire, and most of the West Country produced cider.'[2] Types of husbandry thus varied not merely from county to county but from district to district within each county. Hence farmers depended for their profits upon groups of joint-products which also varied from area to area. For this reason, to deduce the existence of prosperity or depression from the price of a single commodity such as wheat tends to be misleading. Thorold Rogers, for instance, noted that 'we have often recognised the fact that the cheapness of wheat by no means implies the cheapness of other kinds of grains'.[3] And there were large areas in which wheat either was not grown, or was a subsidiary crop. Again, the prices of joint-products could move in the same direction or divergently. Thus the grazier of fatstock was as interested in tallow as in meat, and the fall in the price of one might be partially, or totally, offset by the rise in the other.[4]

A second complicating factor in this period is the existence of a variety of separate markets, particularly for grain. Thorold Rogers, on the basis of Houghton's figures, distinguished six price regions at the end of the seventeenth century. One was based 'on the Thames and its greater affluents, with certain places such as Hitchin and Wycombe near it. . . . The next district is the Eastern Counties, chiefly Cambridgeshire,

[1] Daniel Defoe, *A Tour through England and Wales* (Everyman's edition, 1928), ii, 14.

[2] Ashton, *Eighteenth Century*, p. 32.

[3] J. E. T. Rogers, *A History of Agriculture and Prices in England* (1866–1902), v, 227.

[4] *The Commercial and Agricultural Magazine*, I, ix (1804), 389.

Bedfordshire, Essex, parts of Hertfordshire, Suffolk, Norfolk and Huntingdonshire. The Midlands are less definite, but will comprise the counties west of those last named, generally between the Trent and the Thames. The South is the range from Kent to Devonshire, and includes some Surrey markets. The Southwest includes Falmouth, Plymouth, Bristol and Pembroke, with the valleys of the Severn and the Wye. The North contains the markets north of the Trent and will include Liverpool.'[1] He argued that 'the generally low prices which will be found to prevail in the Northern markets and the highest prices in the Thames valley are due to the very unequal distribution of money in England, a fact sufficiently notorious to be commented on in the literature of the time'.[2] This, however, is only a partial explanation as the divergent price movements in these sectors show. A more fundamental reason lay in the inadequacies of contemporary means of transport, which accentuated the effects both of regional markets and of regional climatic differences. Metropolitan and export demand dominated the corn trade of the Thames valley and of the eastern districts: and the south-western area might well have been divided into two groups of markets, one based on Bristol and the other on the inland clothing towns.[3] It is probable that, because of growing industrial concentrations, the area denominated 'north of the Trent' might also have contained not one, but several markets. At no time, however, were the boundaries of these regional grain markets fixed and definite, especially where there was easy access to coastal shipping. After 1730, the growth of provincial newspapers, which quoted London prices, helped to break down this sectional autonomy; but it was not until the development of canals and turnpike trusts that a major improvement was effected in this respect.

As far as non-grain products are concerned, the influence of the metropolis was far less localized. The counties of Gloucester,

---

[1] Rogers, op. cit., pp. 239–40.

[2] ibid., p. 241.

[3] Warminster, according to Defoe, was 'the greatest market for wheat in England, with this exception only, viz. Where none of it is bought to send to London', op. cit., i, 282. Edward Lisle also makes the distinction between the Thames valley towns and 'Salisbury, Devizes, and the inland towns' which did not send malt to London: *Observations in Husbandry* (1st edn., 1757), p. 430.

Warwick, Wiltshire and Chester supplied its cheese; Suffolk, Yorkshire and Essex its butter; and as London was the 'great object of the grazier', not even Wales and Scotland were unaffected. It is possible that some of the older characteristics of the markets for these products persisted longer in the provinces than in the better-organized London food supplies. The difference between the autumn and spring prices of meat, for example, might have been wider outside the London area than in the metropolis itself. But apart from these minor features, non-grain prices everywhere were closely tied to those obtaining in the capital.

There is, therefore, a danger of assuming that grain prices in one market necessarily moved in the same direction as those in others. The incidence of 'corn riots' in the first half of the eighteenth century points to the same conclusion. This consideration is important not merely in the narrow context of agricultural change, but also in studies on the effects of harvests upon population growth and employment.

If the compilation of price material is itself complex, its interpretation is also fraught with difficulties. Of the many factors which might be mentioned two merit special consideration. The first is that high grain prices did not benefit all classes of farmers. 'Theoretically, it is possible for farm income to increase as a result of a poor crop, if over a given range of output [the elasticity of] demand is less than unity. In view of the complaints of farm distress and the widespread practice of subsistence agriculture, that such was the result for a substantial majority of farmers is highly improbable.'[1] This comment on the condition of American farming during the middle decades of the eighteenth century is no less true of the small English husbandman until well into the nineteenth century. The impact of high grain prices depended upon the size and type of unit farmed. The small arable farmer 'did not share equally with his larger neighbour the benefits of short harvests and scarcity; his surplus was too small after he had provided for his own needs to enable him to make up the loss through high prices'.[2] He was almost as

---

[1] W. S. Sachs, 'Agricultural Conditions in the Northern Colonies before the Revolution', *Journal of Economic History*, xiii (1953), 278, n. 10.

[2] J. D. Chambers, *The Vale of Trent, 1670–1800* (1957), p. 41.

badly affected when prices were low because of extremely bountiful harvests. Either way, for him 'to lose a Wheat-Crop is the ready Way to his Ruin, especially if he be a poor Tenant; for on the Golden Grain Crop chiefly depends the Payment of his Rent'.[1] Where the traditional three-course husbandry was followed, as for example in the Midlands, this dependence seems to have been considerable. 'The Profit of our Wheat is generally reckoned to have two Years Rent dependent on it; that is, the fallow Year and that in which it grows; the third being imployed in what we call *Lent* Grain, as Oats, or Pease, or Beans, that seldom will bear a Reckoning, otherwise, than a Subsistence for our Horses and other Cattle.'[2] This economic precariousness largely accounts for the rapid turnover of small tenants in many arable areas of central England in this, and earlier, periods. Where animal husbandry, on the other hand, was the predominant activity of the small farmer, the effects of harvest conditions were somewhat different. Here grains were mainly grown for consumption on the farm, and less directly affected the husbandman's economic survival. Yet, like the small cultivator, such a farmer suffered grievously when harvests were poor. When he had money, he appeared in the markets as a buyer of food; more often, however, he and his family went hungry. A bountiful harvest, on the other hand, was a benefit shared by family and stock.[3] Farmers of this type were most frequently to be found in the remoter areas of the country, where, there being less pressure for tenancies, dispossessions were fewer. 'There is no changing tenants in this country,' it was reported of South Wales, 'the country is so universally poor and changing is generally for the worse.'[4] And what was true

[1] William Ellis, *The Modern Husbandman* (1750), March, p. 6.

[2] William Ellis, *Chiltern and Vale Farming Explained* (1745), p. 197.

[3] The general argument is applicable, for example, to farming in the French wars between 1793 and 1815. 'In 1799, many farmers could do little more than pay their rents, notwithstanding the amazing prices given for grain.' *Farmers' Magazine*, 1807, p. 38. In parts of Wales, 'The small farmers were obliged for the last two years [1799 and 1800], even till the last harvest, to buy corn, but now all of them without exception have some to sell. And had it not been for the high prices which cattle, butter and cheese bore, during that period of scarcity, most of them would have been ruined.' David Williams, 'The Crop Returns of 1801 for Wales', *Bulletin of the Board of Celtic Studies*, xiv, 65, quoting a contemporary report.

[4] The Steward of St. Donat's Castle, November 1750. Quoted in my *Industrial Development of South Wales, 1750–1850* (1950), p. 17.

of Wales was also true of large areas of western and northern England.

If high grain prices spelt difficulties for the small husbandman, there was also a group of farmers for whom falling prices did not necessarily mean smaller incomes. The outstanding feature of agriculture before the middle of the seventeenth century had been the slowness with which output could be increased. This was changed by the introduction of fodder crops on a field scale, which represented an innovation equal in significance to any subsequently applied to industry. By solving the problem of maintaining (and enhancing) fertility it enabled the farmer to adjust costs to falling prices by more intensive cultivation. In this way a new element of elasticity was introduced into the supply of agricultural products. An impressive list can be compiled of the counties in central and southern England in which, by 1700, clovers, the new grasses and root crops were in use. What is not known is the extent to which these crops had been adopted. Contemporary and other writers do, however, give the impression that there was a much greater improvement of pasture than has hitherto been recognized. Sainfoin, for example, had 'probably become fairly general on the Chalks from Hertford to Dorset by the end of the [seventeenth] century': clover was 'of great advantage in Staffordshire and Worcestershire'.[1] There was also a more intensive use of the fallows. At Toddington in Bedfordshire farmers agreed to 'sow their several Pieces of Land, lying in a common Field, with Beans and Clover-seed', which they either mowed or enclosed with hurdles for the feeding of stock. By the 1730s, clover had passed into common speech as the 'Mother of Corn'.[2] The new crops were clearly being adopted without any fundamental change in the older methods of husbandry, and for this reason the extent of their use is difficult to determine. But it was certainly great enough to have an appreciable effect upon total output and to relax some of the inexorable pressure of diminishing returns in the older arable areas.

It was, however, on the lighter soils of southern and eastern

[1] G. E. Fussell, 'Agriculture from the Restoration to Anne', *Ec.H.R.*, ix (1938), 69 and 71 respectively.
[2] Ellis, *The Modern Husbandman*, February, pp. 31–32.

England, where natural pasture had always been an uncertain quantity, that the new grasses and roots were to be of the greatest value. Such soils were the natural habitat of root crops: they were easy to till and amenable to the use of labour-saving devices like the horse-drawn hoe and the double plough. For these reasons labour costs per acre were lower than on the arable clays. The profits of maintaining large flocks and herds on the 'dry, huskey, hungry, warm, sandy grounds' of eastern England and elsewhere were thus considerable indeed; and it was here that the new fodder crops became the basis of an advanced system of arable husbandry.

That the early development of these new techniques should have been most marked in the counties of Norfolk, Hertford, Suffolk and Essex rose from a variety of circumstances. The possession of large areas of light soil was, of course, important. Secondly, all these areas were within the ambit of the London market: and most of them had easy access to the Continent,[1] where the dislocation of Baltic supplies after 1700 provided a large market.[2] The growth of the Dutch brewing and distilling industry provided similar outlets, particularly for barley, the cereal most closely associated with the early stages of this new husbandry. At the same time, these areas were equally well favoured for the import of new ideas from the Low Countries. It can thus be said that, from 1700 at least, the fortunes of English farming can only be understood in the context of a European agricultural market. Again, much of the lighter soils

[1] The sea voyage from the ports of Norfolk to the Continent was a quicker passage than to London.

[2] 'To all these I may venture to add a remote cause, which probably had some effects at least by raising corn to a better price; every one knows the immense quantities of corn the Dutch used every year to bring from Poland, by way of Dantzick; this having much decreased of late, partly from the destructive wars that laid waste that fertile kingdom; partly, perhaps, from a greater demand for grain in Sweden than formerly; the Russians, since the peace of Nystadt, remaining in possession of the only corn country that ever belonged to that crown, and suffering an exportation of it only when they please.' *Gents. Mag.*, xxii (1752), 454.
Danzig wheat exports in this period were (in quarters):

1670–9	1,014,475	*1700–9*	583,204	*1730–9*	796,971
1680–9	1,521,434	*1710–19*	489,359	*1740–9*	730,193
1690–9	1,114,624	*1720–9*	920,919	*1750–9*	1,212,539

J. Marshall, *Digest of All the Accounts* (1833), ii, 88 and 99.

of these four counties was old enclosure, where changes of technique could be adopted without either institutional obstacles or considerable investment on the part of the landowner.

Here, as later on similar soils in other parts of the country, the new fodder crops enabled farmers to reduce unit costs of production by increasing the yields per acre. The basis of this larger output was, of course, in grains, but the fattening of cattle, the keeping of dairy herds and the rearing of poultry of various kinds provided an important subsidiary income. And as the techniques were new there was considerable scope for improvement. The famous Norfolk four-course system, for example, was the result of almost a century of experiment and adaptation. It was, however, a system of intensive agriculture which required substantial capital investment, and as such was limited to the larger farmers. When prices fell, they were better able to maintain their incomes by increasing the net produce of their farms; and in this way were in a different position from those who cultivated the heavier soils, where, in the conditions of the eighteenth century, there was less room for technical improvement. The comparative position of arable on the two kinds of soils was reflected in several ways. The country increasingly depended upon the grain production of eastern England and southern Scotland rather than, as formerly, upon that of the clays. Secondly, there was a rise in the value of the lighter lands as compared with the heavier ones. 'The general proverbs or wise sayings of our ancestors relating to husbandry seem rather to have been calculated for the vales than the hills; for the hill-country was of less consequence till the late improvement of sowing grass-seeds.'[1] This divergence in values can be traced in the early decades of the eighteenth century in Norfolk, Wiltshire, on the Chilterns and in Lincolnshire, where Wold farmers gave up their extra lowland pastures once their upland farms could support their stock.

The adoption of new agricultural techniques, however, is only one aspect of the question of farming costs—about which, generally, little is known. There seems, for example, to have

[1] Lisle, op. cit., p. 96. See also *Gents. Mag.*, xxii (1752), 503; Joan Thirsk, *English Peasant Farming* (1957), p. 106; and Ellis, *The Modern Husbandman*, March, pp. 80–81.

been a good deal of regional variation in rents. Professor Habakkuk, writing of the Midlands, states 'Rents, which rose considerably between 1640 and 1690, hardly rose at all between
1690 and 1720.'[1] On the northern lands of the Bishop and Chapter of Durham, on the other hand, they 'never varied for the
next century and a half'[2] after the Restoration; and this may
well have been true of other ecclesiastical estates. On the Coke
property in Norfolk between 1718 and 1745, and on parts of the
Greenwich Hospital holdings in Northumberland between 1735
and 1755, rents increased by about 25 per cent. Similarly, there
are marked regional differences in the movements of wage rates.
In the southern and eastern parts of England they seem to have
risen after 1660: in the west they were stationary. Of Anglesey,
for instance, it has been said that 'there is no trace whatsoever
before 1760 of the rise in wages which took place in England in
the second half of the 17th century'.[3] Even the land tax was
heavier in its incidence in the south and east than it was in the
north and west.[4] Variations in costs as between arable and pasture farming are well recognized; but there were also substantial
differences in the expenses involved in growing various cereals.
Wheat was by far the most costly crop, having regard to the
length of time the grain occupied the ground, the costs of
preparation and harvesting, and the yield per acre: oats were
the cheapest. Thus in the early 1730s, when grain prices were at
their lowest, oats proved a profitable crop in the Chilterns.[5]

The factors which have to be considered in determining the
ebb and flow of rural prosperity are, therefore, many and varied.
And in an England which, despite its many rivers and indented
coastline, was still a loosely organized economic entity, where
the typical farm was small, and where agriculture was under-
going important technical advances, the picture must inevitably
be a complicated one.

---

[1] H. J. Habakkuk, 'English Landownership, 1680–1740', *Ec.H.R.*, x (1940), 13.
[2] Edward Hughes, *North Country Life in the Eighteenth Century: The North-East,
1700–1750* (1952), p. 131.
[3] G. Nesta Evans, *Social Life in Mid-Eighteenth Century Anglesey* (1936), p. 154.
[4] W. R. Ward, *The English Land Tax in the Eighteenth Century* (1953), p. 10.
[5] Ellis, *Chiltern and Vale Farming Explained*, pp. 215–16.

II

It follows that much detailed local study is required before an adequate account of agricultural change can be formed for this period. It is, however, possible to illustrate the operation of the more important factors mentioned above and, at the same time, to suggest an outline of events in this great branch of economic activity.[1]

If the pattern of grain prices in the metropolitan market is first considered, it will be seen that the long upward drift came to a halt at the Restoration and was followed by a marked downward trend. The harvest of 1675 introduced sixteen years of relatively low prices, which were at their cheapest between 1686 and 1691. Although the price series are defective for this period, such evidence as there is suggests that both oats and barley were less affected by the fall than was wheat.[2] The two decades which followed brought little relief to those already in difficulties with the price trend. Eton wheat prices, which had averaged 30s 3d a quarter in 1690 and 1691, rose to 41s 9d in the next year; and except for 1695 and 1697, were over 56s for the remainder of the 'Barren Years'. Until the last years of the decade, the rise in spring-sown grains was more moderate, particularly in the eastern counties, suggesting that the increase was due less to crop failures than to the shortage of wheat. For the farmers on the light soils of East Anglia, whose main cereal was barley, this might well have meant a degree of prosperity. But on the largely openfield wheat and bean lands, where the husbandman toiled over sodden clays—his crops still in the fields in the late autumn, his seeding pushed into the last months of the year, and his flocks reduced by footrot in 1696-7—times were less propitious. As far as wheat is concerned, the change from scarcity to plenty came with dramatic swiftness in 1700 and, with the exception of 1704, prices remained low until the

---

[1] I am grateful to Professor E. H. Phelps-Brown and to Miss Sheila V. Hopkins for their kindness in allowing me to use price material collected for their own work; to the Price and Wage History Research, at the Institute of Historical Research, University of London, for the prices of wheat at Exeter; and to the governing bodies of St. Thomas's Hospital and St. Bartholomew's Hospital for allowing me to extract a number of price series from their respective records.

[2] Rogers, op. cit., v, ch. vii.

harvest of 1708. The average price for the decade 1700–9 was 34*s* 9*d*, the same as in 1680–9, and 25 per cent below that of the 'Barren Years'. Barley also fell sharply, although oats were less affected, possibly because of military demand. If the purchases of St. Thomas's Hospital can be regarded as a guide, oatmeal was on average more expensive than in the previous ten years. The cheapness of the two major cereals was, however, sufficient to cause considerable rent arrears in Norfolk and elsewhere. It is clear that many who had little to sell between 1692 and 1699 found the returns of plenty hardly more satisfactory.

Dearth returned in 1709–10 and wheat prices again soared to reach 69*s* a quarter. Thereafter Eton prices declined sharply to reach 31*s* in 1718, and remained about that low level for another six years. There was a very marked recovery in 1725, an equally sharp fall in the following year, and high prices again during the years 1727, 1728 and 1729. The divergency between this pattern and that for barley is very marked, the latter maintaining a relatively higher price than wheat.[1] Within the area influenced by metropolitan prices, conditions were clearly better for the arable farmer than they had been in the decades at the turn of the century; and the barley grower seems to have benefited more than the wheat grower.

When the harvests of 1730 were gathered, London grain prices fell sharply, wheat more precipitously than barley. It was not until the harvest of 1734 that there was a marked, if fluctuating, recovery, culminating in the period of 'Great Frosts' from autumn 1739 until the spring 1742. Wheat was highest in 1740 at Eton, when it reached 48*s* 11*d* a quarter. At this level it was, however, little dearer than in 1711–14, 1725, or 1727–8, largely because of the very heavy crops of barley. Grain prices slumped into a second and lower trough between 1742 and 1747: wheat reaching its nadir in 1743, barley in 1745, and oats in 1747. The subsequent rise was most pronounced in oats, and was followed by a sharp decline in wheat and barley in 1754–5. Finally, there was an immense increase in the values of all cereals in the dearth

---

[1] A series of price relatives, taking the prices of 1731–40 at Bear Key, London, as a base, gives the following results:

	1710–19	*1720–9*
Wheat	113	110
Barley	121	122

of 1756–8, and then a decline into a third trough between 1759 and 1764.

How far can this pattern be regarded as indicative of the country as a whole? The evidence for a comparison between London and provincial prices is not entirely satisfactory, although the admirable collection made by Houghton for the last decade of the seventeenth century forms a convenient starting-point.[1]

REGIONAL GRAIN PRICES
(per quarter)

Region	Wheat		Barley		Oats	
	1691–2	*1691–1700*	*1691–2*	*1691–1700*	*1691–2*	*1691–1700*
	s d	s d	s d	s d	s d	s d
Thames Valley	43 5½	50 9	18 6½	23 4½	15 1¼	16 5½
Eastern	36 3½	44 0½	16 1¾	20 6½	13 4¾	14 2½
Midland	32 8¾	40 2	15 2¾	21 5	9 8½	13 0½
Southern	40 0½	45 4	19 10¼	21 9½	12 3¼	15 7½
South-western	39 11¾	41 3½	23 2	23 11½	10 10	12 10
Northern	29 8¼	39 8	14 3½	21 5	8 9½	13 0

The northern and midland sectors appear, from this table, to have felt the most severe impact of the 'Barren Years'; wheat, and to some extent, barley rose equally in the eastern and Thames valley areas, but oats were hardly affected at all. The southern and, especially, the south-western regions passed through this period relatively unscathed except for the last three years of the decade. This is borne out by the evidence of Thomas Like, a Shropshire gentleman. According to his diary, although prices tended to increase in the years before 1696, there seems to have been no serious difficulty; partly because of an active cattle trade which provided money for the purchase of grain. Crops were 'thin' in 1696, but in the following year 'there was a very bad rye crop in Wales and the bordering counties . . . so that after the Harvest there was scarcely any Bread made of corn only but wt was mixed with Barley, Oates, or Pease, Most chiefly Barley for it proved so kind and likewise

[1] Rogers, op. cit., v, 236 ff.

The Course of Agricultural Change 1660–1760

by reason of its very great crop and ye Tax on Mault'. In 1698 'corne by reason of the badness of the season in the getting of it in was generally dried in the oven or otherwise and made very bad bread'.[1] The last year of the decade was no better in this area, but elsewhere in the south-western region conditions appear to have improved substantially.

For the next sixty years the evidence is less satisfactory. Wheat prices for Exeter might, however, be regarded as indicating the position in the south-west and can be compared with those for the Eton–Windsor market.

WHEAT
DECENNIAL AVERAGE PRICES
(per quarter)

	1660–9		1670–9		1680–9		1690–9		1700–9		1710–19		1720–9		1730–9		1740–9	
	s	d	s	d	s	d	s	d	s	d	s	d	s	d	s	d	s	d
Eton	45	1	43	10	34	10	48	8	34	9	43	6	37	2	31	7	31	11
Exeter	40	10	38	5	31	9	40	10	35	0	34	10	35	7	30	1	29	11

What is immediately striking is the relative stability of Exeter prices. At Eton in the first decade of the eighteenth century, prices are back at the levels of 1680–9, but the fall in the south-west is far less severe: similarly, the divergent pattern for the period 1710–29 suggests an absence of the buoyant conditions then existing in the metropolitan wheat market. It is only in the 'thirties and 'forties that prices converge, and the regional differences become less marked. In individual years, too, there are significant regional differences. In 1725, for example, smut in the wheat and the failure of the French harvest raised prices in the south to a far greater extent than in the northern parts of the country.[2] Fifteen years later, the severest impact of the

[1] Royal Meteorological Society, *The Observations of Thomas Like, 1691–1709*.

[2] 'The summer of this year was the most dreadful for continual rain, cold and tempest that ever any history mentions, not a day from May to October without rain. The fruits of the earth spoiled and according to their different religions, some grumbled, some swore, and some few prayed.' Extract from Parish Register, Sea-salter, Kent. *Quarterly Journal of the Royal Meteorological Society*, lvii (1931), 80. In Lancaster, on the other hand, 'the harvest was got in much better than expected, and also corn proved better fed than expected, and the market settled and potatoes great plenty and cheap'. *Autobiography of William Stout of Lancaster 1665–1752* (edited by J. Harland, 1851), p. 107.

'Great Frosts' was felt in the western areas of the country, where 'there was little less than a famine'.[1] While in the dearth of 1756–8, the only really bad crop in the south-west was in 1756. The harvest of the following year 'produced as much Corne as any year we know of, and it might be expected that Bread should be as cheap as in other Years'.[2]

Comparisons are even more difficult with regard to oats and barley which figured so largely in the cereal crops of the north and west. And it is only by piecing together scattered fragments of information that an outline of conditions in these parts of the country can be formed. Barley was 25 per cent more expensive near Devizes and the 'inland towns' in 1705–6 than in London;[3] and oats were dear in Shropshire in 1703 and, possibly, fairly generally in the north and west between 1708 and 1713. From then until 1728, all the evidence suggests the cheapness of Lent grains in these areas contrasting with the failure of these crops in southern England during the years 1719 and 1720. After 1735–7, however, the situation changes. Henceforth the north and west do not share in the abundance which characterizes eastern England. Fragmentary prices for Oxford and Gloucester show that the recovery of oats and barley prices after 1735 was marked, and Stout noted in the same year that 'corn at London and the south, where [it] is shipped, is cheaper than it is here'.[4] From 1739 until the harvest of 1742 shortages were acute, while in 1744, 'some places, particularly in the North, South and West of England, much of the Harvest, and even some of the Wheat, was spoil'd by the great Rains'.[5] Two good harvests followed, but from 1748 until 1752 oats were as expensive as they had been during the 'Great Frost'. 1751 was reported as 'a dear Year and late Harvest' in Yorkshire, with 'much Corn to

---

[1] Thomas Short, *New Observations on City, Town and Country Bills of Mortality* (1750), p. 350, quoting the diary of Thomas Barker, Lyndon, Rutlandshire. The situation in Anglesey was saved by the arrival in June 1741 of several corn ships from Sussex. G. Nesta Evans, op. cit., p. 185.

[2] *The Western Gazette*, October 1757.

[3] Lisle, op. cit., p. 430.

[4] *The Autobiography of William Stout*, p. 127. The rise in the prices of bread and other provisions is reported to have led to tumults in various parts of the kingdom in 1735; at Leeds eight or nine rioters were killed in clashes with troops. John Mayhall, *Annals of Yorkshire*, (1878) i, 123.

[5] Short, *New Observations*, p. 347.

THE PRICES OF GRAIN AT GLOUCESTER, 1727–60[1]
(quarters)

Harvest year	Wheat		Barley		Oats	
	Glos.	B.K.	Glos.	B.K.	Glos.	B.K.
	s d	s d	s d	s d	s d	s d
1727–8	38 8*	39 6	—	—	15 4*	14 3
1728–9	55 6	39 1	28 8	23 0	19 0	15 3
1729–30	34 0	32 10	17 4	21 6	12 8	14 4
1730–1	30 10	25 8	14 9	17 9	12 5	12 2
1731–2	27 4	22 5	19 1	15 7	12 8	12 2
1732–3	—	—	—	—	—	—
1733–4	31 0*	26 6	18 8*	15 6	12 0*	12 9
1734–5	41 0	31 0	17 0	15 3	14 6	13 2
1735–6	46 1*	30 2	18 4*	15 3	16 8	13 11
1736–7	42 0*	31 4	20 0	15 6	17 0†	12 9
1737–8	—	—	—	—	17 4	12 3
1746–7	34 8	25 3	13 10	11 4	12 6	9 7
1747–8	31 9	24 7	14 11	13 10	12 8	9 4
1748–9	36 9	27 1	18 8	16 8	17 0	15 7
1749–50	35 7	28 1	17 9	15 8	17 8	14 3
1750–1	35 2	27 0	17 4	15 0	15 0	13 11
1751–2	42 5	32 8	21 4	16 2	15 6	14 6
1752–3	42 4	32 1	19 11	15 9	14 9	12 1
1753–4	44 6	26 6	20 11	15 10	21 0	11 10
1754–5	40 6	24 0	18 8	13 10	15 6	12 0
1755–6	38 0	27 6	19 9	14 8	14 7	13 0
1756–7	63 2	47 3	28 8	22 3	22 0	18 7
1757–8	62 11	31 5	30 0	20 7	18 1	17 8
1758–9	39 10	28 6	18 8	16 3	16 6	13 1
1759–60	36 0	26 4	17 9	15 2	15 0	12 0

[1] The authority for these figures is Rogers, op. cit., vii, pt. i. The Gloucester bushel contained 9¼ gallons and it is not explicitly stated whether Rogers adjusted his prices to make them conform to the Winchester quarter. This is, however, immaterial from the point of view of prices at Gloucester itself. Figures which have been marked * represent quotations from Bath and that marked † a quotation from Oxford. Bear Key prices have been included to provide a rough comparison.

get in *October*, and near the Moors much ungot in *November*,[1] and in Anglesey there was a grain shortage relieved by the import of rye.[2] Crops were reported bad in Rutland in 1752[3] and there were shortages again in Anglesey, although harvests were generally good on the eastern side of England. 1754 and 1755 were bad throughout the north and west forming a dismal prelude to the more widespread shortage of the next three years. In Yorkshire wheat which had cost 3s 4d a bushel in 1754 had risen to 5s 4d by the harvest of the following year: oats which had been 10s a quarter in 1752 were 16s in 1755.[4] The dearth which characterized the opening of the Seven Years war arose 'chiefly, if not wholly, from a real scarcity, occasioned by short crops, which for three or four years past have been in the west and north-west of the Kingdom, and from the general shortness of the crops throughout the Kingdom in 1756'.[5] Similarly, when the worst of the shortage was over and prices fell sharply in London, oats remained relatively expensive in the north, where there were corn riots in 1762.

Thus, fragmentary though the evidence is, there are substantial grounds for thinking that London prices are not truly indicative of the grain markets in all parts of the country. How long the price regions suggested by Houghton's figures persisted cannot at present be ascertained with certainty: that some of them lasted until well into the eighteenth century is undoubted. It seems equally true that the areas roughly delimited by the titles Thames valley and eastern regions in Rogers's analysis formed a distinct agricultural sector of the country, closely attached to the European agricultural market based on the North Sea and the Channel. As such, London prices were more powerfully influenced by the stocks maintained by merchants who dealt in the grain trade.[6] If wheat prices for London,

---

[1] Thomas Short, *A Comparative History of the Increase and Decrease of Mankind in England* (1767), p. 100.

[2] G. Nesta Evans, op. cit., p. 185.

[3] Royal Meteorological Society Library. Excerpts from the diary of Thomas Barker.

[4] Short, *A Comparative History*, pp. 100–5.

[5] G. S. Keith, *Tracts on the Corn Laws of Great Britain* (1792), pp. 5–6.

[6] Thus, for example, 'From harvest time through the winter [1705] barley was three shillings in the quarter dearer, near Salisbury, Devizes, and the inland towns, than at Newbury, Reading, and those countries that drove the London trade of

Danzig, Bordeaux and Biscay are compared, the pattern at the four centres is strikingly similar. Except in times of extreme climatic conditions (which tended to create similar harvests throughout north-west Europe), the determining factor in wheat and barley prices in this part of England was the export trade. It is this factor, assisted by the growth of London, which accounts for the divergences between, for example, Eton and Exeter wheat prices. It might well have been the reason why barley maintained a relatively better price than wheat in the metropolitan area between 1710 and 1730. For the most part, north and western England were excluded from a large participation in the overseas grain trade, and cereal prices were accordingly determined by predominantly local influences. This division into an agriculturally active south-eastern region and a more sluggish western and northern England is not new; but its persistence throughout the first half of the eighteenth century needs to be emphasized.

If a claim can, therefore, be made for a degree of regional autonomy in the marketing of grain, the same cannot be asserted for the products of animal husbandry. Here the division was a functional one, between the grazier and the dairyman on the one hand, and the stockbreeder on the other: and the difference in well-being between the two groups was a notable feature of much of the period. Prices of leanstock are difficult to collect and as difficult to correlate, but there are a number of important reasons for thinking that they were generally low during the first half of the eighteenth century. There was, in the first place, the increasing animal population, particularly sheep, which resulted from the use of the new grasses and turnips. 'The lands of England have been much improved since 1670 by cinq-foile and other grasses', stated a Board of Trade report in 1702, 'by which they feed a greater number of sheep than formerly and the state of wool is thereby augmented.'[1] This was not only true of the grasslands but also of the arable areas where these crops were

malting; the reason was, the great stock of barley, the traders in malt to London had provided the year before, had glutted the London market, whereas the maltsters in the inland trade do not provide great quantities beforehand, and therefore, the crops of barley miserably failing this hot summer, barley bore a better price with them than with us.' Lisle, op. cit., p. 430.

[1] *PRO*, C.O. 389/17, October 1702.

grown either on fallows or in a new system of husbandry. And unlike grain, there was no export trade to drain away some part of the extra output. A second reason which affected the returns on sheep-farming was the import of Irish wool and yarn. The effect of this, and of the increase in the number of sheep, was the long downward trend in wool prices after the Restoration, broken only temporarily by shortages caused by weather or footrot. The decisive turning-point in this trend occurs in 1742. Clothing wools which had been 11s a tod in 1737–9 were 17s in 1743 and 20s five years later: combing wools which had sold for 13s in the 1730s fetched 21s in 1744.[1] There was a short break in prices between 1752 and 1756, but thereafter the recovery was marked and sustained. A third factor on the side of supply was the increased influx of Scottish cattle after the Act of Union.

Finally, there was a fourth reason which operated on the demand side: the long succession of dry summers, by reducing supplies of grass, tended to limit the number of livestock sold. The business in animals had been brisk on the Welsh borders between 1693 and 1696, but there were few 'droved from hence' in the period 1697 to 1700. In the next decade, the only years which were not 'droughty' were 1701, 1703 and 1704. In 1702, for example, 'it was affirmed that hay gave £4 at Oxford and £3 at London per tun. . . . There was never less buying of cattle in a summer and former part of winter than was in this.' 1705 was 'a bad year for grasse as ever was known in all parts of England', and as a consequence 'there was never so much hampering of cattle and less selling of them which caused Poor Farmers' conditions to be deplorable. Only there was a great many ewes bought at a low rate and drove to Essex.' Further the border counties 'got very full of sheep which made the price of the wintering of them to be a third of what they were worth'.[2] In the years which followed, the dry summers of 1710, 1714, 1717–1723, 1730–4, the aftermath of the Bubble, and the fall in the value of meat, tallow and wool in the 1730s, continued the pressure upon those whose livelihood depended upon the rearing of animals.

There were occasions, of course, when the price of leanstock

[1] J. Smith, *Chronicon Rusticum-Commerciale; or, Memoirs of Wool* (1747), ii, 463–72.
[2] The Royal Meteorological Society, *The Observations of Thomas Like, 1691–1709.*

moved up sharply; such, for example, would be the end of a prolonged period of drought, of disease, or a particularly heavy frost which had caused losses in herds and flocks. In 1696 when there was widespread footrot in the Midlands, 'Sheep did never live better in this country' was written of Shropshire, 'which caused ye lower countrymen to be buying ye ewes till they were yearning giving 8/– an ewe for the best'.[1] Similarly, after the 'Great Frost', the Aberffraw Fair of June 1741 'proved extraordinary good. Northamptonshire graziers being now come to the country were content with the leavings of our country drovers and gave good rates from £10 to £14 a pair for them and bought a very great number.'[2] But it was not until the 'forties that the fortunes of the breeders improved permanently, and then with sheep in the first place rather than with cattle. For the restrictions on the movement of the latter during the plague led to an 'extraordinary deadness of our cattle fairs'.[3] Yet even the cattle-breeders were beginning to feel the changed conditions by the end of the 'fifties, as the upward movement of rents in Wales and elsewhere shows.

Those who processed animals by fattening them were more happily placed. They benefited from the cheapness of leanstock and also of grain: they could exercise more control over supplies than the breeder, buying more or fewer cattle as circumstances determined. The graziers too were linked to an expanding market. They further gained from the fact that the prices of animal products fluctuated less violently than those of grain: and beef prices less than those of mutton. The peak of London meat prices was reached in 1650–9 and the decennial averages thereafter show a considerable degree of stability. Tallow was also high until 1680, falling slightly in the next ten years, to regain a high level between 1692 and 1702. The disappearance of the seasonal rise in beef prices in the early part of each year by 1680 suggests that the turnip husbandry had by that date sufficiently developed to ensure a fairly steady stream of cattle for the London market. The sharper rise in mutton than in beef during the 'Barren Years' further suggests that it was the clay lands which suffered most during this period. Both meat and tallow fell in value during the first decade of the

[1] ibid.   [2] G. Nesta Evans, op. cit., p. 121.   [3] ibid., p. 122.

eighteenth century, but recovered the loss in the twenty years which followed. From 1734 until 1748 meat prices were extremely low, particularly mutton, although the grazier derived substantial compensation after 1742 from the high price of wool and tallow. The marked increase in sheep sold at Smithfield, which adequately filled the gap in beef supplies caused by the cattle plague, is an interesting commentary on the reserves built up earlier. It was not until footrot in 1754 reinforced the effects of the plague that meat prices began to rise in a marked way.

BEEF AND MUTTON PRICES
(decennial averages)
In pence per 8 lb. stone

	1660–9	*1670–9*	*1680–9*	*1690–9*	*1700–9*
Beef					
St. Thomas's	21·7	23·1	21·9	23·1	19·6
St. Bartholomew's	—	—	—	—	20·1
Mutton					
St. Bartholomew's	—	—	24	27	22·6

	1710–19	*1720–9*	*1730–9*	*1740–9*	*1750–9*
Beef					
St. Thomas's	22	22·1	—	—	—
St. Bartholomew's	21·1	21·5	18·6	20·6	21·5
Mutton					
St. Bartholomew's	23·3	24·3	20·9	21·1	22·2

The pattern of prices for dairy produce—the fourth major division of agricultural activity—differed slightly again. The shortages which characterized the years of the Civil War were over by 1665, and thereafter there was a considerable stability of values. In so far as any decade can be regarded as dominated by low prices it is probably the 1680s. The divergence between butter and cheese prices during the 'nineties might, in some measure, be due to the impact of war upon sea transport. More important, however, is the fact that dairy farmers escaped the difficulties which afflicted many of their contemporaries in the first decade of the eighteenth century and during the 'agricultural depression'. The only exception to this is the fall in

London milk prices during the 'thirties. What seems equally true is that dairy herds suffered more severely from the cattle plague than did beef cattle. And not all farmers were as fortunate as William Rhodes, cowkeeper in Smithfield, who received £869. 1s 9½d together with free grains from various brewers as compensation for the loss of 190 cows and 54 calves between 1745 and 1748.[1] But there were windfall profits for those who escaped the disease. According to one index, dairy produce was 25 per cent higher in the 'fifties than it had been in the period 1730–9, and London milk prices had also risen substantially.

BUTTER AND CHEESE PRICES
ST THOMAS'S HOSPITAL PURCHASES
(In harvest years)

	1660–9	1670–9	1680–9	1690–9	1700–9	1710–19	1720–9	1730–8
	s d	s d	s d	s d	s d	s d	s d	s d
Cambridge and Suffolk Butter (per firkin)	22 6½	24 7½	22 8	25 5	24 8	24 4	25 1	23 10
Cheshire Cheese (per cwt.)	28 2½	28 5½	26 2	33 6	27 7½	28 7½	29 9	28 1

Supplies of butter and cheese never succeeded in catching up demand before the War of American Independence, and these commodities remained more expensive than any other agricultural product, with the exception of wool.[2]

These price movements, combined with the 'stickiness' of costs, inevitably forced adjustments in the practice of husbandry and in the organization of land, where these were possible. And it seems likely that the pressure was the more

---

[1] St. Bartholomew's Hospital, Minutes of the Court of Governors, 1748.

[2] E. H. Phelps-Brown and Miss Sheila V. Hopkins, loc. cit. A decennial average of their indices for butter and cheese comes out as:

1730–9	555·8	1760–9	730·8
1740–9	626·4	1770–9	899·7
1750–9	680·1	1780–9	815·5

powerful because of the downward trend of prices. The increase in convertible husbandry and the continued enclosure of the openfields are expressions of such an adjustment; as is the change in land usage made feasible by technical innovation. In this last respect, there were two major alterations in this period.

On the lighter soils there was a conversion of grassland to arable. The plough gained at the expense of sheep-breeding—the dominant activity of these uncertain pastures. It was in such areas that the new arable techniques were particularly applicable, providing not only large yields of corn, especially barley, but also an important subsidiary income from the fattening of animals and the keeping of dairy herds.[1] Favourable marketing and institutional conditions saw the change well under way in East Anglia by the end of the seventeenth century.[2] The relatively high price of grain after 1710 led to a similar development in Wiltshire where, according to Defoe, 'many thousand acres of carpet ground . . . [were], of late

---

[1] A description of East Anglian farming in the early seventeen-forties has many of the elements of what was subsequently called 'high farming'. 'The Land, which is proper for a Wheat-crop, is not so proper for a Barley-crop; hence it is that most of the *Suffolk* and *Norfolk* Farmers, in particular, who occupy sandy Grounds, are obliged to this Grain for the greatest Part of their Profit; and where they have not Vent enough for it, for Malt-making, they put it to the Uses of Feeding Turkies, Geese, Hogs &c., which enables them to pay their Landlords; and it is in these two Counties beyond all others in *England*, that some fine Improvements in Husbandry may be seen, to the infinite Profit of both Landlords and Tenants: Which have been brought to pass within these fifty Years, ever since they learned the Way of sowing and houghing Turneps in their open, common, sandy, Fields, which has not only proved a Preparative to their succeeding Crops of Barley, but such Turnep-Crops give them a vast first Profit besides, by feeding their horned Beasts with them to the Degree of Fatting; so as to fit them in a compleat Manner for a *Smithfield* Market, where Thousands of them are sold in a Year; and by their cooling, fat Dung, and fertile Urine, that their Runts, Oxen, or Cows leave behind them in the Land, they so dress and prepare their dry, husky, hungry, warm, sandy Grounds, as to cause them to return more plentiful Crops of Barley of late Years than they had formerly.' Ellis, *The Modern Husbandman*, March, pp. 9–10.

[2] 'The soil of the county of *Norfolk* is mostly a light loam, generally pretty deep; the farmers of the western parts, for many years, made it a considerable part of their husbandry to keep flocks of ewes for producing lambs, which they sold for stock to their neighbours. The price of wool has been decaying ever since the prohibition of its exportation. The price of sheep also, when our improvements begun, being lower than they had been formerly, could not but help forward the new method of husbandry, which lessened these commodities, and increased corn, butter and black cattle.' *Gents. Mag.*, xxii (1752), 453–4.

years, turned into arable land, and sowed with wheat'.[1] During the second half of the 1730s the sharp fall in wool, mutton and tallow prices, combined with a sharp reaction in grain prices in the western half of England, caused a substantial continuation of this process. Later, in the 'fifties, there might well have been a further temporary loss of pasture in these areas as a consequence of high grain prices.

The continuing effect of the new arable techniques in adjusting costs to prices can be traced in the period 1730 to 1763, which can be regarded as the culmination of the first stage in agricultural improvement.[2] In this respect, the conditions and the response were very similar to those which characterized another great period of technical advance after 1815. 'Most of our *Chilturn* Farms', it was said in 1744, 'are called *Turnep-Farms*, of late, by some, by Reason our inclosed Fields and Soils are, for the greatest Part of them, proper for this Purpose, and because of our Farmers close Application to improve their Land by this famous Root.'[3] Elsewhere, the same author states 'the *Chilturn* Farmer, who is possessed of an agreeable Soil for it in inclosed Fields, and does not sow it [clover], is deemed one of the worst of Husbandmen: But some carry their Censure further, and closer than all this, and say, that if such a Farmer does not sow Clover, he cannot pay his Rent, as Times now go in the Farming Business; meaning, that as many large Downs in the *West*, and the Commons elsewhere, are of late plowed up, and converted into Arable Land, and by the new Improvement of Husbandry in many Places carried on with great Success, Grain is now become very plenty and cheap and like to continue so'.[4] Of Norfolk it was said in 1753, 'as novel methods of doing business seldom become universal in a small time, it has been 50 years since this husbandry has been introduced, but in the last 20 years the effects have increased so greatly, that it is truly wonderful'.[5] Enclosure coupled with the new techniques gave the farmers new resources with which to meet falling prices. 'We reckon we do not lose a Season, because we get a Crop of

[1] Defoe, op. cit., i, 282.
[2] Despite Arthur Young's remarks in his *Political Arithmetic* (1774–9), p. 29.
[3] Ellis, *The Modern Husbandman*, January, p. 71.
[4] ibid., March, pp. 76–77.
[5] *Gents. Mag.*, xxii (1752), 503.

Turneps, and a Crop of Barley, in one Year, instead of a Crop of Wheat':[1] and there is evidence in East Anglia of a marked increase of yield per acre. The effect of these methods, together with marling, can be traced on a single farm:[2]

Year	Crops in bushels	Value when sold			Butter produced
		£	s	d	cwt.
1731	1,768	143	19	6	11
1732	2,880	227	12	0	—
1733	1,768	194	9	6	—
1734	2,776	219	1	6	—
1735	2,872	283	0	7	48½
1736	1,708	218	15	0	50
1739	2,180	155	5	0	—
1740	3,252	626	3	0	—
1741	3,920	509	4	0	35
1742	5,704	628	10	6	—
1743	6,592	505	1	0	44½

Thus it was that farmers on the clays and in the openfields 'if wheat be at 12*l. per* last they cannot live; at the same time the *Norfolk* farmers get money'.[3] The activities of Lord Townshend and Lord Lovell in this period are well known: but the rise in the Holkham rent roll between 1718 and 1746 is, in itself, evidence that improvements were by no means confined to a few

[1] Ellis, *The Modern Husbandman*, January, p. 75. The same author, in his *The Practical Farmer* (3rd edn., 1738, pt. ii (misdated 1732), 47), writes very illuminatingly about the flexibility of enclosed farms. 'Chiltern Farms letts for more than the Vale Grounds that are in themselves more Richer than the Hilly-Lands, being a black Mould mix'd with a blewish Clay, that will, with half the Dressing of ours, return the most plentiful Crops of Wheat, Barly, and Beans: But then there is this difference, we in the Hill Country have sometimes three Crops in less than a Year and a half; as Clover, Turnips, Wheat, or Barly; or else Peas, Turnips, and Wheat, or Barly, &c. by means of our convenient Inclosures; whilst they in their Valey open Fields are confin'd to lose a Year and a half before they must set on a Barly Crop after their Beans. For which reason it is, That we commonly Reckon, a Wheat or Barly Crop ought to pay two Years Rent.' He however claimed that openfield farmers in the neighbourhood of the Chilterns enjoyed lower rents, had smaller smiths' bills and could hire their servants more cheaply.

[2] R. N. Bacon, *A Report on the Agriculture of Norfolk* (1844), pp. 267–73, cited in Naomi Riches, *The Agricultural Revolution in Norfolk* (University of North Carolina Press, 1937), p. 152.   [3] *Gents. Mag.*, xxii (1752), 502.

aristocrats in whom 'imagination was allied with adequate financial resources'.

The second way in which, in the long run, costs were adjusted to prices, was by the putting down of clay soils to grass. In the Wealden areas of Kent and Surrey, for example, there was a marked development of cattle-rearing in the later decades of the seventeenth century—both on lands newly won from the forest and at the expense of arable.[1] There was, too, a considerable extension of leys and permanent pasture on the Liassic clays of the Midlands, associated in this case with the fattening of animals and with enclosure. Dr. Hoskins estimates that 10 per cent of Leicestershire had been enclosed by 1607; 52 per cent of the county was further dealt with between then and 1730; leaving the remainder for the period of parliamentary enclosure. According to this authority, the grazier had become the dominant figure in the county's farming by 1700, as it is suggested he had become on similar soils from the Chilterns to the Trent.[2] All this was the reflection of the shortage of meat and tallow during the Civil War period, and the divergent trends in meat and wheat prices during much of the subsequent period to the end of the War of the Spanish Succession. Meat was particularly high in the decade 1670–80 and did not share in the fall in prices which affected wheat either in the 1680s or in the first decade of the next century. By changing the use of land in this way, the farmer also reduced his labour costs, especially during harvest: and this was an important element in farm expenses in southern England, where wage rates appear to have been rising in this period. After 1710 it is possible that the pace of conversion from arable to grass slowed down in this region, as grain prices rose under export demand and the grazier's products tended to sag in value.

In areas which were either remote from the larger markets, or where the ownership of land in commonfields was diversified, and hence enclosure difficult, the opportunities of changing the use of land were limited. In such regions conditions were

---

[1] I have to thank Dr. D. C. Coleman and Mr. D. M. Sinclair for this information.

[2] W. G. Hoskins, 'The Leicestershire Farmer in the Seventeenth Century', *Agricultural History*, xxv (1951).

particularly difficult between 1660 and 1710. Falling prices intensified the drive to increase output by the better use of wastes
and fallows in the arable clays; there was a marked movement
towards the consolidation of strips; attempts were made to
increase the number of pasture closes; and there seems to have
been a tendency to switch from wheat to Lent grains which were
less costly to cultivate. These adjustments were, however,
hardly enough when the maintenance of incomes depended
upon a successful attempt to reduce costs. For the small arable
farmer, particularly in central and eastern England, the downward trend in grain prices meant more work in the fields; and
the prolonged fluctuations which persisted for almost a generation between 1685 and 1710 spelt disaster for many such
husbandmen. It is not surprising, therefore, that a large number
of owner-occupiers were ready to sell their holdings after vainly
trying to steer a course between the Charybdis of dearth and the
Scylla of plenty; nor that numbers of the smaller gentry, more
often than not with heavily mortgaged estates, were likewise
inclined, when faced with mounting rent arrears and wartime
taxation. After 1710 conditions were less severe in these areas,
but each recurring period of low prices saw the small arable
farmer in difficulties. This was true of the years 1718–24 and, as
Mr. Mingay has shown, in the seventeen-thirties and 'forties.[1]
When prices were high because of bad harvests their position
was little better. 'The Receiver of rents for the Kingston Estates
in Nottinghamshire reported in 1727 that the small farmers at
Laxton and Kneesall could not pay their last Lady Day rents
and would have to be given until Michaelmas to do so, "for that
they had very bad crops for three years past and their farms all
depending upon tillage".'[2]

III

It is possible that the extension of cultivation over the wastes
and reclaimed fens, together with the slowing-up of population

---

[1] G. E. Mingay, 'The Agricultural Depression 1730–1750', *Ec.H.R.*, 2nd ser.,
viii (1956).

[2] G. E. Mingay, unpublished Ph.D. thesis, University of Nottingham, 1958,
'Agricultural trends in the eighteenth century, with special reference to the estates
of the Duke of Kingston'.

growth, might well have been the significant factors in originating the new trend of prices after the Restoration. Once initiated, however, its impact varied in different branches of husbandry and in different areas of the country. It is to be expected that the greatest effects were to be found in what can be called the primary activities of farming—grain growing and stock rearing—rather than in those which processed agricultural products. The evidence suggests that the greater the farmer's dependence on dairy produce during this period, the less difficult was his position: to a lesser extent the same was true of the grazier. On the other hand, those whose livelihood rested on stock breeding or wool production suffered considerably. Where changes in land usage were difficult to achieve, as in the cattle-breeding areas of the north and west, cheap food between 1700 and 1735 mitigated the ensuing poverty; but the tendency for grain prices to rise in these areas during the next twenty years served only to deepen it. For the arable farmer, particularly from 1700 to 1760, the important factors were access to London and foreign markets and the ability to adopt new techniques. The position of the husbandman excluded from either of these, whether because of geographical, economic or institutional reasons, was less satisfactory. In so far as a particular period can be regarded as critical, that between 1680 and 1710 has perhaps the best claim. After a prolonged downward trend, grain prices were as low between 1686 and 1691 as in any subsequent period, and the 'eighties witnessed years when the prices of meat, tallow and dairy products faltered. This was followed by two decades of extreme fluctuations. It represented the first major price adjustment after a long period of upward movement. Even the 'depression of agriculture', about which Mr. Mingay has written so illuminatingly, failed to affect all sectors of the farming community. Those who depended mainly on dairy produce for their incomes escaped it, so probably did the larger farmers of the light soils of East Anglia and elsewhere; and its impact on the grain growers of the west and the north does not seem to have been anything as great as on the clays of the Midlands.

Taking agriculture generally, the long-term adjustment of costs to prices, which occurred in this period, resulted in a remarkable increase of agricultural output. Evidence has already been given on the increase of animal population on English farms. And this is borne out by comparisons which have been made of Leicestershire and Lincolnshire inventories at the beginning and end of the seventeenth century. It is further supported by the long decline in wool prices despite a growing output of cloth. The fact that England became a major grain exporting country is also important.[1] Changes in public policy towards the overseas corn trade, and also towards the import of Irish produce is not without its relevance in this connexion.

'Since the demand for all agricultural products taken together is inelastic, producers will receive a smaller aggregate sum for the larger than they did for the smaller output. In other words, so long as the number of workers and the amount of capital employed in agriculture remain unchanged, earnings there will be relatively depressed.'[2] This clearly summarizes the general position of English farming after the Restoration, and especially in the first half of the eighteenth century. The terms of trade between agricultural and industrial products tended to move in favour of the latter.

Just as the downward movement of prices had been powerfully affected by real factors, so also the upward swing which began in the middle decades of the eighteenth century. The acceleration of population growth, an increasing industrialism and an improving system of transport provided the underswell of demand. But of equal, and perhaps of more immediate, significance was the failure of agricultural output to increase in proportion. It has been shown that bread grains tended to

[1] Grain exports from England, in quarters, were during the first half of the eighteenth century:

	Wheat	Malt and barley	Rye	Total
1700–9	1,046,294	1,286,605	489,795	2,822,694
1710–19	1,050,952	2,315,308	316,220	3,682,480
1720–9	1,124,098	2,855,818	246,267	4,226,183
1730–9	2,964,694	2,214,436	164,248	5,343,378
1740–9	2,891,307	3,046,478	670,661	6,608,446
1750–9	3,261,761	2,869,073	417,885	6,549,719
1760–4	1,957,350	1,590,677	180,482	3,728,509

Marshall, *Digest of all the Accounts*, ii, 88.

[2] R. Cohen, *The Economics of Agriculture* (1st edn., 1940), p. 131.

rise in certain areas of the country in the 'forties and 'fifties. The demands of war, coupled with the effects of cattle disease and sheep rot, caused shortages of certain types of raw materials by the outbreak of the Seven Years war. 'Lowering the price of soap and candles', stated a petition in 1758, 'would be of great advantage to the woollen manufacture in general and to the poor throughout the nation.'[1] Four years later the shortage of 'stale and dirty butter, not fit for eating, called Grease Butter', was alleged to be causing distress among the makers of broad and narrow bays.[2] Leather was also reported to be relatively scarce. The high price of provisions—as distinct from bread—between 1762 and 1776 was a constant problem to central and local authorities. There were two parliamentary inquiries on the subject in the early 'sixties: Glasgow and Edinburgh banned all exports of tallow and dairy produce in 1766; and in London and Bristol there were associations for 'reducing the exorbitant price of butcher's meat' in the early 'seventies. The frequent recurrence of bad harvests after 1764 only made matters worse. Food riots of one kind or another became common and those of 1766 were outstanding in their extent and severity. When the Special Commissioners went out to try the 'provision rioters' in the autumn of that year, twenty-eight were condemned to death, five to transportation and fifteen to imprisonment at Reading, Newark, Gloucester and Salisbury alone.[3] It is against this background that the parliamentary enclosures of the period must be viewed.

The consequences of these events, and the upward movement of prices associated with them, were twofold. The high values of animal produce generally, and of dairy products in particular, effected a new balance between the breeding and fattening areas. At Holkham, for example, lambs which sold for an average of 4s 4d each in 1732–5 were worth 7s 1d between 1761 and 1767.[4] In Wales, a predominantly breeding area, rents rose sharply after the Seven Years war, and the new affluence was

---

[1] *JHC*, xxviii, 122.
[2] The preamble to 3 George III, c. xx.
[3] *The Scots Magazine*, xxviii, 342.
[4] R. A. C. Parker, unpublished D.Phil. thesis, Christ Church, Oxford, 1956, 'The Financial Affairs and Estate Management of the Cokes of Holkham in the Eighteenth and Nineteenth Centuries', appendix 2.

reflected in splendid additions to otherwise undistinguished mansions. The conversion of arable to grass in the western parts of the country, which seems to have slowed up after 1710, accelerated again. Much of the parliamentary enclosure between 1760 and 1790 was concerned with the growth of ley farming, and in west Lancashire dairying and grazing was being substituted for the plough.[1] Amongst the 'agricultural interest' the emphasis tended to shift from arable techniques to animal breeding. The objective was 'to make the beast, as Mr. Bakewell expressed it, into a machine the best contrived for converting herbage into money'. And with tallow relatively more expensive than meat for much of this period, early maturing Leicesters with ten inches of solid fat on their ribs were not without their attraction to the financially shrewd. At the same time, high grain prices led to an extension of arable cultivation over the lighter soils of north-eastern England and southern Scotland through the adoption of techniques already well established in East Anglia and elsewhere. While this development increased the yields per acre of the country as a whole, it is arguable that the ease with which profits could be earned retarded further improvements in arable methods. It was not until the fall in prices after 1815 forced the intensive use of imported manures and cattle food that the second great step forward was taken by the specialist grain areas of England. Rising incomes from land also tended to divorce the 'agricultural' from the 'landed interest' during the second half of the eighteenth century. In conditions of prosperity, the landowner's position *vis-à-vis* his tenants was strengthened. He was able to demand higher rents, to impose on them the burden of the land tax, and often to induce them to finance improvements which were legitimately the responsibility of the landlord. It was not until after the Napoleonic wars, when prices fell, that a more general interest in farming improvement received a renewed impetus and the distinction between landlord's and tenant's capital was again clearly demarcated.

In the second place, England's changed position within the European agricultural market was not without its repercussions upon her foreign trade and economy generally. The rise in

[1] Arthur Young, *Annals of Agriculture*, vii (1790), 240.

English exports during the Seven Years war was, in a large measure, sustained in the difficult period between 1763 and 1776 by the increased imports of grain, wool, tallow and dairy produce. The new stage in Anglo-Irish trade, which resulted from this need, illustrates the position clearly. When the easier admission of Irish produce was discussed in 1758, in conditions of shortage of tallow, meat and dairy produce, the controversy foreshadowed that over the Corn Laws nearly a century later: and as the *Scots Magazine* observed, 'It was a dispute between the trading interest and the present landed interest of this kingdom.'[1] The effect of the measures then passed, among other factors, was remarkable:

ENGLISH TRADE WITH IRELAND[1]
(official values)
Average Annual Figures £ Sterling

Period	Imports	Exports		
		Manufactures	Re-exports	Total
1722–38	353,124	281,991	299,763	581,794
1749–54	631,493	646,713	500,519	1,147,312
1763–74	1,158,308	882,561	1,047,720	1,950,281

[1] I have to thank Mr. L. M. Cullen for providing me with these figures.

The decision to devote resources to industrial and commercial rather than to agricultural expansion stemmed out of a great variety of circumstances. Among them must be numbered the natural difficulties which faced the expansion of farming output in these years, and this failure of agriculture to respond to the demands made upon it might well have been a contributory factor in launching England upon an industrial revolution.

[1] *The Scots Magazine*, 1758, p. 121.

VII

London Bankers in Wartime 1739–84

ADAM ANDERSON, the eighteenth-century historian of commerce, after making some estimates of the business of the Bank of England, wrote:

Some might possibly indeed be so very inquisitive as to form conjectures, (for they can be no other) concerning the proportion which the quantum of ready cash always necessary to be reserved in this or any other public or private bank, for the circulation of all their cash notes and credit of accounts bears, or should bear to the total amount of those cash notes and credit; and which is the ultimate article in all banking business, and probably also the most considerable one, more especially with respect to our London private bankers, though at the same time an extremely casual and uncertain one: nevertheless as this last mentioned point may be properly termed the fair and reasonable mystery or secret of all banking, we can see no benefit which can arise by any such minute enquiries to the generality of men; neither do we apprehend them proper to be inquired into at all, without there should arise any reasonable suspicion for fraud.[1]

This secrecy surrounding the operations both of the Bank of England and of the private bankers was an accepted commonplace in the eighteenth century. Pamphleteers might guess or fulminate, but the hard facts were kept to the bankers themselves, as closely guarded a secret as the dealings of the individual customer with his banker. It is largely for this reason that the topic was and remains obscure. This essay is an attempt to clarify the behaviour of some London private bankers and of the Bank of England in wartime, and particularly to trace the effects upon their operations of the greatest single borrower of the century, the government.

Though the forty-odd years covered were years of change and expansion in English banking, yet these changes were not so

---

[1] A. Anderson, *An Historical and Chronological Deduction of the Origin of Commerce*, iii (1787), 245.

deep-seated as to make a comparative study of the successive war years impossible. At the head of the system stood the Bank of England, whose position was becoming more central to the operations of the London money market as the years passed. For London and the surrounding area it was the major issuer of notes. Such London private bankers as have been studied were coming to hold more of their cash reserves in Bank notes, and less in specie, a habit which was doubtless assisted by the Bank's maintenance of the convertibility of its notes, and by its successful survival of the 1745 panic conversions of its note issue. As backing for its note issue the Bank held in normal times a substantial reserve of bullion, which probably represented an increasing proportion of the nation's total supply of bullion.[1] And at various times it increased very heavily its participation in the discounting of trade bills and notes. For most of these years the number of private bank partnerships in London was growing, while the size of such individual firms as have been studied was also increasing. Between the City and the West End there was considerable variety of banking practice. Broadly speaking the City bankers were closer to the merchants and tradesmen while the West End bankers either had or developed more aristocratic and gentlemanly customers. These differences often coincided with the differences in the various types of assets in the banker's portfolio; usually there was more bill discounting in the City, while in the West End loans upon bond, mortgage or assignments of mortgage were more the rule.

In these years banks were growing in numbers in the provinces as well. Edmund Burke wrote that when he first came to London in 1750 there were not more than a dozen bankers' shops outside London, and the remark is upheld by modern investigation. After the turn of the half-century the pace of new country bank foundations probably quickened; the years between 1750 and 1784 saw 'considerable growth'.[2] Country bankers were linked to the metropolis by their London agents. London bankers

---

[1] Sir John Clapham, *The Bank of England* (Cambridge, 1944). For a discussion of the role of the Bank, together with estimates of the volume of its discounts, see M. C. Lovell, 'The Role of the Bank of England as Lender of Last Resort in the Crises of the Eighteenth Century', *Explorations in Entrepreneurial History*, x (1957), 8–21.

[2] L. S. Pressnell, *Country Banking in the Industrial Revolution* (Oxford, 1956), pp. 5–7.

had private country clients. Clearly a more unified financial structure for the whole country was coming into being, and this was assisted by the improvements in transport that were taking place.

In this loosely jointed system, it is not to be expected that all reactions should synchronize closely, particularly at first. Each banking house had its own rules and traditions, and granted the differences among the habits of customers, the differences in the esteem they felt for the credit worthiness of particular bankers, and the absence of universally accepted conventional ratios of cash to liabilities, there was obviously scope for variations in individual banking reactions. An early document of private banking policy, dated 22 January 1746, at a time of acute banking crisis, is worth quoting at length, as it reveals both elements of orderliness and the latitude left to private judgement.[1] It also shows the personal nature of banking activity at the time, for it is an interesting mixture of plain horse sense (maxim 11), advice upon the personal conduct of the partners (maxims 6, 10, 13), rule-of-thumb guidance for particular occasions (maxims 7, 8, 9, 12), combined with a grasp of the need to arrange and proportion the assets of a firm with a clear emphasis upon degrees of liquidity (maxims 1 to 5 and 12).

PROPER CONSIDERATIONS FOR PERSONS CONCERNED IN THE BANKING BUSINESS
JANUARY 22ND 1746

1. Some Judgment ought to be made of what sum is proper to be out at constant interest.
2. A proportion of Bonds, Land Tax tallies, and silver, to be ready on sudden demand.
3. A proportion of Government securities, as Navy Bills.
4. Not to lend any money without application from the borrower and upon alienable security that may be easily disposed of, and a probability of punctual payment without being reckoned hard by the borrower.
5. All loans to be repaid when due, and ye rotation not to exceed six months.

[1] J. B. Martin, *The Grasshopper in Lombard Street* (1892), p. 46.

6. Not to boast of great surplus or plenty of money.
7. When loans do not offer, to lend on stocks or other securities, buy for ready money and sell for time.
8. When credit increases by accident upon an uncertain circulation, the money may be lent to Goldsmiths, or discount Bills of Exchange.
9. 'Tis prudence and advantage of a Goldsmith, that depend upon Credit, to endeavour as near as possible upon the yearly settling accounts, to have the Investure of that money in Effects that are easy to convert into money.
10. To appear cautious and timorous contributes very much to give persons in credit an esteem among mankind.
11. Avoid unprofitable business, especially when attended with trouble and expense.
12. 'Tis certainly better to employ a little money at a good advantage, if safely lent, in order to have a greater cash by you, tho' possibly you may extend your credit safely.
13. When it shall be thought proper to call in old loans, the demanding of them ought to be in the names of all the Partners.

Yet there were definite limits upon the lending activities of bankers. For the whole system was based upon bullion, and Professors Clapham and Ashton have both suggested that in time of prolonged war the balance of payments was liable to turn against England, and that the rates of exchange would become adverse.[1] Though the higher costs of freight and insurance in wartime may have limited the tendency to export bullion, yet the possibility of a bullion outflow remains. The Bank of England, directly concerned with government remittances, would feel the strain first, but the private bankers would not go unaffected. Secondly, the war years saw an increase, sometimes a massive increase, in the volume of government paper issued, both long and short. This provided an obvious incentive for customers to convert bank balances into government paper, for deposits with London bankers did not yield interest, while government paper did. Thirdly, there is the less calculable but none the less significant increase of uncertainty in wartime. Panics of liquidity, triggered off by commercial crises, fears of war or internal rebellion were not uncommon in eighteenth-century England, and were certainly not confined to war years.

[1] Clapham, *Bank of England*, i, 233. Ashton, *Eighteenth Century*, p. 195.

But the general presumption is that bankers as well as customers might well take a less sanguine and more cautious view of business prospects.

The effects of war conditions from 1739 to 1748 can only be sketched in lightly, partly because the statistical records of such London private bankers as have been unearthed are incomplete, but also because for these years no bank correspondence has been found to provide a running commentary. At least the indicators available enable one to divide the war fairly sharply into two distinct periods.

From the declaration of war upon Spain in October 1739 until the French entry into the war in March 1744, the financial pressure was barely noticeable. Government borrowing was light in this period. Just how light is attested by observing that the three per cents stayed close to their par value from 1739 to January 1744. The Bank of England began the war in an extremely strong position, with its note issue completely covered in bullion; only after 1741 did the long slow drain of bullion out of the Bank begin. The three private banks whose records are available during these years did not behave at all uniformly, either in regard to lending policies or fluctuations in the size of their business.[1] At Martin's, a City bank, there were year-to-year fluctuations from 1739 to 1744, but no clear trend. Nor is any clear pattern visible for Gosling's, at that time a small West End bank, for the years from 1742 to 1744, which is all the records cover. Only Hoare's, a substantial West End house, with a long tradition behind it, showed a clear movement and policy. Their deposits rose almost continuously, from £460,000 in June 1740 to £601,000 by June 1745. Yet the partners were cautious, pushing up their cash reserves continuously, and after 1742 reducing their loans as well.

Clearly there were no forces in these years sufficiently strong

---

[1] These and other statements are based on the surviving account books and manuscripts of four London private banks. I am greatly indebted to Messrs. Charles Hoare and Company of 37 Fleet Street, for kind permission to use their magnificent collection of records; to Glyn Mills and Co., 1 Fleet Street, for kindly permitting me to consult the available records of Child's Bank; to Mr. W. D. Gosling of Gosling's Branch of Barclay's Bank for permission to use the eighteenth-century records of the firm; to Martin's Bank Limited for similar permission to consult records in their possession.

to prompt a general reaction, or a common restriction of credit. The marked change in credit conditions resulted from the entry of France into the war in March 1744 and from the Jacobite rebellion of the following year. War with France implied heavier government borrowing, while the rebellion brought panic. As Sir John Clapham remarks, the rebellion of 1745 found the resources of the Bank of England strained by six years of war and of borrowing, and with its stock of bullion 'dangerously low'.[1] After the Jacobite victory at Prestonpans on 21 September the Bank was forced to protect itself by limiting its discount to bills with less than a month to run, and then only for its own clients. A run on the Bank began, slowed down by paying out in sixpences, but checked by the declaration of merchants of the City that they would accept and pay in its notes whenever possible. Matters worsened again in December when the Bank made a call upon the 'Subscription to the Circulation', further shortened its discounts to fifteen days, and on 12 December raised its discount rate on foreign bills to 5 per cent. Higher, the usury law forbade it to go. In January it made a call upon its capital which was successful, and thereafter, with its treasure rising, the worst appears to have passed for the Bank, as victory in February eased the strain. On 1 May 1746 the Bank was able to reduce its discount rate upon foreign bills to 4 per cent. Matters were equally serious for the government, as it was negotiating a new loan in the black months of December 1745 and January 1746, when the 'three per cents' were falling and about to touch their lowest point of 75 in February 1746. The normal loans in anticipation of the Land Tax failed, and a public subscription to make up the deficit was only partially successful. The picture of the panic for liquidity has been amplified by Professor Ashton's demonstration that heavy sales of foreign exchange drove up the value of sterling to a peak in January 1746.[2]

The private banking evidence is unfortunately even more fragmentary for this period than the preceding one, but there is

[1] Clapham, op. cit., i, 233.

[2] Ashton, *Eighteenth Century*, p. 194. See also L. S. Sutherland, 'Samson Gideon and the Reduction of Interest, 1749–50', *Ec.H.R.*, xvi (1946), 15–29. Quotations of prices of the 'Funds' are taken from Sir John Sinclair, *History of the Public Revenue*, ii (1790), appendix, pp. 49 f.

no doubting a general reaction. Gosling's deposits fell from £43,000 in September 1745 to £37,579 by March 1746. This seems manageable enough, but it should be noticed that between March 1745 and September 1745 they had reduced their loans and bought securities; in the next period from September 1745 to March 1746, which were the months of acute crisis, they held their loans down, even decreased them slightly, and sold securities heavily. In this way they raised their holding of cash from £10,174 in September 1745 to £15,801 by March 1746; as a percentage to their total liabilities this represented an increase from 26 per cent to 42 per cent. It is little wonder that they showed a loss from March 1745 to March 1746, or that money should have been scarce in the half-year from September 1745 to March 1746 if others raised their liquidity in the same proportion. For Child's bank the loan ledgers show no fresh loans from 10 September 1745 until 3 May 1746, together with heavy sales of securities from October to December 1745. The pressure on Hoare's bank must have been enormous, but it is less easy to follow in detail, owing to the date of balancing the accounts. They began strongly enough, for in June 1745 their cash was already 49 per cent of their liabilities. They had gone liquid early, but the justification of their caution is the extent of the subsequent fall in their deposits which nearly halved from £601,000 in June 1745 to £349,000 in June 1746. In this period they pulled in loans heavily and emerged quite safely, despite the pressure, with the highly creditable ratio of cash to liabilities of nearly one-third in June 1746.

The acute crisis was over by May 1746, and from then until 1749 the dominant theme is the effect of government long-term borrowing and its expenditure. Over the loan for 1747 there was no difficulty, as the two major City factions collaborated in floating it. They did so again in 1748, but this time there were difficulties early in the year, and the time granted for the payment of instalments on the loan had to be extended. Thereafter, with peace, the easing of credit conditions is shown by the rising price of the three per cents: from a low point of 76 in March 1748 they had risen to touch par in June 1749. Long-term borrowing was not the only way in which the government affected the money market, for with increased expenditure on the armed forces came heavier issues of departmental bills to contractors. Delays in payment rose; the gap between the registration and payment of Navy bills grew markedly greater from 1744 to 1747. In the latter year the delay was between nineteen and twenty-five months, so the discount on the sale of such bills was probably substantial, and they made an attractive investment for those able to wait until they were paid off.[1]

The indicators for banking all suggest a low level of activity for these years. The Bank of England was not in further difficulties, and its reserves were substantial. Yet its note issue did not recover greatly from 1746 to 1748, and in 1748 its 'drawing accounts' were barely half their volume in 1741. Interestingly enough, in its private business the discounts expanded markedly in the years from 1746 to 1749.

What was happening among the private bankers is more difficult to perceive, as the records of only two, Hoare's and Gosling's, are continuous. But they are now consistent and move closely in step. Deposits recovered from the trough of 1746 to a steady level in 1747 and 1748; then they recovered further and began to increase in 1749. Both firms made some loans to customers in these years, but in both cases repayments of old loans exceeded new lending from 1746 to 1748. With the weight of long-term government borrowing and the low level of resources available the rate of interest charged upon mortgages was driven up. In 1747 and 1749 Hoare's were consistently charging the maximum legal rate of 5 per cent, though they lent at 4 per cent (to favoured customers?) in 1748. Both firms switched their resources into securities, which accounted for half of Gosling's assets in September 1748 and a fifth of Hoare's assets in June 1749. From an isolated list of securities, it looks as though Martin's achieved a parallel switch. While the behaviour of the two West End bankers is a doubtful guide to what was happening in the City proper, it is at least suggestive that the Bank of England's discounts rose markedly in these years, when there were profits to be made by shrewd speculation in government securities, and probably a high yield upon say Navy and Victualling bills. If the City bankers behaved as they did in the next war, then it is a reasonable deduction that they switched

[1] Sir William Beveridge, *Prices and Wages in England* (1939), i, 515–28.

resources away from discounts and unsatisfied clients went to the Bank of England.

How severe in general the contraction of banking activity was we cannot tell. But the offsets to the increased volume of government paper which might circulate as 'money', and to its deficit spending must have been substantial, for the lift in prices in the later years of war was very slight. To take the Bank of England first; its circulation fell from just over £5 million in August 1742 to £3¾ million in 1748; its drawing accounts almost halved from £3·2 million in 1741 to just short of £1·7 million in 1748. Such evidence of private bank deposits as we have suggests only a partial recovery after the panic of 1745. The slow recovery was only partially due to more restricted lending; many customers must have shifted from holding large bank balances which earned no interest to holding government securities which did, and to working with smaller bank balances.

That the effects of war from 1745 to 1749 created tighter conditions for would-be borrowers in London is clear. Measured by the yield on long-term government securities the pressure on would-be borrowers cannot have been too acute; with yields never much above 3½ per cent, a mortgage at 5 per cent may well have looked quite attractive throughout this period. The behaviour of short-term interest rates is less easy to follow, and here we can only suggest that private bankers may well have been attracted away from discounts of commercial bills by the higher yields on departmental issues, and that the Bank of England helped fill in the gap. And for this relatively slight reaction compared with the two subsequent wars three broad reasons may be advanced. First that in absolute terms government long-term borrowing was not enormous, and on the whole could be absorbed by a nation that had benefited from the long years of peace, commercial prosperity and gently falling interest rates of Walpole's era. Secondly that the pressure upon long-term interest rates was markedly lessened by tapping the resources of Dutch investors to a significant extent during these years.[1] And lastly, with the exception of the rebellion of 1745, the economic dislocation caused by the war was limited. Foreign

[1] See C. H. Wilson, *Anglo-Dutch Commerce and Finance in the Eighteenth Century* (1941).

trade did not fall off significantly, except in 1746, so that mercantile incomes, and in all probability activity in the major export industries, were not falling away.[1]

The intervening years down to 1755 were a period of exceptionally low interest rates, marked by Pelham's successful consolidation and conversion of the 4 per cent Funds into the Consolidated Stock, upon which 3 per cent was to be paid after 1757. Yet they were years of uneasy peace, and Englishmen were fighting Frenchmen long before the official declaration of war on 18 May 1756. As early as 28 January 1755 Martin's wrote to a customer: 'The stocks are still heavy in general, occasioned by the Press for sailors, but we think the vigorous methods which seem to be taking are a great security to the Funds.' By 7 August they were more gloomy, one of the partners remarking, 'I cannot but think we shall soon have war declared.' A month later they were even more apprehensive and wrote: 'People in general seem to think that the French will soon declare war and likewise may attempt something of a descent upon this Island the next dark night, but that we think we are very well prepared against them.' On top of these alarms came the Lisbon earthquake, whose repercussions were felt in the City. On 2 December Martin's were refusing to lend and were pleading that 'We must excuse ourselves from parting with any money upon loan at this time, as the Calamity which has happened at Lisbon will cause a very great demand for money.' It was a year of the jitters. The price of the three per cents slid downward particularly sharply from June to September. The Bank of England, relieved by this fall from the pressure of the repatriation of Dutch capital in the Funds which had marked the previous years, strengthened its free treasure and bullion generally. In August 1755 its bullion backing for its note issue was over 90 per cent, and by August 1756 the bullion had risen still further to over £4 million, though as a ratio to its note issue it was fractionally less.[2] The figures both for Martin's and for Hoare's suggest nervousness; the loans and investments at Martin's in December 1755 were lower than at the previous

---

[1] For a general discussion of the economic effects of war, see A. H. John, 'War and the English Economy, 1700–1763', *Ec.H.R.*, 2nd ser., vii (1955), 329–44.

[2] Clapham, op. cit., i, 235.

Christmas, and though their deposits were much higher, the cash had piled up until it was two-thirds of the liabilities at Christmas 1755. The movement is less marked for Hoare's, but it is visible; though they lent money from June 1754 to June 1755, their new lendings were slightly less than repayments, and their cash reserve was much higher in June 1755, at 35 per cent of liabilities, than it had been since the previous war.

The Bank of England, having begun in an extremely strong position in 1755, was not in serious difficulties during the war itself. The bullion was substantial enough, despite adverse exchange rates late in 1760, which persisted for the next two years. Heavy strain on the Bank came with the post-war crisis in 1763. During the war the note issue was steady from 1757 to 1761, and markedly higher in 1761 and 1764. As in the previous war its drawing accounts moved downwards. Even more pronounced was the secular rise in discounts, which finally overtopped £2 million from August 1763 to August 1764, when the Bank came to the support of the market during the crisis.[1]

Government borrowing was rather limited down to 1758, but then expanded rapidly. The peak was in 1761, when, according to Mrs. Schumpeter, over £12 million 'net receipts from loans' was reached.[2] Investors needed to be tempted, so the bill for 'douceurs' mounted.[3] It was an expensive war, and the pressure on the market can be gauged by looking at the price of the three per cents and at the discount on Navy bills for short-term rates. Consistently with the figures of borrowing, the three per cents, after their initial slide in 1755, remained steady until 1759. The first financial crisis is shown by the slide of over ten points from 91 in November 1758 to 79 by June 1759. As government borrowing increased they fell again, drastically, from 83 in October 1760 to 73 by February 1761. The worst was still to come, a long slide downwards from 76 in August 1761 to hit the bottom at 63 in January 1762. This was the second year of acute stringency, which coincided with the peak of government borrowing, the fall of Pitt (October) and the entry of Spain

---

[1] Lovell, op. cit.

[2] E. B. Schumpeter, 'English Prices and Public Finance, 1660–1822', *Review of Economic Statistics*, xx (1938).

[3] Sinclair, op. cit., ii, 87.

into the war (January 1762). As early as 28 May 1761, a London merchant wrote to the Duke of Newcastle, 'Private credit is at an entire stand in the City, and the great houses are tumbling down one after the other, poor Touchet stop'd yesterday and God knows where this will end, for private paper has now no subsistence, everyone is afraid of his neighbour.'[1] From early in 1762 the stocks recovered, stayed up well even in the crisis of 1763, and began an emphatic upward climb in 1764. The movements in the discount on Navy bills are equally interesting, and confirm the chronology, as an increase set in during the second half of 1759, and reached 10 per cent discount in June 1760. A heavy discount remained until late in 1762, and reappeared again from October 1763 until the summer of 1764. Thereafter the combined effect of funding and prompt payment reduced it to a negligible amount.[2] These figures at least confirm the suggestion of varying degrees of stringency from 1759 to 1764.

What was happening among the private bankers?

For Hoare's the picture is a fairly full one, as bank correspondence survives to illuminate the statistical changes, and the trends are clear. Down to June 1758 no major change is visible. The bank's deposits were still high at that time, having been even a little higher in June 1757. Until June 1758 the partners continued to lend, it would seem fairly freely, as new loans exceeded repayments. The cash was kept high at least to June 1757 (37 per cent to liabilities), though the price of this was some realization of securities.

The turning-point came between June 1758 and June 1759. The volume of business shrank enormously; deposits fell from £763,000 to £515,000 (June 1759). Stocks were realized to keep the bank liquid, and over this period the partners called in a substantial number of loans, and only re-lent a fraction of the amount. Thereafter from June 1759 to September 1764 the comparative stagnation of banking activity is clear. During these years the deposits remained consistently near the low level of 1759. In all these years new lending was small, and was

---

[1] L. B. Namier, *The Structure of Politics at the accession of George III* (1st edn., 1929), i, 211.

[2] Beveridge, op. cit., i, 523.

exceeded in nearly every year by repayments. Having reduced their loans upon mortgage and bond in this way, the firm shifted back into the market for securities, holdings of which rose to just a quarter of their assets by September 1764. This movement into liquid assets probably enabled the partners to work with rather lower cash reserves from 1761 to 1763. Interest rates charged to borrowers moved in sympathy. They appear never to have been below 5 per cent for fresh borrowings from 1760 to 1764, though on previous loans the partners were often content with less, so long as the interest was punctually paid.

How did their customers fare? Some of the answers are revealed in the letter books, which give a consistent picture of tightening and at times acute credit conditions.

On 11 September 1758 a large borrower was advised that the rate of interest on an existing mortgage had been raised to 4 per cent, and the letter added:

So great a sum as £40,000 advanced on one security is rare, nor was it ever usual to us to do it. Such a sum in our power would enable us to supply persons who keep their cash with us, and whose occasions often require sums from £1000 to £10,000. It is to oblige those also that we are desirous of a reduction in the Principal. A larger interest is not what we have in view, though I can affirm that so great is the scarcity of money that at this time 5 per cent is offered every day on the best of securitys.

A few days later another client was told that his loan was 'now attended with great inconveniency, owing to the demand for public loans and the late fall in the Stocks'. The reason was clear; faced with shifts of customers' balances into the stocks, and with pressing applications for help, the firm was being forced to replenish its cash by the sale of securities, 'the losses', added one of the partners on 21 November, 'were upon my word real'. By January 1759 the tone is even stronger (and fits in with the fall in loans visible in the balance sheets).

At present we do not advance Money to anyone on any security. Yours is most unexceptionable. The uncommon supply of millions upon millions granted and now to be raised obliges all of our Profession to be prepared for the Payments coming on, so that instead of lending out money, we have called it in on this occasion.

The year 1759 witnessed a crisis for private as well as for government credit, and by 15 October a clear note of apprehension can be detected. Refusals to lend could reasonably be blamed upon

the Necessity of the Times and the obligation we are under to be prepared for the Call of 13 or 14 millions to be raised yearly. These immense sums granted are such as no former times ever knew, nor could the Present foresee, and outgo all calculation, but we must with others bear our share in the Publick Troubles.

Conditions eased slightly until the next crisis late in 1761 but the firm continued its policy of recalling loans, particularly if interest payments were in arrears. March 1760 was a 'time when 5 per cent and a Premium is given every day for Money on the best securities, and when everyone is punctual in the Payment of interest under 5 per cent for fear of being raised or the principal demanded'. Such comments continue until the final easing of conditions in 1764.

The mechanism of short-term issues of paper by the departments, and the way it might affect bankers' decisions to lend, or even let clients overdraw, is clear. 'Interest, My Lord, I never had in view, or my Partners, in those proofs we have given of our inclinations to serve you, for at the time we consented to your drawing for the £3000 we could undenyably have made 15 per cent of it in Navy bills at 10 or 11 per cent Discount, carrying 4 per cent Interest beside, and commanded our money again in a year.' In addition to pressures from customers who ran down their balances and invested in the stocks came pressure from others who wanted at all costs to avoid selling their holdings in the 'Funds' at a heavy loss, when the price was low. 'We were solicited by such numbers to advance them money, to prevent their selling out of the Stocks that no ways and means were left untryed to effect it, even by selling my own Property for them, in the Stocks.' That money was generally scarce was accepted by the partners, who knew that promises of repayment could not 'reasonably be expected to be kept to in this Crisis of Stagnation of Money, and consuming war without present prospect of end' (9 June 1762).

Sometimes rent incomes were moved up to London to help

pay off existing mortgages. It is at least probable that funds moved in from the provinces to take advantage of the low price of government securities; it is certain that in 1761 a withdrawal of funds from Scotland to take advantage of an acute fall in the Funds precipitated a banking crisis in the northern kingdom.[1] That liquid resources were scarce is not in doubt, but the borrower had alternatives to bank loans. In these years Hoare's, using their knowledge and connexions, were able to find private lenders willing to accommodate many of the borrowers who were asked to repay as well as others whom they themselves could not satisfy. Yet an overall impression remains that from 1759 to 1764 there were considerable difficulties in raising fresh, substantial sums on mortgage in London.

The evidence for Gosling's is fragmentary, but the general shape of the movement is similar to that for Hoare's, and resembles the behaviour of the firm at the end of the previous war. In September 1761, in the middle of acute financial crisis, their deposits stood at £115,214; they were slightly lower still in March 1762, but then recovery set in by March 1763 (£169,018), only to be checked again in the following year before the removal of the government from the market enabled them to recover. Yet this uneven recovery from what was probably the abnormally low figure in 1761 implied no increase, either absolute or relative, in the totals of their loans and discounts for private customers. Together these two items were just short of 20 per cent of assets in September 1761; by March 1763 they were down to a mere 6 per cent of total assets. After this a slow, irregular movement in their favour seems to have begun. What gained was a perceptible rise in the investments in securities and in the cash. Either because of their high yield, or because of the expectation of capital gains on the coming of peace, the securities had risen to make up just half the assets by March 1763. Obviously we cannot time the beginning of the switch for Goslings, yet clearly in the late years of the war the desire to purchase securities together with the need to hold the cash high for emergencies, overrode any demands from private customers.

---

[1] H. Hamilton, 'Scotland's Balance of Payments Problem in 1762', *Ec.H.R.* 2nd ser., v (1953), 344.

Lastly Martin's, a City bank. Though no balance sheets are available until 1761, a series of monthly balances enables us to estimate the overall movements quite accurately. Despite considerable short-term fluctuations, two unmistakable trends are visible which fit in reassuringly with the behaviour of Hoare's bank. The two years 1756 and 1757 were a period when on the whole deposits were high, touching two peaks in November 1756 (£393,000) and again in April 1757 (£363,000). Again during these two years the total figures for discounts, loans and investments (a composite figure which cannot be broken down) show a considerable expansion over the level in 1755, and touch a peak of £165,000 in August 1757. There follows a marked contraction. Deposits dropped irregularly to a low point of £198,000 in July 1758. Thereafter they fluctuated within a remarkably fixed upper limit of a few thousand pounds more or less than a quarter of a million pounds. The minimum point reached was during the crisis of 1761, a mere £162,000 in December 1761. The items headed 'Discount Book' also fluctuated, but the downward trend is evident, and yet again the bottom point was reached in December 1761 and January 1762. After a brief recovery later in 1762, the years 1763 to 1764 appear as the doldrums before the gradual post-war expansion began. The cash, an uncertain item, which undoubtedly included short-term government paper, is the major item after 1758. Not only had the bank, like the others, gone liquid. If its behaviour is at all typical, it reveals a story of contraction in the City parallel to the contraction in the West End. Thomas Mortimer's embittered remark that the profits made from 'the pawning of Scrip' were so large that bankers in Lombard Street had since 1760 refused 'to discount bills, to the great detriment of the commercial interest of this city' points in the same direction.[1] So, as has already been suggested, does the marked increase in the Bank of England's commercial discounts.

Considering the expense and duration of the war, it is again worth remarking that only for periods in 1761 and 1762 was the yield on the three per cents higher than 4 per cent, in short that the rise in long-term interest rates was to some degree modest. At least during Pitt's regime the war was highly popular in the

[1] Thomas Mortimer, *Every Man His Own Broker* (1762), p. 201.

City, and his successful strategy results in a marked accession of trade which were a 'substantial element in financing of war expenditure'. Prosperity characterized not only the metallurgical industries but also the growing cotton trade. And again the ability to draw in supplies of Dutch capital reduced the strain.[1]

For the American War of Independence no such offsets existed. Instead of Pitt, with his following in the City and his plans for a large-scale war of commercial strategy, there was only the weak government of Lord North. He could not rely, as had his predecessors, upon Dutch investors to alleviate the burden. After 1780 the Dutch were at war with England, and even before this, in 1777, there had been substantial repatriation of Dutch capital, and there was to be more withdrawn in 1783. Though North might plead with some justification that the loan contractors were driving hard bargains, particularly in 1779 and 1781, yet there was little justification for his financial methods, the continued borrowings in stocks bearing a low rate of interest, which brought in to the government far less than their par value and so constituted an extra burden upon the capital of the national debt. And these borrowings took place in an economy which, so far from being made to flourish by war, was feeling the burden of the first continued fall in foreign trade in the century, a long decline which began to be felt in 1776 and continued until the end of hostilities.

It is not surprising that government borrowing should have proved more expensive and more onerous. After the entry of France into the war in 1778, not only were the sums borrowed very substantial, with net borrowings continually over £10 million from 1780 to 1785, but the terms were unfavourable to the government. Except in 1783, the government was forced to pay well over 5 per cent for its borrowings from 1779 to 1784; the effect of this upon private borrowers unable to evade the legal maximum of 5 per cent is obvious. The same story of a financially embarrassed government is revealed by the discount rate on Navy and Victualling bills. As delays in payments

---

[1] For a discussion of the relations of Chatham and the City, see K. F. Hotblack, *Chatham's Colonial Policy* (1917). On the importance of Dutch investment, see Wilson, op. cit., pp. 158–66. The effects of the Seven Years war are discussed in John, op. cit.

extended, so the discount rate increased. By January 1779 the discount had reached 11½ per cent, and it was to remain high, almost invariably over 10 per cent until June 1785. In January and February of 1784 it was as much as 20 per cent.[1]

The Bank of England's position early in the war is difficult to assess, as its bullion figures were swollen by the recoinage of 1774 to 1778. It appears to have acted fairly generously in the crisis of 1778, for both its circulation and discounts rose sharply from August 1777 to August 1778. After 1780 its treasure drained away, largely as the result of adverse exchanges. It got through the war; but the crisis of 1783 was severe. Sir John Clapham remarks: 'Whether through good fortune or high intelligence, the Bank's conduct of affairs in 1783 was justified by the event.'[2] After 1784 its position was secure. Taking the years after 1778 as a whole, its note issue seems to have declined slightly, while the drawing accounts remained stable. After the sharp increase in 1778, there is, as in the previous wars, a continued expansion of its discounts.

The private bankers reacted in what by now must be regarded as the familiar fashion. First Hoare's. Their deposits touched a peak in 1777, at £861,000, moved downwards to £726,000 by 1780, and remained close to this figure until 1784. The fall in deposits is less marked than upon previous occasions, but the shape of the movement is similar, a downward slide, followed by years at a consistently lower level. As previously, only this time more promptly, the partners recalled loans in excess of their new lending, starting in 1777. From 1777 to 1780 the reductions in loans upon mortgage and bond were heavy; thereafter they remained steady, either because they were deemed low enough or because at the lower level they were more incompressible. Again interest rates were driven up: from 1780 to 1783 the firm never charged less than 5 per cent. Rates eased in 1784. The expected switch was made into government securities, with greater speed and continuity than in the Seven Years war. By 1784 the holdings of stocks and short government paper had risen to nearly one-third of the assets, whereas in 1776 they

---

[1] For the financial statistics, see Schumpeter, op. cit.; Beveridge, op. cit., i, 524–526; see also below, p. 175.

[2] Clapham, op. cit., i, 256.

were less than one-tenth. Cash holdings were steadily raised to 1780, being particularly high (30 per cent) in 1779. They were, as might be expected, rather lower thereafter as the proportion of readily marketable securities rose. That the firm was in a highly liquid condition is evident from the fact that from 1779 to 1784 the combined totals of cash and securities were usually over half the total assets. It is unnecessary to repeat the literary evidence, as the tale of called-in loans and scarcity of money in wartime has already been given.

Gosling's behaviour was broadly similar. Their deposits show a peak (as do Hoare's) in 1777 (December) at £474,000. In the crisis year of 1778 they were abnormally low, below £400,000, rose again to December 1779 (£484,000), and then fell again, remaining at a consistently lower level until 1785. The contraction is less marked than in Hoare's, but the direction and timing of the movement are similar. A second similarity is clear in the loans to private customers, which were reduced after 1777 and remained low until after the war was over. But there is not such a pronounced shift into the Funds, which remained fairly constant. What varied rather more were the discounts, which rose to a first peak in December 1777, and recovered again from the subsequent fall. In June 1783 and 1784 they were about one-fifth of the assets. Nevertheless the movement towards greater liquidity is clear in Gosling's as well as Hoare's. The cash, which was under 20 per cent in June 1777, was raised to over 40 per cent by December 1778, and stayed at a high level until June 1783.

For Martin's the coverage is unfortunately briefer, so that the behaviour of a City banker is not available for the whole war. Their deposits, as in the other two cases, were lower for 1778 than in the succeeding years, but their movement thereafter is distinctive, as a recovery set in late in 1781 and was maintained until the middle of 1782, where the record ends. Discounts and loans followed a similar course, contracting to 1780 and then expanding again. Some correspondence for 1779 and 1780 shows that the partners were calling in overdue loans, and were being selective in accommodating their customers. Refusals were prefaced by allusions to the 'scarcity of money' and 'the precariousness of the times'.

The general conclusion, as previously, is of a contraction of bank deposits as government lending became heavy, presumably as customers switched some of their resources. For the merchant seeking discounts, there were probably other firms like Gosling's, who kept up or even extended their volume; and there was the same significant increase in the Bank of England's discounting. But for long-term borrowers upon mortgage there was less relief. True some gentlemen may have relieved the situation by the sale of undervalued annuities, but the evidence of unsatisfied borrowers is considerable. Not only the bank correspondence, but the testimony of others coincides. In 1779 William Pulteney wrote:

Our manufacturers, our traders, our farmers and even our landed gentlemen know to what a degree this expectation of Government premiums has affected them. Money cannot now be borrowed on mortgages, on the former terms. The price of land has fallen, the quantity of circulating cash in the hands of our merchants, manufacturers, builders, improvers, is remarkably diminished.[1]

Years later, in 1818, Joseph Kaye, a solicitor, told the Select Committee of the House of Commons on the usury laws,

I am old enough to recollect those inconveniences so long ago as the American War, when money was very scarce, and the discount upon Government securities, such as Navy and Victualling bills and Ordnance debentures, were as high as 15 or 16 and sometimes nearly twenty per cent, and when it was impracticable for an individual, in the best credit, and having the best landed securities to obtain money at the legal interest of 5 per cent.[2]

The behaviour of these private bankers in wartime is remarkably consistent, though the limited coverage must be emphasized. In years of heavy government borrowing the secular rise in bank deposits was checked, as customers purchased securities and the bankers restricted their loans to private borrowers. Because government paper, long or short, was an alternative to loans upon mortgage, as well as to discounts, the effects were communicated to both markets. For discounts of commercial

---

[1] William Pulteney, *Considerations on the Present State of Public Affairs* (1779), p. 30.
[2] Report of Sel. Comm. on the Usury Laws, 1818, in *BPP*, 1845 (375/611), XII, Q. 540.

paper there emerged in each war a major alternative source of finance in the expanding discounts of the Bank of England.

In the mortgage market some existing mortgages were transferred from bankers to private lenders, the banker acting as intermediary. But in the long run the stream of loans on mortgage diminished in volume as potential lenders who had invested in the Funds were rendered less willing to oblige by the heavy capital loss incurred as the price of the Funds fell. Furthermore, the positive attraction of government securities increased with their rising yield, and at the very end of the war, the prospect of capital gains with the coming of peace. But before any correlation of tightness in the London market with the major fluctuations in investment can be attempted, there are several reservations to be made. A considerable proportion of aristocratic borrowings upon mortgage were for marriage settlements, for the consolidation of debts incurred by extravagance, and for building. Such borrowings may have been easily postponable. Secondly, while we need more information about the financing of turnpikes and enclosures, it is clear that the sources of finance for much improving activity were local, rather than metropolitan. Professor Ashton has suggested that in normal times interest rates ruled higher in the provinces than in London; if so, it is at least arguable that the yield on government long-term securities might need to rise very close to 5 per cent before funds would seek London rather than local employment. Only a detailed study of provincial lenders can throw any clear light upon these problems, but they may help to explain the rather limited fall in private investment that seems to have occurred prior to the American war.

While it is broadly true that the major investment booms fit in to the periods of peace, yet the damping down of private investment in the later years of war, when there was a clear shortage of funds in London, is limited. In London itself there was a definite fall in the level of building activity from 1743 to 1748, and again during the later years of the Seven Years war. While it is possible to observe a fluctuating volume of enclosures and turnpiking from 1744 to 1749 it is doubtful how much weight should be attached to a shortage of finance in view of the rather moderate lift in interest rates. A marked fall in such investment does not occur until the very end of the next war, in 1762–3. For the American war of Independence the case is clearer. Exports fell, and one would expect some investment to fall consequently. Yet the sharpness with which the totals of turnpikes, canals and enclosures all turned down after 1778 suggests that, in addition, the government was deflecting resources on a substantial scale away from private borrowers. But in these matters we are at present, like Anderson, only able to form probable conjectures.

VIII

The Rate of Interest in the Eighteenth Century[1]

I

FOR some years there has been a controversy among economists about the contemporary significance of the rate of interest. There has been a parallel, though less organized, debate among economic historians about its significance in the eighteenth century, due largely to Professor Ashton's initiative; but, if less indifferent than formerly, economic historians remain sceptical of the stress he has placed upon it. One consequence is the continued dearth of special studies of the problem, upon which alone a reasoned judgement can be based. This essay seeks to distinguish some of the issues and, by the analysis of some factual material, to take the discussion a little further.

II

The marked fluctuations in interest rates during the eighteenth century raise many questions, the first of which concerns the nature of the rate of interest. How far was it merely a *real* rate, reflecting the changing profitability and changing supply of capital? To what extent was it a *money* rate, reflecting changes in the supply of and demand for money? As a money rate—the cost of liquidity—the rate of interest may have affected the pace of economic activity; were individuals and the economy as a whole in fact sensitive to interest rates? If so, did apparently small changes really matter, and, further, what explanation can be offered for the relative stability of rates that is frequently found in monetary transactions? Such stable rates apart, are the

[1] I am grateful to the Central Research Fund of the University of London for a grant which has facilitated my research.

commonly cited yields of securities in the London money market in any way representative of trends beyond the metropolis?

A cautious assessment indicates four points of especial relevance. First, monetary factors were undoubtedly of considerable general importance in the eighteenth century, whether or not attention was given specifically to the rate of interest. Second, the allied influences of liquidity and of potential capital gain or loss must probably be sought behind the fluctuation of any interest rate. Third, it is arguable that there were sufficient links between London and provincial centres, and between provincial centres and their hinterlands, for London rates to indicate broad monetary trends in the country as a whole, at any rate at the margins of economic activity. Finally, small changes in the long-term rate are deceptive indicators. The degree of flexibility in the money supply, together with investment opportunities, helped to determine the range within which interest rates fluctuated; moreover, apparently small variations in the long-term rate look quite different when viewed as part of a constantly changing complex of interest rates.

III

During the eighteenth century, the long-term rate of interest, as indicated by the yields of Bank of England stock and of government securities ('the Funds'), tended to fall.[1] There was a marked decline during the first thirty years of the century, notably between 1710 and 1720, and then something of a flattening out from the mid-1730s to about 1750. Then came a few years of cheap money, followed by a rise during the Seven Years war (1756–63). From the mid-'sixties to the early 'seventies the rate fluctuated around a fairly low level, rising again thereafter, especially during the war of American Independence (1776–83). From the mid-'eighties to the mid-'nineties it fell again, reaching almost record low levels in 1792. Subsequently the rate rose again; it fluctuated around the high level of 5 per cent during the revolutionary and Napoleonic wars (1793–1815).

The costs of long-term governmental and private borrowings varied in rough harmony with these broad trends. From time to

[1] Ashton, *Eighteenth Century*, table xiii, p. 251.

time the interest on the national debt was reduced by some major conversion operation, or by an adjustment in the terms on which the Bank of England or the South Sea Company managed the national debt.[1] For private borrowing mortgage rates in particular showed a long-run flexibility throughout the country; this appears in the records of estates, of London insurance companies,[2] and of London bankers.[3] Rates on personal bonds and promissory notes displayed less flexibility, but moved from plateau to plateau in sympathy with major trends. Rates of interest paid by public utilities, such as turnpike trusts, canal companies, and public improvement trusts, resembled those on private mortgages in fluctuating in rough harmony with the yield of the Funds.

Short-term assets followed similar paths, though with differing amplitudes of variation. As every wartime government in the eighteenth century appreciated, investors displayed discomforting agility in moving between the short and long ends of the money market when the Treasury's reluctance to pay high long-term rates drove it to borrow heavily on short-term. Some short rates, e.g., those on Navy bills, proved to be extremely volatile, leaving the legal maximum of 5 per cent far behind.[4] The East India Company's popular and more liquid short-term securities followed a similar but more subdued pattern of movement.[5] Information on rates for commercial paper is scantier, but, inasmuch as businessmen used India bonds and elements of the floating debt as money, the phrase 'commercial paper' must be interpreted widely. The return on such means of payment was calculated as a yield on their prices, which were free to fluctuate; this quite legitimately short-circuited the usury laws, so that businessmen employing such instruments paid or took the market rate of interest. In contrast, the commercial bill was technically discounted, so that the rate of interest, being the relevant consideration in discount, brought it within the usury laws. In conditions when the market rate exceeded the legal maximum, the

---

[1] E. L. Hargreaves, *The National Debt* (1930), ch. ii–viii.

[2] A. H. John, 'Insurance Investment and the London Money Market of the Eighteenth Century', *Economica*, new ser., xx, no. 78 (May 1953), 149–50.

[3] According to Mr. D. M. Joslin.

[4] For Navy bills, see Sir William Beveridge, *Wages and Prices in England*, i (1939), 523–5.   [5] John, op. cit., diagrams on p. 149.

market for commercial paper might in consequence be starved of funds. There were, however, conventional means by which businessmen registered changes in the cost of money without necessarily varying formal interest rates; these arose particularly from the internal balance of payments, and from the practice of granting trade credits and trade discounts (below, pp. 197–201).

In terms of the economy as a whole, the possible significance of these variations can be approached as reflections first of the real rate, and second of the money rate. Adam Smith's views are probably of general acceptance on the interpretation of the real rate. 'According . . . as the usual market rate of interest varies in any country, we may be assured that the ordinary profits of stock [i.e., capital] must vary with it, must sink as it sinks, and rise as it rises.' Smith points out that, where the market rate is high, the country is poorer and wages are lower than where the rate of interest is low. In short, he argues that a low rate reflects capital accumulation, which is a key to the wealth of a country.[1]

The accumulation of capital in the eighteenth century, which the declining trend of interest rates (until the French wars at the end of the century) clearly indicates, appears in this light as a major social and economic achievement. The falling rate of interest, itself owing much to technical progress, further facilitated it; lower rates brought into view many worthwhile projects, such as the improvement of town life, which could not otherwise have been undertaken because of their low rate of return as investments.

The monetary aspect of interest rates poses difficult problems. In the longer run, a favourable balance of payments, an increased supply of marketable 'near-money' assets with the growth of the national debt and of investments in public utilities, and an improvement in banking facilities, may all have eased the money supply and depressed the rate of interest. In the shorter run, one might expect interest rates to reflect changes in the liquidity position: if the public's views of the expected future value of money changed, then more or less money to hold would have been demanded than previously, with consequent effects on the level of interest rates; equally, changes in interest

[1] Adam Smith, *Wealth of Nations* (2 vols., Cannan edn., 1903), i, 90–93.

rates may have been induced from the supply side, through changes in the volume of money and/or of alternative assets.

To assess the impact of general monetary conditions upon the economy as a whole, it is necessary to distinguish between the technical defects of the monetary system and what might be called monetary factors proper. In the first category come institutional factors, changes in the currency, and so on. In the second come changes in the availability and cost of money, whether by variation of interest rates or in other ways.

On the technical level, there was much to cause dislocation: financial crises, the occasional recoinages,[1] seasonal fluctuations, and the frequently uncertain nature of payments over any distance. Until the road improvements of the later eighteenth century, transport difficulties drastically reduced trading in winter months, so that payments would move slowly;[2] the tax receiver for part of north Wales said in 1743 that he had 'very few opportunities of remitting the money but by the Drovers, that from the latter end of November till after Candlemass is quite a dead time with them, so that till then 'twill not be possible to make any Return'.[3] Each district had its special problems, expressed simply enough in the differing premiums that government departments might recognize as legitimate for tax collectors to pay for remittance to London;[4] or even in the need so late as 1742 to consider the bodily, and expensive, transport of cash under armed guard.[5] Even where remittance facilities were found they were not always reliable. Between 1714 and 1735 a Carlisle land agent habitually remitted to London by drover as other means were dearer though less risky. 'They are as brittle as glass', he moaned; after one remittance (possibly by drover) he was worried 'for about 10 days & could

[1] In July 1773, before the enactment of the recoinage, Thomas Bland was touring the north of England, and wrote that 'People . . . are all in Confusion about the Act (wch suppose by this Time has had the Royal Assent) to put a stop to the circulating of light Gold . . . all payments may be said to be totally at a stand', Gurney MSS. (Friends' House, London), i, 507.

[2] See, e.g., J. D. Chambers, *The Vale of Trent, 1670–1800* (1957), p. 8. See also *BMAM*, 27420, for the Newcastle lead trade: 'Trade is now at a stand, & no money to be got till ye Spring is further advanced' (9 February 1731/2).

[3] *PRO*, T.1/310, fol. 50, and *Cal. Treas. Books & Papers, 1741–5*, pp. 225–6 (7 January 1742/3).

[4] *Cal. Treas. Books & Papers, 1739–41*, pp. 45–46 (10 August 1739).

[5] ibid., *1741–5*, p. 101 (14 December 1742).

neither Eat nor sleep well'.[1] Professor Ashton registers the point lucidly in his study of Peter Stubs; he appropriately opens a chapter on 'The Medium of Exchange' with the remark that a modern firm's history would not contain such a chapter, since nowadays we take for granted the adequacy of monetary facilities. 'But in the days of Peter Stubs a manufacturer could never be quite certain of getting cash for the payment of wages; and the instruments by which purchasing power was normally transferred from one person and place to another frequently operated with a great deal of friction and sometimes failed to work at all.'[2]

In face of such serious technical difficulties in the money supply, monetary factors proper would indeed need to be strong to be significant. Strong they certainly appeared to be. Substantial switching of resources between money and other assets, and between different types of securities, was likely to accompany marked changes in interest rates. Alternatively, some investors might be 'frozen in' if a change in rates reduced the capital value of their assets; this result depended upon the asset involved and the availability of other attractive outlets.

These movements were seen most clearly when the free market rate of interest, as registered in the stock markets, reached or passed the legal maximum; the approach to the legal ceiling cramped existing or would-be borrowers. Mortgagors might have to repay their debts so that mortgagees could reinvest profitably beyond the reach of the usury laws and also make capital gains: a situation that is said to have led the courts to prevent foreclosure during the Seven Years war when interest rates were high.[3] Idle balances were tempted into attractive securities: invited in 1760 to lend money to the river Weaver trustees, Lord Derby regretted his inability to do so. 'I have disposed of my money . . . upon a good security at £4 per cent. The lowness of the stocks at present is the occasion of several monied men purchasing into those funds in hopes of a great rise whenever we shall be blessed with a peace. . . .'[4] Other potential

[1] *PRO*, C.109/356, 15 April 1727 and 2 March 1716 respectively.

[2] T. S. Ashton, *An Eighteenth Century Industrialist* (1939), p. 99.

[3] John, op. cit., p. 143, n. 4.

[4] T. S. Willan, *The Navigation of the River Weaver in the Eighteenth Century* (Chetham Society, 1951), p. 196.

sources of loans were 'frozen in'—in 1757, Jedediah Strutt found his friend Dr. Benson unwilling to make a loan to finance a newly invented stocking frame, because he would have incurred a capital loss by selling out his stockholdings to raise cash.[1] Some people might be able to borrow only on unfavourable terms, if at all: mortgages were unobtainable for long periods during the American and Napoleonic wars, those in need of money sometimes being driven to raise it by the sale of annuities at costly rates.[2] Yet others, needing the money for themselves, would shoulder the capital loss of realizing assets (equivalent to a savage rate of interest), echoing sadly Edward Gibbon's lament in 1778, when the Funds were sliding, 'In spite of the War I must sell.'[3] With *low* yields on the Funds, the mechanism worked in reverse. It seems likely that the government's reduction of the rate of interest in the early 1750s encouraged a close comparison between the advantages of investment in the London money market and in provincial estates.[4] Forty years later, Chalmers recorded a similar impact of a rise in the price of the Funds.[5] At first, in the boom of the 1790s, this drew money to London, but its continuance drove back 'vast sums' to the country where it formed the base of the remarkable credit expansion that characterized the pre-war boom.

The existence of switching implied a sensitivity to changes in

---

[1] Ashton, *Eighteenth Century*, pp. 28–29. A similar problem of potential capital loss clouded a London attorney's efforts to sell a Leicester estate of the Carringtons in 1747. His contacts had located a prospective purchaser in Twickenham (Middlesex), who had had £50,000 'Left to him to Lay out in an Estate in the County of Leicester . . . he was willing to purchase y.̊ Estate' but he was unwilling to buy at that moment because 'his money was in y.̊ Stocks & they were now so Low that should he now draw it out he might Loose foure Thousand pounds by it'. *PRO*, C.103/164.

[2] Report from the Select Committee on the Usury Laws, 1818, in *BPP*, 1845 (376/611) XII, evidence, QQ.61–69, 86, 91–96, 123–7, 131–6, 188–203, 262–350, 538–40, 565–75. The secretary to an insurance company that had been accustomed to invest in mortgages recollected that in the Napoleonic wars 'for the period of, I think, six or seven years, mortgages were not to be obtained; the term "mortgage" had become almost obsolete' (Q. 197).

For the attitude of London bankers to mortgages see above, pp.168, 175–6.

[3] J. E. Norton, *The Letters of Edward Gibbon* (3 vols., 1956), ii, 179.

[4] See below, p. 194.

[5] G. Chalmers, *An Estimate of the Comparative Strength of Great Britain* (1794), pp. lii–liii.

the rate of interest.[1] That sensitivity took three forms. First, as borrowers or lenders, people might take direct account of it; second, holders of money and of liquid assets in general might be affected by changing capital values; third, individuals or enterprises would have been affected indirectly through their dealings with those in the first two groups, or by the change in general monetary conditions when variations in interest rates registered the public's changing preference for money compared with other things. Only the first two forms justify close attention, because the third follows logically from them.

IV

Much lending and borrowing was small scale, local, and personal, to oblige friends and relatives and neighbours. To the example of William Stout's master, during his apprenticeship, whom people confidently entrusted with their surplus cash,[2] two Yorkshire cases may be added.[3] Arthur Jessop (1682–1751), an apothecary and farmer at New-mill in the West Riding, clearly combined lending at interest with his daily business: 'Mr Dobson was here,' he records in his diary in May 1730, 'and paid me for physic & the interest for £20 on a promissory note this day.' Other lending for varying amounts had been made on bond. Ralph Ward, a gentleman dealer in cattle and a land agent, received bills and money in the course of his business, and actively conducted borrowing and lending among his friends and neighbours and business contacts besides exchanging for them bills and cash. On a somewhat busy occasion in March 1756 he ran a fair gamut of this kind of activity: he records that

Mr Scottow and Mr preston came about 11 Oclock. with the former I settled some accounts and I paid him £219.5.2 In Ballance, also Mr preston paid 31.7 from Mr peirse for Interest which with 30:13 Oliver presswick is to pay for a Bill I had from Mr peirse is for one year's Interest for all he owes me, then also Mr John Ward of

---

[1] For switching by London bankers, see above, pp. 163, 168, 170,173–6.
[2] Ashton, *Eighteenth Century*, p. 181.
[3] *Two Yorkshire Diaries: The Diary of Arthur Jessop and Ralph Ward's Journal.* Edited by C. E. Whiting (Yorks. Archaeol. Soc., Record Series, cxvii, 1952).

Billingham & his Son came here and paid me £100 he had of mine on Bond & all Interest due thereon, they all dined here and went away afternoon.

Other lending was on notes and on an occasional mortgage, sometimes for four-figure sums.

This unprofessionalized lending was done at interest. That charged by Jessop is not clear, but Ward appears to have charged 4 per cent between 1754 and 1756: a reasonable premium of about 1 per cent over the contemporary yields of three per cent government stock.

In lending of this nature, the rate would probably have been determined partly by convention, partly by the nature of the security, and partly by the confinement of such transactions to the highly personal circles of friends and relatives. In such circumstances, interest sensitivity was likely to be comparatively low, or to be restrained where in a more impersonal market it might have asserted itself. The initial rate presumably mattered (or else why did people bother about a rate at all?), but it was likely to remain fairly static subsequently in default of substantial shifts in the return from alternative employments—if these existed. Moreover, inertia in respect of an investment once made is notoriously the characteristic of the small saver. The retired servant, the moderately affluent widow or spinster, the tenant lending his savings to his landlord—these were lending for an income and for security, not for capital gain; they were hardly the most interest-conscious members of the community. Thus, the Lloyds of Aston Hall in north Wales maintained over long periods payments of interest at the maximum legal rates between 1692 and 1733: first 6 per cent and then 5 per cent on most of their many bond debts.[1] Later in the eighteenth century, improved institutions and a wider range of assets appear to have increased interest sensitivity. For instance, the grandfather of Robert Lowe ('ex luce lucellum') was to have a rather less easy time in similar transactions. His notebook records some thirty borrowing transactions in Nottinghamshire between 1781 and 1800.[2] From time to time, alterations in the rates allowed were agreed with the maidservants and spinsters

[1] *NLW*, Aston Hall MSS., 4502, 4845, 2729.
[2] Notts. *CRO*, DD.SK.191/46.

and labourers from whom he borrowed. The changes showed some correlation with movements in the long-term rate of interest, as indicated by the yield of three per cent Consols, although they were not common to all the loans, nor did they coincide precisely in time; nevertheless, the fact that they were made at all leaves no room for doubt that the parties to the transactions attached weight to the rate of interest.

Much the most important means of raising money privately in the eighteenth century was the property mortgage. For this the market was almost of necessity wider and more sensitive to interest rates than localized and personal loans, though many quite small and medium-sized mortgages had a local market. The large sums often involved necessitated a search beyond the immediate vicinity, by both the prospective borrower and the prospective lender, usually with the aid of knowledgeable attorneys. The interest element would loom more largely: a difference of one-half per cent on a £20,000 mortgage amounted to £100 per annum. Moreover, as a real security the mortgage was superior to the personal security of notes and bonds: mortgagors could expect to give and mortgagees would be willing to receive commensurately lower rates.

Two features of mortgage transactions registered sensitivity to interest rates. First, some agreements specified an abatement of interest if it were paid promptly. Second, mortgagors had the habit of redeeming or of threatening to redeem their mortgages if the rate did not follow market rate downwards; with equal insistence, mortgagees might recall or threaten to recall their loans unless it followed it upwards.

An abatement of interest was clearly a reward to the diligent borrower and a measure of the greater value of money in the present over money in the future. 'The time of my Great paym[en]t now draweing neare', wrote a nagging steward to a Montgomeryshire land agent in 1727, 'is the occasion of my Writing this to remind you of itt; for if I should not be able to pay the Int^t by the 8th or tenth of August; which is the last Day but two; there will be halfe p Cent Difference; so pray begin Getting up Lady Days rent . . . of such as are able to pay it.' Came the great day, and the money had been gotten up. The agent must have read with relief that 'By your . . . enabling me to pay so punctually I shall not only keep the money . . . last Borrowed at 4½ p Cent but I shall Reduce the 12,000 formerly borrowed . . . from 5 to 4½ which is a considerable advantage in so large A sum.'[1]

Ten years later, the same principle was at work in a loan of £10,000 on lands in Leicestershire and Lincolnshire: 4½ per cent with a reduction to 4 if interest were paid within the half-year.[2] Henry Hindley, a Wiltshire merchant, negotiated several loans with similar provisions between 1760 and 1776, the abatement varying between ½ per cent and 1½ per cent; the larger amount possibly implied the sanction of a heavy penal rate against the day when money became scarcer, though Hindley did not exact his full pound of flesh for tardy payment in 1778–9.[3]

That provision for a variable rate was a common device is a legitimate deduction from the wording of a security to be given in 1774 to Lady Isham of Lamport in Northamptonshire.[4] It would bear interest 'at 4 p C^{t.} wch. will of course be made at 4½ or 5 if not paid within 3 Months after each ½ year becomes due'. The historian Edward Gibbon proposed in 1789 a comparable arrangement—unsuccessfully, because the security was good—when contemplating a loan of £8,000 on mortgage, and displayed here as elsewhere an anxiety to secure the maximum yield from his money.[5] 'Let four and a half or rather five per cent be stipulated in the Mortgage deed, with a proviso in a separate act that as long as the interest shall be paid on or before the day appointed I shall be satisfied with four percent.'

In the absence of a specific clause to vary the interest rate in this manner—which gave a cushion against rises or falls in the market rate—there was a simple means of adjustment: either party to a mortgage could threaten to terminate the loan. When interest rates were shading downwards in 1727, a Shropshire gentleman pestered his mortgagees for several months to reduce the charge from 5 per cent to 4 per cent.[6] He called in aid the principle of abatement. 'Hope Considdering how well I pay y^r

[1] NLW, Powis Castle MSS., 1070, 1068.　　[2] PRO, C.103/164.
[3] Information from Professor T. S. Ashton.　　[4] BMAM, 29602, fol. 236.
[5] Norton, op. cit., iii, 154–5, 161.
[6] NLW, Nat. Lib. Wales MSS., 9350 D.

The Rate of Interest in the Eighteenth Century

Intrest you will be so good as to take 4 and half p cent for y^e· time to come', he wrote, adding, however, 'I must wholly rely upon y^r· goodness: but hope you will Consider y^t full 5 p Cent is ye utmost extremity of ye law: and y^t you will mittigate y^r Interest for ye future.' The request was backed by the threat to repay by selling some of his South Sea stock; a step which, unless purely vindictive and self-wounding, suggested a balancing of profitability against a 5 per cent mortgage. Unfortunately, the correspondence ends without revealing the conclusion of the protest. There are much more explicit cases, however, to be found in the records of turnpike trusts.[1] Amongst private borrowers, the response of the shrewd Lady Kinnoull to easier money conditions in 1732 was quite clear.[2] £1,800 had been borrowed from Joseph Banks II. She now gave notice that, unless the existing rate were reduced to 4½ per cent, she would re-borrow more cheaply elsewhere in order to repay the loan:

Brodsworth, 11 November 1732. I am very credibly informed from divers hands that money is very plentyfull to come by in the country at £4.10.0 per cent upon good land security, as I very well know ours to be; and some I hear has got money on the like security at £4 per cent. I therefore ordered my steward . . . to acquaint you at the payment of the last halfe years intrist before this . . . that I expected this intrist money to be reduced to £4.10.0 per cent., or otherwise I should be looking for money another way and give legal notice for paying in this £1800 thats due to you, but he missing the oppertunity when last at London is the occasion of these lines to request a positive answer whether this intrist may be reduced as above, for the time to come or not, and it will oblige, Sir, your humble servant,

A. Kinnoull.

We do not know if Lady Kinnoull successfully beat down her mortgagee. The financially calculating Earl of Egmont, has, however, left in his diary an adequate account of his successful efforts in 1737 to make the most of a fall in interest rates.[3] The rate of interest on private lending was running at around 4 per

[1] L. S. Pressnell, *Country Banking in the Industrial Revolution* (1956), appendix 30, pp. 554–7.
[2] J. W. F. Hill (editor), *The Letters and Papers of the Banks Family of Revesby Abbey 1704–1760* (Lincoln Record Society, 1952), p. 141.
[3] Hist. MSS. Comm., *MSS. of the Earl of Egmont, Diary of the First Earl of Egmont* (3 vols., 1923), ii, 380–97.

cent, and the Funds were yielding less than 3 per cent. Egmont therefore arranged to sell out South Sea stock, and told the mortgagee of his house that he would repay his 5 per cent loan, adding however that he might care to relend the money in 'an even better security' at 4 per cent. In less than a fortnight after selling his stock, Egmont had repaid the loan, and arranged for his son to borrow the money, though he had to agree to $4\frac{1}{2}$ per cent.

V

If a change in the rate of interest merely resulted in an adjustment of existing rates, there might be comparatively little more to say. In fact such adjustments often were not made or, because of the usury laws, could not be made. Above all, the occurrence of 'switching' clearly altered the availability of money against certain assets. To what extent did this affect economic activity? Interest rates had an uneven incidence, depending not only upon individual sensitivity but also upon the degree to which a project was externally financed and upon the expected rate of return. The slower and lower yielding the investment, the greater the ratio of interest costs to the annual rate of amortization of capital, and the greater therefore the likely significance of interest rates.

Public utility investment provides the clearest cases. This was marginal investment. Capital had to be raised from outside, and on much of it the rate of interest, being technically a return on a loan secured by a mortgage, was limited to 5 per cent, although canal companies were to develop share capital which sometimes earned very high dividends. By and large, returns were slow to come, and amortization was prolonged. The overall picture is of sympathy between falling interest rates and high investment, at least at the major turning-points: there were bursts of activity around 1720 and 1726; in the early 'fifties; in the second half of the 'sixties and in the early 'seventies; and in the early 'nineties. Not surprisingly the sympathy is incomplete. A change in the rate of interest might be offset by a change in the expected profitability of investment in some regions. This was particularly the case in wartime, when rising interest rates squeezed some, but not those favoured by the demands of war production—hence, possibly, the spate of turnpike activity in Midland counties during the Seven Years war. These influences apart, interest rates might run along a prolonged plateau between major turning-points because of reluctance to disturb established rates; the effect was to bring in adequate money when market rates dropped, up to the point when it was possible to contemplate the reduction of the going rate; and, when market rates were high, the enterprise struggled along as best it could until driven to raise the rate, or in face of the usury laws or inadequate profit expectations or both it had to forgo planned activity.

The records of river navigations, canal companies, turnpike trusts, and local improvement commissioners all bear emphatic witness to concern with monetary problems, with interest rates, and with the clog to activity that was sometimes involved. Turnpikes, for example, seized their chances to reduce their interest charges, and Devon[1] saw such fine shading as 3¾ per cent in 1753 and—by a kind of auction of securities—3·95 per cent in 1772.

The history of the Whitehaven Harbour Trust[2] between 1709 and 1782 gives instructive glimpses of these problems. Its organization and the general impression left by its minutes closely resemble those of other public utilities; further, after beginning as a harbour improvement trust, it was from 1762 also associated with local turnpike and town improvements. In common with such enterprises it drew finance from varied sources—four in all, apart from ordinary harbour dues: from the general public; from the local 'Sick and Wounded Seamen's Fund'; from a fund imposed to help the improvement of the harbour, the 'Voluntary Duties'; finally, and of especial importance in early years, there was constant help from the local territorial magnates, the Lowthers, who acted as a cross between fairy godmother and lender of last resort.

Rates of interest in the early years accorded broadly with trends registered by the London money market. At its establishment in 1709, the full legal rate of 6 per cent was paid. This rate

[1] Devon *CRO*, Exeter, minutes of the Exeter Turnpike Trust, 7 August, 2 October 1753; 3 March 1772.
[2] *PRO*, C.107/117, minute book of the trustees.

was cut to 5 per cent in 1716, lagging behind the new usury law limit of 5 per cent; a further reduction—in clear parallelism with London trends and the effort to cut the legal rate to 4 per cent[1]—was made, to 4 per cent, in 1718. The next important change did not come until September 1752, when the rate was cut from 4 to 3½ per cent; this had to be restored in the following March. The cut, though not the restoration, accorded well with current cheap money trends. The last change to be recorded came in 1775, when the trustees offered 4½ per cent in an unsuccessful attempt to borrow £4,000. These were the rates for ordinary lenders; those allowed to the Lowthers and to the special funds, and on occasion to a group of comfortably placed ladies, diverged somewhat and varied less.

The long plateaux of virtually unchanged rates reflected in part the access to special sources of finance; they also reflect, however, a conservatism towards established rates—paralleled by the modern building society movement, for instance—that preferred to risk being starved of funds rather than disturb the *status quo*. This was unavoidable when the rate was already at the legal peak. Thus, in 1711, the trustees recorded that 'under the present Discouragement of Trade it is found difficult to raise any more Money upon the Credit of the Act'. They therefore enhanced the security by adding their personal guarantee to potential lenders and resorted to the Lowthers. At other times, they simply gave up the effort to raise money at the established rate. 'It being represented that Numbers of Masons sufficient for carrying on so large an undertaking are not likely to be gott this Summer, And that there may be a difficulty in procuring Money at an Interest of 4 p Cent Sufficient to answer the Expence of the same', the Trustees resolved in March 1747 to limit work on a new pier to the foundations, but to go on seeking money at 4 per cent. Still short in September after advertising for loans, they decided to approach merchants elsewhere, but it seems that they did not succeed. In the 'seventies, the easy early years of the decade gave the trust sufficient momentum to carry investment past the crisis of 1772–3, but work had eventually to be slowed down in 1775 for monetary reasons. Having raised the rate from 4 to 4½ per cent, the Trust obtained only £200—

[1] *JHC*, xviii (1714–18), 1716–17, pp. 631, 653, 658, 661, 668, 683.

half from Sir James Lowther—of the £4,000 they had sought. This combined with the unfavourable season to delay the execution of plans and led the trustees to order that 'all the workmen now employed at the New Works . . . be discharged on Saturday . . . and remain discharged till the Duties accumulate or a sufficient Sum be lent upon securities to carry forward the New Works'.

Both for the lender on mortgage and for the landowner acquiring land for his own use the balance of expected cost and gain might be very carefully weighed. During the seventeenth century, it is true, a clear link between the rate of interest and the price of land is not to be discerned,[1] but the situation evidently changed during the following century.[2] Admittedly the effect of interest charges was muffled to the extent that the direct purchase of estates overlaid the lure of monetary reward with a search for social prestige; but the balance had to be struck somewhere—and very finely for estates with narrow margins between income and outgoings. Switching between assets with competing yields clearly had its part here. The alert Earl of Egmont again shows the way.[3] In May 1743, with the Funds higher than they had been since 1737, he travelled to London to sell £1,350 (nominal value) of Old four per cent annuities belonging to his niece. At 114⅜ they yielded £1,544. 1s 3d. He was to lay out £1,500 of this on a mortgage on the Earl of Salisbury's estates (in which in earlier years he had invested a much larger sum), noting that on this 'the interest at 4 per cent for 100 l. is better . . . than 4 per cent for 114⅜ in the stock' which in settled times the government would repay at only £100. His move was based upon a comparison between the

---

[1] H. J. Habakkuk, 'The Long-term Rate of Interest and the Price of Land in the Seventeenth Century', *Ec.H.R.*, 2nd ser., v (1952), 26–45.

[2] Apart from the evidence in the text, see, e.g., W. Marshall, *The Rural Economy of the Midland Counties* (2 vols., 1790), i, 16, on land purchase:
'Some years back, the same species of frenzy—*Terramania*—showed itself here, as it did in other districts. . . . At the time . . . the interest of the funds was extraordinarily high. . . . The *interest* of the funds will always have more or less influence on the price of land.'
See also the comment of the historian Gibbon, who was well-experienced in land negotiations: 'The miserable state of the funds must excuse the lowness of the price' realized on the sale of one of his estates. Norton, op. cit., iii, 5 (18 October 1784).

[3] *Diary*, iii, 272.

firm capital value of the mortgage and the precarious inflated one, which had doubtless yielded a capital gain, of the stock: he had sold when he had, his diary records, 'the stock being high, and subject to a fall in case of any bad news from abroad'. He had chosen his moment well; a sale three months earlier or three months later would have reduced the proceeds by a sum equivalent to more than a year's dividends.

From the north-east a concentration of examples drives home for a single region the weighing of alternative yields and the parallelism between trends in the stock markets and in private investment.[1] 'Tho' this is a time for extraordinary advantage of money', a London attorney advised a client purchasing land, 'I doubt not of your quick return.' This was in 1711 when low stock prices offered good yields and a chance of capital gain. Seven years later, a local gentleman was advising his mother to buy land in view of the continued fall in interest rates, even if she had to give as much as twenty-two years' purchase. A comparison of yields was evident in another land purchase, this time in 1733, with the Funds yielding less than 3 per cent. The agent told his client that she ought to make $4\frac{1}{2}$ per cent on her purchase 'very easily' and $5\frac{1}{2}$ 'God willing' when the commons had been enclosed. Fourteen years later an apparently reverse situation confronted those wishing to raise money on land because government securities had been drawing off money. As a final example, in the halcyon cheap money days of 1752 a correspondent from London was inclined to recommend his Gateshead friend to purchase an estate for around £6,000 since the rent would exceed the yield of a similar sum in the stocks.

The possible connexion between investment in enclosures and changes in the rate of interest has become a familiar subject for speculation. There is good reason to expect such a connexion. Enclosure schemes were likely to be marginal investments; their cost was substantial; the period of investment and of awaiting returns was often prolonged; and the prospects of profit possibly less enticing than those of alternative investments. They might therefore be expected to react sharply to a marked fall in interest rates, to a sizeable jump in expectations of returns, or to a

[1] E. Hughes, *North Country Life in the Eighteenth Century: The North-East, 1700–1750* (1952), pp. 79–81 and 133.

varying mixture of each of these influences. There is a rough correlation of this kind during the second half of the century between Enclosure Acts (admittedly an imperfect guide to enclosure activity) and such factors. As with public utility investment, there are so to speak kinks in the curves compared because of local differences under the stress of wartime conditions, not to say in soil and cropping possibilities.[1]

The significance of interest rates for industry and trade is one of the great unknowns of eighteenth-century history. Much investment was internally financed or came from local or family sources with limited sensitivity to interest rates. Moreover the investment process was not always so long, nor the expected returns so low, as in public utilities or in agriculture. Long-term interest costs might not therefore bulk so large, and short-term rates ranked for closer consideration. Perhaps in recognition of this, the classical economists concentrated almost exclusively on circulating capital, Ricardo embodying a chapter on 'Machinery' only in the third edition (1823) of his *Principles*.

To attempt a statistical correlation between the rate of interest and the level of industrial activity is not yet possible. There are, however, numerous clues to the consideration the businessmen accorded directly or indirectly to the rate of interest. Some had contacts, through their asset holdings, with the money market; others had indirect contacts in so far as bills and mortgages (which were sometimes used to raise capital) competed with other assets for the favour of the potential discounter or mortgagee; and there were investment contacts between industrialists and traders on the one hand, and public utilities and agriculture on the other. Thus, the switching movements induced by fluctuating interest rates would have rippled across the world of industry and trade, affecting some at least of those engaged in these activities. Direct reactions apart, changes in

---

[1] The plausibility of connexion between enclosures and interest rates has been accepted for Leicestershire for the 1760s, 1770s, and 1780s, but has been questioned for the period from 1789 to 1794, because a burst of enclosure *preceded* the bad harvest and high grain prices of 1795: see H. G. Hunt, 'The Chronology of Parliamentary Enclosure in Leicestershire', *Ec.H.R.*, 2nd ser., x, no. 2 (December 1957), 267–8. In fact, the doubted years centred on a spell of exceptionally low interest rates, when Leicestershire seemed to be so flush with money that it was a focus for the canal mania (Pressnell, op. cit., pp. 273–4).

the value of money were changes in the relative valuation placed upon goods, and hence in effective demand. Businessmen were therefore likely to weigh anew the relative advantages of liquidity compared with investment in long-term capital, in raw materials, and in stocks of their own products.

Industrialists raising finance externally expected to pay *some* rate of interest. 'We desire you will apply to the following people, or any other you think likely as soon as you conveniently can to know if they can lend us any, and what sums of money at Candlemas next when annual settlements were made, and at what rate of interest', a Furness iron company wrote to a partner in 1772.[1] Should the value of money change, however, lenders would not necessarily translate this into revised interest rates. They might prefer—like the borrowers on the other side of the fence—not to disturb settled rates; instead they might vary the intensity of credit rationing. To adopt Lord Keynes's illuminating concept, lenders undoubtedly acted upon the principle that at any rate of interest there was always a 'fringe of unsatisfied borrowers', which they widened or narrowed by varying their standards of eligibility.[2] This was and still is characteristic of British banking and of British financial institutions in general. It is implicit in the arrangements offered by Evans and Co., the Derby bankers, to Samuel Oldknow in 1786: they were well aware that the going rate might fluctuate, but they preferred to average out high and low to a stable 5 per cent, to pick and choose from the 'fringe', and to lay down the amount of accommodation they would grant at a fixed rate. They explained:[3]

Our rule is to take common interest [i.e., 5 per cent] for what bills we discount, we never take more nor less and on those terms we can generally choose our customers; which is more satisfactory to us than any trifling advantage we could make in time of necessity. . . .

There were many ways in which money could become costly and more difficult to obtain without an overt variation of the rate of interest. When would-be borrowers—such as Strutt,

---

[1] A. Fell, *The Early Iron Industry of Furness and District* (1908), p. 333.
[2] J. M. Keynes, *A Treatise on Money* (2 vols., 1930), i, 212, and ii, 364–7.
[3] G. Unwin and others, *Samuel Oldknow and the Arkwrights* (1924), p. 177.

disappointed in 1757 by Dr. Benson—had to seek money else-where, the delay itself imposed an extra cost, since profits are a function of time. Equally, where assets had to be realized to raise money, a resultant capital loss was equivalent to a swinge-ing rate of interest. Those who failed to procure funds might swell the bankrupts' queue—it varied, after a lag, with interest rate movements—or enter the debtors' prison.

Perhaps the most important of these indirect means of varying the cost of money involved the paper credit and the trading credit that businessmen provided for themselves. Bills and drafts were widely used in payment. The tenor of those circulating was conventional, according to the trade; any departure from it was likely to be appropriately offset. Searching for a London bill, a Lincolnshire land agent wrote[1] in 1730 that he could not 'be certaine to procure bills under a month after date unless by accident it fall out other wayes, which I shall imbrace as often as may be. But I know from experience, returning betwixt 5 and 6000 pounds intrest to London every year . . . [? that] substan-tiall merchants in Leeds with whom I usually make my returns, will not break their custome of drawing a month after date for any man's pleasure without they give them a premium to serve some necessity.' It is true that there was not normally a nice adjustment for every bill or draft that differed from the con-ventional tenor, but according to Henry Thornton, writing in 1802, this would be corrected in an agreed fashion when periodic settlements were made between businessmen.[2]

Paper credit was chronically scarce in the provinces during the first three-quarters of the eighteenth century; there were seasonal shortages; and its availability varied with the general state of trade. The long-run problem doubtless reflected the unevenness of regional economic development and the swelling of London's wealth.[3] Variations in trade produced fluctuations in the balance of payments between the provinces and London: slacker trade reduced the supply of claims on London, so that those in need of them might be unable to obtain bills of the

[1] Hill, op. cit., p. 113.
[2] Ashton, *An Eighteenth Century Industrialist*, p. 103, and H. Thornton, *An Enquiry into . . . Paper Credit* (1802, ed. F. A. Hayek, 1939), p. 93.
[3] E. J. Buckatzsch, 'The Geographical Distribution of Wealth in England, 1086–1843', *Ec.H.R.*, 2nd ser., iii (1950), 180–202.

customary tenor; or they would have to pay premiums for them; or, what amounted to paying a higher price by having to wait longer for effective payment, they might have to take bills at longer than the customary dates. On the other side of the balance, bills on provincial people were correspondingly *less* valuable: the Newcastle agent of a lead-mine explained in 1730 that he hoped to send London bills in ten days' time; the alternative for his creditor was to draw on him 'at 30 Days wch I presume can't be done without paying a premium'.[1] In short, payment in provincial paper was more costly than payment in London paper, a sign that the balance of payments was unfavourable to Newcastle. In good times, the pattern was reversed. Bills were available at shorter dates and could be discounted at longer dates, whilst premiums were reduced or disappeared. These swings in the balance of payments would have been emphasized by the impact of capital movements between London and the country. This was a likely conjuncture, given the occurrence of asset-switching; given the substantial involvement of London investors in provincial activity; and given also, in the later years of the century, the run-down and build-up of country bankers' London funds during boom and recession respectively.

It may be difficult to estimate the effect upon businessmen of changes in the cost of credit, but their awareness of it and their sensitivity to it are frequently evident. For instance, slacker trade meant reduced receipts, less easy payments, and more reluctant debtors; eyes were sharpened to the value of money. 'Inclosed are three bills . . . if they are at too long a Date to answer your Demands and you cant Discount them on easie terms please after acceptance to return them, & I shall send ye money by the Carrier'. Thus the Newcastle agent of Sir William Blackett in April 1731. The following day, in place of a separate sum he had planned to send in any case by carrier (the cheaper though riskier method), he was able to send it instead by a bill, on which, however, he had been 'obldged to pay . . . ½ p Cent preem^m . . . good bills not being now to be got here at par'. Some days later, he clearly indicated that scarce and therefore dear

---

[1] *BMAM*, 27420, letter book of J. Richmond, agent to Sir W. C. Blackett, letter of 3 February 1729/30.

bills, which he disliked buying, sprang from bad trade: 'Trade continues so very dull that I have not . . . been able to get sixpence either in Money or Bills.' Sales might bring bills but at present he could meet with 'no good bills under one p Cent^m.' premium.[1]

With poor trade debtors stumbled in payment; they were sometimes tolerated in this for the sake of goodwill. Nevertheless, this taking of credit was a strain to those providing it. For instance, the proprietors of Kirkstall Forge, near Leeds, made periodical rounds lasting about two weeks to collect orders and debts. Between 1796 and 1799 they experienced the prevailing trade difficulties and with them, in the efforts to collect cash, 'many disappointments', 'very bad success', 'very indifferent success' and 'not . . . a prosperous journey'. Some of these diary comments were the product of an engrained sourness, but they appeared to rest mainly on the sheer impossibility of mobilizing debts when trade was sluggish.[2]

In general, businessmen formalized in a considerable degree the credit they granted amongst themselves.[3] The practice focused their attitudes to the value of money and to changes in it; most clearly of all, it reflected a direct association between the expected returns of enterprise and the rate of interest. To discuss this is necessarily to drive a route through virtually unexplored country; all the evidence, however, points in the same direction. Each trade and each commodity was likely to have a conventional period of credit. Earlier payment was rewarded by an appropriate discount. In bad times, the discount might be enlarged, thereby to stimulate debtors by granting them the equivalent of a high rate of interest for money now rather than in the future. It was in effect a substitution for or an addition to a variation in price. (The rates were superficially large, but discount granted and discounts received tended to cancel each other out except for the residual which was the entrepreneur's net trading income; overall, they represented the valuation placed on ready money.) In good times, these broad principles

---

[1] ibid., 23 April, 24 April, 7 May 1731.

[2] A. E., B. F., and H. M. Butler (editors), *The Diary of Thomas Butler of Kirkstall Forge, Yorkshire, 1796–1799* (privately printed 1909), *passim.* I am grateful to Mr. D. M. Joslin for drawing my attention to this book.

[3] Cf. above, p. 197.

worked in reverse. At all times, they were liable to vary with the businessman's appraisal of his debtor's credit-worthiness and of the value of his custom. In the Newcastle lead trade, for instance, Blackett's agent declared in 1730 that the normal period of credit was two months 'unless in consideration of a better bargain'. This was written during a downward pressure upon prices. Whilst he was accumulating unsold stocks, was fearing labour troubles through wages being in arrears, and was striving to maintain prices, a rival was doubly undercutting with reduced prices and the grant of three months' credit, 'so little Lead remains at this market'.[1]

There is further instructive evidence from the Somerset woollen firm of Were and Co. in the 'sixties and 'seventies, and from the cotton business of Evans and Co. of Derby during the Napoleonic wars. In 1764 the Somerset firm[2] granted 3 per cent discount to a customer 'for remitting in 2 mo. from date of Invoice'. Three years later, in paying a local supplier they paid by a forty days' bill, taking 3 per cent discount; they noted 'By disct. for good pay at 3 p Ct. this discount to be a Standing Article for future.' In other dealings the arrangements were less firm. Seeking in 1769 a discount of 3 per cent from a dyestuffs supplier, they could obtain only 2½. Five years later, against the ledger entry was a note that 'Friend Lidiard was here & as he would not allow any Dis[count] or abatement paid him the sum of £3–9–9 & taken his receipt in full.'

Evans and Co., cotton-spinners and much else besides, were alert to the usefulness of trade discount.[3] Writing to an agent in 1796, they stressed that 'In respect to yarn you must be Governed a little by the demand and what others are selling for.

[1] op. cit., 11 November and 23 October 1730. Other examples: in 1756, Robert Plumsted, a Quaker commission merchant, told a correspondent that 'for thy Governance the Credit for Lead Shott & Gunpowder Is Six Months' (Camb. Univ. Lib., Add. 2798). In 1765, a Welsh purchaser of iron ore wrote that 'the usual time of pay . . . is allways 3 months, except when it is agreed other ways . . .' (*NLW*, Add. MSS., 478ᴱ). A West Indian produce broker, with thirty-two years' experience, told the Usury Laws Committee in 1818 that the usual length of credit on sugar was two months, on cotton three months and fourteen days, and on coffee one month (evidence, QQ.351, 374–7, in *BPP*, 1845 (376/611), XII).

[2] Subsequently the present firm of Fox Brothers and Co., of Wellington, from whose general ledgers these examples are drawn.

[3] Jean Forrest, 'The Darley Abbey Cotton Spinning and Paper Mills, 1783–1810' (unpubl. thesis, M.Sc.(Econ.), Univ. of London, 1957), pp. 74–76, 79–82.

If you find the demand slacks you may find it Needful to deduct ten p. cent for particular numbers, and on condition of their taking a quantity of those numbers. . . .' Eleven years later they were explaining that on sewing cotton the usual terms were eight months' credit or 7½ per cent discount, and on candle-wicks six months or 7½ per cent. If goods did not sell at the same price as that charged by their competitors, the Strutts, then they were willing, on the excuse of quality, to tolerate 'a small con-cession in the discount say 2½ per cent more'. When trade was recovering by early in 1809, they were less ready to yield on dis-count. As trade boomed later in the year they could not meet all orders and had less use for ready money; they became stricter about discount. 'The demand has been so good', they wrote, 'that we have lessened our discount much in the country as selling at heavy discounts when we cannot supply our orders is out of the question.' Only if it were necessary 'to indulge a particular customer' should it be raised above 7½ per cent.

VI

In some firms and during some periods, changes in costs other than those of capital may have predominated. It is hardly to be doubted, however, that many people, entrepreneurs and others, were in varying ways exercised over the cost of borrowing. There remain, nevertheless, many outstanding questions. Atten-tion can be given here to three of these. How far were London rates of interest broadly representative of conditions beyond the metropolis? Why were fluctuations comparatively small at some periods, and rather larger at others? And, finally, can serious importance really be attached to what seem somewhat slight flutterings in the long-term rate?

There may appear reason enough, particularly in the con-centration of financial development in London until the later part of the century, to expect at best a remote connexion be-tween London and provincial trends. In fact, there were quite close sympathies of movement. Some allowance has first to be made for local asymmetry. The industrializing areas were anxious for capital; elsewhere, it was less easy to employ. The result was a disparity of interest rates between, for instance, the south-west and the Midlands. Movements in diverse regions were, however, broadly parallel with those in London and the main points of inflection lagged little if at all. Allowance has to be made also for lags when trying to correlate changes in interest rates with changes in those marginal investments in public utilities. Months, sometimes years, of planning and scheming and parliamentary lobbying might precede the passage of the Act which registered the intention to invest. With adverse changes in the economic weather, an unwillingness to write off such outlays was likely to provide sufficient momentum to drive a project over and some way along any hump in the rate of interest well into a recession. Eventually, the flow of new Acts would peter out.

The links embodied in asset-switching by those with feet in London and in the country were primarily personal in nature and therefore of limited significance in terms of local economic structure. There were firmer links in the all-important field of short-term credit, as illustrated in the earlier discussion on the internal balance of payments. Moreover, long before the emergence of formal country bankers there were connexions of a banking type between the provinces and London in the persons of quasi-bankers. We could with advantage know very much more of them than at present; they faced outwards to the metropolis and inwards to their own hinterlands; by couplings of varying flexibility even remote parts of the country might become aware of financial trends in London. The provincial towns in which they were found were in some senses miniature financial centres for a region. Newcastle and possibly York may have been such centres for remittance to London by the 1660s.[1] Exeter was clearly such a centre for the whole south-west.[2] During the early years of the eighteenth century Joseph Quash, a Devon land-tax receiver and an Exeter trader, remitted revenue for his own collection and also for that of the receiver for Cornwall,[3] besides acting as banker to a local landed proprietor.[4]

[1] *Cal. Treas. Books*, ii (1667–8), 275 (Newcastle), and iii, pt. i (1669–72), 89 (York).
[2] ibid., iii, pt. i (1669–72), 555, and Pressnell, op. cit., p. 78.
[3] W. R. Ward, *The English Land Tax in the Eighteenth Century* (1953), p. 161.
[4] *PRO*, E.134/4 Geo. I/Easter 22.

The Rate of Interest in the Eighteenth Century

With regular bill-accepting arrangements in London[1] he must have been a useful man; after his bankruptcy about 1714, remittance from the south-west appears to have become more difficult.[2] Probably comparable with Quash, and bankrupted about the same time, was John Wallis, formerly a maltster at Hertford.[3] He had been employed by the excise and malt collectors in the district to make remittances; it appeared that he 'had been a person of great credit, a constant returner for many years and had remitted money for the several Collectors of Hertfordshire'. Bristol, by evidence of 1738 (and undoubtedly earlier), was another centre and so was Leeds.[4] Any commercial town, in fact, was a natural centre for financial contacts with the world beyond.

The existence of these financial centres necessarily qualifies the restricted views propounded in 1734 by a Welsh gentleman, who urged that, outside the great maritime towns and areas near London, the provinces were remote from monetary influences.[5] The case must not be spoilt by exaggeration: the contacts were loose and imperfect, but they were sufficiently substantial to modify the view of eighteenth-century England as a parcellated jumble of little-related economic regions.[6] The existence of widely disparate local economies by no means ruled out the existence of close links between them, as indeed the theory of comparative costs suggests.[7]

These connexions apart, it may well be asked whether the fluctuations in interest rates, the primary concern of this paper, were sufficiently large to be meaningful. In the first instance,

---

[1] *PRO*, B.1/No. 2/fols. 230 ff., and letters of Quash to Oswald Hoskyns of London (in the Foxwell Collection of the Kress Collection at the Baker Library, Harvard; I am grateful to Professor A. H. Cole for drawing my attention to these letters).

[2] *Cal. Treas. Books & Papers, 1735–8*, pp. 314–15.

[3] *Cal. Treas. Papers*, xxvii, 182 (22 March 1713/4).

[4] *PRO*, T.1/298, fols. 137–8, 141.

[5] W. Allen, *Ways and Means to raise the Value of Land* (written 1734, edition of 1742), pp. 8–9.

[6] For other views, see above, pp. 127, 176.

[7] Mr. J. K. Horsefield has kindly drawn my attention to three lists suggestive of the importance of certain provincial towns as financial centres: (i) provincial mints, 1696–8; (ii) towns for which banks were proposed in *A Proposal for Erecting a General Bank, which may be fitly called The Land Bank of England* (1695); (iii) towns for which Daniel Defoe proposed banks in his *Essay upon Projects* (1697). York, Exeter, Norwich, and Bristol occur in all three.

there is the problem of the varying range of fluctuation. This may have been due largely to the combined effects of changing profit expectations and of the flexibility of the supply of money. The first two decades and the second half of the century (barring the American war) had the marks of a persistently high or rising level of expectations, the intervening period the marks of dampened expectations. Corresponding with these aspects, the earlier and later periods witnessed a surge of formal and informal banking which brought greater flexibility in the supply of money. On the one hand, the state of expectations would have limited the feasible rise in interest rates in *real* terms; on the other hand the flexibility of the money supply would have largely governed the feasible rise in *money* terms. More explicitly, the demand for money fell into two parts: that for current needs, depending upon income, and that for idle balances on the chance of future gain. In a boom, whether characterized by stockjobbing or by a canal mania or by war expenditure, income rose and so did prices as factors of production became scarcer. To sustain these higher incomes and prices, businessmen were able to increase the supply of money in bills, and devised their own favourite means to speed the velocity of circulation in the characteristic boom phenomenon of accommodation or finance bills; bankers responded to demand by compressing their highly elastic cash ratios. Only when these means failed to meet the demand for more money was it necessary to tap by higher interest rates the money held under the second, speculative, head. Moreover, in so far as prices rose, they diminished the real burden of a rise in interest costs. Consequently, the higher were expectations, and the more flexible was the supply of money, the higher would interest rates need to rise to check a boom. It is in such terms that the explanation of the differing amplitudes of variation of the long-term rate may lie.

VII

Whether the range of fluctuation were wide or small, and whether the explanation proffered be acceptable or not, it may yet be questioned whether a rise or fall of 1 per cent or so really mattered very much to businessmen. It is conceivable that the questionings miss the main issue. It may be necessary to view the long-term rate, not alone in solitary domination, but as part of a structure of interest rates. The concept of a structure of rates opens, indeed, the possibility of explaining more forcibly much that has hitherto been explained piecemeal by reference largely to a single rate; but it is so much more a possibility than a probability, so much less than a certainty, at the present stage of research that it has seemed preferable to let the preceding arguments stand on their own legs, and to leave to the end what is primarily a suggestion for further explorations.

The concept of a structure of rates hinges upon the public's attitude to a 'normal rate of interest'. By and large, the public has fixed ideas about what the long-term rate ought to be. This subjective approach can readily be detected in the abortive debt-conversion scheme of 1737 and in the successful conversion initiated in 1749.

With the Funds yielding less than 3 per cent, Sir John Barnard presented a Bill to Parliament in 1737 to reduce the rate of interest on the national debt. This proposal raised fears that a reduction of rentiers' incomes would cut consumption outlays and therefore profits, and that frightened foreigners might withdraw their capital.[1] Political motives were doubtless mingled with these hostile reactions. There was a short sharp run on the Bank of England. The Funds fell, and in the City 'every face appeared confounded by the proposed reduction of interest'. When the prime minister, Sir Robert Walpole, rallied to bring the Commons to defeat the Bill, the mob burned Barnard in effigy and raised the cry, 'Long live Sir Robert Walpole for ever'.[2]

The conflict of opinion about the proper level of the rate of interest emerged clearly enough when Pelham proposed in 1749 to reduce gradually the burden of servicing the debt, by the conversion of 4 per cent securities to 3 per cent. This was a difficult time to choose, for money was none too cheap.[3] Soon after the proposal, in December 1749, Dean Cowper of Durham

[1] *A Speech without Doors addressed to the National Creditors* (1737), p. 17.

[2] Hist. MSS. Comm., *Egmont's Diary*, ii, 380–97.

[3] Hargreaves, op. cit., p. 53. See also L. S. Sutherland, 'Samson Gideon and the Reduction of Interest, 1749–50', *Ec.H.R.*, xvi (1946), 15–29, for the fullest account yet available of the conversion.

opined to his brother, the second Earl Cowper, that 'the Legal Interest of Money will likely sink' and encouraged him to persist in efforts to reduce his own interest payments. 'Money'd folks', he continued, 'are very angry at the Intended reduction of Interest, but I beleive you Landed Men are as much pleased.' For his own part, he was ready to help towards easing the government's task in financing future wars.[1] A more hesitant attitude was reflected in a letter written soon after this, in 1750, by Eustace Isham at Oxford to his brother, Sir Edward Isham, M.P., in London. He declared that he would be 'glad to know what a prudent man should do who has a small property in ye Stocks about this Subscription to the lowering of Interest. The general run seems to be against it; is that likely to produce an alteration in the Act^t if so we sit still; if not, we must I think do, as the generality does.'[2] Eventually, the balance of opinion swayed by the government's determination, permitted the consolidation of the debt upon a lower rate, much as originally planned.

When the long-term rate was more or less at the level which the public regarded as 'normal' one would expect other rates of interest to have been a simple function of time, differences in the risk element apart. The shorter the period of the loan, the lower the rate; the longer, the higher. In such conditions it would be safe as well as convenient to cite a single rate of interest as an indicator of the monetary situation. Professor Ashton thus treats the various rates as forming a harmonious whole. 'Frequent mention will be made of *the* rate of interest', he advises his readers.[3] 'The reference is to the yield on government stocks. Other rates were generally higher. . . . But all rates rose and fell together.'

In truth, harmonious variation is no more accurate as a picture of interest rates in the eighteenth century than in the twentieth. At some times short rates were below long rates, at others noticeably above. The concept of a 'normal rate' is strong today and was evidently strong when Thomas Mortimer

---

[1] E. Hughes (editor), *Letters of Spencer Cowper, Dean of Durham 1746–74*, Surtees Society, clxv (1956), 118.

[2] *BMAM*, 29602, fol. 1.

[3] Ashton, *Eighteenth Century*, p. 28.

wrote in 1761; he pointed out that three per cent stocks were the most popular, because they were the stocks least likely to be converted to a lower rate.[1]

A marked deviation of the long-term rate from its 'normal' level would have changed the pattern of rates. When it rose above the 'normal' borrowers may well have tended to borrow short rather than long, in order to postpone long-term borrowing until the long-term rate had slipped back to 'normal'; this was the standard reaction of wartime governments in the eighteenth century, which borrowed at very high rates on short-term, through the floating debt, rather than commit themselves into an indefinite future with 'abnormally' high long-term rates. The alternative to more short-term borrowing was to cease or postpone activity, particularly where the project could not sustain increased interest charges. As for lenders, they presumably wished to take advantage of the high rates while they lasted; some could safely shift to short lending, others remained at the long end of the market. The movement of borrowers away from the long towards the short end of the market, and the slower move of the lenders, tended to narrow or even to reverse the 'normal' positive spread between short and long rates, driving marginal borrowers off the market altogether.

If this approach through the structure of rates be appropriate, one would expect surges of investment and general activity to have coincided with periods when short rates tended to be continuously below long rates; in such a conjuncture the public would appear to have been satisfied with the 'normalcy' of the long rate. Conversely, unwillingness to invest for long periods, and slack activity, would have been reflected in the rise of short rates above long.

This approach may throw useful light upon the problem of interest rates in the eighteenth century. Some leading rates of interest are presented in the diagrams at the end of this chapter (pp. 211–14). The *yields* of Bank stock and of government securities indicated movements in long rates. There are three important clues to short rates. The *nominal* interest rate offered on issues of India bonds reflected current trends in short rates, and their *yields* (for which a continuous series is not available) the

[1] Thomas Mortimer, *Every Man His Own Broker* (3rd edn., 1761), p. 108.

current fluctuations. Finally, the market's evaluation of government short-term obligations appeared most notably in the *discount* on Navy bills, during those war and immediate post-war years of the second half of the century preceding the regularization of their redemption early in 1797. Indeed, the swamping in volume of India bonds by Navy bills at these times makes the latter a stronger indicator than the former of short-term rates.[1] (Unfortunately, it does not yet appear possible to utilize for a similar purpose the even more inflated issues of Exchequer bills, which were widely held, and the prices for which were regularly quoted in the press; nor, equally unfortunately, do we possess a continuous series of discount rates or premiums for commercial bills.)

Within this structure, it is possible to discern some apparent sympathy between rate relationships and changes in economic activity. The rise and fall of public utility investment, for example, appears to fit broadly into a framework of a widening and a narrowing respectively of the 'normal' spread between interest rates. The years in which the short darted to and fro across the long were, as one might expect, years of difficulty; and where, for a considerable period, they exceeded long rates, there was economic depression.[2]

The concept of a structure of rates together with that of changing profit expectations makes it hazardous to discuss in isolation a particular *level* of the long-term rate, or particular changes in it. A specific example, involving the fortunes of

[1] Sources of statistics: Prices of Bank stock and of government long-term securities from J. E. Thorold Rogers, *A History of Agriculture and Prices in England* (7 vols. in 8, 1866–1902), vi and vii, pt. ii, and also from Sir John Sinclair, *The History of the Public Revenue of the British Empire* (3 vols., 3rd edn., 1803–4), ii, appendix, 28–46.

Discount on Navy bills from Beveridge, op. cit., i, 523–5. I wish to thank Dr. A. H. John for lending me his own assembly of statistics, particularly of the volume of India bonds outstanding, and of their market yields.

To avoid unnecessary overcrowding in the diagrams, a single representative quotation of long-term rates is given, that of the yield on Bank Stock.

[2] In the diagrams, the structure of rates during the boom of the early 'nineties appears to contradict this analysis, since it shows India bonds yielding more than long-term securities. This is undoubtedly due to the inappropriateness of India bonds for short-term quotations during the last decade or so of the eighteenth century. The premiums on Exchequer bills, and the low discount rates on commercial bills (see John, op. cit., p. 142, n. 5, and Pressnell, op. cit., p. 93) clearly indicate the 'normal' spread between short and long rates to be expected in a boom.

agriculture, appears to be offered by the course of investment on the Duke of Kingston's estates.[1] Professor Ashton's comment that 'the depression period of the eighteenth century, 1730–1750, was one of extremely low rates of interest and that this was a condition favourable to . . . investment' in repairs and improvements was explored with no tangible result. In fact, the estates provide evidence of a sort for the present thesis. Between 1726 (when the records commence) and 1735 'the expenditure on repairs and new buildings, etc., was relatively low'. The dates cited (unfortunately, we do not know what was happening before 1726) flank a period during much of which short-term rates were close to or above long rates. These are exactly the indicators one would expect in conditions unfavourable to long-term investment. It is no matter whether or not the landlord had in fact to borrow; rates of interest indicated the value of money alike to those who had it and to those who had not.

The argument may be further elaborated in the light of the comment[2] that 'It is difficult to believe that a temporary rise of 1 per cent would by itself have weighed heavily with landowners compared with other influences upon investment, so long as loans were available at some rate, as they usually were in times of peace.' Does the difficulty possibly lie in that phrase 'by itself'? A higher rate of interest possibly concealed the operation of a substantial pair of scissors, reduced profit expectations being one blade, a higher cost of borrowing the other; a higher rate represented a rise at the margin in the relative value of money, and a fall in the relative attractiveness of other means of holding wealth. Marginal investment may well in consequence have been adversely affected. To the extent that an 'abnormally' high rate appeared, the consequent distortion of the rate structure would have heightened these effects. It is true that the interest on some loans might be readily revised, so that a possible future fluctuation in interest rates might thereby be discounted in advance; but would there ever have been an 'abnormal' pattern of short and long rates at all if expectations

---

[1] G. E. Mingay, 'The Agricultural Depression, 1730–1750', *Ec.H.R.*, 2nd ser. viii (1956), 330.

[2] H. J. Habakkuk, reviewing Ashton, *Eighteenth Century*, in 'The Eighteenth Century', *Ec.H.R.*, 2nd ser., viii (1956), 435.

had been fully discounted? The appearance of a hump pattern (short rates higher than long, and medium higher than both) was a strong hint that past expectations of the trend of the long-term rate had been falsified.

VIII

Beyond the initial distinction between real and monetary factors, this study has not attempted to explore the causes of changes in the rate of interest. It should suffice at the present preliminary stage of investigation to register the importance of interest rates. The evidence is substantial—too substantial, it may respectfully be submitted, to warrant the somewhat summary treatment in an article devoted to 'The Entrepreneur in the Industrial Revolution in Britain'.[1] For some undertakings there is indeed no obvious clue that it was considered. For others, particularly those at the margin, it was certainly relevant at some stage. In general, the cost of money in its various forms was liable to be watched with varying concern by those proposing to borrow, to invest their own or others' money, to remit, or to realize capital assets. It seems safe to say that the rate of interest entered into a significant proportion of decisions to undertake economic activity. The pattern is not necessarily a tidy one, although a little imagination may not perhaps be ruled out of court. Our forebears were surely not so indifferent to the value of money as the virtual silence of economic historiography until recent years has tended to imply; we might well have studies of some of the unexplored sources of information about interest rates in estate records, public utility records, business firms' ledgers, and in mortgage agreements (usually, alas, calendared by archivists in complete neglect of the interest rates cited therein). There is no case for asserting the primacy of interest over other costs; there is a case for asserting that any interpretation of economic trends which overlooks the role of monetary factors is inevitably incomplete.

[1] Charles Wilson, in *History*, xlii, no. 45 (June 1957), 106, states baldly, 'The falling rate of interest was certainly an important factor in expansion: but it seems to me to have been rather in the nature of an enabling condition for those prepared to take advantage of it. It did not prevent the decline and virtual extinction of well-established industries in some areas.'

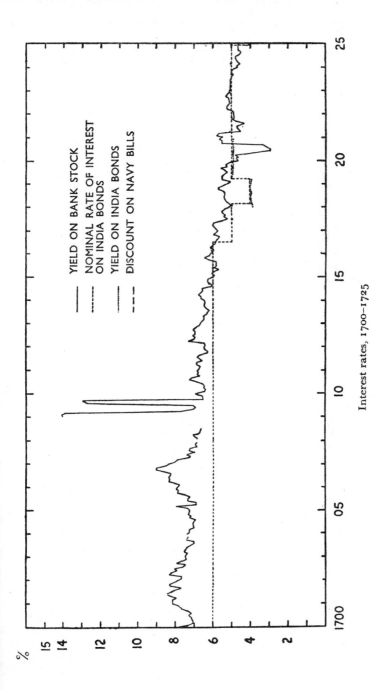

Interest rates, 1700–1725

%

15
14

12

10

8

6

4

2

1700   05   10   15   20   25

——————   YIELD ON BANK STOCK

----------   NOMINAL RATE OF INTEREST
              ON INDIA BONDS

··········   YIELD ON INDIA BONDS

— · — ·   DISCOUNT ON NAVY BILLS

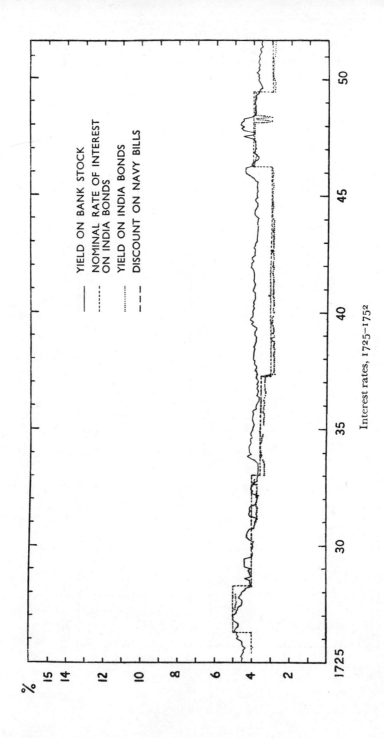

Interest rates, 1725–1752

YIELD ON BANK STOCK

NOMINAL RATE OF INTEREST
ON INDIA BONDS

YIELD ON INDIA BONDS

DISCOUNT ON NAVY BILLS

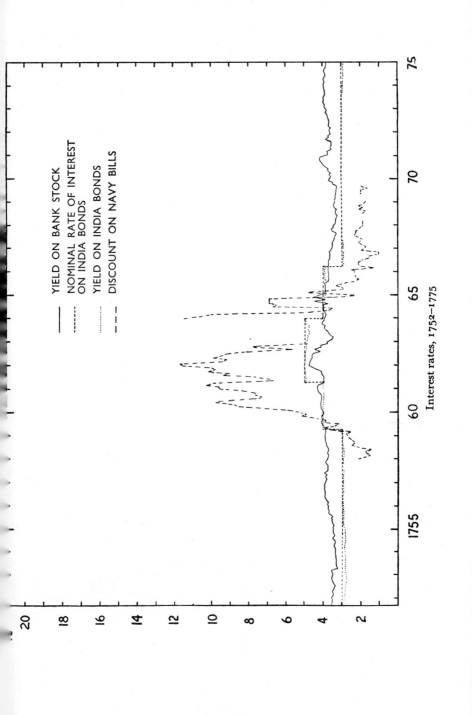

Interest rates, 1752–1775

YIELD ON BANK STOCK

NOMINAL RATE OF INTEREST
ON INDIA BONDS

YIELD ON INDIA BONDS

DISCOUNT ON NAVY BILLS

20 18 16 14 12 10 8 6 4 2

1755   60   65   70   75

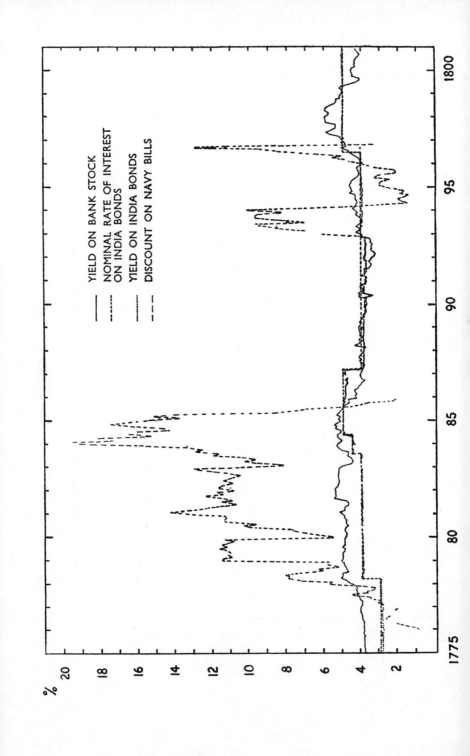

The Sub-contract System in the British Coal Industry

I T is thirty years since Professor Ashton and Professor Joseph Sykes in a short but vivid essay[1] examined the origins and development of the sub-contract system in eighteenth-century coalmining. This form of organization, by no means peculiar to coalmining, occupies a significant place in the evolution of the British industrial order. Its relationship to the development of capitalist institutions and of labour relations has been examined, among others, by D. F. Schloss, G. C. Allen and A. H. John.[2] In this essay an attempt is made to reassess the significance of the system in the light of these studies and with particular reference to the experience of the coal industry in Staffordshire and north-eastern England.

I

The sub-contract,[3] or butty, system, it has been said, 'consists in the workmen being the servants, not of the proprietor or lessee of the colliery, but of a contractor, in Staffordshire familiarly called a *butty*, who engages with the proprietor of the mine to deliver the coal or ironstone at so much the ton, himself hiring the labourers requisite, using his own horses and supplying all

---

[1] T. S. Ashton and J. Sykes, *The Coal Industry of the Eighteenth Century* (1929), ch. vii.

[2] D. F. Schloss, *Methods of Industrial Remuneration* (1892), pp. 82–140; G. C. Allen, *The Industrial Development of Birmingham and the Black Country, 1860–1927* (1929), pt. ii, ch. vi and vii; A. H. John, *The Industrial Development of South Wales* (1950), pp. 76–80.

[3] For a distinction between contracting and sub-contracting, see Schloss, op. cit., p. 105. ('The distinction between the "contractor" and the "sub-contractor" is that the former is not an employer, while the latter is, *being a sub-employer working under a superior employer*.' [My italics.])

the tools necessary for working the mines'.[1] In Staffordshire,[2] where the system was to prove most tenacious in its hold upon the industry, the mine owner himself sank the pits, 'opened out' the work and installed 'all the necessary "plant" of the colliery', the butty for his part recruiting the men and providing the working capital. The men were paid either by the piece, in the case of the *pickmen* working at the face, or by the day, in that of the *bandsmen* or hauliers; but the rate of wages for both piece and day work was determined by the coal owner in accordance with 'the market price of coal or the demand for labour', and it was this which regulated the charter price paid to the butty for the coal produced.

Sub-contracting had its roots deep in the early history of the coal industry and at different times seems to have been found on every coalfield. By the end of the eighteenth century the system was operating in districts as far apart as western Scotland and south Wales, but in most areas it was already a dying force. In Staffordshire, however, sub-contracting on an extensive scale persisted in full vigour, and it is to this area, therefore, that we may best turn for a first appreciation of the forces making for its growth and survival.

Coal had been mined in the Black Country since at least the thirteenth century, but before the last quarter of the eighteenth century the great mineral resources of this inland coalfield had been little exploited. Under the quickening influences of the development of canal transport and the advent of machine-industry, however, the coalfield sprang into vigorous life; and the protracted wars with France served rather to stimulate than to depress an area which could produce ordnance as readily as locks and nails. The output of pig-iron in Staffordshire, a mere 7,000 tons in 1788, rose to 50,000 tons in 1806, to more than 200,000 tons by 1830, and finally reached a peak of 777,000 tons in the mid-'fifties. The fortunes of coal were closely linked to those of iron, and from an output still countable in hundreds of thousands of tons in 1790, production mounted until the

---

[1] Report of the Midland Mining Commission, *BPP*, 1843 (508), XIII, p. xxxiii.

[2] For the remainder of this paragraph, see especially Census of 1861, *BPP* (3221), 1863, LIII (pt. 1), pp. 236–7.

The Sub-contract System in the British Coal Industry

coalfields of the Black Country and neighbouring Cannock Chase were yielding over ten million tons by 1875.

At the turn of the eighteenth century the Black Country coalfield was distinguished among the coalfields of Britain not only for the rapidity but also for the ease of its exploitation. In the so-called Ten Yard seam there existed close to the surface vast quantities of coal whose winning and working required no large investment of capital. Neither shaft-sinking nor haulage machinery made heavy demands on the mine owner's pocket, and this factor, together with the prevailing system of landownership, encouraged a proliferation of small enterprises. As a result areas of working of less than ten acres were common, and those of twenty acres or more comparatively rare.[1] By the middle of the nineteenth century close on four hundred collieries were operating in the Black Country, each on average representing a capital commitment of no more than £3,000, producing some 15,000 tons of coal annually, and giving employment to between sixty and seventy men and boys.[2]

The presence of a multitude of small enterprises on the Staffordshire coalfield brought with it fierce and unremitting competition. The strong ebb and flow of the business cycle made life for the coal owner a constant battle in which success and disaster alike were always close at hand. The Black Country was essentially a 'frontier' territory, and its economic life displayed that turbulence which is characteristic of a frontier society. Labour was undisciplined and restless, and frequently difficult to obtain;[3] and a premium, therefore, was placed upon efficient and forceful management. Yet the headlong advance of industrial activity and the accompanying forward movement of population had far outdistanced the growth of those educational facilities upon which trained leadership and a disciplined labour force ultimately depend. In consequence industry had to turn for its managers to men schooled only in the craft which they practised, and lacking both the rudimentary general training and the discipline which formal education of the most elementary

---

[1] T. E. Lones, *History of Mining in the Black Country* (1898), p. 37.

[2] Estimates based on Census Returns 1851, 1861; *Mineral Statistics*; and on 1863, LIII (pt. 1), p. 237. See also 'Mid. Min. Com.', p. civ.

[3] See, e.g., Report of the Commissioner on the State of Population in Mining Districts, *BPP*, 1850 (1248), XXIII, p. 11.

kind would have afforded.[1] Where even a modest competence in the three Rs was little in evidence, the absence of men trained for managerial duties or in the principles of mining engineering was no more than to be expected. In earlier and more slowly developed districts, like north-eastern England, the industry itself had raised up its own informal schools of management; but neither time nor the circumstances of the industry's growth had permitted such a development in the Black Country. In such conditions it is not surprising that the Black Country mine owner should have turned to those who, out of their own experience as working colliers, could be relied upon to bring to their task both a 'knowledge of the business' and 'acquaintance with the habits of the men'.[2] When in addition the butty could be expected to bring much needed working capital to the enterprise, it is no cause for wonder that the small mine owner should have found in the system of sub-contracting not only the most feasible but also the most desirable solution to his managerial and labour problems.

The butty did not commit himself to his employer at the price of a manager's salary. Neither his upbringing nor the interests of the mine owner suggested such an arrangement. Management, as it has developed in modern industrial society, has become essentially professionalized and is imbued with those values which are associated with professional service. The butty, raised in a harder if no more exacting school, responded only to the stimulus of profit, and was encouraged to drive his men to the utmost in its pursuit. The great advantage of this system, as Schloss pointed out, was that it supplied 'a self-acting stimulus', which dispensed with the necessity of incessant supervision of the managing-foreman by the employer.[3] In a society lacking a professional managerial class, and inhibited by the small size of its business units from creating one, this form of delegated responsibility clearly had its place.

By the middle of the nineteenth century, however, the butty

---

[1] Cf. Census 1861, loc. cit.: 'His [the butty's] general characteristics are a knowledge of the manual operation of mining, considerable shrewdness, and energy enough to act on the wills of other men; his general intelligence is not often his characteristic, for many cannot write, and there are not a few who cannot read.'

[2] Rep. Com. Population Min. Dist., *BPP*, 1859, Sess. 2 (2566), XII, p. 8.

[3] Schloss, op. cit., p. 104.

system no longer held unchallenged sway in Black Country mining. The system had come under attack both from the miners, who saw in it an instrument fashioned for their exploitation, and from those enlightened mine owners who perceived its inherent wastefulness and inefficiency. The grievances of the men were real enough and found expression in the strike of 1842;[1] but the attack from below lacked both force and cohesion. That from above, if less general, was more dangerously corrosive. The intelligent mine owner had come to appreciate that even if he contrived to drive a successful bargain with his butty, he could not prevent the latter from operating the colliery to his own short-term rather than to the mine owner's long-term advantage. Thus not only were the men overworked, but the colliery was exploited for its choicest pickings rather than for its fullest yield, and development work was seriously neglected. James Foster and D. G. Round both testified that the abandonment of sub-contracting had led to more economical mining, greater output, more regular working and fewer accidents in their pits.[2] Yet this was not a universal experience. Many employers who had operated both systems maintained that, with direct labour, they 'could not get their men to do them justice', and that only under the butty system 'could they obtain coal at the cheapest rate'.[3] Contemporaries were not altogether blind to the reasons for this diversity of experience. The butty system was patently expendable in thick-coal working,[4] but its successful replacement by a system of direct labour depended in the last resort on the ability of the employer to find an efficient and conscientious salaried manager.[5] In the middle of the nineteenth century, though the supply of such men was slowly increasing, there were as yet by no means enough to go round.

Far from declining, the butty system, in the third quarter of the nineteenth century, tended to increase its hold on the south Staffordshire industry.[6] This was in part the result of the added vitality which railway construction in Britain and overseas brought to the coal and iron trades: but it was also in part the

[1] Mid. Min. Com., pp. xxiii ff.
[2] ibid., p. 69; Rep. Com. Population Min. Dist., 1859, Sess. 2, p. 10.
[3] ibid.   [4] ibid., p. 7.   [5] ibid., p. 10.
[6] ibid., p. 9. The number of butties in the Black Country *c.* 1848 was estimated to be 900. In 1858 they were 'more numerous'.

outcome of an inevitable shift of activity to thinner seams and a consequent increase in the employment of longwall methods of coal extraction. The longwall system, by contrast with pillar and stall or square working, makes work at the face essentially a collective operation. Thus even in those larger collieries, where it was found necessary to commit the overall direction of the mine workings to the hands of a salaried manager, it proved expedient to maintain a system of collective piecework at the face—the so-called 'little butty system'.[1] Thus until the final quarter of the nineteenth century a combination of forces contrived not only to perpetuate but to strengthen the hold of the butty system in south Staffordshire. When, moreover, the activities of the coal industry are set in the wider context of Black Country industry in general, dominated as it was by the small master and sub-contract systems,[2] it is less surprising that the butty system survived than that its days proved to be numbered. It declined, in company with the Black Country coal industry itself, only in the last quarter of the nineteenth century.

II

In mining experience, organization and technique no two areas of coal working show such contrasts as the Black Country and north-eastern England: indeed when Thomas Tancred made his survey of the Staffordshire coalfield in 1843, it was to the great northern coalfield of the Tyne and Wear that he turned to emphasize the deficiencies of Staffordshire. The Northumberland and Durham coal district had for centuries claimed pre-eminence in the British coal industry not only in terms of output —already exceeding three million tons in 1800—but still more in terms of mining technique and organization; and this superiority tended to increase rather than diminish with the passing of the years. Increasing depth of working—coal was being won from 792 feet at Hebburn before 1800, and from 1,674 feet at Monkwearmouth forty years later—meant increasing calls on capital, but the industry experienced no

---

[1] This system was particularly prevalent in the east Midlands, but it lacked the capitalist elements which are essential to the true butty system.
[2] See especially Allen, op. cit.

difficulty in meeting these demands. Wealth flowed into the coalfield from landowners like the Ravensworths, Lambtons and Tempests; from trading families like the Russells; and from London merchants, drawn into the industry along the channels of commerce. Whereas in Staffordshire limited capital resources were spread thinly over a large number of competing undertakings, in the north-east concentration of investment was the rule: so that while at the middle of the nineteenth century the typical Black Country colliery represented an investment of some two or three thousand pounds, the majority of north-eastern collieries had cost up to ten times this amount to win and equip, and some few, like Gosforth, involved a commitment of upwards of £100,000.[1] Likewise, where south Staffordshire collieries counted their employees in scores, north-eastern collieries numbered theirs in hundreds. At Jarrow in 1843, 502 miners were employed at a single pit, while 857 men and boys were working at the two pits of Haswell colliery.[2]

The large-scale organization to which these statistics bear witness had been of slow and steady growth. It had involved the gradual creation of a hierarchy of officials and workers ranging from the check-viewer responsible for the general oversight of a group of collieries to the humble door-boy stationed in some remote corner of the pit. The greatest of the colliery viewers—men like Thomas Barnes, John Watson and the elder Buddle—had their 'schools', and from these had flowed a stream of under-viewers and engineers trained in the discipline of sound mining practice. By the early nineteenth century there was a two-way traffic of men moving into the north-east to serve their apprenticeship with the great viewers of the coalfield, and of others going south to apply northern methods in newly developing districts.

Enough has already been said to indicate the clear distinction which existed throughout the nineteenth century between mining conditions in Staffordshire and in the north-east. The distinction was, moreover, one which extended to the method of working at the face, for whereas the extraction of the thick, and even more of the thin, coal in the Black Country demanded techniques which put a premium on the undifferentiated

[1] Mid. Min. Com., pp. cv, cvii.   [2] ibid.

activities of the group, the system of working universally employed in the north-eastern field—that of pillar and stall—readily lent itself to division of labour and individual piece-work. If environmental factors had dictated the growth and survival of the butty system in the Black Country, therefore, no such fertile soil existed in the north-east. Yet there is evidence that as late as the beginning of the nineteenth century sub-contracting was by no means unknown even on this coalfield. The reasons for its development and persistence under these seemingly unfavourable conditions clearly merit closer examination.

Contracting had been known at Elswick[1] and elsewhere in Northumberland before 1700 in undertakings which probably differed little in size and efficiency from the Black Country collieries of the nineteenth century. Whether thereafter the system had fallen into disuse is not clear—the argument from silence is scarcely to be trusted here—but when in 1756 John Watson, viewer to Sir Francis Delaval, the proprietor of Hartley colliery, recommended his master to employ the sub-contract system in his pits, he was commending a system which, while not unknown, does not seem to have been generally practised in the district at this time. The circumstances attending this particular development are illuminating. Watson was concerned about the high charges for unproductive shift-work—as distinct from the productive labour of coal getting and conveying—at the colliery. On 28 November he wrote to Delaval:[2]

> To remedy this Sort of Imposition I would recommend you to have the Pitts let by the Score [*a measure of quantity*] to the Overmen who now work them, or if they cannot be bro: to reason to some others, to find their own wages, Headways, Shiftwork, Candles, Cutting Stone and Holeing Walls. This method keeps you clear of paying wages to the Overmen and Stone Cutters when the Pitts are idle and will induce the Overmen to keep their Pitts more constantly at work and raise a greater quantity of Scores as their Wages will depend entirely upon it.

Within a year Watson was able to report that 'the Pitts are let to the Person who had the lowest Proposal, and who really turns

---

[1] J. U. Nef, *Rise of the British Coal Industry* (1932), i, 424.
[2] Newcastle Public Library, Delaval MSS., 34.A.10.

out an Industrious, Sober and Carefull Man, and carries forward his Business extreamly well';[1] and a reduction in costs would seem to have confirmed the wisdom of his advice. As a result the viewer found himself in a position to recommend that not only work at the face but also the drawing, putting and sledding of the coal should be put out to contract.[2]

Watson's efforts, however, do not appear to have established sub-contracting as a permanent feature of this colliery's economy. From time to time proposals similar to Watson's were made by his successors, and for similar reasons. In 1789, for example, Delaval was being warned that 'several things which has the appearance of rogrey has been found out and made proof. . . . I am apt to believe that overcharging the pit bills has been long practised in Hartley Colliery';[3] and again in 1797 an attempt was being made to let the working of the colliery to undertakers on the basis of a seven-year contract.[4] Under this arrangement the full responsibility for productive operations at the colliery was to be placed in the hands of the undertakers but the disposal of the coal was to remain in the hands of Delaval or his agent.

The record of contracting at Hartley though stretching over half a century is not continuous nor can it be clearly drawn. At the Durham collieries of the Lambton family, by contrast, though undertakers were apparently not employed until as late as 1784, the system thereafter had an unbroken life of almost thirty years.[5] The first contractors, Messrs. Featherstonhaugh and Co., entered into an eight-year agreement with William Lambton in 1784. In return for a payment—determined annually—in respect of each chaldron of coal delivered at the pit's mouth, the contractors undertook to work the coal and to 'keep and uphold' the wagon-ways and wagons. All other charges, including the maintenance of the general stock of the colliery, were to be met by Lambton, who also retained the responsibility for the disposal of the coal in the coastal and in land markets. The extra charges which fell for payment to the

[1] ibid., 25 November 1757.
[2] ibid., 1 January 1758.
[3] ibid., 34.A.4. Samuel Haggerston (Overman) to Delaval, August 1789.
[4] ibid., 34.A.4.
[5] North of England Institute of Mining Engineers, Buddle MSS. III, 197 ff.

The Sub-contract System in the British Coal Industry

proprietor consisted in the main of additions to the working stock of the collieries, but they also included subsidies paid to the contractors in respect of excess payments made by them for oats, hay, bread, corn and the binding of colliers. In all during the ten years 1800–9 these extra charges totalled almost £110,000, of which perhaps 60 per cent may be regarded as addition to the stock of the collieries, while the payments made to the undertakers for coal delivered at the pit's mouth in this period amounted to rather more than £500,000. Messrs. Featherstonhaugh renewed their undertaking for seven years in 1792 and again in 1799; but, at the end of 1803, the discovery that the undertakers had financial interests in another colliery led to the summary ending of their contract.[1] Messrs. Fenwick and Co. who took their place remained in the service of the Lambtons until 1813, when Mr. Lambton 'resolved to take the working of the Collieries into his own hand'.[2]

At the neighbouring collieries of the Tempest family, the contracting system was also in operation at the end of the eighteenth century. The Tempests then stood second only to the Lambtons among the colliery owners of County Durham. From their pits at East Rainton, Pensher and Harrington Mill little short of 100,000 tons were sent each year from Sunderland to the London coal market. In 1801 tenders were invited from undertakers for the working of these three collieries. The conditions on which the undertaking was to be let were stipulated under twenty-six heads and may be summarized as follows:

1. The agreement was to be for five years, and provided for an annual vend from the collieries of 36,000 Newcastle chaldrons (c. 95,000 tons).[3]
2. The contractor was to take the 'dead' and the 'live and using' stock of the colliery at valuation, and was to be reimbursed at the end of the term.[4]

[1] ibid., XIV, under *Twizel*: 'In May 1802 it was reported that Messrs. Featherston [*sic*] and Croudace had purchased their shares in the lease thereof, and that they were in possession, which proved to be true, and in consequence of which they were shut out of their shares in the Lambton Undertaking; as being contrary to the spirit of their engagement with the Lambton family.'
[2] ibid., XXVIII, 114.
[3] ibid., VIII. *Conditions on which the Workings of Sir Henry Tempest Vane, Bart's Collieries, at East Rainton, Pensher, and Harrington-Mill are to be let to an Undertaker* (printed leaflet). Clauses 1 and 2.   [4] Clauses 3 and 4.

3. The undertaker might make 'new erections' or remove any machines 'at his own cost and charges'.[1]
4. The colliery owner might sink new pits, drive drifts, etc., 'making compensation to the undertaker for the use of his machines, and other matters and things necessary for such purposes'.[2]
5. If the price of oats should exceed 5s a boll or that of new hay £3 a ton, if it should be necessary to provide rye for the workmen, or if the expense of the yearly binding of pitmen should exceed 3d per chaldron on the year's workings, the excess in each instance was to be met equally by owner and contractor.[3]
6. The contract-price from year to year was to vary according to the changing cost of labour and materials. (This was not explicitly stated in the Tender notice but it was the basis on which the undertaking worked in practice.)

Before the end of the year an agreement was entered into between the proprietor and Messrs. Longridge, Leviss and Watkin for the working of the three collieries. The contract was given a further five years' life in 1806, but there is no evidence of its subsequent renewal. It seems probable, though not certain, that on the Tempest estates as elsewhere contracting did not survive far into the nineteenth century.[4]

The record of contracting which is here revealed on three important north-eastern estates might be supplemented by a number of similar examples. Two further illustrations will perhaps suffice to indicate the ubiquity and variety of the system. At Harraton Outside, a colliery in the possession of Sir Ralph Milbanke, first Robert Wade in 1797, and then, five years later, Messrs. Longridge and Watkin, two of the partners in the Tempest undertaking, contracted to work the colliery.[5] The agreement, although similar in general terms to that offered by Tempest, differed from it in certain important points of emphasis. It was expressly provided that the undertaker should be required to 'lay no new way, nor sink any pit', nor should he 'keep the Colliery fire-engine' (i.e. supply the engine with coal at his

---

[1] Clause 5.   [2] Clause 15.   [3] Clauses 22–25.
[4] Cf. M. Dunn, *History of the Viewers* (unpublished MS.), p. 10, where it is stated that Sober Watkin, viewer for Longridge and Co., undertakers of the Tempest Collieries, continued to act as viewer 'after they became again into the Tempest family'.
[5] Buddle MSS. XIV.

own expense). Whereas at the Tempest collieries, the undertaker was to pay for damaged ground and to be responsible for all taxes except the land tax, at Harraton he was expressly relieved of these responsibilities. In brief Milbanke was offering different and more favourable terms to those given by Tempest.

The agreement for the working of Cowpen colliery, also effected in 1797, presents further interesting features.[1] The owners of the Cowpen royalty were Mrs. Bowes and Rev. Robert Croft and the colliery was let to a partnership, two of whose nine shares were held by Croft himself. The working and leading of the coals were in their turn let to a group of four undertakers—Messrs. Clark, Gray, Hodgson and Smith—one of whom, Clark, was also a shareholder in the principal concern. It was expressly stated in the terms of agreement that the undertakers engaged to find not only horses and materials for the colliery but also men, and that the pitmen were to be bound not to the colliery owners but to the undertakers.

This necessarily brief and random survey of the practice of contracting in the northern coalfield prompts an immediate question. How far can this form of business organization be equated with the butty system of south Staffordshire? Patently the difference in scale of operation which distinguished the two districts from each other in the early nineteenth century extended to the field of contracting. Whereas a pair of butties in the Black Country seldom had more than one hundred men and boys under their control, Messrs. Longridge and Co. in 1810 employed 880 miners at the Tempest collieries alone;[2] and while a butty might be expected to bring at most a few hundred pounds into a Midland mining concern, the larger northeastern undertakers must have been required to command much more substantial capital resources. The implications of this difference in scale are by no means unimportant, but they leave the fundamentals of the contract system untouched. In both districts the contractor assumed broad responsibilities for the production, but not for the distribution, of the coal; for the provision of the working, but not of the fixed, capital of the colliery; and for the maintenance, though not necessarily the initial

[1] ibid.
[2] A. Bailey, *General View of the Agriculture of Durham* (1813), p. 12.

recruitment, of the labour force. North-eastern undertaker in short was but Black Country charter-master writ large.

To what then may we attribute the existence and persistence of a sub-contracting system in soil seemingly so unfavourable as the north-east? In attempting an answer to this question it is necessary to sketch, however briefly, the basic conditions affecting the economy of the north-eastern coal industry in the later years of the eighteenth century. For the coal owners of the Tyne and Wear as for those of other districts the second half of the eighteenth century was a period of expansion. The evidence of the growing pressure of demand after 1750 is to be seen not only in the statistics of exports from the Tyne and Wear—these increased from some 1,200,000 tons in 1750 to over 1,600,000 tons a quarter of a century later—but also in the upward movement of coal prices.[1] The profitability of the coal trade, however, inevitably encouraged investment both from within and from without the ranks of the existing colliery owners. Thus, although exports from the area continued to increase in the closing years of the century, prices both at Newcastle and in London proved far less buoyant. The gains of a decade of rising prices between 1773 and 1782 were lost in the single year of 1783, and thereafter until the outbreak of the French war ten years later the price of coal remained persistently low. In so far as this fall in price was the reflection of an increase in sales, there was no loss to the north-eastern area as a whole; but individual entrepreneurs suffered severely as a result of the increased competition which the prosperity of the previous decade had brought in its train. Competition was felt not only in the market for coal, but also in the demand for labour—the prime item in every colliery's costs—and for materials. The daily earnings of hewers increased by at least $12\frac{1}{2}$ per cent between 1780 and 1790, while at the same time the cost of horses rose by 40 per cent and that of feeding stuffs by more than a quarter.[2] The following decade, while it saw a continued upward trend in output and a welcome recovery in prices, also brought an even more spectacular rise in costs. The daily wage of hewers rose again, this time by a quarter, and the cost of materials advanced even more sharply, timber and cordage, for example, each

---

[1] Ashton and Sykes, op. cit., pp. 250–3.　　　[2] Buddle MSS. III, 192.

doubling its price within the decade. At the same time a first penetration of the rich resources of the lower Tyne valley, involving the winning of the important Willington, Wallsend, Hebburn and Percy Main collieries, had widened appreciably the area of supply and denied to the older collieries the full fruits of the expanding market.

The eighteenth-century expansion of the north-eastern coal industry was determined primarily by the growth in the population of London and of the coastal districts of eastern and southern England which the industry supplied. The coming of the canal, which had so quickened the activity of inland coalfields, had been less beneficial to the north-east, and geographically at least had restricted rather than enlarged the market which the coalfield served.[1] In so doing it had tended to confirm the area's status as a supplier of domestic rather than of industrial fuel. The demand for north-eastern coal was consequently less elastic and less volatile than that for the coal of inland fields, principally concerned with supplying the ironworks and factories of an expanding industrial economy. In these circumstances the north-eastern coal owner was torn between policies aiming on the one hand at expansion and on the other at stabilization; but, as the pressure of competition grew, his preference for the certain rewards of stability and assured prices, as against the headier but more uncertain gains of rapid expansion and open competition, tended to increase.

The attempt to ensure stability involved the coal owner in efforts to restrict the movement of both prices and costs. The policy of maintaining prices by an agreed restriction of output and sales lay deep in the gild origins of the coal trade, and it only required revival in 1771.[2] But the practice of limitation—the so-called Regulation of the Vend—demanded from coal owners a loyalty which was not consistently forthcoming in the expansionist years of the late eighteenth century. Thus the collapse in prices after 1782 was the result of a temporary abandonment of the Regulation;[3] and the coal owner who rested his hopes of

---

[1] Rep. Sel. Com. (H. of L.) on Coal Trade, *BPP*, 1830 (9), VIII, p. 98.

[2] On the history of the Regulation of the Vend see especially P. M. Sweezy, *Monopoly and Competition in the English Coal Trade, 1550–1850* (1950).

[3] Sweezy, op. cit., p. 39.

prosperity on a policy of sales restriction was building his future on shifting sand.

A second approach to stability lay through the cost conditions of the industry. Here also a well-tried instrument was ready to the hand of the coal owners, namely the annual binding of colliers. When, at the turn of the century, the opening of the new collieries of the lower Tyne was increasing the demand, and the pressure of naval and military recruiting was reducing the supply of colliery workers, the owners combined to regulate and to restrict their intake of labour and to fix the terms on which they were prepared to bind their men.[1] But this combination did not prevent the miners from exacting handsome sums from their employers by way of 'binding money'; and in the exceptional conditions of the binding of 1804, as much as twenty guineas was paid to hewers over and above their guaranteed fortnightly wages.[2]

The attempt to maintain conditions of stability in the industry by collective action was not, therefore, wholly successful, an outcome to which the erratic and often unrelated movement of costs and prices bears eloquent testimony. The individual coal owner, in consequence, had to trim his own sails to this uncertain wind, and it was in this context that the contract system commended itself to him. By contracting out the productive side of his enterprise to an undertaker, the coal owner not only divested himself of the responsibility for controlling and maintaining an increasingly turbulent body of workmen, but also introduced a measure of stability and predictability into his labour and general costs. In particular the provision in the Tempest, Lambton and Harraton agreements that half of the excess charges for feeding stuffs and for binding money should be met by the undertaker offered an automatic hedge against cost inflation. In 1800, for example, the total bill for excess charges at the Lambton collieries was £22,209. 6s, and the coal owner was thus able to limit his liability by more than £11,000.[3] In 1806, a less exceptional year, his saving was

[1] N. of Eng. Inst. of Min. Eng., Minute Books of the Regulation of the Vend, c. 1800–10, passim.
[2] Buddle MSS. XIII. Hewers were bound at the Lambton collieries for amounts ranging from 17 to 20 guineas, drivers at from 5 to 10 guineas.
[3] ibid., III, 197 ff.

£2,000. Nor did the gains to the coal owner cease at the point of labour cost and control. Although a system of fourteen-day settlements between owner and undertaker largely relieved the undertaker of the responsibility for providing cash capital for the concern,[1] the practice of determining each year's getting-costs in advance placed the onus of meeting the rising charges for colliery materials squarely on the shoulders of the undertaker.

If the gains of the coal owner were as substantial as they thus appear, what incentive induced the undertaker to go forward with his enterprise? It is clear that the undertaker, like his employer, was a capitalist seeking profitable employment for his capital and his managerial abilities. The annual computations of the contract-price at the Lambton collieries included an item 'for the undertaker's risk and trouble', but as this would appear to have represented no more than 3 per cent of the contract-price,[2] it is evident that the undertaker's profit could only have been assured by efficiency and economy in the day-to-day operation of the colliery. Profit there must have been, but it is doubtful whether many fortunes were made by colliery contracting. The upward movement of undertakers into the owner class, though perceptible, is limited in terms both of the number and of the wealth of the subsequent enterprises; and at least one undertaker, Lewis Legg, is known to have lost heavily by his activities as a contractor.[3] Contracting, in the inflationary conditions of the French wars, offered much hazard for small reward.

III

If this view of the factors conditioning the growth and survival of contracting in the Black Country and the north-east has validity, one might expect to find confirmation in the history of its decline. As late as the 1870s the butty system is said to have prevailed in 'all coal-mines in Staffordshire, north and south'.[4] By 1908, however, the system had disappeared in north Staffordshire, and in the Black Country fewer than two thousand colliers —between a fifth and a quarter of the labour force—were

---

[1] ibid., VIII, Tempest Undertaking, Clause 16.
[2] ibid., XIII, 146.   [3] Dunn, op. cit., p. 5.
[4] Roy. Com. on Mines, *BPP*, 1908 (4349), XX, Q.36708.

employed under butties.[1] The reasons for this decline were in part technological. The exhaustion of the shallow seams and the consequent necessity to sink deeper, more highly capitalized, and more heavily manned collieries had gone far to remove those physical and economic conditions in which the butty system had hitherto thriven. Though gang-labour and the 'little butty system' could be, and still were, in some measure employed, the traditional butty—of limited means and education, and unschooled in the problems of deep mining—could have no place in a colliery in which upwards of £250,000 might be invested and up to nine hundred miners employed.[2] Public opinion was also playing its part. The butty system encountered growing disfavour among trade unionists; employers were becoming increasingly aware of its wastefulness; and from the standpoint of the mines inspectorate it was being argued that the 'system conduces to working of the pits in an unskilful way, and to the neglect of discipline and measures of safety'.[3] Legislatively, too, the system had been placed in an increasingly disadvantageous position. As a result of a decision in the case of *Regina v. Cope* in 1867 it had been established that liability for injury sustained in a butty-operated colliery lay not with the contractor but with the coal owner.[4] Five years later the Mines and Collieries Act of 1872 made it a statutory obligation for every colliery to employ a duly trained and certificated manager, and at the same time strengthened considerably the code of safety regulations applicable to all mines. Safety was thus made the first watchword in colliery management, and technical training became as significant as mining experience in the make-up of the colliery manager. Management in short was given a professional status, which, in the Black Country at least, it had hitherto conspicuously lacked, and the requirements of the law expedited a change in organizational and managerial institutions which the technical and economic needs of the industry were already beginning to demand. In the 'new

[1] ibid., Q.36795, 36853, 36911.
[2] The three major collieries in South Staffordshire in 1913 were Sandwell Park (248 men), Hamstead (697) and Baggeridge Wood (903). The smallest, Sandwell Park, had a capital of over £250,000.
[3] Roy. Com. on Mines, *BPP*, 1907 (3549), XIV, p. 404.
[4] Lones, op. cit., p. 82.

model' coal industry of the late nineteenth century the butty could at best hold only a limited and questioned place, and subcontracting survived from force of habit rather than from any virtue it had once possessed.[1]

In the north-east the decline of contracting is less easily charted; but the View-Books, so eloquent of the existence of the system in the early years of the nineteenth century, are wholly silent about its survival in the years after 1815. If it is true, as seems likely, that the system fell into abeyance with the ending of the Napoleonic wars, the explanation may lie in the passing of those conditions which had given such vitality to contracting in the period of war and inflation. In the fifteen years after Waterloo coal prices held surprisingly firm in face of general deflationary tendencies.[2] The price of coal from Tanfield Moor colliery, for example, which had increased by some 60 per cent between 1798 and 1809, subsequently remained at 25s per Newcastle chaldron for twenty years.[3] This happy development was in part a result of the nature of the coalfield's market, in part a consequence of the comparative firmness with which the ranks of the Regulation of the Vend were maintained in the immediate post-war years. At the same time labour was increasingly abundant. At Jarrow, for example, in March 1817 men were said to be 'plentiful' and a wage reduction was effected;[4] and by 1830 the supply of labour in the north-east was more than adequate for the general colliery demand.[5] The price of materials was also falling, and these cost-reducing tendencies in a period of growing markets were sufficient to give a rewarding stability to the coal owners of the Tyne and Wear. Under such conditions the contract system would appear to have lost its primary *raison d'être*. When, with the opening up of the south Durham coalfield, equilibrium was again upset after 1828, the roots of the system had been largely cut away. It was left to a new world to find new remedies for the problems to which the contract system had proved only a partial answer.

[1] Roy. Com. on Mines, 1908, XX, Q.36859. ('It is a dear-loved system they have had, and they stick to it.')
[2] Rep. Sel. Com. (H.C.) on Coal Trade, *BPP*, 1830 (663), VIII, p. 294.
[3] Buddle MSS., XXII, 280.   [4] ibid., XXXVI. Entry dated 17 March 1817.
[5] Minute Books of the Regulation of the Vend, 13 March 1830; Rep. Sel. Com. (H.C.) on Coal Trade, *BPP*, 1830, VIII, p. 315.

IV

It will have become apparent that no simple explanation can be given for the emergence, survival and decline of the contract system; yet certain common forces may be discerned influencing the growth of the system even in coalfields so dissimilar as those of the Black Country and the north-east. In the Black Country the wide diffusion of limited capital resources, the size and nature of the working unit, the shortage and the recalcitrance of labour, and the lack of a managerial class and tradition, all combined to favour the development and continuance of the system; and where, as in Shropshire, south and north Wales and western Scotland, similar technical and economic forces were at work, sub-contracting showed a like persistence. In the north-east comparable conditions may initially have applied. The introduction of sub-contracting at Hartley is a case in point, for here were conjoined the factors of a relatively small labour force, recruited and maintained with difficulty, and of an acknowledged lack of efficient and honest management by the colliery overmen. But other, more specific reasons may be suggested for the reappearance of contracting at the larger collieries towards the end of the eighteenth century. Once again there was a crisis of management, but of a peculiar and transitory kind, brought about by severe competition for markets and men, and the consequent development of conditions of increasing costs. That contracting in these circumstances represented a temporary adoption of a once-tried but perhaps discarded type of organization is suggested by the diversity of forms in which the contract was expressed. Whereas the form of contract between coal owner and butty in the Black Country had by the middle of the nineteenth century been largely standardized,[1] the north-eastern contracts admitted a wide variety of formulation. Such a hypothesis would explain why a relatively highly sophisticated mining economy like that of the north-east at the end of the eighteenth century exhibits forms of organization more usually associated with less mature economic societies; and this would also help to explain the relative freedom of the north-east at this time from those social evils—truck, the exploitation of pauper

---

[1] Mid. Min. Com., pp. 53–55.

labour and the like—which seem to have been the almost inevitable concomitants of the butty system in its Black Country stronghold.

Set against the wider background of the general development of industrial organization in eighteenth-century England, the sub-contract system in the coal industry reflects a common movement in economic society. Contracting in a variety of forms was prevalent almost to the point of ubiquity in eighteenth-century England. For example, in the small metal industries of the Midlands, in the construction and operation of turnpikes, in the building of canals and in the management of workhouses, the contractor was a familiar figure. There are significant differences of form and purpose in these varied examples of contracting practice, but collectively they represent the strivings of an expansionist society seeking to maximize output and minimize cost. The adoption of piece-work practices was an obvious means to these twin ends. Early in the nineteenth century Thomas Hodgskin commented that in recent years 'the plan has become general throughout the country to pay people according to their work instead of according to the hours they are employed'.[1] Piece-rate foremanship or management was the corollary to piece-work labour. But just as piece-work and high standards of workmanship have frequently proved to be mutually incompatible, so the development of the highest qualities of management was inhibited by a system of piece-rate foremanship. Sub-contracting, in short, both from a narrowly economic and from a managerial point of view, was a form of organization peculiar to the adolescence of industrial society and destined to disappear as the British economy grew to maturity. Where the system has persisted, as within the ship-building and constructional industries, it has done so on the basis of advantages of occupational specialization and division of labour rather than of piece-rate management. In the early stages of industrial growth and at times thereafter when cost and price tendencies subjected management to conditions of special strain, the advantages of the system asserted themselves; but in the long run the logic of industrial organization has tended to

[1] Hodgskin to Francis Place, 20 August 1816; quoted by E. Halévy, *Thomas Hodgskin* (Engl. trans. 1956), p. 38.

favour those integrating forces to which sub-contracting is alien both in principle and practice. The rise and decline of sub-contracting in the coal industry conforms to this general pattern, and as such it may be said to exemplify a significant stage in the development of a managerial society.

X

Atlantic Economy, 1815–60: the U.S.A. and the Industrial Revolution in Britain

'England and America are bound up together in peaceful fetters, by the strongest of all the ligatures that can bind two nations to each other,—viz. commercial interests. . . .'(Richard Cobden, English advocate of Free Trade, *England, Ireland and America*, 1835, p. 105.)

'The Iowa farmer can make no exchange with the Mississippi planter, until after the corn and cotton have travelled to Manchester, there to be converted into cloth to be returned to Iowa and Mississippi. . . .' (Henry C. Carey, American advocate of Protection, *Letters to the President of the United States, 1857–8*, Philadelphia, 1858, p. 123.)

THE complementarity of the American and British economies during the first half-century and more of American independence is almost self-evident. It is platitudinous to repeat that political independence did not bring economic independence to the new nation, and that the characteristics of Anglo-American trade in the middle of the nineteenth century were the same as in the colonial period, based on the exchange of primary produce for manufactured goods.

Yet the insistence that the early decades of American nationhood are only understandable when American development is studied in the whole context of an Atlantic community is a comparatively recent feature of American historiography. The view involves an abandonment of certain well-established introspective attitudes towards American history and an admission that for most of the nineteenth century the American frontier was also the European frontier of expansion for both labour and capital.

It has been more instinctive for European historians to view American history in this light and to regard the Atlantic as 'less of a great divide and more of a pond'.[1] Indeed, for too long American history was studied in England merely as an extension of British history and not at all for its own sake and interest. At the present moment, with the recent increase in the attention paid by British historians to the U.S.A., there is perhaps more common ground between historians in the two countries than ever before.[2]

The main interest naturally lies in exploring the implications of this Atlantic community for America herself. The U.S.A. as the underdeveloped economy stood to gain more from the partnership than the mature metropolis. The argument of this essay is, however, that this partnership was mutually beneficial and that consequently there cannot be a full understanding of British developments either, except in the Atlantic context. What did the Atlantic economy of the first half of the nineteenth century mean for Great Britain and, in particular, what was its influence upon the process of industrialization? If the period traditionally demarcated as that of the Industrial Revolution was also, in Mr. Thistlethwaite's words, 'the golden age of Anglo-American commerce', it is perhaps surprising that British economic historians have not paid more attention to this fact. The influences obviously did not operate on one side of the Atlantic only. This essay investigates the importance to Britain of American supplies of primary produce and the significance for British producers of American markets. It is concerned only with the most obvious feature of the partnership, the exchange of goods. The main purpose is to call attention to the dominant importance of the American component in British foreign trade

[1] H. Heaton, 'The American Trade', in *The Trade Winds* (ed. C. Northcote Parkinson, 1948), p. 214.

[2] It is unnecessary to draw attention in detail to the inestimable contributions of D. W. Brogan to the study in Britain of American history. The idea of an Atlantic community in the first half of the nineteenth century has been most fully explored in recent years by F. Thistlethwaite in two articles, 'Atlantic Partnership', *Ec.H.R.*, 2nd ser., vii (1954), 1, and 'Commercial America', *British Essays in American History* (ed. H. C. Allen and C. P. Hill, 1957), and in his book, *The Great Experiment* (1955). This present essay could not have been written without the stimulus and assistance of Mr. Thistlethwaite's pioneer work. At this point I would also like to record my gratitude to my colleague Charlotte Erickson for helpful criticisms and suggestions.

and to suggest that one of the most important fields of research, hitherto largely neglected, in the study of British economic growth in the period of the Industrial Revolution is the significance of the Atlantic economy in that process. The scope of this essay is necessarily limited: it is confined to presenting the basic raw materials with which all research in the field must work, the trade figures themselves, drawn from the official Trade and Navigation Accounts. Clearly, however, these are only the starting-point; the trade must be studied industry by industry and, where possible, firm by firm. Studies of the organization of trade have limited value unless they are seen in perspective, through an understanding of the quantitative significance of the branches of trade in question. Finally, it should be emphasized that there exists in the U.S.A. itself an abundance of documents, both official and private, which have great relevance to our studies of British industrial history.

I

THE ATLANTIC COMMUNITY

For half a century or more after the U.S.A. gained independence and nationhood, her economic fortunes remained heavily dependent on her relations with the economically more advanced parts of the world. The most profitable employment for her available supplies of both capital and labour was in producing raw materials or simple manufactured goods, and in creating means of transport for the conveyance of such goods to outside markets. Seen from America at the end of the eighteenth century, Britain appeared an advanced, industrialized country. She offered an example of a manufacturing economy to be followed or shunned, according to the image in American minds of what constituted a desirable future for the new nation. By and large, the proponents of policies designed to promote industrialization were also admirers of Britain while the opponents of such policies saw Britain as a deplorable, even vicious, urban-industrial society. But one thing was clear: for the time being there was no immediate prospect of America's competing with Britain in 'the manufacturing arts'.

Atlantic Economy, 1815–60

The economic relationship between Britain and the U.S.A. in the half-century which followed the ending of the Napoleonic wars was much closer than that normally achieved between sovereign nations in the usual channels of international trade. What came into existence may in fact be regarded as a single, integrated Atlantic economy in which North America—the area as a whole, not merely the U.S.A.—was the 'colonial' unit producing raw materials which fed the needs, and were exchanged for the manufactures, of the advanced 'metropolitan' unit, north-western Europe and predominantly Great Britain.

This unique relationship did not arise simply from predestination. It could scarcely have been foreseen in the middle 1780s when passions were still inflamed and when, as John Adams wrote to Jay from London in the late summer of 1785, British manufacturers seeing that 'the demand for their merchandises from all parts of Europe is greater than ever' were disposed to 'think little of American commerce'.[1] To Americans themselves, the renewal of commercial relations with the former oppressor could only be looked upon with mixed feelings. Political attitudes remained, to say the least, equivocal. The revival of trade in the late 1780s and the 1790s was set back by the troubles of the 1800s which culminated in the war of 1812, delaying still further the healing of the wounds. Nevertheless the extent of the revival and the effects of the new breach were indicated by Baring in the House of Commons in 1812:

It might be well to direct the notice of members to the proportion of trade these manufacturing places carried on with the United States, compared with the amount of their whole business. In Birmingham, it was supposed to be one-third or one-half; in Wolverhampton, one-half; in Sheffield, one-third; in the potteries, one-fourth in value; and one-third in bulk; in Leeds, one-half, or one-third; in Dewsbury, one-half; in Rochdale, two-fifths; in Bury, one-half; in Manchester, one-third or one-fourth; in Leicester, one-third; in Hinckley, two-thirds; and from the salt works of Cheshire, 50,000 tons were annually exported. In all these places the demand stated had ceased; the consequence was, that those who formerly were engaged in the foreign trade, were thrown upon the home

---

[1] Letters of John Adams to John Jay, quoted in G. S. Callender, *Selections from the Economic History of the United States, 1765–1860* (Boston, 1909), p. 215.

market. . . . The stock on hand was stated to be of an immense amount, having been gradually augmented by the unwillingness of the masters to turn off their men, and . . . it was apparent, that many workmen were still kept on from charity, to manufacture articles for which there was no sale. . . .[1]

Despite the continuance of political differences, many factors combined after 1815 to encourage an intimacy between the U.S.A. and Britain without parallel between two sovereign states.[2] More than any other single factor, the unifying agent, unforeseen in the 1780s, was America's ability to produce, and to produce in ever expanding quantities, the raw material, cotton, required by Britain's leading industry. The North Atlantic cotton trade of the nineteenth century was of fundamentally different significance from the tobacco trade of the eighteenth century. The tobacco import and re-export trades had certainly been profitable undertakings, but their direct effects were limited to a narrow sector of the British economy. By contrast the expansion of the cotton industry depended absolutely upon imports of raw cotton. At the same time American markets were widened for British manufactured goods of all sorts. For four decades before the American Civil War cotton was king not merely of the American South but also of the Atlantic economy. By the end of the 1820s, South Carolina and Georgia had become practically the only source of Lancashire's raw material; at about the same time, raw cotton became America's leading export. For almost forty years, British cotton manufacturers depended upon the U.S.A. for well over three-quarters of their raw cotton supplies. For most of the period after 1820, raw cotton accounted for considerably over half the value of all American exports; by 1860 its value represented two-thirds of

[1] Debate on Brougham's motion for the repeal of the Orders in Council, 16 June 1812. (Parliamentary Debates, 1st ser., vol. xxiii, col. 532.)

[2] A curious commentary on the relationship is afforded by the manufacture in Staffordshire, for export to the U.S.A., of plate, etc., bearing emblems to commemorate the great American generals and victories of the Revolutionary War. Cobden, with his sharp nose for anti-American sentiments, commented: 'If [some Englishmen] be told that the people of the United States constitute our largest and most valuable commercial connection, that the business we carry on with them is nearly twice as extensive as with any other people, . . . they will express surprise; but then they will predict that no good will arise ultimately from trading with Yankee republicans. . . .' (R. Cobden, *England, Ireland and America*, 1835, p. 102.)

total American exports, a figure which indicates a far greater dependence upon a single export commodity than has existed at any other time in American history. The application of the power loom in British cotton factories depended upon the application of the cotton gin on American cotton plantations, and British imports of American raw cotton provide an index of the development of British cotton manufacturing.

The importance of Britain to American merchants, producers and consumers was obvious to contemporaries, but it would not be relevant to this essay to list examples of the extent to which American economic life depended upon exports to and imports from Britain. Professor N. S. Buck in 1925 presented the main trade statistics in his book *The Development of the Organization of Anglo-American Trade, 1800–1850*, showing that in the years examined the United Kingdom was the supplier of around 40 per cent by value of American imports and the market for between one-third and one-half by value of American exports.

Seen from the British side the percentage figures for the American share of British trade are less spectacular. Clapham, one of the few historians who has shown awareness of the importance of the Atlantic trade, estimated the American share of U.K. exports as having varied between one-sixth and one-quarter,[1] but made no estimate of the proportion of imports which came from the U.S.A. The aggregate figures are, however, much less significant than the strategic nature of the goods and the particularly close relations with the U.S.A. of whole branches of industry. Nevertheless even in aggregate terms, in almost every year the U.S.A. provided Britain with a greater value of imports than any other single country and similarly took a greater value of exports than any other single country.[2]

[1] J. H. Clapham, *An Economic History of Modern Britain, I, The Early Railway Age, 1820–1850* (1926), p. 483.

[2] Such a statement begs the question of course whether political units have great economic significance. Porter's tables, for example, set Britain's trade with the U.S.A. alongside her trade with northern and southern Europe, with the result that the American figures are generally inferior (G. R. Porter, *The Progress of the Nation*, 1851 edn., pp. 359–60). But if size of population is considered in relation to trade, imports from and exports to the U.K. per head of population in the U.S.A. and British North America make even more emphatic the predominating role of North America in British trade; there is nothing to compare with it until the rapid growth of the Australian trade in the 1850s.

It is not self-evident what geographical divisions—if not political units—are appropriate for comparisons of this sort. It is strongly arguable, for instance, that it would be economically more meaningful to consider the trade with North America as a whole, not merely the U.S.A. The trade of the U.K. with the British West Indies and the North American colonies was sustained at a remarkably high level in both directions, sometimes equalling that with the U.S.A.[1] The total figures for British trade with the whole of North America, including the West Indies and the Canadian provinces, set beyond any doubt the strategic economic significance of that sub-continent. Total figures of British exports to North America are given in Table VIII, but to examine fully the entire North Atlantic trade would be a much larger project than that which has been undertaken for this article.

II

BRITISH IMPORTS FROM THE U.S.A.

The problems of constructing British foreign trade statistics comparable over time are considerable. Wherever possible, quantity figures will be used in this survey, though even these may imply unwarrantable assumptions about the homogeneity of the goods concerned.

The first compilation of total import figures based on current values was made in 1854. For earlier dates attempts at aggregation must rest upon the official values found in the Returns, computed according to more or less fixed scales of value for separate commodities. These ignore current market prices and therefore do not reflect the marked fall in prices, especially of manufactures, but they do provide some index of the volume of imports.[2] For the years 1854–6, the Returns show both

---

[1] In addition, national trade figures do not disclose illicit trade. There is no doubt that American tariffs encouraged the smuggling of British goods into the U.S.A. from the Canadian provinces. See, for example, the Cambreleng *Report on the Commerce and Navigation of the U.S.*, 8 February 1830. (U.S. 21st Congress, 1st Session, Rep. No. 165), p. 26.

[2] The methodological problems are discussed in detail by W. Schlote in *British Overseas Trade from 1700 to the 1930s* (Eng. trans. 1952, by W. O. Henderson and W. H. Chaloner), pp. 3–40.

'official' and 'computed real' values; Schlote's figures show that official values in 1854 slightly overestimate the North American share of the British import trade when compared with actual values and underestimate the European share.[1]

TABLE I. Official Value of Imports of Merchandise into the U.K. Annual average in each 5-year period.[1] £ million

	Total	From U.S.A.	Imports from U.S.A. as % of total
1816–20	31·7	3·3	*11*
1821–25	35·8	4·8	*14*
1826–30	43·6	6·7	*15*
1831–35	47·7	9·4	*19*
1836–40	60·5	13·5	*20*
1841–45	72·1	18·2	*25*
1846–50	85·2	21·7	*25*
1851–55	116·9	27·5	*24*
1856	131·9	32·7	*22*

[1] In all tables, figures are given to the nearest whole number or first decimal; percentages have been calculated from the original, not the rounded, figures.

Most figures in the tables presented in this article are given as annual averages over five-year periods. Such averages of course obscure cyclical fluctuations of trade. The complete tables have been deposited in the Library of the London School of Economics. The tables have been compiled almost entirely from British Parliamentary Papers, and a list of the volumes consulted is appended to the complete tables. Sparing use has also been made, for occasional information, of J. Macgregor, *Commercial Statistics* (1847), J. R. McCulloch, *Dictionary of Commerce* (1849), G. R. Porter, *The Progress of the Nation* (1851), W. F. Reuss, *Calculations and Statements relative to the Trade between Great Britain and the United States of America* (1833), and Timothy Pitkin, *A Statistical View of the Commerce of the United States of America* (1835).

Table I gives the official value of total imports and of imports from the U.S.A. in the years for which these figures are available.

[1] ibid., p. 35. The detailed figures for the three years for which both 'official' and 'computed real' values are available are as follows (£ million):

	Official			Computed real		
	Total	U.S.A.	%	Total	U.S.A.	%
1854	124·1	30·1	24	152·4	29·8	*19*
1855	117·3	27·0	24	143·5	25·7	*18*
1856	131·9	32·7	22	172·5	36·0	*21*

The official values for 1855–6, not noted by Schlote, appear in *BPP*, 1857, Sess. 2 2286), 427.

Thus, by the 1830s, the U.S.A. was providing one-fifth, by official valuation, of all imports into the U.K. This proportion increased to one-quarter during the 1840s, returning to one-fifth after 1850 and remaining at about that level, however calculated, until the American Civil War. Imports from the U.S.A. between 1815 and 1830 increased much more rapidly than total imports and after 1830 kept pace with the general increase.[1]

A clearer picture is to be obtained for the years after 1854 for which 'computed real' values are available. The aggregate imports from the main supplying countries for the eight years 1854–61 were:

Computed real value of imports from	£ mill.	Computed real value of imports from	£ mill.
U.S.A.	287·3	Holland	56·7
British East Indies	126·7	Prussia	53·2
France	107·7	British North America	50·9
Russia[1]	83·7	British West Indies	47·5
China (incl. Hong Kong)	73·0		

[1] The loss of trade occasioned by the Crimean War may be estimated at about £16 million.

Thus in the middle and late 1850s, when the American share of total British imports appears to have declined somewhat by comparison with the 1840s, the computed value of imports from the U.S.A. was nevertheless considerably more than twice as great as that of imports from the second supplier; the computed value of all imports from all other countries except three was *less than one-quarter* of that of imports from the U.S.A.

The next task is to analyse the constituents in the import trade from the U.S.A. Table II summarizes the relative importance of the main components in the same eight years, 1854–61.

It has been necessary to use value figures to this point in order to establish approximate relative magnitudes. In the remaining

[1] Total imports during this period, and therefore imports from the U.S.A., expanded more rapidly than the British population. As estimated by official value, total imports per head of population for the U.K. as a whole expanded as follows: 1821, £1. 10s; 1831, £2; 1841, £2. 8s; 1851, £3. 4s.

TABLE II. The main categories of imports
into the U.K. from the U.S.A., 1854–61

Percentage of total imports. (Computed real values)

	1854	*1855*	*1856*	*1857*	*1858*	*1859*	*1860*	*1861*
Raw cotton	59	64	60	61	72	82	67	54
Corn, etc.	21	13	25	12	10	1	15	25
Provisions	6	6	5	6	3	3	4	5
Tobacco	3	4	4	3	5	4	3	3
Other items	11	13	6	18	10	10	11	13
Total	100	100	100	100	100	100	100	100

part of this examination of the import trade, in which the main
categories will be considered separately, it is possible to use
quantity figures.

RAW COTTON

To this, the most important item in the trade, least attention will
be paid, as the role of raw cotton in the Atlantic economy has
already been stressed in the introductory remarks. Table II
shows the relative importance of raw cotton in British total
imports from America. The relative importance of the American
supply in total British imports of raw cotton is greater still, as is
seen from Table III.[1]

Cotton dominates the whole trade for the whole period. It was
the most valuable item which the U.S.A. could supply to
Britain; re-exports were negligible and British cotton manufacturers relied almost exclusively upon the U.S.A. for the supplies
which kept their factories working.

CORN

Table II shows that in some years of the 1850s corn accounted
for as much as one-quarter of the computed real value of all
imports from America. British trade returns do not permit the

[1] Lancashire merchants and manufacturers did not regard this dependence on
the U.S.A. for their supplies of raw cotton as healthy and strove hard to find
alternative sources. See A. Redford, *Manchester Merchants and Foreign Trade, 1794–
1858* (1934), pp. 217 ff.

compilation of a complete and comparable time-series for imports of grains and flour from the U.S.A. before 1830.[1] It is clear,
nevertheless, that considerable quantities were coming in from
the very beginning of the century. In 1801, 1807 and 1817 well
over a quarter of a million quarters of grain were imported from
the U.S.A. The annual average importation of grain from
America for the period 1801–25 was 81,000 quarters, in which
wheat amounted to 74,000 quarters. Although total grain
imports from the U.S.A. were surpassed by those from Russia,
Prussia, Germany, the Netherlands (and, in considering Great
Britain, from Ireland), wheat imports from the U.S.A. were
surpassed only by those from Prussia (157,000 quarters) and
Ireland (187,000 quarters). Wheat and particularly wheat flour
were from the start the main commodities in the Atlantic grain
trade; in 1829–31 about six-sevenths of all wheat flour imported
into the U.K. came from the U.S.A. Similarly, as Table IV
shows, in the early 1830s Britain was the chief market for
American wheat flour.

   Grain imports fell off in the 1830s and flour imports varied
enormously from year to year. In 1831 seventy-five thousand
tons of wheat meal and flour entered the U.K. from America,
90 per cent of the total import. In the six years 1833–8, however,
wheat flour imports from the U.S.A. fell off much more than
those from other countries, amounting to a mere five thousand
tons out of seventy-five thousand tons. The position changed
again in 1839 and 1840 when the U.S.A. supplied 51 per cent
and 64 per cent respectively of British flour imports.

   It was in the middle 1840s, however, that Britain's grain
imports from the U.S.A. began to assume such proportions that
one can speak of a shift in the pattern of trade. The early 1840s
saw a quite unprecedented increase in the productivity of
American agriculture, the total output of wheat, barley, rye,
oats and maize increasing by about 40 per cent between 1840
and 1847; the years 1843–7 brought greater harvests than
ever before known in the United States.[2] Table V shows quite

---

[1] The opening years of the century are treated in detail in W. F. Galpin, *The Grain Supply of England during the Napoleonic Period* (New York, 1925).
[2] See, e.g., H. C. Carey, *The Working of British Free Trade* (New York, 1852), pp. 16–17, 29–30.

TABLE III. Imports of Raw Cotton into the U.K., 1815–61

Average annual quantity in each 5-year period

	1815	1816–20	1821–5	1826–30	1831–5	1836–40	1841–5	1846–50	1851–5	1856–60	1861
Total imports mill. lb.	100	141	169	229	314	461	612	615	872	1,129	1,257
From U.S.A. mill. lb.	54	66	114	174	246	368	485	499	683	869	820
U.S. supply as % of total	54	48	68	76	78	78	79	81	77	76	65

TABLE IV. Exports of Grain and Flour from the U.S.A., 1821–31

Annual average	Wheat (thousand bushels)	Wheat flour (thousand barrels)	Indian corn (thousand bushels)	Rye flour (thousand barrels)	Corn meal (thousand barrels)	Destination of wheat flour (thousand barrels)				
						U.K.	West Indies	South America	British North America	France
1821–4	14	909	661	25	144	45	463	231	72	—
1825–8	24	850	765	22	163	30	401	279	75	1
1829	4	837	898	34	174	221	248	236	91	17
1830	45	1,226	444	26	145	326	281	347	150	57
1831	405	1,805	567	19	204	879	372	320	151	24

TABLE V. Imports of Grain and Flour into the U.K., 1840–61[1]

Note. This table has been arranged so as to throw into relief the various constituent items and groups of items. In consequence, sections (1) and (2) are partly self-contained, partly overlapping; they cannot therefore be added horizontally in order to reach the summary totals in section (3).

| | (1) GRAIN | | | | | | (2) WHEAT | | | | | | (3) GRAIN AND FLOUR | | | | | | |
| | Wheat (mill. Q.) | | | Total all kinds (mill. Q.) | | | Flour (mill. Q.) | | | Grain and Flour (mill. Q.) | | | Total all kinds (mill. Q.) | | | | | | |
	TOTAL	FROM U.S.A.	FROM PRUSSIA	TOTAL	FROM U.S.A.	FROM RUSSIA	TOTAL	FROM U.S.A.	FROM BRIT. NORTH AMERICA	TOTAL	FROM U.S.A.	FROM RUSSIA	TOTAL	FROM U.S.A.	FROM RUSSIA	FROM PRUSSIA	FROM FRANCE	FROM BRIT. NORTH AMERICA	FROM DENMARK AND THE DUCHIES
1840	2·0	0·07		3·5	0·1		1·5	1·0	0·5	2·5	0·4		3·9	0·4	0·4	1·2			0·4
1841	2·4	0·01		3·3	0·01		1·3	0·4	0·6				3·6	0·1	0·1	1·1			0·4
1842	2·7	0·02		3·4	0·03		1·2	0·4	0·5				3·7	0·1	0·4	0·9			0·2
1843	0·9			1·3			0·4	0·1	0·3				1·4		0·1	0·7			0·2
1844	1·1	0·02		2·7	0·02		1·0	0·3	0·3				3·0	0·1	0·2	0·7			0·7
1845	0·9			2·2	0·03		0·9	0·2	0·7				2·4	0·1	0·2	0·5			0·7
1846	1·4	0·2		3·8	0·4		3·2	2·2	0·9	4·5	1·8	0·8	4·8	1·1	0·5	0·5			0·4
1847	2·7	0·4	0·5	9·4	2·5	2·0	6·3	4·9	1·0	3·1	0·3	0·5	11·9	4·3	2·2	0·7	0·3	0·5	0·6
1848	2·6	0·1	0·5	6·9	1·0	0·7	1·8	0·8	0·6	4·8	0·3	0·5	7·5	1·3	0·7	0·8	0·5	0·2	0·7
1849	3·8	0·1	0·6	9·7	1·3	0·9	3·3	1·8	0·5	5·3	0·5	0·6	10·7	1·8	0·9	1·4	1·0	0·2	1·0
1850	3·7	0·1	0·8	7·9	0·6	0·9	3·8	1·5	0·3	4·2	0·9	0·7	9·0	1·1	0·9	1·3	1·3	0·1	1·3
1851	3·8	0·2	0·7	8·1	0·5	1·3	5·3	2·5	0·4	6·2	1·2	0·7	9·6	1·2	1·3	0·9	1·6	0·1	1·1
1852	3·1	0·5	0·5	6·6	0·7	1·3	3·9	2·6	0·3	3·2	1·6	1·1	7·7	1·4	1·3	0·6	0·7	0·1	0·8
1853	4·9	0·7	1·1	8·8	0·9	1·7	4·6	3·0	0·3	4·5	1·2	0·5	10·2	1·8	1·7	1·2	0·7	0·2	0·8
1854	3·4	0·4	0·7	6·9	1·4	0·7	3·6	2·6	0·1	5·2	0·4	0·7	7·9	2·1	0·7	0·7	0·2	0·1	0·9
1855	2·7	0·2	0·5	5·7	0·9		1·9	0·7	0·01	4·0	1·1	0·7	6·3	1·1		0·6	0·1	0·03	0·9
1856	4·1	1·2	0·2	8·2	2·3	1·2	4·0	2·9	0·3	5·3	1·1	0·6	9·3	3·1	1·2	0·4	0·2	0·3	1·0
1857	3·4	0·4	0·9	8·6	1·1	2·0	2·2	1·5	0·2	5·0	0·1	0·7	9·2	1·5	2·0	1·7	1·7	0·2	0·6
1858	4·2	0·6	0·6	10·2	1·0	2·2	3·9	1·8	0·2	7·3	2·1	1·3	11·3	1·5	2·3	1·0	2·2	0·2	1·0
1859	4·0	0·04	0·8	9·3	0·05	2·4	3·3	0·2	0·1	8·9		1·0	10·3	0·1	2·4	1·0	1·4	0·1	0·6
1860	5·9	1·5	1·1	13·0	2·0	2·8	5·1	2·3	0·4				14·5	2·6	2·8	1·8	0·4	0·5	1·0
1861	6·9	2·5	1·0	14·3	4·3	1·9	6·2	3·8	0·8		3·6		16·1	*5·4*	1·9	1·5		1·2	0·8

[1] Leading supply italicised.

unmistakably America's ability to take immediate advantage of the repeal of the Corn Laws. In 1846 the U.S.A. became for the first time the main provider of British imports of all grains and flour. In the 1·1 million quarters imported, wheat and wheat flour were the principal items. Over 100 American ships, including 64 from New York, 18 from New Orleans and 13 from Baltimore (against 3 British ships, one from New York and 2 from Boston), were mustered into service[1] and the trade expanded even more markedly in 1847.

It will be seen from Table V that in the sixteen years between 1846 and 1861 the U.S.A. was the main supplier of wheat flour in every year except 1859, the main supplier of wheat grain in four years, the main supplier of all grains (the American total being made up largely of wheat and maize) in seven years, and in no fewer than ten years the main supplier of grains and flour in total. The Crimean War of course greatly strengthened the American position in the British market; although total grain and flour imports sagged in the middle 1850s, the quantity imported from the U.S.A. increased greatly. America lost her position of primacy for four years thereafter with the return of Russia into the market on an unprecedented scale but, as many writers have pointed out, the sudden and massive increase in British grain imports from the U.S.A. (as well as from the North American colonies) in 1860 and 1861, on the eve of the Civil War, was a clear portent of things to come.[2]

[1] *BPP*, 1847 (183), LX. The exports in 1846 from the main American ports were:

	Wheat	Wheat flour	Oats	Indian corn
	000 qrs.	*000 cwt.*	*000 qrs.*	*000 qrs.*
New York	11·5	177·2	5·5	2·8
New Orleans	2·5	58·6		1·0
Baltimore		106·4		2·0

The fact that there was a very considerable drop in cotton shipments in 1846 and 1847 suggests very strongly that some of the normal cotton tonnage was diverted to grain in those years; the American cotton crop was short in 1846 (after a series of good years since 1842), but excellent in 1847. W. L. Thorp, *Business Annals* (New York, 1926), pp. 123–4.

[2] But in saying this one does not automatically accept the simplified view that the American Civil War resulted from a race between corn and cotton in which corn won.

PROVISIONS

From the early 1840s imports from the U.S.A. of foodstuffs other than grain began to achieve growing importance. In the years for which computed real values are available, 1854–61, the aggregate import into the U.K. of bacon, salted and fresh pork, lard, and salted and fresh beef was valued at just over £25 million, the U.S.A. accounting for almost £14 million. In those eight years, 55 per cent of all imports of the foodstuffs named came from the U.S.A.

Some details of imported provisions are given in Table VI. Although the figures are not quite complete, the picture is clear enough. In terms of computed real values after 1854, bacon was the most important item coming from the U.S.A., followed by lard, beef, pork, cheese and hams, generally in that order. It will be seen in particular that imports into the U.K. of bacon and ham increased from virtually nothing in the early 1840s to an average of about 250,000 cwt. per year in the late 1850s and that the U.S.A. made by far the greatest contribution to this increase. The increase in beef and pork imports was almost equally spectacular, the U.S.A., supplying salted meat only, again playing a very large part, especially as far as beef was concerned. Lard, however, was the commodity in which the American share of total imports was the greatest.

The rapid increase in the importation of most foodstuffs in the 1840s reflects the reduction and eventual repeal of British tariffs during that decade as well as the tremendous expansion of American production. The tariffs on bacon, beef, hams, lard, pork and cheese were all reduced in 1842, being transformed at the same time from a uniform to a discriminatory tariff, giving a preference to produce from British possessions. In 1846 the tariffs on bacon, beef and pork were repealed, the duty on cheese being reduced from 11s 0·3d (foreign) and 2s 7½d (British) per cwt. to 5s and 1s 6d respectively. After 1852, cheese was the only item examined here which still bore any duty; the preference was lowered in 1852 when the foreign duty was reduced to 2s 6d.[1] There can be no doubt that without these

[1] The details of these tariff changes are to be found in BPP, 1845 (599), XLVI; 1846 (417), XLIV; 1852–3 (504), XCIX.

TABLE VI. U.K. Imports of various Foodstuffs, 1840–61
Annual average quantity in each 5-year period, thousand cwt.

	1841–5	*1846–50*	*1851–5*	*1856–60*	*1861*
BACON					
Total import	0·3	205	218	255	477
Import from U.S.A.		(–)[1]	162	187	368
U.S. supply as % of total		*86*[2]	*74*	*73*	*77*
HAMS					
Total import	0·2	11	11	19	39
Import from U.S.A.			3	11	28
U.S. supply as % of total			*27*	*58*	*72*
LARD					
Total import	45	193	139	167	325
Import from U.S.A.	44	127[3]	124	117	276
U.S. supply as % of total	*98*	*77*[4]	*90*	*70*	*85*
PORK					
Total import (salted and fresh)	39	224	154	134	136
Import from U.S.A. (salted)	13	176[3]	62	54	45
U.S. supply as % of total	*33*	*55*[4]	*40*	*43*	*33*
BEEF					
Total import (salted and fresh)	65	137	170	198	153
Import from U.S.A. (salted)	42	128[3]	139	158	125
U.S. supply as % of total	*65*	*89*[4]	*82*	*79*	*82*
CHEESE					
Total import	222	371	360	431	706
Import from U.S.A.	37	108	54	84	323
U.S. supply as % of total	*16*	*29*	*15*	*20*	*46*

[1] Average of 308 cwt. for 1849–50 when total imports averaged 360 cwt.
[2] Percentage in 1849–50.
[3] Average for 4 years. No figures available for 1848.
[4] Percentage excluding 1848.

tariff reforms, the vast expansion of food imports into the U.K. in the late 1840s and in the 1850s would not have occurred. Indeed it is arguable from a comparison of the quantity figures shown in Tables V and VI that the increase after 1846 in imports of the items considered in this section was greater and more significant than the increase in grain imports. Re-exports of these items were insignificant throughout.

TOBACCO

The tobacco trade has no central significance for this essay. Table II suggests that, at any rate at the end of the period under review, the value of tobacco imports was less than 5 per cent of total imports from the U.S.A. Table VII summarizes the quantities imported.

TABLE VII. Imports of Tobacco into the U.K., 1816–61

Annual average quantity in each 5-year period. Million lb.

	Total imports of tobacco, manufactured and unmanufactured	Imports from U.S.A.	U.S. supply as percentage of total
1816–20	31·8		
1821–25	30·7		
1826–30	26·5[1]	25·7[1]	97
1831–35	30·5	27·4	90
1836–40	37·4	35·8	96
1841–45	40·1	38·8	94
1846–50	41·3	37·1	90
1851–55	37·8	29·6	78
1856–60	50·9	37·1	73
1861	52·8	35·1	66

[1] 1826 figures missing.

OTHER ITEMS

In addition to the major items of importation, Britain also obtained from the U.S.A. a very large range of items of much smaller value. With some of the items, the importance lay not so much in their absolute value as in the fact that the U.S.A. was the only, or the leading, supplier. America supplied, for instance, almost the whole of Britain's imports of turpentine and oil of turpentine and of resin; she was the leading supplier of spermaceti oil and, in growing amounts in the 1850s, of seed cake oil. In addition, the annual official valuation of the imports of a number of other commodities generally exceeded £100,000: tallow, staves, wood not sawn or split, logwood; and occasionally manufactures of caoutchouc, copper unwrought or part wrought, guano and hops. To make a complete inventory of all items imported from the U.S.A. would involve listing a great many other commodities, but for the most part the value imported was negligible. But among the list one might in conclusion note the old colonial staples, pot and pearl ashes, indigo, hides, skins and furs, and rice, together with a motley assortment of goods including chromate of iron, manganese ore, beeswax, flax— and rhubarb.

III

Exports to the U.S.A. of British and Irish Produce and Manufactures

This section must begin with a brief outline of American tariff history during the period under review. Unfortunately, there is no wholly satisfactory account of this subject. Most writers draw upon F. W. Taussig's well-known book, *The Tariff History of the United States*, first published in 1892 and subsequently republished several times in revised editions. This work certainly gives a clear summary of American tariff legislation, but when one wishes to look at the incidence of American tariffs in any detail, the information is not always to be found. Average rates for groups of commodities are not very useful when one wishes to examine the trade in specific items. What concerns us here is the effect of American tariffs, and of changes in tariffs, on exports to America of different British products.

The main Tariff Acts which have to be considered are those of 1816, 1824, 1828, 1832–3, 1842, 1846 and 1857. The mere fact that they are so numerous had effects upon trade.[1] The first of these tariffs, however, established the framework of the American tariff system for the whole period down to the Civil War. It imposed *ad valorem* duties of between 20 and 25 per cent on most manufactured goods, and 15 to 20 per cent on raw materials. The level of 20–25 per cent on manufactures represented a tax that did not at that time prevent the entry of many commodities or even bring about an equalization of foreign and domestic prices. Moreover, the tax on imported raw materials—especially raw wool—placed a serious obstacle in the way of the expansion of certain domestic industries.

The main effect of the Tariff Act of 1824 was to raise all import duties to a level at which some of them began to be protective, though at the same time certain duties on raw materials were increased; we may remind ourselves that in the same year Huskisson reduced the British tariff on certain imported raw materials. The Tariff of Abominations of 1828—never intended to be passed, as Taussig relates—raised all duties on both manufactures and raw materials.[2] By this time, the tariff question had become a major political issue in the U.S.A., and one over which there was a broad difference of opinion between North and South.[3] The matter was settled for the time being by

[1] Great anxiety was caused to British merchants and manufacturers by each change, or rumour of change, in the American tariff. See, for example, *BPP*, 1828 (578), XIX, pp. 1–247, 'American Tariffs', and various evidence before the Select Committee on Manufactures, Commerce and Shipping, *BPP*, 1833 (690), VI.

[2] Cf. Cambreleng *Report* (1830), pp. 8 ff., '. . . the provisions of our tariff are so singularly and ingeniously contrived, that the only result of our taxation must be to perpetuate the ascendancy, even in our own markets, of the manufactures of Great Britain. . . . While England cheapens the cost of her manufactures by admitting wool, hemp, flax, iron, lead, copper, dyestuffs etc. etc. etc. at the least possible duties, and while we raise our imports on raw materials to rates which almost forbid their importation . . . it is manifestly impossible that American should ever be as cheap as British. It is idle to suppose that, because we have levied duties on some manufactures as high as 75, 100 and 200 per cent, that we have therefore protected them. . . .'

[3] See C. W. Harris, *The Sectional Struggle: Early Tariffs and Nullification* (Philadelphia, 1902); G. R. Taylor (ed.), *The Great Tariff Debate, 1820–1830* (*Problems in American Civilization*, Amherst College Selected Readings, Boston, 1953). A great deal of contemporary polemical literature reached a climax, or anti-climax, in the retrospectively amusing document *Collectanea* (Philadelphia, 1833), by the aged Matthew Carey, occasioned by the attempt by South Carolina to nullify the tariff proposals of 1832. The sectional division was, however, not yet complete if already clearly defined. The interests of northern manufacturers did not coincide at this

the so-called Compromise Tariff of 1833 which stipulated a graduated decrease of all tariffs to a general level of 20 per cent by 1842. This level was reached by the intended date but was only maintained for two months before a new Tariff Act was passed, again restoring the level to one which might be considered generally protective. This Act did not have the popular support of the earlier acts and was passed after two vetoes by President Tyler. Four years later, in 1846, the Walker Tariff was introduced, again lowering the general level. Four schedules were drawn up, A, B, C and D, taxed *ad valorem* at 100, 40, 30 and 25 per cent respectively. Schedule C was the main category, including iron and other metals, metal manufactures, wool and woollens, and manufactures of leather, paper, glass and wood. Cotton manufactures were in Schedule D. By 1857 the justification for tariffs on grounds of the need for revenue was weaker than it had ever been and the rates were reduced, that of the main category, C, to 24 per cent. At this level tariffs remained until the Civil War.

It will be necessary, as the separate trades are examined, to look at these different tariffs in greater detail. Many problems of interpretation are involved which cannot be discussed at any length in this essay: these concern the complicated interactions between cyclical fluctuations and tariffs, and, more broadly still, between economics and politics in the U.S.A. Were tariff changes caused by, or did they cause, changes in the economic climate between good and bad years? Were the development of American political parties and the complexion of governments determined by, or largely irrelevant to, the immediate economic situation?[1]

. . .

time with the interests of northern merchants who stood to gain from low tariffs, and the northern shipping interest was still strong.

[1] The problems are particularly complex in the 1840s. The brief interlude of Whig rule, brought about by the election of Harrison to the Presidency in 1840, ended with Harrison's death in 1841; John Tyler, the first Vice-President to take over the Presidency, was a Virginia Democrat but at first retained the Whig cabinet. The election of Polk in 1846 confirmed the ascendancy of the Democrats and the alignment of parties along lines determined largely by the slavery issue.

The year 1842 saw the lowest point in the post-1837 depression, the serious threat of a third war with Great Britain, the beginnings of economic recovery in the spring and the passage in August of the Tariff Act. Crops had been generally good (except cotton in 1841) since 1839, and continued so in the middle 1840s. From the end of 1842 or early in 1843 moderate or rapid recovery is recorded in almost every

Table VIII shows the main destinations of exports from the United Kingdom. The valuation of exports is based on current prices.

These calculations set in perspective the main markets for British exports.[1] With remarkable regularity the continents of Europe and of America took about equal shares of this trade. While the U.S.A. was throughout the largest single national market, her share of British exports approximated closely to the share going to southern Europe, but exceeded that of northern Europe in only four years, 1815, 1831, 1835 and 1836. That it did so at all underlines the main argument of this article. The apparent decline of the American share in the decade 1836–45 results mainly from the aftermath of the 1837 crisis in the U.S.A., total exports to America being particularly low in 1837, 1840 and 1842.

Total exports of British products to the main markets of the world in the same eight years, 1854–61, for which import figures were given on p. 244 were as follows:

Declared real value of exports to	£ mill.	Declared real value of exports to	£ mill.
U.S.A.	147·5	France	45·6
East India Company's		Holland	44·7
Territories	111·3	Brazil	32·5
Australia	81·8	British North America	31·5
The Hanse Towns	73·3	Turkey	31·0

American leadership in the export field in these years is perhaps not so marked as with imports, as three territories took

statistical series (see W. B. Smith and A. H. Cole, *Fluctuations in American Business, 1790–1860* (Cambridge, Mass., 1935), pp. 37 ff., and Thorp, op. cit., p. 124); 'so magical a resuscitation', wrote H. C. Carey (*The Working of British Free Trade*, p. 37), 'the world had never seen'. The prosperity continued, despite a mild recession in 1847–8 before the tariff reductions, until 1854–5.

The Whigs came back into power, though only for four years, in 1848, with the election of Taylor on a free-soil, anti-slavery programme; Taylor also died in office and was succeeded by Fillmore in 1850.

The chronicle offers almost endless possibilities for interpreting causal connexions according to initial predispositions.

[1] It is recognized that the data presented here give no indication of the ratio of exports to total production. Some rough assessments are to be found in W. G. Hoffmann, *British Industry, 1700–1950* (Eng. trans. 1955, by W. O. Henderson and W. H. Chaloner), pp. 82–89.

S

TABLE VIII. Exports from the U.K. of British and Irish produce and manufactures

Annual average declared value in each 5-year period. £ million

(Parentheses indicate that the figures are the average for *less* than 5 years, due to gaps in the statistics)

Destination	1805–9	1816–20	1821–5	1826–30	1831–5	1836–40	1841–5	1846–50	1851–5	1856–60
U.S.A.	9·5	7·0	6·3	5·7	7·9	7·8	6·1	10·9	18·7	19·9
British North America				(1·7)	2·0	2·5	2·7	2·8	4·1	3·8
British West Indies				(3·3)	2·7	3·7	2·6	2·1	1·5	1·7
Germany				(4·5)	4·6	5·0	6·1	5·8	7·3	9·7
Holland (with Belgium to 1832)				(2·1)	2·4	2·8	3·5	3·3	4·2	5·8
France				(0·5)	0·9	2·0	2·8	2·1	3·3	5·5
Russia (north and south ports)				(1·4)	1·5	1·8	1·9	1·7		
East India Company's Territories (with China to 1834)				(4·0)	3·2	4·5	6·3	6·2	7·8	15·2
China (after 1834)						0·9	1·6	1·5		
Turkey					1·0	1·4	1·8	2·5	3·1	4·0
Brazil				(2·7)	2·0	2·5	2·3	2·4	3·3	4·3
Australia				(0·3)	0·6	1·3	1·1	1·8	7·9	10·6
TOTAL EXPORTS	40·2	40·3	37·3	35·9	40·4	50·0	54·0	60·8	88·8	124·1
U.S.A. as % of total	*23*	*17*	*17*	*16*	*19*	*16*	*11*	*18*	*21*	*16*
North America as % of total		*35*	*34*	*32*	*34*	*30*	*24*	*24*	*25*	*26*
Central and South America as % of total		*7*	*12*	*13*	*11*	*11*	*10*			
North Europe as % of total		*27*	*22*	*23*	*23*	*23*	*26*			
South Europe as % of total		*18*	*22*	*17*	*17*	*18*	*19*			

exports at a total declared value which was more than one-half the American figure; nevertheless, apart from these three, the declared value of exports to all other countries was *less than one-third* of that of exports to the U.S.A.

The significance of American markets for British industries cannot be judged, however, from these aggregate figures alone, indicative though they are of America's importance. The U.S.A. never took more than a fraction of Britain's main export, cotton textiles, but for many other commodities the American market was completely dominant. The point is illustrated by the calculations presented in Table IX, in which exports of cotton textiles have been removed from the aggregate export figures.

Thus, although cotton manufactures made up over 40 per cent (line a) of total U.K. exports in every quinquennium down to 1850, only about 10 per cent (line b) of these manufactures went to the U.S.A. and cotton goods made up, on the average, 25 per cent (line c averaged) of exports to the U.S.A. The greatest discrepancies are found in the years 1841–5 when the cotton goods content of exports to the U.S.A. was only 16 per cent, compared with total averages of 45 per cent, the U.S.A. taking much less than one-twentieth of cotton goods exported. In the 1850s it is seen that the trends move slightly in the reverse direction: although cotton goods declined in their relative importance in the export trade as a whole, the share of cotton exports going to the U.S.A. was restored to about 10 per cent. Indeed, as Table X will show, exports of cotton manufactures to the U.S.A. were greater in the 1850s than any other single item, surpassing even woollens.

It can also be seen from Table IX that, when exports of cotton goods are subtracted from total exports, the American share of all other exports varies between 17 and 28 per cent (line d), averaging 23 per cent over the whole period. It will be seen later, however, that when a number of particularly significant items are examined separately, the American share of the market is considerably greater than one-quarter.

Table X shows the main categories of exports to the U.S.A., listed in the order of relative importance in the quinquennium 1856–60. It will be seen that woollens were generally the leading

TABLE IX. Exports from the U.K., distinguishing cotton and other manufactures

Annual average declared value in each 5-year period

		1816–20	1821–5	1826–30	1831–5	1836–40	1841–5	1846–50	1851–5	1856–60
Total exports	£ mill.	40·3	37·3	35·9	40·4	50·0	54·0	60·8	88·8	124·1
Total exports of cotton manufactures	£ mill.	16·4	16·7	17·2	19·2	23·7	24·1	25·3	31·8	38·3
Cotton manufactures as % of total exports	(a)	*41*	*45*	*48*	*47*	*47*	*45*	*42*	*36*	*31*
Cotton manufactures exported to U.S.A.	£ mill.	1·8	2·0	1·9	2·1	1·7	1·0	2·0	3·1	4·0
Percentage of total exports of cotton manufactures exported to U.S.A.	(b)	*11*	*12*	*11*	*11*	*7*	*4*	*8*	*10*	*10*
Cotton manufactures as % of total exports to U.S.A.	(c)	*26*	*32*	*33*	*26*	*22*	*16*	*18*	*17*	*20*
Total exports less cotton manufactures	£ mill.	23·9	20·6	18·7	21·2	26·3	29·9	35·5	57·0	85·8
Exports to U.S.A. less cotton manufactures	£ mill.	5·2	4·3	3·8	5·8	6·7	5·1	8·9	15·6	15·9
U.S. share of total exports less cotton manufacture %	(d)	*22*	*21*	*20*	*27*	*26*	*17*	*27*	*28*	*19*

category, being surpassed by cottons only in 1826–30 and 1851–1860. Neither of these items, however, expanded in value terms as rapidly as the total trade over the period as a whole. Many items show considerable stability for a quarter of a century from the mid-1820s until 1850, the expansion of the iron and steel trades in the late 1840s being the outstanding exception. Several items increased rapidly in the 1850s to reach quite unprecedented proportions, especially linen manufactures, clothing, tin and pewter products (above all, tinplate), hardware and cutlery; iron and steel exports expanded enormously in the early part of the decade but fell off somewhat in the second half—an obvious reflection of American railroad building activity.

The final task is to examine in greater detail some of the major categories listed in Table X. It is only when one looks at the British economy sector by sector, industry by industry, even firm by firm, that the significance of the American market can be fully appreciated. British exports were extremely heterogeneous and the dependence upon American markets varied greatly even within industries. Several factors combined to determine the ability of British industries to sell their products in the U.S.A.: the nature and needs of American markets; the existence, and the degree, of competition from domestic or from other foreign suppliers; the commercial and financial organization; and the varying incidence of American tariffs.

COTTON MANUFACTURES

The average annual declared values of exports of cotton manufactures have already been given in Tables IX and X. It will be noted that the quinquennium in which the U.S.A. took her greatest share—12 per cent—of British exports of cotton goods occurred early in the post-war period, between 1821 and 1825, years of particular prosperity and expansion for the cotton industry.

Perhaps the first point to be made is that the cotton industries in the two countries were competitors for American raw cotton. By the mid-1820s, American cotton manufacturing had taken a firm hold and from that time the consumption of raw cotton in the U.S.A. increased at about the same rate as did the British

TABLE X. The main categories of exports to the U.S.A. of British and Irish produce and manufactures

Average annual declared value in each 5-year period. £ million

	1816–20	1821–5	1826–30	1831–5	1836–40	1841–5	1846–50	1851–5	1856–60	1861
Cotton manufactures and yarn .	1·8	2·0	1·9	2·1	1·7	1·0	2·0	3·1	4·0	1·5
Woollen manufactures and yarn	2·2	2·0	1·2	2·1	1·9	1·7	2·1	2·9	3·5	2·0
Iron and steel, wrought and un-wrought			0·2	0·3	0·6	0·5	1·7	3·8	2·8	1·0
Linen manufactures and yarn .			0·7	0·9	1·0	0·8	1·2	1·8	1·9	0·7
Clothing, etc. . .			0·1	0·2	0·2	0·1	0·4	1·1	1·4	0·7
Hardwares and cutlery . .	0·6	0·5	0·7	0·8	0·7	0·6	0·8	1·1	1·0	0·7
Tin and pewter wares, unwrought tin and tinplate .	0·1	0·1	0·1	0·1	0·2	0·2	0·4	0·8	1·0	0·4
Earthenware			0·2	0·2	0·3	0·5	0·4	0·5	0·6	0·2
Silk manufactures . .			0·1	0·3	0·3	0·2	0·3	0·4	0·5	0·2
Alkali soda . .								0·3	0·4	0·2
Brass and copper manufactures.			0·1	0·2	0·2	0·2	0·2	0·3	0·1	
Salt			0·1		0·1	0·1	0·1	0·1	0·1	
Glass manufactures . .			0·1					0·1	0·1	
Other items . . .	2·3	1·7	0·2	0·7	0·4	0·2	1·3	2·7	2·5	1·5
TOTAL . . .	7·0	6·3	5·7	7·9	7·8	6·1	10·9	18·7	19·9	9·1

importation from the U.S.A.[1] Supporters of a high tariff system in the U.S.A. made much of the argument that, by curtailing imports from Britain by means of a tariff, America could reduce British demand for, and therefore the price of, American raw cotton and thus stimulate the progress of cotton manufacturing in the U.S.A. not merely through direct protection but also by a consequential reduction of the costs of cotton production.[2]

The tariff of 1816 imposed a duty of 25 per cent on imports of manufactured cottons. But in addition to the general *ad valorem* rate, a minimum duty was also imposed which meant that the incidence of duty on the cheapest cloths was much greater than 25 per cent. The effect of this minimum duty was to debar entry to the coarser cloths and to afford American producers of these cheapest cloths with almost complete protection. The range of goods so affected was widened with the increase of the minimum duty which was brought about in 1824 and 1828.

With this protection, the American cotton industry made such progress that by the early 1830s it had little to fear from foreign competition in certain grades of cloth. In 1833 Mr. Nathan Appleton, an American cotton factory promoter, stated that even if there had been no import duty, England could not have sold coarse cottons in the U.S.A. and that she could compete with American producers only with difficulty in many finer cloths.[3] The reputation of English cloth, ignorance and market imperfections were more important factors than the tariffs. By the 1830s various American writers were claiming that the American cotton industry was as advanced technically as the British and that its much greater employment of female labour—especially in Massachusetts—involved a more efficient use of the labour available. That this general view was not wholly

---

[1] U.S. consumption of raw cotton (thous. bales): 1830, 150; 1840, 300; 1850, 600; 1860, 800; U.K. imports of raw cotton from U.S.A. (mill. lb.): 1826–30, 174; 1836–40, 368; 1846–50, 499; 1856–60, 869. By 1833 fears were being expressed in Manchester that American raw cotton production might eventually be sufficient only for American factories. (Redford, op. cit., p. 80.)

[2] See especially Matthew Carey, *Appeal to Common Sense and Justice* (Philadelphia, 1822) and the work already mentioned, *Collectanea displaying the Rise and Progress of the Tariff System of the United States* (1833). The complementary argument was that low tariffs meant high prices for raw cotton (and also for flour) and correspondingly slow industrial growth in the U.S.A.

[3] Quoted in Taussig, op. cit., p. 136.

unfounded seems to be confirmed by the evidence of Kirkman Finlay, a Glasgow merchant, before the Select Committee on Manufactures, Commerce and Shipping of 1833:

Of all the improvements... that have been made for the last two years, the invention has been in America; . . . if the American manufacturers are in possession of an important improvement, it follows as a matter of course, that unless the manufacturer of this country not only gets hold of that improvement, but works it also in a manner at least equal, or perhaps superior, that with the advantage that the manufacturer in America has of the position for the lower price of the raw material, an advantage would be given to him, in some kinds of cotton goods, of a perfectly overwhelming character.[1]

The *ad valorem* duty remained unchanged at 25 per cent, except for the reductions under the Compromise Tariff of 1833 to reach 20 per cent by 1842. The 25 per cent level was restored by the Tariff Act of 1842 and maintained under the 1846 Act, to be reduced insignificantly to 24 per cent when cottons were transferred from Schedule D to Schedule C in 1857.

In all those circumstances it was inevitable that the American market was much stronger throughout the period for the more expensive prints and patterned cloths. Indeed, the prosperity induced by the development of manufacturing in the U.S.A. greatly increased the demand for those British manufactures which American industry could not yet produce.[2] Although the total value of British exports of such high-quality cottons rarely accounted for more than one-quarter of the total value of all cotton exports, it was regularly one-half, and in some years two-thirds, of the value of cotton exports to the U.S.A. Before 1830

---

[1] *BPP*, 1833 (690), VI, Q.640. Another witness, Joshua Bates, a partner in Baring Brothers and an American by birth, stated that America had been competing in South American markets with British exports in the coarser cloths. 'But I think in the case of the American domestic manufacture, being less perfect in their knowledge of manufacturing, they used none but the very best cotton; consequently the cotton was more durable; . . . *at Manchester they now make an imitation of the American domestic*, which is nearly as good, and at rather a less price.' (My italics.) Ibid., Q.892.

[2] This was argued before the 1833 Committee by the banker Timothy Wiggin who stated firmly that many British cotton manufactures could find no market in the U.S.A. at current rates of duty (ibid., Q.2047) but that 'employment in factories furnishes additional means for the consumption of articles of British production, which suit the convenience of the inhabitants' (Q.1997).

and again after 1850, America was the main single market for such products.

The progress of the American cotton industry is most clearly marked in the decline of her imports from Britain of white and plain calicoes. In the immediate post-war years, down to 1822, she was the leading market, taking up to 30 per cent of exports. From about 1830, America's relative share of British exports dwindled, though continuing to expand slowly in absolute figures. A marked spurt occurred in the 1850s, presumably because American domestic production was unable to expand rapidly enough to meet demand in this period of extremely rapid general growth in the U.S.A. But by this time, the U.S.A. was taking less than 5 per cent of Britain's exports; even so in some years, e.g. 1858, the value of such exports to the U.S.A. amounted to over one million pounds.

The sporadic nature of the Trade Returns makes it difficult to construct detailed tables of exports for the whole period. The occasional glimpse one gets, however, suggests that America was the main market in most years for cotton stockings.[1] Though the value of this trade rarely exceeded half a million pounds, the U.S.A. regularly took over one-third of all exports; in 1857 she took 729 out of 1,016 thousand dozen pairs. Similarly, the U.S.A. appears in occasional years as the leading market for counterpanes and bed quilts, lace and patent net, and sewing cotton. In the late 1850s America was the main market for the groups described as fustians, velvets, etc., and mixed stuffs. Exports of cotton yarn to the U.S.A. were negligible throughout.

A marked characteristic of several categories of cotton goods is that America was a leading, or the leading, market until about 1825 or 1830. A decline, sometimes absolute, always relative, then followed for about two decades, until the late 1840s when there began a sharp improvement, which was both relative and absolute and continued throughout the 1850s. The timing is such that it is difficult not to believe that the changes in the American tariff had a considerable influence on these trends.

[1] Mrs. Trollope observed in New York in 1829: 'Broadway might be taken for a French street, where it was the fashion for very smart ladies to promenade. The dress is entirely French; not an article (except perhaps cotton stockings) must be English, on pain of being stigmatised as out of the fashion. . . .' (Frances Trollope, *Domestic Manners of the Americans*, p. 310.)

But the development of American production on the one hand and the condition of American demand on the other were also important determinants; and the causal relationship between these two factors and the state of the tariff is not a simple one.

WOOLLEN MANUFACTURES

The American tariff of 1816 imposed a 25 per cent duty[1] on woollen imports as on cottons, but no minimum duty was imposed. There was therefore no discrimination at first against cheaper cloths. On the contrary the Act of 1824 retained the level of 25 per cent for cheaper woollens but increased it at once to 30 per cent and after 1825 to 33⅓ per cent on all others. Raw wool was subjected to a tariff of 15 per cent in 1816; the Act of 1824 increased this, for qualities costing over 10 cents a pound, to 20 per cent at once, 25 per cent in 1825 and 30 per cent in 1826. The Act of 1828, after amendment, raised the general level of duty on woollens to 45 per cent, while imported raw wool was taxed at 4 cents a pound plus 50 per cent *ad valorem*.[2]

In 1832 the duty on manufactured woollens was raised still further to a level of 50 per cent *ad valorem*; the duty on raw wool remained generally at 4 cents per pound plus 40 per cent, but cheap wools costing under 8 cents a pound were freed. The general reduction of the Compromise Tariff brought the tariff on woollen manufactures down to 20 per cent, along with the reduction for all other commodities. It was restored to 30 per cent (Schedule C) in 1846 and lowered again to 24 per cent in 1857.

The inferiority of American raw wool and the high tax on imported raw wool were important reasons—but not the only ones—why American woollen manufacturing was slow to develop. As with cottons the production of high-quality grades, especially worsteds, made the slowest progress. As late as 1860

---

[1] Provision was made for a reduction to 20 per cent, but this was not implemented.

[2] The initial proposals were for a specific duty on different types of cloth at about 40 per cent, and for a raw wool tax of 7 cents plus increment. The point of the flat rate on raw wool was to tax lower quality wools. These were used in the manufacture of carpets and some cheap flannels and cloths. They were imported from Asia Minor and South America, costing only 4–10 cents a pound at the place of exportation.

there were only three worsted factories of importance in the
U.S.A. and the value of imported worsteds was about four times
that of American home production. One of the main reasons for
this was the high level of duty—30 per cent—on imports of
long-staple wool.[1]

Not surprisingly, American markets commanded a very much
larger share of British exports of woollens and worsteds than of
cottons. In almost every year, a greater value of woollens went
to the U.S.A. than to any other single country and in many years
the U.S.A. took more than twice the amount going to the second-
largest market. Generally, between one-quarter and one-third of
total woollen exports went to the U.S.A., compared with a
maximum figure of 12 per cent for cotton goods.

Table XI shows the total figures for all exports of woollens
and worsteds and the details of the different qualities and
categories. The table excludes items of which the export to
America was negligible: these were mainly napped coatings,
etc. (total declared value in the 1820s about £200,000, but
declining to virtually nothing), baizes (total declared value
£200,000–£300,000 in the 1820s), flannels (of which the U.S.A.
took 5 million yards out of a total of 7·3 million yards in 1815,
declining to 1 million out of 2·5 million yards in 1827, and to
negligible proportions thereafter), sundry items (returned by
value; the U.S.A. took about one-quarter of total exports, but
the value involved never exceeded £100,000), and woollen and
worsted yarn (negligible exports to the U.S.A.).

The main items by value in the woollen export trade were the
categories 'cloths of all kinds', 'stuffs, woollen and worsted' and
'woollens mixed with cotton'. In the late 1810s and the 1820s,
the first of these was much the most important; by the 1850s the
three categories accounted for approximately equal shares of
total exports, with declared values of between £2½ and £3 million each; in the late 1850s exports of woollen and worsted stuffs
expanded continually and became the leading category. By
comparison, the value of total exports of blankets and carpets
was considerably lower; in the 1850s the total value of the
export of each was about half a million pounds. Exports of
woollen and worsted stockings were worth still less, rarely

[1] With exemption for imports from Canada after the Reciprocity Treaty of 1854.

TABLE XI. Exports from the U.K. of British woollen and worsted manufactures

Annual average in each 5-year period

		1816-20	1821-5	1826-30	1831-5	1836-40	1841-5	1846-50	1851-5	1856-60	1861
CLOTHS OF ALL KINDS											
Total export	000 pieces	437	389	357	554	465	248	323	564¹	565	566
Export to U.S.A.	,, ,,	157	144	104	217	186	40	75	184¹	183	73
U.S. share of total	%	*36*	*37*	*30*	*39*	*40*	*16*	*23*	*33*	*32*	*13*
STUFFS, WOOLLEN OR WORSTED											
Total export	mill. pieces	0·8	1·1	1·3	1·6	1·4	2·2	1·8	2·1¹	2·5	2·2
Export to U.S.A.	,, ,,	0·2	0·3	0·2	0·5	0·3	0·4	0·4	0·5¹	0·7	0·4
U.S. share of total	%	*30*	*24*	*18*	*30*	*23*	*19*	*20*	*23*	*27*	*17*
WOOLLENS MIXED WITH COTTON											
Total export	mill. yds.	0·8	1·2	0·9	1·5	2·2	13·5	34·8	56·7¹	70·7	61·1
Export to U.S.A.	,, ,,	0·1	0·2	0·1	0·4	0·7	5·6	16·8	33·5¹	35·1	20·8
U.S. share of total	%	*12*	*17*	*11*	*26*	*34*	*42*	*48*	*59*	*50*	*34*
BLANKETS AND BLANKETING											
Total export	mill. yds.	2·0	1·9	1·8	2·6	2·9	2·4	4·5	6·6¹	7·9	8·8
Export to U.S.A.	,, ,,	1·3	1·1	1·0	1·7	1·7	1·2	3·1	4·4¹	5·2	5·2
U.S. share of total	%	*65*	*58*	*56*	*65*	*58*	*50*	*69*	*66*	*66*	*60*
CARPETS AND CARPETING											
Total export	mill. yds.	0·8	0·9	1·0	0·7	0·9	0·9	1·3	2·9¹	4·6	4·1
Export to U.S.A.	,, ,,	0·5	0·5	0·6	0·4	0·3	0·2	0·4	1·0¹	2·3	1·0
U.S. share of total	%	*55*	*62*	*64*	*51*	*37*	*21*	*32*	*35*	*50*	*24*
STOCKINGS, WOOLLEN OR WORSTED											
Total export	000 doz.	122	114	116	182	124	175	141	201¹	215	129
Export to U.S.A.	,, ,,	55	68	64	110	64	99	75	95¹	119	35
U.S. share of total	%	*45*	*60*	*55*	*60*	*60*	*56*	*53*	*46*	*58*	*27*
KERSEYMERES											
Total export	000 pieces	89	103	72	31·2	31·7	25·3	24·5	14¹	3·6	
Export to U.S.A.	,, ,,	26	26	9	3·9	9·4	6·3	12·2	5¹	0·5	
U.S. share of total	%	*39*	*25*	*12*	*12*	*30*	*25*	*25*	*35*	*14*	
WOOLLENS AND WORSTEDS TOTAL except yarn											
Total export	£ mill.	7·6	6·3	4·9	5·8	5·9	6·7	7·0	8·8	10·8	11·1
Export to U.S.A.	,, ,,	2·2	2·0	1·2	2·1	1·9	1·7	2·1	2·9	3·5	2·0
U.S. share of total	%	*29*	*32*	*24*	*36*	*32*	*25*	*30*	*33*	*32*	*18*

¹ Figures for 1854 have not been traced

exceeding one-quarter of a million pounds, and tending to decline throughout the period.

Of the three main items indicated above, the U.S.A. took, between 1816 and 1860, 31, 24 and 33 per cent respectively of the total quantity exported. Such overall averages, however, are not very meaningful except as giving the very broadest indication of the distribution of the trade. Until 1840 America was in every year the main market for 'cloths of all kinds', reaching a peak in 1836 when she received 356 out of 720 thousand pieces (or almost exactly one-half of the entire export). In most years the export to the U.S.A. of this class of cloth was more than twice that to the next largest market. The high level of exports to the U.S.A. was maintained until 1839 but fell by two-thirds in 1840; it remained relatively low throughout the 1840s, 1842, 1843, 1846 and 1848 being particularly bad years. Signs of recovery were to be seen in 1849, and by 1850—and throughout the 1850s—the absolute figures were roughly the same as in the late 1830s, the relative figures being slightly below.

The U.S.A. and Germany were the two main customers for 'stuffs, woollens and worsted', alternating in pre-eminence from one year to the next. The decline in the American trade in the 1840s is less marked here, though 1846 was again a particularly bad year. In almost every year in the 1850s, by which time the item is classified in the Returns simply as 'stuffs, worsted', the U.S.A. was the leading market; in 1859, the best year, she took 813 out of 2,722 thousand pieces exported, or about 30 per cent of the total. The trade as a whole, and the American sector of it, expanded fairly steadily over the whole period.

The mixed stuffs, or 'woollens mixed with cottons', present a different picture. Their export was negligible in the early years of the period, often amounting to a value of less than £100,000. By the 1850s, however, their value was generally over two million pounds and exceeded three million in 1852, 1854, 1856 and 1860. The tables leave no doubt that the American market was by far the most important factor in this massive expansion, since it absorbed 48 per cent of the total export in the late 1840s; in the 1850s the American share of the trade was regularly more than one-half and in 1859 reached almost 60 per cent, with a value in that year and the next of no less than £1·3 million.

Of the less valuable items, the one which stands out quite dramatically is the blanket trade, of which the American share was never less than half; between the middle 1840s and 1860 it was two-thirds or over. This trade also shows a steady expansion, the export to America keeping pace almost exactly with the total trade. The export of blankets to the U.S.A. was nearly always twice as great, and often ten times as great, as the export to the second customer (British North America until the late 1840s, Australia thereafter).

The carpet trade shows somewhat greater fluctuations, there being a marked decline in the total trade in the early 1830s (especially 1834) and a sag in the American trade in the early and middle 1840s (with 1846 the worst year). Although the U.S.A. was the main customer in almost every year except a few in the 1840s, she gradually lost her complete predominance (of around 60 per cent) of the pre-1830 period. Before 1830 she took between eight and ten times as much as the next most important customer (Germany until the mid-1820s, British North America thereafter). Although the export of carpets to the U.S.A. expanded remarkably from 1849 onwards, America did not recover such a supremely dominant position.[1] Nevertheless, her share of the trade was still half of the total in the late 1850s, so that the decline was only relative.

In the last important section of the woollen export trade also, that of hosiery, the U.S.A. was the leading market in every year in the entire period, with British North America a very poor second. The percentage figures speak for themselves: the quinquennial averages show that the U.S.A. took between 45 per cent and 60 per cent of all exports of woollen and worsted stockings (as well as a similar share of the hosiery itemized in the Returns as 'Sundries').

IRON AND STEEL MANUFACTURES

The third main category is that of iron and steel. As will be seen from Table X, during the American railroad-building boom of the early 1850s, these products accounted for a higher value

---

[1] The decline must be attributed to domestic American production following the introduction of the Bigelow loom in the early 1840s.

of exports to the U.S.A. than either woollen manufactures or cotton manufactures; in both 1853 and 1854, indeed, their declared value was over £5 million, compared with about half a million pounds only a decade earlier. In 1853 almost exactly one-half by value of all British exports of iron and steel went to the U.S.A., and iron and steel accounted for 23 per cent of the total value of all exports to the U.S.A. The importance of iron and steel in British-American trade in the 1850s is indicated by the fact that 1853, the best year for iron and steel exports, was also the best year for British exports to the U.S.A. in the entire period before 1861, with a total declared value of £23·7 million (out of total exports of £98·9 million—or 24 per cent). The same two years, 1853 and 1854, were also the best years throughout the entire period for exports to the U.S.A. of the allied products, hardwares and cutlery, with £1·3 million and £1·4 million respectively.

The fall in the average exports of iron and steel to the U.S.A. in the late 1850s is heavily weighted by the low value of £1·5 million in the post-crisis year of 1858, when total exports of iron and steel manufactures fell to £11·2 million. In the other four years of this quinquennium, the declared value of iron and steel exports to the U.S.A. certainly did not reach the heights of 1853–4, but was always above £3 million. Iron and steel lost the prime position in American trade, however, to the two main textile categories, though if hardwares and cutlery are included with iron and steel, the value of those products then is greater than that of woollens and only just behind that of cottons.

The tariffs imposed on iron manufactures in 1816 were at a level of 20 per cent on bar iron and pig iron, somewhat higher on rolled bar iron. In 1818 (when the proposed reduction of duty on cotton and woollens was postponed) these rates were actually increased to specific duties of 75 cents and 50 cents per cwt. on bar and pig respectively. These duties became proportionately heavier as the price of iron fell after 1818–19. The 1824 tariff raised the duty on bar iron to 90 cents per cwt., that on rolled iron remaining at the 1816 level of $1.50 per cwt. Further increases were imposed in 1828 but the 1832 tariff restored the level of 1824. The Compromise Tariff retained the

1832 level for two years and provided thereafter for a gradual return to 20 per cent by 1842, the reduction becoming really effective in 1838/9. On the whole, it does not seem likely that these high levels, especially in the late 1820s and early 1830s, greatly impeded imports and it appears that the proportion of imported iron to domestically produced remained fairly constant from 1815 to 1840. Certainly the increase in the rate of duty in the 1820s and early 1830s was not reflected in any marked fall in imports from Britain any more than the reduction after 1833 was reflected in any marked increase. Nevertheless, it appears certain that the effective American market for British iron was kept below the potential market by these duties.[1] Imports before 1842 probably supplied a smaller proportion of the total American consumption of iron than they did after 1846, despite the fact that all railroad iron was admitted duty free. The most effective part of the tariff was the heavy discrimination against imported rolled bar iron, the specific duty on which was equivalent to about 100 per cent of value.[2]

Iron manufactures were included in the sharp increase of duties in 1842 and British exports to the U.S.A. show a distinct fall in the years 1843–6. After 1846, however, with the level of duty at 30 per cent and at 24 per cent after 1857, British iron exports to the U.S.A. show a quick response. The British iron industry benefited enormously from the heavy railroad building of 1852 to 1857; in 1853 and 1854 American imports of iron almost equalled domestic production.

American charcoal pig iron was as effectively protected as hammered iron. The protection was in force for most of the 1830s and the brief reduction was succeeded by the high level imposed in 1842, including railroad iron, hitherto free. At the same time anthracite began to be used for the production of pig iron in the U.S.A. and American output doubled from 300,000

[1] There was, however, an expansion of American imports from Sweden. See above, pp. 58–9.

[2] This kept out iron made in Britain by the Cort puddling and rolling process and continued the American method of production by hammering. The tariff protected American producers of hammered iron, kept the prices of rolled iron high (though this was later modified by the free entry of railroad iron) but did not hasten the introduction in the U.S.A. of the puddling and rolling processes. These processes did not take hold in America until after 1840 when anthracite began to be used as an iron-making fuel.

tons in 1840/1 to 650,000 tons in 1846/7. During this period American output of iron rails expanded considerably though a start had already been made in the 1830s. The reduction of duty on pig iron to 30 per cent in 1846 had little immediate effect, partly because of the high demand for iron in Britain; the consequent high price made the *ad valorem* duty high. But by the early 1850s, imports were expanding rapidly, especially with the railroad-building boom.

The details of the British-American iron and steel trade are presented in Table XII. In value terms, the first item is by far the most important, accounting for between three- and four-fifths of the entire trade. Unwrought steel increased greatly in importance in the 1850s, when the declared value of the export to the U.S.A. was about half a million pounds annually.

Exports of bar iron to the U.S.A. began to expand rapidly in the early 1830s, and from 1831 onwards America took in almost every year a greater share of exports than any other country. The expansion continued almost without set-back until a period of slackness in the middle 1840s. The turning-point occurred in 1848 in which year the U.S.A. took 162 out of 339 thousand tons, or almost one-half, while the next largest customer, Italy, took less than one-tenth of the American figure. Between 1848 and 1853 the quantity increased annually; by 1853 it had reached 410 out of 645 thousand tons, or 63 per cent of the total quantity exported, with a declared value of £3·5 out of £5·6 million. Railroad iron was the main component in this category. There was a considerable decline in the late 1850s, very strongly marked in 1858 when the export of railroad iron to the U.S.A. slumped to a mere 30,000 tons, but even so in every year except 1858 the U.S.A. remained the main market.

The other main item in which the American market was wholly dominant throughout the entire period was unwrought steel. In every year after 1821, the U.S.A. was the principal market. By 1830 America was regularly taking one-half or more of the total exports; in 1839, for example, she took 2·7 out of 3·9 thousand tons, or almost 70 per cent, while the next largest customer, France, took only three hundred tons, one-ninth the American quantity. Both 1842 and 1843 were poor years but the trade expanded year by year, except for a slight set-back in 1848, until 1854 when 15·3 thousand tons out of a total export of 20·8 thousand tons went to the U.S.A., no less than 74 per cent of the entire trade! This level was not sustained in the next few years and 1858 was a bad year (though America still took 50 per cent of the total export, 8·6 out of 16·4 thousand tons). The trade built up rapidly in the last two years of the decade, reaching 22 thousand tons, out of a total export of 32 thousand, in 1860; in that year the declared value of steel exports to the U.S.A. was £653,000.

From unwrought steel it is appropriate to pass to the trade in hardware and cutlery where the story is not wholly one of success. Until the middle 1830s, Sheffield had a virtual monopoly of the American market, supplying agricultural and domestic tools and implements of all kinds. About half of the total exports of the British manufactured steel industry went to the U.S.A. The trade expanded annually, with only occasional slight set-backs as in 1826. The American tariff was successively increased to a peak of 50 per cent in 1828. Despite this, the trade reached its highest point in 1825–6. The level then achieved could not long be maintained, however, although the tariff was reduced in the 1830s; domestic American production was increasing and in addition German steel products became highly competitive in the American markets.[1] Both total exports and exports to the U.S.A. slumped badly in 1837 and 1838; total exports did not regain their 1835–6 level until 1844; the American tariff was restored to 33 per cent in 1842 and from the 1840s on British exporters were compelled to concentrate on a number of specialized products; exports to the U.S.A. did not again regain the level of the mid-1830s before the American Civil War. Nevertheless, despite this absolute as well as relative decline, the U.S.A. remained the most important single market in practically every year down to 1860, taking, as Table XII shows, about one-quarter of total exports; the figures of declared values correspond fairly closely with the quantity figures given in the Table.

[1] See Peter C. Garlick, 'The Sheffield Cutlery and Allied Trades and their Markets in the 18th and 19th centuries' (unpublished M.A. thesis, Sheffield University, 1951). Mr. Garlick quotes Alfred Gatty, *Sheffield, Past and Present* (1873): 'The fortunes of the town rose and fell with the temperature of the American market.'

TABLE XII. Exports from the U.K. of British iron and steel manufactures

Annual average in each 5-year period

		1816-20	1821-5	1826-30	1831-5	1836-40	1841-5	1846-50	1851-5	1856-60	1861
BAR IRON[1]											
Total export	000 tons	40	41	49	76	112	181	304	567	468[a]	378[a]
Export to U.S.A.	,, ,,	4	3	7	21	42	41	149	322	123[a]	28[a]
U.S. share of total	%	10	8	15	28	38	23	49	57	26[a]	8[a]
BOLT AND ROD IRON											
Total export	000 tons	7·4	8·5	7·3	8·8	11·8	17·9	19·4	16·4	29·3[a]	25·8[a]
Export to U.S.A.	,, ,,	0·6	0·9	0·8	0·4	0·4	0·4	1·0	2·1	2·5[a]	1·9[a]
U.S. share of total	%	9	11	11	5	3	2	5	13		
PIG IRON											
Total export	000 tons	4·9	7·0	8·5	21·6	44·0	102·4	163·0	274·0	360·0	388
Export to U.S.A.	,, ,,	0·8	1·2	2·0	9·6	10·9	17·7	61·6	102·8	64·8	32
U.S. share of total	%	16	17	24	44	25	17	38	37	18	8
CAST IRON											
Total export	000 tons	7·4	7·1	7·2	12·8	13·6	17·3	20·7	53·3	75·9	75·0
Export to U.S.A.	,, ,,	0·8	0·6	0·6	5·1	3·1	0·7	1·2	2·7	2·5	1·1
U.S. share of total	%	11	9	8	40	23	4	6	5	4	2
STEEL, UNWROUGHT											
Total export	000 tons	0·7	0·7	0·7	1·7	4·2	4·5	8·8	17·1	23·3	21·8
Export to U.S.A.	,, ,,	0·2	0·2	0·3	1·1	1·9	2·3	5·1	11·7	14·8	0·9
U.S. share of total	%	34	32	44	65	46	49	58	68	63	5
IRON WIRE											
Total export	000 tons	0·2	0·3	0·2	0·5	0·7	1·6	2·6	6·7	11·4	11·6
Export to U.S.A.	,, ,,	0·1	0·1	0·1	0·2	0·1		0·6	2·2	2·7	2·0
U.S. share of total	%	36	41	50	31	8		21	32	23	17

		1816-20	1821-5	1826-30	1831-5	1836-40	1841-5	1846-50	1851-5	1856-60	1861
IRON HOOPS											
Total export	000 tons		3·6	8·1	10·9	11·2	14·4	21·8	29·0	39·2	31·8
Export to U.S.A.	,,		0·3	0·5	0·5	0·6	0·4	3·5	9·1	11·5	3·4
U.S. share of total	%		8	7	5	6	3	16	31	29	11
IRON NAILS											
Total export	000 tons	3·8		4·1	5·0	6·3	6·5	6·8	8·0	12·5	10·2
Export to U.S.A.	,,	1·2		(0·2)	0·2	0·6	0·3	0·4	0·5	0·4	0·2
U.S. share of total	%	32		5	4	10	5	6	6	3	2
ANCHORS AND GRAPNELS											
Total export	000 tons	2·6	1·0	1·3	1·7	2·9	3·1	9·9	21·0	21·0	14·9
Export to U.S.A.	,,							3·1	6·1	3·5	2·4
U.S. share of total	%							31	30	17	16
OTHER WROUGHT IRON											
Total export	000 tons		8·1	11·5	19·0	25·7	44·4	59·5	89·5	109·8	124
Export to U.S.A.	,,		1·1	1·4	4·3	3·2	3·6	11·7	27·1	17·4	6
U.S. share of total	%		13	12	23	13	8	20	30	14	5
TOTAL IRON AND STEEL, WROUGHT AND UNWROUGHT											
Total export	£ mill.		(1·8)	1·2	1·3	2·4	2·9	4·9	8·9	12·5	10·3
Export to U.S.A.	,,		(0·1)	0·2	0·3	0·6	0·5	1·7	3·8	2·8	1·0
U.S. share of total	%		(6)	17	23	25	17	35	43	22	9
HARDWARES AND CUTLERY											
Total export	000 tons	9·7	10·6	12·1	17·0	17·2	18·7	21·5	28·8	37·3	35·1
Export to U.S.A.	,,	4·4	4·4	5·9	8·9	7·7	5·7	7·6	8·3	7·6	3·8
U.S. share of total	%	45	42	49	52	45	30	35	29	21	11

[1] Includes railroad iron up to 1855.   [2] Railroad iron only.   [3] Bar, bolt and rod iron.

The rest of the iron and steel trade consisted of a large miscellany of less valuable items. The fact that they were of diminutive significance in the whole of British foreign trade should not be allowed to obscure the importance of such an import as iron nails in the American economy of the early nineteenth century. From about 1830 on, the U.S.A. was in most years the main market for British exports of pig iron; in the early 1850s she took three or four times as much as the second-largest customer. From the late 1840s, the U.S.A. provided the main market for British exports of iron wire, iron hoops, anchors and grapnels, and other wrought iron. The U.S.A. was an important market for cast iron only between 1829 and 1839.

OTHER ITEMS

The values of exports to the U.S.A. of the other main items in British-American trade were shown in Table X. No single item was comparable in total value with the three major groups. It is still true, nevertheless, that with many of the commodities in question, the U.S.A. took as large a share of the total British export as with the major groups. The figures are given in Table XIII; owing to problems arising from the calculation of totals or from discontinuities in the quantitative trade returns, the data in this Table are given as declared values.

The remaining textile groups, linens, silks and clothing, together accounted for £3½ million of exports in most years of the 1850s. Exports of linens increased steadily from the mid-1820s to the late 1850s, the American share remaining fairly constant at about one-third of the total. The main relapses in the American trade occurred in 1832, 1837, 1842, and in decided contrast to iron and steel, 1854 and 1855, but in every year the U.S.A. was the principal market, generally taking between twice and three times as much as the second market. It has not been possible to isolate Irish from British linen, but figures for 1810–20 suggest that in that decade Irish linen made up about one-third of the total export.

Exports of British manufactures of silk expanded much more rapidly than those of linens. The American market was proportionately the largest in the late 1830s, declining to about

TABLE XIII. Other important exports to the U.S.A. of British and Irish manufactures and products

Annual average in each 5-year period

		1816-20	1821-5	1826-30	1831-5	1836-40	1841-5	1846-50	1851-5	1856-60	1861
LINEN MANUFACTURES											
Total export	£ mill.			2·0[1]	2·4	3·0	3·8	3·7	5·0	6·2	5·5
Export to U.S.A.	,,			0·7[1]	1·0	1·0	0·8	1·2	1·8	1·9	0·7
U.S. share of total	%			*32*	*42*	*33*	*21*	*32*	*36*	*31*	*13*
CLOTHING, ETC.											
Total export	£ mill.			0·8[1]	0·8	1·1	1·4	1·9	4·6	5·9	5·6
Export to U.S.A.	,,			0·1[1]	0·1	0·2	0·1	0·4	1·1	1·4	0·7
U.S. share of total	%			*16*	*18*	*13*	*11*	*20*	*24*	*24*	*12*
SILK MANUFACTURES											
Total export	£ mill.		0·4	0·3[1]	0·7	0·8	0·8	0·9	1·6	2·5	2·3
Export to U.S.A.	,,			0·1[1]	0·3	0·3	0·2	0·3	0·4	0·5	0·2
U.S. share of total	%			*30*	*38*	*43*	*24*	*31*	*27*	*20*	*8*
TIN AND PEWTER WARE AND TIN PLATES											
Total export	£ mill.	0·1	0·1	0·3[1]	0·3	0·4	0·5	0·7	1·1	1·5	0·9
Export to U.S.A.	,,			0·1[1]	0·1	0·2	0·2	0·4	0·8	1·2	0·4
U.S. share of total	%			*37*	*41*	*52*	*50*	*63*	*70*	*79*	*44*
EARTHENWARE											
Total export	£ mill.	0·5		0·4[1]	0·5	0·7	0·7	0·8	1·2	1·4	1·1
Export to U.S.A.	,,	0·1		0·2[1]	0·3	0·3	0·3	0·4	0·6	0·5	0·2
U.S. share of total	%	*28*		*37*	*47*	*47*	*39*	*45*	*53*	*39*	*20*
SALT											
Total export	£10,000			15	16	20	21	20	27	33	37
Export to U.S.A.	,,			6	6	8	6	9	11	12	8
U.S. share of total	%			*31*	*35*	*38*	*30*	*43*	*40*	*36*	*21*

[1] 4-year average: no figures available for 1826.

one-quarter of the total in the 1850s; in that decade exports to the U.S.A. were very stable, at around half a million pounds, with the exception of 1855 when they fell to £294,000. Exports to the U.S.A. of clothing, on the other hand, increased rapidly from the late 1840s, reaching a peak in 1856 when their official value was £1·7 million (out of a total export of £5·5 million). This trade was very sensitive to business conditions in the U.S.A. The 1836 level of exports was not regained for ten whole years but rapid expansion began in 1847 and continued until 1856, years of great vitality in American economic life.

The earthenware trade is one of the best-known examples of close Anglo-American connexions during the nineteenth century. The U.S.A. was in every year the main market for Staffordshire products, taking generally between 40 and 50 per cent of total exports. The relative insignificance of the trade in the aggregate figures—exceeding £600,000 to the U.S.A. in only three years, 1853, 1854 and 1860—cannot conceal its tremendous importance for the Potteries.

No other commodities approached in value the British-American trade in those which have been examined. This is not to say, however, that the American market did not exert a powerful influence on other sectors of the British economy. The U.S.A. was the main market for British exports of salt (a particularly welcome return cargo because of its bulk), taking at least twice as much as the second customer, and maintaining a share of the trade of between 30 and 45 per cent until 1860. In the late-developing industry of alkali soda, the American market expanded rapidly in the 1850s, and was the only important foreign market.

It would be tedious to present a wholly comprehensive list of the remaining exports in which the U.S.A. was the main or an important market. Some of these—printed books, for example—are not at all surprising. Many commodities found a ready market in the U.S.A. for a few years only; among these are coal, of which America took about 15 per cent of total exports in the 1820s and as much as 300,000 tons in some years of the 1850s; leather products, also especially in the 1850s; and window and plate glass in the late 1820s and middle 1830s.

IV

Conclusion

The intention of this article, as stated at the outset, was as much to raise questions as to provide answers. Many aspects of the Atlantic economy have been wholly ignored, not least the migration of labour, especially skilled, and of capital. The data presented would admit a much more exhaustive analysis than has been attempted here. The five-year averages override cyclical fluctuations and other trade movements. The development of separate industries, especially from a technological point of view, needs to be examined in both countries with a view to discovering to what extent, for example, the lines of development were competitive and to what extent complementary. There are of course many excellent studies of the growth of separate industries on both sides of the Atlantic, but these generally provide only partial explanations of the trends indicated in this essay. One interesting feature is that some British industries which depended heavily on the American market were not yet factory industries in the period examined.

The period which above all merits further study is the 1850s when, as the figures given earlier have shown, British-American trade reached its climax. This was a decade of tremendous economic expansion in the U.S.A. and of intensification of development in Britain. It saw a closer approximation to a North Atlantic free-trade area than has occurred at any other time, with tariffs at their lowest in the U.S.A., with British tariffs virtually removed, and with the inauguration of the brief period of American-Canadian reciprocity. The statistics showed the massive expansion in this decade of British imports from the U.S.A. of grain and other foodstuffs, although American raw cotton continued to dominate Atlantic trade. On the export side the 1850s saw a tremendous increase in the exports of both old and new British products, above all of iron and steel.

The American trade in the late 1850s contained portents for the future. America had already become Britain's main supplier of foodstuffs. The U.K. had had an unfavourable balance of visible trade with the U.S.A. from the middle 1840s at least and in the late 1850s the deficit reached formidable proportions; in 1860 the computed real value of imports from the U.S.A. (including the cost of conveyance to the U.K.) was slightly more than twice the declared value of exports (excluding the cost of conveyance to the U.S.A.), £44·7 million compared with £21·7 million. While many British export industries continued to look to America for their main markets, the vast development of American transport and industry in the 1850s, stimulated still further by the Civil War, was drastically to change the performance of the American economy. The imposition of the highly protective tariff of 1864, more than any other single act, announced the severance by the U.S.A. of her ancient commercial links with the old world and constituted a declaration of American economic independence.

XI

A Yorkshire Mechanic Abroad

THERE is nothing intrinsically noteworthy in the experiences of a Yorkshire—or even of a Lancashire—mechanic abroad. But if the man happened to be a bit of an inventor, or at least a skilful improver of major inventions; if he spent a dozen years during the mid-nineteenth century in France and northern Italy, installing new types of British machines for French, Italian, and British firms, managing the mill and training the operatives; and if at his death he left a very large tin trunk crammed full of diaries, petty-cash books, and thousands of business or personal letters and memoranda,[1] then he may merit attention as a member of the teaching staff in the decades when 'Britain's role as the schoolmaster of industrial Europe was coming to an end'.[2]

His name was John Barraclough, his home base Triangle, near Halifax, and the first document is dated 1845. By that year two important recent developments, the one political, the other technological, were influencing the outflow of British labour and equipment. The first was the sweeping away in 1843 of all bans on the exportation of machinery—'the last prohibition which deforms the statute book',[3] as Labouchere described it. There had been some hope this might happen in 1824, when the kindred policy of forbidding the emigration of artisans was abandoned. Certainly the evidence gathered by Hume's select committees of 1824 and 1825 had proved conclusively that the laws were being evaded by divers tried and trustworthy stratagems, and had failed dismally to prevent foreigners from obtaining either the men or the machines they desired. But while no vested interest opposed the select committee's recommendation

---

[1] These papers are in the possession of descendants residing at Crosshills, near Keighley, and in Bath.

[2] W. O. Henderson, *Britain and Industrial Europe, 1750–1870* (1954), p. 212.

[3] Hansard, 3rd ser., lxxi, 509–10.

that artisans be made free to emigrate and return at will 'in the same manner as other classes of the community now go and return', there was no such lack of interest, or harmony of interests, on the other issue. Machine-making was still virtually an infant industry which was only just learning how to talk. The London engineers were almost alone in urging free exportation of their products. Many of their provincial counterparts and virtually all machine-using industries, especially textiles, were so violently hostile that Hume's group dared do no more than recommend that 'until an alteration be made in the laws' the Board of Trade should continue to exercise its discretionary power to license the shipment 'of all such Tools and Machinery now prohibited as may appear . . . not likely to be prejudicial to the trade or manufactures of the United Kingdom'.[1]

For eighteen years there was no 'alteration of the laws'. Customs officers continued to wrestle, for the most part spasmodically and ineffectually, with smuggling, deceptive descriptions, and the mingling of parts of prohibited machines with those of legally exportable or licensed equipment.[2] The Board of Trade faced a rising tide of applications for licences, mounting from 23 in 1826 to 251 in 1842. Of the total for that period, 2,160 in all, about 1,930 were granted and only 230 rejected, of which 185 concerned textile machines, especially those for spinning and weaving.[3]

In 1841 it was the North Country machine-maker's turn to clamour for repeal. The depression which began in 1836–7 and plunged deeper after 1839 was starving them of domestic orders, so the foreign market must be made accessible. Of the machine-users, cotton and woollen manufacturers were now indifferent or mildly favourable, and opposition was confined to two relatively small interests, Nottingham lace and Ulster linen. A select committee which studied the matter in 1841 recommended repeal, but further action was delayed by the cabinet change from Melbourne to Peel in 1841 and the concentration on Peel's Corn

[1] Select Committee on the Exportation of Tools and Machinery, *BPP*, 1825 (135), V, p. 135.

[2] The total number of seizures and detentions in 1824–39 was less than 400, of which only half resulted in confiscation and sale. *BPP*, 1841 (201), VII, p. 395.

[3] Figures compiled from the Board's registry book in the Public Record Office, B.T.6, vols. 151, 152.

Law, tariff reform, and income tax in 1842. A measure of administrative relief did come in late 1842, when the Board of Trade began to license the export of spinning and weaving machines that were intended for making cottons, woollens, and silks—but not for linen and lace. In August 1843 parliament found sufficient time to repeal the laws and abandon the policy.

This new freedom was especially valuable to the textile engineers. For them the 'thirties and 'forties were marked by some major inventions as well as minor refinements. In the central processes spindles were being made to turn more rapidly, while the power-loom was passing on from the production of coarse cottons to that of middle and even high-grade fabrics and was capturing the worsted industry. Possibly more significant, and certainly more revolutionary, were the changes taking place in the 'preparatory' processes which rid the raw material of its dirt, grease, or gum (in the case of silk), then by carding, combing, roving, hackling, and the like disentangled the fibres and laid them together in such manner that they could be spun.

The most famous achievement in this field was the surmounting of technical difficulties which had long thwarted efforts to design a satisfactory wool-combing machine. In Alsace Heilmann wrestled fairly successfully with the problem. In Yorkshire at least half a dozen men, including Donnisthorpe, Fairbairn, Holden, and Lister, did likewise, working alone or in pairs. By 1845, through 'a complex cross-fertilization of ideas',[1] the chief problems had been solved and combing machines came into widespread use during the next ten years.

The wool-combers' triumph overshadowed another development which had far-reaching effects by rendering low-grade or waste materials capable of profitable treatment. While the shoddy-makers were more efficiently salvaging woollen rags and waste or inferior wool, the linen men were designing or adapting machines which enabled them to convert inferior or waste tow into yarn almost as good as that made from the better fibres of flax or hemp. This development, apparently initiated in the late 'twenties by Peter Fairbairn, mechanic and machine-maker

---

[1] E. M. Sigsworth on 'Bradford' in C. R. Fay, *Round About Industrial England, 1830–1860* (1952), p. 125.

at Marshall's large mill in Leeds,[1] had gone far by the early 'thirties.

The salvaging of waste silk was a still more revolutionary step, since it gave birth to a new branch of silk manufacture. Waste silk came from two sources: first from cocoons which were naturally imperfect or had been so crushed, torn, or pierced that their slender fibre could not be reeled from them; second, from the material that was damaged in the basic reeling, winding, and throwing processes. The combined supply was large, yet little or no use was found for it—save perhaps for manure—until after 1815, when men familiar with the new machine methods of treating cotton, wool, or flax began patiently to apply them to waste silk. They rid it of its gum, bleached or dyed it, loosened up and rearranged the fibres by combing or carding and got them ready for spinning. The 'spun silk' thus produced might look as bright as did the yarn made from perfect material and evidently wore well.[2]

These experiments were conducted chiefly in the Leeds–Manchester area. In the former town Fairbairn adapted his flax machines for processing waste silk, while many mechanics in the Bradford–Halifax region and across the Pennines made their contributions. By the mid-'thirties considerable success had been achieved, though there was still need for many more experiments, conducted patiently in face of frequent failure. Not till 1859 did Lister succeed in adapting his wool-combing machine to the treatment of Indian waste silk, but he thereby found a use for material which hitherto had been offered in vain at $\frac{1}{2}d$ a pound and had been refused as manure because farmers found it would not rot.

These innovations continued to keep parts of British textile technique far ahead of that in use on the Continent. Consequently French, Belgian, German, or Italian manufacturers who wished to make yarn 'on the English principle' must,

---

[1] It was based on Fairbairn's improvements on machines designed in France by de Girard, which in turn were considerable improvements on earlier English machines. A. L. Dunham, *The Industrial Revolution in France, 1815–1848* (1955), pp. 293–7; also W. O. Henderson, op. cit., p. 32.

[2] See Ratain Rawley, *The Silk Industry and Trade* (1919), Swire Smith, *The Manufacture of Textile Fabrics* (1885), or Frank Warner, *The Silk Industry of the United Kingdom* (1921), for accounts of the various kinds of silk.

as in the recent past, buy these new models and employ British workers to install them, keep them running, and teach the natives how to operate them. By the early 'thirties they were trying to buy so many of Fairbairn's tow-dressing machines that the Board of Trade, alarmed by the flood of applications for licences, resolved in 1835 to refuse all such requests. By 1837 they were ordering Fairbairn's machines 'for dressing and cleaning refuse and waste silk', and since the waste silk industry possessed no strong protesting voice the Board readily granted licences. Further, some British manufacturers might wish to jump Continental tariff walls, whether French or Zollverein, or to protect their patents, by establishing factories abroad, and for this purpose must send out a small body of skilled mechanics and foremen, or even departmental and general managers.

It was in this world of technological change, of emigration of skilled friends and neighbours, and of legal or illicit exportation that John Barraclough had grown up. In 1853, when he applied for a new job, he described himself as follows:

From long experience I don't think there is a man in the trade that is a better judge of all kinds of silk waste. I understand the manufacture of spun silk of all kinds, both long and short, having worked as a workman at nearly every operation, and having filled different situations as manager for these last ten years. I have had a verry great deal of experience with nearly all kinds of machinery. I have a verry good idea of book-keeping, having allways been acustomed to keep mill accounts.

To this self-portrait he might have added that he was now forty-one years old; that years of travel and residence across the English Channel had taught him how to write French fluently and to speak it with a West Riding accent; and that while his spelling in any language was frequently phonetic, his handwriting was in such excellent early Victorian style that one might deduce his education had gone well beyond the elementary school. On his passport he described himself as 'Manufacturer'.

Of Barraclough's first sojourn abroad in the early 'forties we know only that the conditions and salary offered him must have seemed very seductive, for he sold his furniture and took his whole family with him to France; also that the job turned out so disastrously that he soon had to sell all his new furniture and take his family back home, disgusted, disappointed, almost penniless. In October 1845 came his second invitation to emigrate. A friend who was *contremaître* of a French mill gave his name to Charles Revel, operator of a spinning mill at Amilly, near Montargis (Loiret), about sixty miles south of Paris. Revel was anxious to improve his plant by adopting the newest British machines and methods. He therefore fired a battery of questions at Barraclough: what qualities of waste silk are used, and what are their prices; what kind—Italian, Spanish, Indian, or Chinese—gives the best results; where are the largest British mills? He wound up with the news: 'I am coming to England to collect the most thorough information on the industry, and wish to see you.'

By the time Revel arrived in Manchester in May 1846, he had learned much from Barraclough, including the fact that the latter was willing to return to France. The two men met, drew up a list of the equipment Revel needed—it was to cost over £1,100— and struck a bargain which Revel put into writing as follows:

You will be in charge of the silk combing and the other operations of which you have the requisite knowledge. I shall allow you 40 francs a week and *logement* in the *établissement*. I shall pay your expenses to France. When you have passed some weeks with me you will bring your wife and children. . . . Until you come I will give you 5/- a week on condition that you keep me *au courant* of all you can learn about the spinning of long silk.[1] You will give me three months notice if you wish to leave me, and if you go to another French factory you pay me all I have spent in bringing you out. If I wish to send you back to England I must give you three month's notice and pay your fare, unless I dismiss you for bad conduct.

On these terms Barraclough went to Amilly and remained there as *contremaître du peignage* (combing) till 1853. The machines ordered in Lancashire and the West Riding were promptly delivered and erected. But the family did not join him after 'some weeks'. His appointment was too indefinite to make safe the transplanting of wife and six children. The salary of 32s a week left little margin for saving after an infrequent £5 note

---

[1] This was a new development in which Revel was particularly interested and Barraclough especially expert.

had been sent home to augment the scanty earnings of the four youngsters who were old enough to work in mills. By mid-1847 he was hinting in letters to his wife that his tenure would soon be made good enough for him to say 'Come!' but this forecast was falsified by the depression of 1847 and the disturbances in 1848. His wages were reduced, and as the trickle of £5 notes almost stopped, his wellnigh penniless wife lamented that she 'could not be more miserable if [she] were in Vandemen's Land'. Not till early 1851 did the terms of tenure and income make it seem safe, as well as financially feasible, to reunite the family.

Through Barraclough's Amilly papers we get intimate glimpses of the industrial *émigrés* and of the conditions in which they lived and worked. The landscape seems to be swarming with English mechanics and cloth-making specialists, not to mention men in such other occupations as metallurgy and railroad construction or operation. Barraclough's acquaintances, many of them neighbours he had known in the West Riding, were sprinkled throughout the textile areas of central and northern France. In a visit to Paris he tried to call on at least a dozen of them, including a 'railway driver' and members of the group of Yorkshiremen brought over by Lister and Holden to manage or operate the wool-combing factory they had opened in St. Denis in 1849.[1] Letters passed between him and friends in Roubaix, Lille, Essonnes, and elsewhere, including three Salt brothers who settled first in the village of Crécy, then moved to Roubaix.

Many forces mingled to pull or push these men abroad. Some, like Barraclough, had been sought out personally by Continental manufacturers. They in turn, having proved their worth, might be sent back home or be asked to hunt by correspondence for more men. In mid-1843, for example, a Bradford overlooker engaged to go to Prussia. By Christmas he was back in Bradford looking for three more men.[2] During his Amilly years, especially the good ones which dispelled the gloom of 1848, Barraclough was occasionally authorized by Revel to hire more Englishmen and was asked by fellow-countrymen in other mills for help in filling vacancies. In 1851 he requested his brother in Yorkshire to find him a dresser. A year later Matthew Salt wrote from

---

[1] See Henderson, op. cit., pp. 83–88.   [2] *Leeds Mercury*, 30 December 1843.

Roubaix, 'Are them inglish that come to your place gon back to ingland? if thear shold be any that wishes to come to me I shold be very glad.'

In good years this hunting was not always easy among men fully employed at good wages in their homeland. The wage bait would need to be temptingly large when compared with British figures, yet many of the French firms were so small in scale, as well as so inadequately capitalized, that they might not be disposed or able to offer more than six or seven francs a day for a superintendent. The reply to Barraclough's request for a dresser was: 'We cannot hear anything of one that is in the mind for coming.'

In the lean years the position was reversed. The emigrants, faced with the prospect of reduced salaries or even of dismissal if a cheaper foreigner or native could be found, were inundated with gloomy reports and applications for jobs from England. For example: 'Trade is only indifferent in this part and money very scarce. There are hundreds of Mechanicks tramping the road in quest of work'; 'We are only working two days a week and I wish to come to France if you could give me a situation as silk dresser'; 'Can you find a job for the young man that lives next door to your wife? He is out of work.' Since Barraclough's own situation was so insecure that he was searching for another one, he could offer little comfort to the suppliants.

The migration to the Continent, like that to more remote lands, doubtless contained its share of escapists, of men who were a step or two beyond reach of the hand of the law, and of those who were worried by some moral, marital, or extra-marital problem. Commenting on one departed Yorkshireman, a Halifax correspondent wrote:

I think he should not have left England, for he was doing well, and a very good wage he had. He has got a bad character for leaving the way wich he did. But I hope he will send some money toward keeping that child of his wich has been born since he left England.

The engineers who gave evidence to the Select Committee in 1824 insisted that it was 'invariably the best ones' who were induced to emigrate,[1] but we may safely assume that 'best'

---

[1] *BPP*, 1824 (51), V, p. 10.

referred to their skill rather than their general conduct. As Henderson puts it: 'The relatively high wages paid to Englishmen on the Continent attracted not only good but also bad workers',[1] and in this case 'bad' could cover character as well as craftsmanship.

Barraclough's letters reveal a strong community of interest among the scattered emigrants. It was not organized formally in a combined friendly society and union club, as was that of the Nottingham lace-makers settled in Calais and Lille; but it was perhaps more pervasive in consequence. The men had known one another across the Channel, and some had been brought over by those who came earlier. In a strange land—strange in language, manners, food, and religion[2]—they must stick together. Even those who held contracts assuring tenure for a fixed term did not feel very secure, since the 'dismissal for bad conduct' clause might be stretched or broken if employers deliberately provoked a quarrel or determined to supplant them with cheaper substitutes when natives had been adequately trained. They had the skilled producer's characteristic low opinion of the importance attached to managerial, commercial, and financial ability. For these reasons, they were unlikely to feel a deep loyalty to the firm that employed them and were ready to consider any invitation from another foreign manufacturer who offered them better terms elsewhere.

More important still was their awareness that the textile industry enjoyed a very high birth rate. It swarmed with men who had stepped out of the employed ranks, established small firms with scanty capital or credit, yet had succeeded in building up flourishing middle-sized or even large enterprises. Since the émigrés' positions were at least one rung above the ordinary wage-earner's level and they had learned to enjoy a modest measure of prestige and power, why not go higher, why continue to serve others? If only they could scrape together a little capital somehow somewhere, their skill, know-how, and trade secrets could be put to better use in starting a business of their

---

[1] Henderson, op. cit., p. 8. See also his account (pp. 10–11) of a Swiss engineer's non-employment of British workmen and his reasons therefor: 'Not only do they cost a damned lot of money, but they are often drunkards.'

[2] Barraclough had to take his youngest child, born in France in 1852, to Corbeil, fifty miles away, for baptism by a Protestant parson.

own, in France[1] or back in England. The fact that the textile industry's death rate, especially that of infants, was high tended to be persistently forgotten.

Barraclough's sense of obligation seems to have been somewhat stronger than that of many of his correspondents. Within six months of entering Revel's service he was approached by another French manufacturer eager to do all the latest things with raw silk, who offered a higher salary, a year's contract, and a bonus of three hundred francs at the year's end 'if I am satisfied with you'. Scarcely had this offer been declined when a Basle mill owner asked for confidential information about the processes and machinery Barraclough used, also for samples of his product, then invited him to change masters. When business conditions improved in 1851–3 several similar temptations came to him, the strongest and most prolonged of them from a fellow Yorkshire mechanic, Matthew Salt.

Salt was feeling a strong urge to independence. He had already built four combing-machines, but lacked the capital for acquiring the rest of the equipment for spinning waste silk as well as the expert knowledge of how to operate it. For nearly two years he bombarded Barraclough with requests for technical tips and with proposals that the two enter into partnership. In August 1851 he wrote: 'I oneley wish you was at liberty at this time. Whe would try what whe cold do with the comeing masheens that I have.' Five months later he reported: 'I am alwase thinking of you comeing with me. . . . I have sevrel good places offred to me. . . . I think thear would be A good place for whe boath', especially as he had interested some 'very rich men' in a plan under which he was to contribute his four machines and they provide capital for the rest.

Within a month he is back again, urgent and insistent. He has got his mill in Roubaix, found 'a very rich man, one of the finest gentlemen ever I met with', who has provided 50,000 francs, and is ready to rush to England to buy what he needs for the firm of *Matthew Salt et Cie*. 'I must see you before long. I alwase wanted you to come in with me and now is the time. Don't you be fritened if your master was to turn you away tomorrer. I will

---

[1] In France there were countless small mills, suitable for such ventures, in the rural or small town textile areas.

give you my word and honer I will niver leave you.' In April, on his return from England, where he has spent over 100,000 francs—so he says—he finds a letter containing Barraclough's refusal to join him. He accepts this decision ruefully:

You think you have don right by stopping whear you are because Mr. Reavil as gave you A little more. You have never don so rong. Reavil as gave you more because he was forced to do so, if he ad not somebody hels wood have don. I miself i would not stop at Montargis for twice the mony he gives you for it is a pore place. Where I am i can go to parris verry often for six francs almost every month by the trains of pleager [*trains de plaisir*, excursion trains].

He winds up by inviting Barraclough's brother, Edwin, who had recently come to work at Amilly, to transfer to Roubaix; by urging Barraclough to meet him soon, so that the two of them can 'speke about sevrel things witch wold do me a great deal of good'; and by hinting that he might be willing to pay a thousand francs in return for 'every pertickulier conserning silk' processes.

Barraclough's refusal to leave Amilly may have rested on his suspicion of Salt's competence. It was also due to the fact that the 'little more' which Revel had given him included a salary increase and a contract that was to run till 1855. Yet despite these more pleasant conditions, he quarrelled with Revel in early 1853, behaved 'unreasonably'—according to his own later admission—and quit his post. Vainly he scoured Paris, Lille, Roubaix, and other places seeking a new employer. Salt no longer needed him, nor did any of the men who had been after him during the preceding years. By the summer he and his family were back in Triangle. France had failed him for the second time.

Perhaps England would not, for it was offering him a grand opportunity to start afresh, this time as master rather than servant. Since early 1852 his stay-at-home brothers, Joseph and William, had been consulting him. They were 'thinking of starting in the silk business' in the usual tiny way 'with two pair of frames'. Joseph's two brothers-in-law 'will lay down the mouney[1] and us to pay them so much per sent till we can pay

---

[1] One of them talked about lending £200, but failed to provide anything.

up'. They sought John's advice about materials, machine-makers, costs, and so forth; then wound up with the remark: 'We should be very glad if you could throw in with us.'

Barraclough gave the advice, but thought little more about the matter until, during the months of job-hunting in mid-1853, his brothers reported that a very suitable little factory called Swamp Mill was vacant and could be rented for £40 a year. To Barraclough, eating his heart out under a foreign sky and hearing the complaints of his family immured in a flea-infested Roubaix tenement, that empty mill looked like a temple in the promised land. From France he promptly lined up his brothers and two others as partners in the firm of John Barraclough and Company, signed the lease for the mill in August, hurried home and flung himself into his duties as manager.

The story of this little firm is a far from unusual tale of grim courage and fantastic foolhardiness. The five partners agreed to provide both the capital and the labour. Actually they did little of the former, for the total investment up to 31 December 1853 was a mere £127. 13s 1d. Most of it may have been in cash, but the odd shillings and pennies suggest that some of it represented the partners' salaries earned by working for the firm but ploughed back as capital. Barraclough had no spare money for investment after his retreat from France. His contribution of £7. 12s 2½d therefore consisted of out-of-pocket expenses, petty cash, travelling costs, and his uncollected salary, at two shillings a day, for the forty-nine long days which he spent constructing four combing-machines, assembling other kinds of equipment, and getting the mill ready to start operations.

This shoestring, or rather this silk fibre, was too slender to hold the firm up for long. In the first quarter of 1854 a little waste silk was processed and sold, and some was dressed for a customer. Barraclough ran the machines, packed the product, wrote letters to potential buyers at home and abroad, visited prospective clients, and generally served as manager, secretary, salesman, and operative all in one. The receipts in those three months were only £56. 10s, while the expenses, not including a penny of wages to Barraclough, ran to £54. 9s 9d. The capital was all gone, and there was only £2. 0s 3d left in the till. The Swamp Mill venture therefore died young and quickly.

As Barraclough calculated his uncollectable claim for salary, he uttered the prayer, 'And may God preserve us from being swamped again.'

Without awaiting the funeral, he and his brother Thomas dashed off to accept positions in a mill at Fourmies (Nord). His first impressions were mixed, for while 'we are verry comfortable here . . . living with the master at the same table', he felt irked by the awareness that 'we keep no other company, in fact they look after us verry closely, for there is another silk mill beginning in the same village, and they are afraid of us seeing any of the other firm'. There were no second impressions, for in mid-April he accepted an offer to tour France, Switzerland, and Italy as waste silk buyer for Edward Briggs, a Rochdale manufacturer. For this purpose he made three tours of these countries during the next fifteen months, thereby extending greatly his knowledge of the Continent and of the silk-producing or manufacturing regions. The travelling was often strenuous and fatiguing, especially when it involved an all-night sleigh ride over the Mont Cenis pass. The payment was not large—£2 a week and travelling expenses. The buying was not easy, for Briggs's remittances of cash were spasmodic and his credit rating was poor. 'When he writes,' reported Barraclough to his wife, 'he gives orders to buy lots of silk, . . . but sends no money, and he knows that he has no credit here, so we can do nothing.'

To 'do nothing' during three wintry months (November 1854 to January 1855) spent in Milan was a dreary experience. Barraclough laid in a stock of Italian books and worked hard studying the language. 'I think if I was to stay here a few more months longer it would be no more trouble to me than the french.' He was 'verry lonely' among 'a verry shy mistrustful people'. By way of relief he took advantage of a festival which closed the silk market to visit a small group of North of England exiles stationed about thirty-five miles away in a silk mill at Meina, near Arona, on the southern tip of Lake Maggiore. John Dean had come there some months before from the West Riding, accompanied by his wife, to install some imported machines and get the old dilapidated ones back into operation. A cousin and his son, both of them silk dressers from Macclesfield, had just arrived to tend the carding- and dressing-machines.

On one of the Borromeo Islands opposite Arona lived an Italian family which had once operated a silk mill in Manchester, there acquiring a Lancashire daughter-in-law and a fortune sufficient for comfortable existence on an island long famous for its gardens full of tropical plants. Magistrini, the managing partner of Dean's mill, was most gracious and cordial, and pressed Barraclough to spend a few days with him in his island home.

The first visit to this Anglo-Italian colony was followed by an invitation to come for Christmas, then for a third and longer visit in January. By the end of the third (23 January 1855) Barraclough had sized up the industrial possibilities of that particular bit of Italy and decided to urge Briggs to establish a silk factory there 'either in his name or in mine'. More important, his hosts had sized him up and realized that he possessed a technical *expertise* far beyond theirs. Dean, with whom he lodged, hinted that the two of them might join hands to run Magistrini's plant, or go off together to some more rewarding employer, and meanwhile look forward to the day when they could 'be on their own'. Magistrini asked him to secure price lists from half a dozen English machine-makers, and in addition to ascertain whether a Parisian silk-yarn dealer called Marquis, who had become Barraclough's close friend during the Amilly years, would care to throw his lot in with the Meina mill. Other textile manufacturers in the area requested him to look for a British manager of a worsted-spinning mill they intended to set up, to find a head for their dyeing department, and to supply names of the best makers of worsted-spinning equipment.

Thus fully charged with commissions and ideas, Barraclough returned to England, there to tinker with machines and spin fine yarns in Briggs's mill until spring sent him back on the road again. But the seed sown in him and by him at Meina quickly began to sprout. In late February Magistrini wrote asking whether Marquis was disposed to come to Italy.

If he is not, I pray you to find me a person furnished with all the knowledge necessary to carry on the direction of this enterprise and to assure me of the perfection of the work. His intervention will do no harm to Mr. Dean, as it is our intention to retain him and give him a better place when he has acquired more knowledge. If any properly qualified English entrepreneur wished to associate himself with me I would readily accept him *pourvu qu'il ait des connaissances spéciales*, since that is the one thing I lack.

This letter may have carried a bait. Certainly Barraclough thought it did and snatched at it. He reported that Marquis was very content and immovable in Paris; that he would search for 'a man with the knowledge and the disposition to associate with you'; but that he had little hope of success, 'for in our spinning mills there are few masters who have travelled abroad, and they are afraid of risking their funds in a country which they do not know'. Then came the bite at the bait:

If I find no one, and you think that John Dean has not enough knowledge for directing your establishment, and if you think I would be useful, I am disposed to make an arrangement with you for a fixed salary, or for a salary plus a share of the profits, or for a salary a part of which would remain in the firm so that I became a partner. I leave it to you to make the choice and the offer. I am beginning to fear that my health necessitates Italy or France. But I do not wish to hurt Dean at all.

In the four months of negotiation that followed, two questions had to be answered. The first concerned the duties and compensation of the 'director in chief of the spinning mill in Meina of the House of Merzagora, Defilipi and Company of Arona'. The second involved the relative positions and powers of Dean and Barraclough. Dean was eager to welcome a new colleague. He wrote in early April: 'We are already discussing your coming and joining me in the concern. We could take into our hands everything connected with the concern, correspondence and the commercial part.' He took it for granted that Barraclough's arrival would involve no reduction in his authority or salary. Barraclough in return was insistent that any arrangement must be beneficial to them both, and said this to both Dean and Magistrini. But Dean's letters soon began to voice a suspicion that his employers intended to reduce his rank and pay, or even to dismiss him. His language grew angry and defiant: 'Such a set of fools or ignoramuses I never met'; in view of their 'dirty action' and 'mean underhand ways' he would gladly 'go away and leave them in the lurch'. From that attitude it was an easy step to suspect Barraclough of playing him false. When, however, the latter succeeded in refuting the charge and

Magistrini said he wanted the two of them to manage the mill jointly—though he omitted to say 'as equals'—Dean suggested that they agree to do so for a year 'and in the meantime be preparing our other project.[1] It would give us a nice chance.'

With Dean temporarily mollified, Barraclough went ahead with his negotiations. Since Briggs had sent him to Milan in April he could discuss matters in person or quickly by correspondence. By the terms of the contract, signed 1 August, Signore Giovanni Barraclough became *Direttore della Filatura*. In that capacity he undertook 'all the disposition and direction of the work in the mill in such a manner that the yarns . . . will be of the best quality and such as will bring honour to the establishment'. He was to control all employees, assign their work, and fix their wages on the basis agreed between himself and the firm. He could not employ any person, still less give admittance, to anyone who had not been furnished with a pass from some member of the company. He would 'teach, or cause to be taught, the workpeople how to do the work that may be assigned to them in the best fashion, and to dismiss them for inability and insubordination'. At the end of each month he would prepare a table showing all work done or in process, and the cost thereof. He would record in a book all entries and deliveries from the warehouses, along with 'other accounts that may be necessary in order to give a regular statistic account of the establishment'. He would not absent himself without leave for more than a day, but could be sent anywhere when his employers felt it desirable 'in the interests of the society'.

The contract was valid for one year and thereafter renewable from year to year. The 'recompense', set out in Article VIII, was to be £3 (75 francs) a week plus a bonus of 1,000 francs (£40) at year's end for each 5 per cent of profit, without any ceiling. If, however, 'the statistic table at the end of a month' revealed results 'compromising the interests of the society', his employers could 'stop the work, and in that case consider as non-existing the Article VIII so far as regards the stipend based upon the profits'.

[1] Both men used the phrase, 'our other project', when referring to their plan for setting up their own firm, financed by an Italian capitalist who was vaguely discussing it with them.

With this document in his pocket, Barraclough hastened to England, there to purchase and supervise the construction of fifteen new machines and nearly three hundred necessary parts for the Meina mill. The ten weeks spent on this task would normally have been pleasant, since he was doing the kind of work he liked and was receiving his salary and travelling expenses. Instead, they were darkened by conflicting reports of renewed discord between Dean and his employers. Dean alleged that part of his wages for many months past were unpaid; that the firm was trying to get him and his cousin to sign new contracts—'as long as the title deeds of a manor'—at far lower rates of pay than formerly; and that rather than consent the two men would find jobs elsewhere and turn their backs on 'these damned fools'.

This news disturbed Barraclough so deeply that he wrote an angry letter to Magistrini:

If you do not fulfil your engagements with [Mr. Dean] I am very little assured that you will fulfil them towards me, and I have no fortune, I have a family, and if the [salary] is not more sure I begin to think I ought better search another place. . . . I have ordered all the machines. . . . But until I receive some news more encouraging I shall not make any preparations to return.

Awaiting your reply.

The reply was prompt and blunt. The firm owed no unpaid wages to Dean; the revised contract offered him 'new advantages' in piece-rate earnings which might make his total 'recompense probably superior to your own'; and the real trouble was his refusal to 'share with anyone else a direction which he thinks belongs solely to him'. Barraclough could have whatever additional guarantee he desired to give him peace of mind, but in return he must recognize that his contract called for his speedy return if he did not wish to deny all his principles of honour and wreck his reputation as an honest man. Close on the heels of this chiding came word from Dean. He had made his peace with the firm in a compromise agreement which apparently would give him as much income as he had received before. He wound up cheerfully: 'I hope you will take the job they offered you. We shall then be together again and plan our other affairs.' Whereupon Barraclough sent an apology for his outburst, asked only for an assurance that he would receive his salary on a fixed day each month, and announced his almost immediate departure.

He arrived at Meina in mid-October 1855, accompanied by his eldest daughter, Elizabeth, to serve as housekeeper and companion. The two went to live with the Deans, and Barraclough flung himself into his work at the mill. It was a heart-breaking task, for the factory and the firm alike were in a bad way. The owners 'were very disspirited and down of it, as they had done nothing but lost Money since the Biginning'. The quality of their yarn had been too poor to attract sales, and production had been negligible since late 1854.

Barraclough quickly became aware of this grim situation and of its causes. After two months' experience, he wrote his wife:

I begin to think this place will never be a comfortable place either for me or for anyone else so long as it is in the hands of the same company, for they know nothing of the Busness and seem determined not to learn, for without men it is not likly that I ever shall be able to make it pay and they won't consent to let me have them. They are like the Farmer who durst not trust the seed in the ground for fear he should not get it back again. I want a mecanic, a man to teach the dressers and look after them, and a carder. But they insist on doing without all these and say they cannot afford to pay them.

The result is that one half of the machinery is standing and god knows when we shall be able to get it to work. Dean and me are at it from 7 in the morn till 9 at night, obliged to do all sorts of work or else it will be undone. That part which is working we have no time to look after it properly as there is always some machine or other wants some repairs, and then we have all the new to set up and put to work.

Conditions were not improved by the dispute between Dean and his employers. As friend, lodger, and superior, Barraclough was in the middle of the brawl, vainly attempting reconciliation. Dean finally quitted his post in March 1856, bearing a grudge against Barraclough for the turn events had taken. Relations became so strained that the lodgers had to find another shelter, and the whole affair degenerated into an unseemly quarrel conducted by correspondence. At last the Deans departed, and Barraclough moved into their house. To his wife he wrote: 'I never passed 6 months ever in my life half so uncomfortable as I have done these last . . . and I am sure if you saw me you would say I look older by many a year since I came.'

Gradually conditions improved, though too slowly for Barraclough to satisfy his wife's desire that the rest of the family should come to Italy. He could, however, send her a thousand francs, and soon gained authority to bring out his son Alfred as *macchinista Inglese* at five francs a day. The monthly 'statistic table' became more encouraging, the firm participated in the general boom of the mid-'fifties, and when the 1856 financial statement showed a profit of at least 5 per cent, Barraclough was entitled to a bonus of 1,000 francs. True, he did not receive it in cash, but in a national debt bond which yielded 50 francs interest per annum. He had already received two similar bonds in part payment of his wages during the fall and winter of 1856–7, and apparently liked the appearance (or repute) of the documents so much that he bought one for himself. Sufficient of his weekly salary of 75 francs came in cash to defray the living costs—about 100 francs a month—of himself and his daughter, while Alfred earned more than the cost of his keep. Some saving was therefore possible. After every pay day he 'counted our money on hand', and in early 1858 found that in addition to four bonds he held 2,130 francs in gold pieces. He thereupon spent 1,800 francs of this sum in buying two more 'certificates of Piedmont loan of 1849'. These bonds had come to mean a little more to him since his one glimpse of Italian politics. In the summer of 1856 he reported: 'We have had the Count di CAVOUR here. I have been through the mill with him and have had a deal of conversation with him. He is *Prime Minister* here.'

Yet the money did not compensate adequately for separation from his family or for the unremitting hard work by which it was earned. In the latter respect Barraclough felt at one with his employees, of whom he wrote in June 1857:

From the following you may judge what a set of unfeeling Masters I have to deal with. Our workpeople are a set of poor things, a great part of them barefoot and barelegged, and they have to climb up and down these Mountains night and morn on roads worse than you ever saw in your life. A many of them have 2 or 3 miles to go home, and we have been working a long time from ½ past 4 a.m. till 7 at night, stoping one hour and a halfe for meals, but [the Masters] don't consider that long enough. Last week they sent up an order that I must begin and work them from 4 a.m. till 11 p.m., and stop 3 hours in the middle of the day on account of the heat. But I told them it was impossible and I could not think of it, and after a great ado they agreed (but only for a short time) to allow us to stop 2 hours at noon and ½ an hour at breakfast and give up at 7.30.[1] The wages are the same as before and they don't pay anything more for overtime. . . . Alfred does not like it and I have great difficulty in getting him to submit to it, and I made so much ado about it with some of the partners that I don't think we are likely to ever be good friends again. It is not because the place is not paying, for they are making great profits. You know a deal of my wages depends on the profits, and I am satisfied and I know no reason why they should not be.

The domestic situation also imposed its strain, especially on the daughter.

Our Elizabeth has no companion. She never goes out except with Alfred or me. We keep no company with anybody except on Sundays or Holidays, when we generaly go to see Mr. and Mrs. Ward [the only other British residents nearby] or they come to see us. She has her school-mistress who comes one hour a day to teach her Italian and that is the only company she keeps, but she has a deal of work cooking, mending, looking after the house, etc. . . . She has so much work that I would have got her a servant before now, but if I did I know she would be only a spy in the house and would tell all kinds of tales to the Roman Cath^c. parson and probably make us in the end a deal of mischief as they did for the Deans.

The only cure for homesickness was a job in England. A few reports of suitable vacancies were promptly investigated, but without any happy result. Barraclough therefore had to be satisfied with his Italian masters, and they gave him a little respite after two years of virtual incarceration by sending him on an inspection tour of French factories in October 1857. His list of 'Things to be remembered' indicates the considerable number of changes that had taken place in silk-spinning machinery and methods since he had left England in 1855. New inventions were making his technical knowledge obsolescent in

---

[1] These figures work out at actual working totals of 13 hours, 16 hours, and 13 hours respectively.

some spots and he must refresh it by trying to get inside mills housing the latest patented devices. For instance, he must 'take particular notice of the fineness of the screws and diameter of the rollers in Ramsden's preparing if I get to see them'; and 'If we see that Donnisthorpe's machine is too much like Lister's to be allowed here, to ask him if he has no plan by which he can avoid the patent taken out here by M. Vanzini.'[1]

From this trip he returned with much useful information, a dress and shoes for Elizabeth, a watch with 'a minuit hand' for Alfred, a pair of revolvers 'one for me, the other for the book-keeper', a few artificial fish for bait, and 'three safety belts for the water'. His employers were waiting for him with the draft terms of a new contract to replace the 1855 agreement. Their basic proposal was that he receive a regular wage far below the original £3 a week and depend on a share of the profits for the greater part of his income. These terms he bluntly refused to accept and gave his reasons. Profits depended on skilful buying and selling as well as on efficient production. While he had no control over the former, those in charge of it received good fixed salaries and 'some of them must be given jobs whether they understand the business or not'. Let them give him control of that branch of the firm's work and some good machinery as well; pay the cost of bringing his family from Yorkshire; then he would accept the terms.

He waged a losing battle, for in the deep depression which burst on the world in late 1857 he had no chance of finding another position, and in April 1858 accepted a compromise 'convention'. Or rather he and his son did so, for they were given a joint appointment, with the father as Technical Director of Spinning, the son as Master Mechanic. Their fixed salary was to be 3,000 francs, beyond which they got the house rent free and were to receive 8 per cent of profits, up to a maximum of 8,000 francs. Since the former basic pay of the two men had been about 5,500 francs (£220), the reduction thereon was drastic. The 3,000 francs were worth about £120, and the son could scarcely be expected to accept less than a third of that sum. The father's sure income therefore fell from the former £156 to about £80—on his income tax return he put it at only

[1] Presumably Vanzini had bought Lister's patent rights for Italy.

£60. The house may have been a modest supplement, but the chief compensation and consolation must come from the share of profits, if there were any. In 1858 there were not likely to be.

Having won this battle, the directors called on Barraclough in June to apply the lessons he had learned in France. He was presented with a list of drastic improvements, some of them amounting to a virtual rebuilding of at least seven machines. His reply was sharp: 'I deeply regret you have not more experience in spinning machinery, for many of the changes you command me to make are totally impossible.' He then dealt with each item. The remodelling job on the first began ten days ago, but the carpenter lacks some necessary tools, and if he had them it would take three months of undisturbed labour to complete the task. The second is impossible, because the machine needs a cast-iron base and we have no casting equipment. As for the third, calling for the copying of a Fairbairn machine, 'to do this one would have to see a Fairbairn machine, [and] I have not seen one'. The fourth would remedy some defects in another Fairbairn model, but 'these are defects which Mr. Fairbairn hasn't yet found a way to remove, and I haven't found one either'. And so on, all down the list. 'I don't know how long it will take to do the things that are possible, but it will be a long time and much more money than you have ever been able or willing to provide.' Consequently,

since it seems to me that I advance too slowly and that I am not big enough to do all that you desire, and as I don't wish to retard you, if you think you can find anyone who can do better and more quickly, you are free to seek him, and the sooner you find him the happier I shall be. . . . If I am slow, it is often because of your economizing, for I can do nothing without spending money. . . . Often you demand what I know will cost far more than you think; and I try to be as economical as possible to avoid your reproaches. If you have a man more hardy, you would perhaps feel better.

As no 'more hardy' man was available, Barraclough remained, subjected to steady pressure and pinpricks. In September, for example, his masters complained that the quality of the spun silk had deteriorated greatly, and called for intensive training of the new hands, whose lack of skill was admitted to be the cause of the defects; the offering of prizes 'to excite the spirit of *emulation reciproque*'; and the extension of the working day to 11 p.m. This continued strain and the lengthened hours affected his health and made him determined to escape. His friends in England, worried by the signs of imminent war in northern Italy, wrote him: 'We would advise you to get your money into good old England. . . . Your wife is thin, all the children have had the fever, but are coming round very nicely.' Finally, he was playing with a new idea which might give him a better job, perhaps even a small fortune.

For years past he had been trying to devise a machine for dressing silk on a better principle than any in current use. After endless experiments he was actually building it on the eve of his trip to Paris. There he evidently saw a new wool-combing machine made by Donnisthorpe, whereupon he scrapped his own, persuaded Magistrini to buy one of Donnisthorpe's, installed and adapted it to incorporate some of his own notions, and by March 1859 had run it day and night for three months. His employers, impressed by its performance, completely changed their tune. They urged him to build others like it, to stay with them, to accept a better contract. When he refused to do so, an acrimonious discussion ended his days at Meina, and in late April the three Barracloughs departed from the house by the mill. Father and daughter had spent three and a half years there, the son about two. From the experience the father had learned Italian, lost some of his good health, and acquired six Piedmont bonds with a face value of 6,000 francs. He was succeeded by a Belgian machinist who built the machines he had refused to construct. The firm went into liquidation in 1864.

Having convinced himself that the adapted machine would 'dress silk better than any other machine ever put to that purpose', Barraclough reported his achievement to the inventor. 'I have altered it a little, but the alterations would cost nothing if they were made in the original machine.' He therefore offered, after leaving Meina, to visit silk mills in Switzerland and France, where he had no doubt he could find many customers. 'If I undertake it, I will make it a machine necessary to every silk spinner.' He would then come to Leeds, supervise the making of the first model embodying his adaptations, then return to the Continent, set up each machine when it reached its purchaser, and put it to work—all for a commission sufficient to pay for his trouble and expenses. As an alternative, he was willing to start a small mill in Yorkshire on his own account, as partner with Donnisthorpe, or as his manager, and dress silk there with the adapted machines. He actually preferred this latter plan, but as Donnisthorpe chose the former, he sent his children home, selling one of the bonds to raise the fare, and began his tour as Donnisthorpe's salesman at £2 a week. For a year he went the rounds, but to little avail. Buyers were very few indeed, and by May 1860 the job—the fifth in fifteen years —came to an end.

The search for the sixth did not last long, for on 1 July Barraclough signed an agreement 'to serve as manager or assistant-manager in the preparation of spun silk, and as traveller in buying the raw material for spun silk, and in selling silk or other yarns, or in any of these capacities for five years' at a salary of £3 a week and travelling expenses. His new employer was perhaps the most colourful inventively minded entrepreneur in the West Riding, Samuel Cunliffe Lister. Throughout the 'forties and 'fifties Lister had been the driving force in the mechanization of wool-combing. By 1853, as Mr. Sigsworth has pointed out,[1] he had one inventor (Donnisthorpe) under close contract, and another (Isaac Holden) as his partner in three French wool-combing firms; he had bought the patent rights of Heilmann's and Noble's machines for Britain, and held several of his own, thereby monopolizing the market for such equipment. He owned or was a partner in five Yorkshire combing mills, had one in Germany, and provided the capital for the French factories at St. Denis, Croix (near Roubaix), and Reims. Now, after being checked in his stride by the crisis of 1857, which closed his Halifax mill and forced him to sell his French interests to Holden, he was turning to the waste-silk industry, and Barraclough's varied experiences might be helpful in converting his Manningham mill from wool-combing to the spinning of waste silk.

Of Barraclough's three duties—managing, buying, and selling—the first proved the least important, and his wife's hope

---

[1] E. M. Sigsworth on 'Bradford' in Fay, op. cit., p. 126.

that the family would be united at last was only partly realized. An initial personal survey of the British market revealed that most sellers of waste silk already served regular customers, while the buyers of spun silk were not impressed by the wares Barraclough offered them. A similar survey of France proved equally disappointing, especially in view of the expectation that the recently signed Cobden-Chevalier Trade Treaty would lay that market wide open to British exporters.

Lister's first response to these rebuffs was to give Barraclough authority to do whatever was needed at the mill to raise quality and reduce production costs. Soon he had a better idea. He would jump the still fairly high tariff wall by establishing a mill, equipped with his own machines, on French soil. Barraclough was dispatched in March 1861 to scour a wide area of countryside around Lyons in search of a suitable building. For three months he hunted, often on foot, talking with farmers, village notaries, machinists, and builders, and tracking down any mill advertised in local papers. Most places were too far from the railroad, lacked adequate power, or were in bad disrepair. When at last he reported that he had found the perfect spot, Lister wired 'Take it if we can have the whole mill and the house and if the rent is right.' The owner said its rent was 7,500 francs a year; Lister said, 'Offer 5,000', and the owner asked for a week's grace to consider the figure. By the time he was ready to give his decision Barraclough had received two other messages from Lister. The first said 'Offer 4,000', the second read, 'Four thousand is too much and 3,000 is nearer the mark.' Hence when the owner announced that 5,000 was acceptable, poor Barraclough had to say it was far too much. A few days later Lister ordered him to 'let the matter stand over' and come home. When he arrived in Lister's office, he learned that his master had dropped the whole idea. Two days later he was told that it had not been dropped.

What could one do with such a changeable employer? In retrospect Revel and the Meina masters began to look less baleful. 'I don't think I can stay long at Lister's', he wrote in his diary. For a while he flirted with the idea of joining hands with Jessen, the mill cashier, and another fellow employee to start a factory in Switzerland. When, however, he sought release from his contract Lister refused, and kept him busy for the rest of the year experimenting with Persian knubs—waste silk from Asia—under instructions to persist in his efforts till he achieved success or found that failure was unescapable.

The new year (1862) brought new duties. Lister revived his plans for a French factory, and this time he swore he was in earnest. In it he would install his famous double-nip wool-combing machine, recently adapted for treating waste silk. It would process material for sale in France and in addition establish his patent rights in that country. To do the latter he must get permission to import one machine, erect it, and operate it in the presence of credible witnesses who would then sign a declaration that they had seen it moving and producing. All these steps must be taken within a certain length of time, or the claim for the patent would lapse.

In mid-April Lister went to Paris to secure the necessary import permit and was given until 30 July to establish his claim. True, no mill had yet been found, and it was therefore decided to erect the machine in some small northern factory, run it there for the benefit of the witnesses, then dismount it for transfer to its permanent home. Barraclough was assigned this task, and on 5 May he left Bradford, accompanied by a mechanic, for Lille. There he found John Ward, the Yorkshire machinist who had been his only *émigré* neighbour during the last years in Meina. Ward occupied a mill, actually 'a miserable place not much bigger than a barn'. He offered to lease part of it with steam power and shafting, for 500 francs a month for six months. 'Too much and too long', said Lister; try elsewhere, but as a last resort 'try Ward for one month or, failing that, for two'.

Discussion of terms and time had not ended when Barraclough was confronted by a more serious problem. On 12 May the machine reached Dunkirk. While Case Number Two was being lifted from the hold the chain broke and it 'fell into the bottom of the steamer. It is a wonder it did not go through.' Barraclough and his man rushed to Dunkirk to survey the damage. One whole end of the machine was shattered beyond repair. The case and its contents must be sent back to Bradford and on 23 May another case containing the needed replacements was sent off. It reached Dunkirk on 31 May to join the undamaged cases still lying in the customs shed under a ruling that part of a machine could not be released. The officials asked for the certificate to prove British origin of the shipment. Barraclough did not have it and was told that failure to produce it would raise the tariff charges to an exorbitant figure. He wrote asking for it and finally got it on 6 June.

At last things could move, but only after he paid a bill of 801 francs (£32) for sundry charges, and he was hard put to raise that amount, since he had left Bradford with only £50 in his pocket a month before. The work of assembling the machine in Ward's mill was quickly completed, and on 7 June Ward promised to have the shafting fixed up ready to deliver power on the ninth. Since those days were a week-end, nothing was done. By 11 June all was ready, but when Barraclough said, 'Let her go', the machine refused to budge, because the shaft was not delivering sufficient power. A broader strap and larger shaft wheel were installed by the thirteenth, whereupon the strain was now so great that the shaft threatened to fall down and its supports had to be strengthened. On the fourteenth the machine really worked and combed some silk 'after several mishaps'. On the fifteenth, a Sunday, its guardians rested. On Monday and Tuesday it ran fairly smoothly, apart from a breakdown in the engine on Monday afternoon.

Now for the demonstration before witnesses! Barraclough already had obtained from the Paris Patents Office the certificate 'which must be filled in and signed by as many respectable people as possible'. He rushed into Lille and asked two *huissiers* to come, see, and sign. 'But one of them made so many observations about the patent that I saw he wanted to run up a bill, so I left them' and went to discuss this new *impasse* with a friend who had some knowledge of French bureaucracy and its ways. The advice given him was 'Work the machine where it is for a few weeks, sell the combed silk, do all your business by correspondence, keep copies or originals of all letters and invoices, and these will be better than a certificate for securing the patent and shewing that the machine was working in time'.

The only defects in this advice were, first, that Barraclough had received only enough silk from Bradford for the trials and demonstration, and Lister would send no more. In fact, Lister sent little of anything, including money. Secondly, to work the machine for a few weeks in Lille meant that Ward's mill must continue to be used, and Ward was being 'difficult'. He was eager to extend the lease beyond the original unwritten one or two months' contract. It was evident that he wanted to keep the machine there for a long time in the hope of making its kind for France, and had the notion of adapting it for combing tow as well as silk. 'In fact he makes himself too Buisey in the affair for me.'

Lister's reply to this news was, 'I will not work it at Lille and be careful not to let anyone see it. I am afraid of Ward copying it if he can. You must guard against this.' He suggested that Lepointre of Roubaix, with whom Barraclough's brother Edwin had worked for more than a decade, might be invited to take it in and let the brother work it in secret. 'Or you can let Revel [Barraclough's employer in the mid-century years] have it, *as I have decided not to have a place in the south for the present.* Of course I leave it with you to do as you think best. If it is found to answer they can either buy it or pay a licence of so much per lb.'

'Do as you think best.' No 'best' was possible at this stage in the tragi-comedy of errors, and Barraclough was scarcely in a condition to 'think', now that his master had once more abandoned the plan for a French factory. The strain of frustrating events since early May had brought him near to physical and nervous exhaustion. Now, a sick man, he must get rid of the accursed machine somehow. With no patent certificate signed and the expectant permanent home destroyed by the latest whim of the great entrepreneur, the machine was like a castle in the clouds. Yet in every letter Lister nagged him to clear up the sorry venture and come home, for 'I do not like the daily expense that is incurred'. And Lister's cashier was deaf to all requests for money.

Lepointre was offered the use of the machine, but declined. So also did Revel and others. 'I cannot give it away', reported Barraclough. 'Nobody will have it. I have offered it to all the silk-spinners that are likely, and not one of them will have anything to do with it, though I offered it on trial for a year for nothing.' Lister's reply was, 'Sell the machine either through a broker or by auction. Do let us have an end of it, as I am sick of the expense.' That sad fate was averted when Barraclough found a refuge for the unwanted equipment in the Croix mill of Isaac Holden, Lister's partner from whom he had parted company in 1858. This may have been magnanimity on Holden's part, but it must have been gall and wormwood to Lister.

Barraclough reached England in mid-August, thus ending one of his sorriest ventures or wild-goose chases abroad. Yet there was a comic sequel. Revel soon repented his refusal and asked for the machine. 'Too late,' replied Barraclough, 'I am verry sorry things have taken this turn, for you could have got the first machine very cheap.' Then two others who had rejected the offer changed their minds. Barraclough chuckled over this turn of events, but was not seriously concerned, for already he was being tempted to let his mind run on another track, or rather on the old track that promised to lead him to management of a mill and of a firm which would in part be his own.

The voice of the tempter came, as he convalesced in Ostend, in a long letter from Jessen, Lister's cashier:

Lister is talking of going out of business, and if he does you and I will be out of work. If he does not, you have not much chance of selling his machines in France and Italy. I am tired, and desirous with all my heart of a change. I have a chance of representing a large house in India, but that's rather far and too hot for a stout man. Besides I could not take my dear little girls with me, and would have to take them for a time to grandmama in Berlin.[1]

I may toss the ball as I like, it always falls to the ground and hits upon our plan to open an establishment in France in connection with you and your brother and families. I have various new ideas in machinery for carding and dressing, and you have your sorting machine to separate long from short fibres. Our establishment would soon tell a tale in the way of profits.

Capital. I will give what I can spare, and calculating what you and your brother might produce I think we could raise £2,000 amongst us, which is amply enough and will leave a handsome sum to buy materials. The financing job I am willing to undertake and I am sure we shall not be fast [short of money]. Now or never is the opportunity to make a rapid fortune in silk.

[1] Jessen was a member of the German colony which settled in Bradford during the second quarter of the century.

Perhaps the summer sun and sea breezes at Ostend explain why Barraclough was exhilarated by this letter. Otherwise, apart from incorrigible optimism, how account for the failure to sniff any warning odour from Swamp Mill, or to recall how remiss Jessen had been in sending money to defray the expenses of the combing-machine fiasco in Lille? The venture into which he plunged, as partner in the firm of Jessen, Barraclough and Company, as soon as he returned home and was released from his contract by Lister in August 1862, collapsed within a year completely and more cruelly than any of the others to which he had pinned his hopes or devoted his energies.

There were all the usual difficulties, only this time much larger. The mill, leased not in France but a few miles from Halifax, was high in rent but low in industrial conveniences. Of the machinery, which cost at least £1,000, only a third had been delivered by June 1863, and as that third did not include the spinning units no yarn could be made, no goods sold, no commissions accepted. 'We have a great expense going on and nothing coming in.' The capital supply was to be £1,800, surely more than ample. But while Barraclough immediately contributed most of his £300 investment and soon added the balance of it, Jessen doled out only a small part of his promised £1,500, and that only when importuned, in snippets of £5, £10, at most £30. By June 1863 he had provided only £270, and his last-minute addition was only £400. Hence the familiar picture of Barraclough paying his wages out of his own capital, and when that ran out, getting virtually none, as was the case with his son and his brother Edwin, who were working for him; of having to borrow £1 from his wife to pay the wages of one of his men; and of being called on to 'pay so many things that I did not expect today that I was left with 11/- in hand and my wife 3/6, all the money in the house'.

This grimly ridiculous situation could not last long, especially when the machine makers began to ask for instalments of payment. In mid-August 1863 the partnership was dissolved, but the liquidation was terribly complicated, with assignment of the property to a trustee, countless lawyer's letters, a suit in chancery, writs served, and trouble over a bill of exchange for £1,000 drawn by the machine makers and 'accepted' by Jessen.

Nearly two years elapsed before *Finis* was written to the sorry episode.

Through the manœuvrings of those years Barraclough moved bewildered, disillusioned, bitter. The only bright spot in dark days was a brief letter from Lister dated April 1864. It read: 'I shall be glad if you will give me a call if you have not yet got a situation.' Eagerly Barraclough waited on the master he had left so gladly twenty months before, and was appointed travelling waste-silk buyer and seller of silk products at £3 weekly with travelling expenses. Once more his dream of enterprise had faded. Once more he was on the old roads at the old salary, and he was now fifty-two years old.

We need not follow him closely on his itinerary, which covered southern France and northern Italy every winter and summer and took him round the British silk-manufacturing regions each spring. There was little new in his experiences. He faced again the thankless task of compromising between high market prices in sellers' markets and the upper limits imposed by his employer. Replies to his letters and telegrams were long delayed when Lister, now climbing high on the social ladder, was away shooting birds on the moors or enjoying other aristocratic pleasures, without delegating anyone to make decisions in his absence. There were the discomforts of travel: the hot humid summer nights in Marseilles, when he 'doubted if [he] could live till morn', and the cold wintry days when the mistral swept over southern France; the endless struggle in lodging-houses and hotels with fleas and bugs which sometimes drove him to sleep on the floor and on one occasion tormented him so much that 'he had to keep a light on all night and read Bradshaw'; the occasional attack of mild malaria, and the teeth broken on French breakfast rolls; then, by way of contrast and compensation, the joy he experienced in gazing at some landscapes in Ireland, the Cotswolds, and the west of England, in eating a 'chimney dinner' with a glass of rum for a shilling, or on finding at the Crown Inn in Chard 'ham and eggs for tea, cheese and ale for supper, the best of beds, and a big breakfast, all for three shillings'.

In the summer of 1868 all this came to an end when Lister announced:

After fully considering all things I have come to the conclusion that your services will not be further required. We have such very large purchases [of raw silk] coming from India that we shall require very little buying in the home market. Consequently your proposed journey to France would be lost time.

Barraclough declined an invitation to carry on as machine supervisor in one of Lister's factories, since he could 'no longer stand the dust and stink in the mill'.

So ended his connexion with big business, machines, and foreign mills. By 1870 western Europe's demand for British mechanics and textile experts was reaching vanishing point. Brother Edwin, who had gone back to his old post in Roubaix after the fiasco of 1862–3, talked as if Russia was now the only country offering attractive terms to such emigrants. When occasionally he was commissioned to ask John to find a dresser or two for a French firm, he urged his brother to reply that he could find none or that the only ones available 'would not come because of the language difficulty. I give no encouragement to come here.'

John therefore stayed in England. He served a few months as buyer of silk waste and seller of yarn for a Lancashire mill; then started selling goods on commission. In 1870 and 1871 he conducted small parties from Yorkshire on tours of France, Italy, Germany, and Scotland. After a gap of fifteen years in the records, we find him and his son operating in 1885 as 'cotton, cotton waste, warp and yarn merchants'. By that time he was seventy-three years old. He died ten years later, in 1895.

XII

The Return to Gold, 1925

ALTHOUGH its subject is a single brief episode, this paper is rather to be regarded as a plea for the systematic study of recent monetary history. I am pleading for a trade I have made my own, because its very nature causes it to be neglected, although it is of high importance to a full appreciation of problems of economic policy. To develop a taste for monetary history a student must have a pretty good grasp of monetary theory, and the expert in monetary theory is apt to succumb either to the fascination of highbrow theory or to the temptation to expend his energies in controversies about current policy; in either event he has no time for history. The historian, on the other hand, with plenty of other aspects of the past to study, is disinclined to get himself involved in a subject in which he fears the professional economists may easily catch him out.[1] So monetary history falls between the stools.

What is the result? It is not that we have no monetary history at all, but that we have a lot of bogus monetary history, largely composed of the old skins thrown off by the snake of controversy. No matter how unhistorical they are, most people engaged in the controversies of economic policy do use arguments avowedly based on an interpretation of recent events, and this interpretation, being bandied about in current controversy, tends to harden into the accepted view of history. Yet it is most unlikely to be a sound view: it will have been based on the evidence of the moment alone, and its shape may well be influenced, if not dictated, by the more striking phrases of the controversialists. One of the qualifications of the effective controversialist is ability to coin the striking phrase; these phrases and the evidence of the moment form the basis of the view commonly taken of an

[1] The eminent scholar in whose honour this volume is published is the exception who proves the rule.

episode as it slips back into the past. Though this process may be repugnant to the scholar, it would not greatly matter were it not that this accepted view itself becomes one of the arguments bandied about in the next phase of monetary controversy. The policies of tomorrow are influenced by today's slipshod history of yesterday; this is the evil we should seek to correct by turning our searchlights on to the recent past.

That completes the generalities that lie behind my review of an episode in recent monetary history. Through the remainder of this paper I shall be dealing with the restoration of the gold standard in 1925, because I believe that this episode provides a sharp illustration of the traps into which we may fall when we neglect the systematic study of monetary history.

The restoration of the gold standard in itself can be described very shortly. After being pegged by official dealings through the latter part of the war, at a rate close to the old parity, the dollar rate was allowed to slide from March 1919, and reached its low point of 3.20 in February 1920. The restoration of the gold standard, at a tacitly assumed rate of 4.86, was government policy throughout, and corrective measures for the low exchange were taken from the autumn of 1919 onwards. The wartime measures modifying the gold standard had been replaced in 1920 by the Gold and Silver Export Embargo Act. The term of this had been fixed at five years, ending 31 December 1925. There was no special significance about this period (it is a common period for temporary legislation when one year is obviously too short); but when 1925 came round something had to be done about it. Policy in the intervening years had been directed, though not in an extreme way, to restoration of the gold standard, and in 1924 reasonably favourable conditions had helped the exchange towards par. A decision had then to be taken, and the decision was announced in the Budget Speech at the end of April 1925. The gold export embargo was effectively suspended forthwith, and the Gold Standard Act established a gold bullion system, the old parity of $4.86 to the £ being the basis.

The commonly accepted view of this step is that it was a grave mistake, made by Churchill after he had been misled by his official advisers; that the interests of British industry were, in some measure, sacrificed to the interests of the City of London as an international trading and financial centre; that it was a gamble on a rise in American prices that did not materialize; that the resulting international disequilibrium was the prime cause of the relative stagnation of the British economy through the second half of the 'twenties; that the resulting weakness of sterling was a major factor in the international currency collapse of 1931 and that the policy of 1925 was thus one of the remote causes of the cruel waste of the 'thirties. It is this view that has become part of the background of all recent argument on both short-term and long-term policy for sterling; it has given an air of historical justification to the case against any measures of exchange rigidity. I am going to suggest that, when all the evidence now available is reviewed, it is possible to interpret events quite differently.

But first I must say a few words about how the common view developed. It was by no means the immediate reaction of the commentators. *The Times* (29 April) claimed that the great majority of businessmen would rejoice in the return to gold. *The Economist* (2 May) expected it to effect 'a definite broadening of the base of British commerce'; the new policy was subject for congratulation to the Chancellor and was 'the crowning achievement' of Montagu Norman. The *Yorkshire Post* (2 May) and the *Manchester Guardian* (5 May) were equally comfortable. The President of the Federation of British Industries had much more to say about other (now forgotten) aspects of the Budget, but did find a moment in which to welcome the return to gold as a step towards a revival of foreign investment and the conquest of new markets. Criticism in the House of Commons had the empty ring of the formal duty of His Majesty's Opposition, and was not pressed.[1]

During the summer of 1925 opinion began to change rapidly. Keynes wrote a series of articles in *The Nation* and the *Evening Standard*, and these were reprinted as a pamphlet with the stinging title *The Economic Consequences of Mr. Churchill*;[2] Stamp lent his weighty support to Keynes's main thesis in his Addendum

---

[1] The chief Opposition spokesman was Philip Snowden, who was in such matters always a pillar of 'orthodoxy'. The account given in his *Autobiography* (1934), ii, 721-2, was written in the light of later troubles and gives the impression of stronger doubts than were in fact voiced in 1925.

[2] Hogarth Press, 1925.

to the Report of the Court of Inquiry concerning the Coal Industry Dispute.[1] Keynes treated the whole thing as a blunder; his explanation of why Churchill did 'such a silly thing' was that 'he was gravely misled by his experts'. Churchill's repentance gathered strength until he has almost come to believe that it was 'the greatest mistake of his life, and that he was bounced into it in his green and early days by an unholy conspiracy between the officials of the Treasury and the Bank of England'.[2] In fact it was an exceptionally well-considered step, Churchill's final decision only coming after a long series of official papers and, at the end, a dinner-party that was a kind of Brains Trust with opposing views voiced by the most eminent authorities. The argument of the case may be said to begin with the Cunliffe Report in 1918; after that date every government had proclaimed its intention of working towards the earliest possible restoration of the gold standard.[3] At the Genoa Conference in 1922 British delegates had taken the lead in advocating a universal return to gold, at previous parities where possible. The Bank Chairmen had pronounced in its favour (though not ignoring difficulties) and as lately as March 1925 the Federation of British Industries addressed to the Chancellor an Open Letter advocating restoration of the gold standard and not even referring to any disequilibrium in the international price situation.[4] The only real opposition came from a small group round Keynes, and there were critical noises in the Beaverbrook Press. The critics had their representatives in Churchill's private circles, and they worried him. Consequently, despite the overwhelming pressure of opinion in favour of restoration, the whole

---

[1] *BPP*, 1924–5 (2478), XIII, 21–23.

[2] P. J. Grigg, *Prejudice and Judgment* (1948), p. 180. The following account of Churchill's consultations is based on Grigg's pages 180–6; Grigg was at the time in the Treasury and was the Chancellor's Principal Private Secretary.

[3] On the views of the Bank of England, see Sir Henry Clay, *Lord Norman* (1957), ch. iv.

[4] In view of this document, I find disingenuous the 'I-told-you-so' element in the evidence tendered by the F.B.I. to the Macmillan Committee in 1930. (Committee on Finance and Industry, *Minutes of Evidence*, i, 186–210.) This evidence included reproduction of the written evidence tendered by the F.B.I., July 1924, to the 'Bradbury Committee', urging delay and caution in the return to gold, but the Open Letter of March 1925 would seem to indicate that the F.B.I., like many others, came round to the policy of immediate return as conditions seemed in the winter of 1924–5 to become more propitious.

The Return to Gold, 1925

subject and all possible courses of action were thoroughly argued out in official circles and put before the Chancellor both in written memoranda and in oral discussions. In these discussions there was no concealment of the pains of adjustment.

Finally Churchill gave a dinner-party, Niemeyer and Bradbury invited to represent the Ayes and McKenna and Keynes the Noes; Grigg was there as the Chancellor's Private Secretary, and it is from him that we have the story. Plenty was said about the risks of unemployment, falling wages, prolonged strikes and the contraction of some of the heavy industries. I suspect that Keynes was not at his most effective: he did not in those days carry his later weight, and he was always liable to have an 'off-day'. At any rate, Churchill was not completely convinced by Keynes's gloomy prognostications and turned to McKenna, who had wobbled somewhat in his latest public pronouncements. Churchill in effect asked McKenna: 'This is a political decision; you have been a politician, indeed you have been Chancellor of the Exchequer. If the decision were yours, what would it be?' McKenna, after wobbling to the end, replied, 'There's no escape; you have got to go back; but it will be hell.'[1]

So much for the story that Churchill was misled by his official advisers. I must now turn to two elements in the case that was made. First, there is the idea that the interests of British industry were sacrificed to the interests of the City of London: in effect, that Montagu Norman cared more for top-hats in the City than for cloth caps in the streets of Lancashire and the valleys of South Wales. Nothing could be further from the truth, for the Gold Standard policy was essentially an Employment Policy. The post-war slump in Britain had reached bottom in 1922, and the slow revival thereafter had halved unemployment in the next two years, bringing it to around a million in 1924. At that level, or a little higher, it got stuck, and it was clear that Britain had an unemployment problem going beyond anything that could be explained by reference to the trade cycle. Analysis of the unemployment total revealed that the bulk of the remaining unemployment was in a few great export industries: coal, textiles, iron and steel, shipbuilding, which had

[1] This is reported by Grigg as the substance of Churchill's question and McKenna's reply: naturally no verbatim record was made of the discussion.

been the staples in the terrific expansion of British exports in the generation before 1914. By the beginning of 1925 informed opinion therefore regarded the abnormal unemployment as a symptom of the difficulties of the staple export trades. Why were the export trades depressed?

This question, greatly debated up and down the country, was systematically tackled in the winter of 1924–5 by the Balfour Committee on Industry and Trade, a Committee predominantly of industrialists and traders, appointed by the MacDonald Labour Government in 1924. Its most important conclusions were published in mid-1925, after the actual return to gold, but the operative document is dated 12 March[1] and represents the views of intelligent businessmen during that winter when the gold standard policy was under consideration. The Board of Trade had provided the Committee with statistics showing that the proportion of British exports to total world exports had, if anything, risen since pre-war; the decline in Britain's export industries therefore appeared as an effect of causes operating not peculiarly upon Britain but upon the whole volume of world trade. For this general decline in world trade, the Committee found two sets of cause, one temporary and the other more permanent. The permanent cause was the growth of local manufactures; this was a tough one, to be countered only by continuing inventiveness in the most advanced products and, as it was then argued, by 'rationalization' of the old industries.[2] Temporarily there was the dislocation of markets by wartime conditions; prominent among this set of causes was 'financial dislocation and the disorganization of currency and exchange'.[3]

The Committee itself did not there and then point the moral, but it was widely appreciated. Britain's unemployment problem was due to depression of world export markets; this was partly due to currency disorganization; therefore get the world's currency instability removed, the former foreign exchange stability restored, and export markets could be expected to

[1] It is printed as an Introduction to the *Survey of Overseas Markets* by the Committee on Industry and Trade (H.M.S.O., 1926).

[2] cf. Clay, op. cit., especially pp. 166 and 356–7.

[3] The violent exchange fluctuations of the early 'twenties had discouraged the export trades in much the same way as uncertainties of U.S. tariff policy operate today.

revive and Britain's unemployment would dwindle. The world was waiting on the decision Britain had to take in 1925;[1] Britain's return to gold would give the lead and so give tremendous impetus to the movement towards international monetary stability.[2] A decision to return to gold at a lower parity would probably have had almost as good an effect. I must come back to this alternative in a moment; my immediate point is that the decision to go back to gold, far from being neglectful of the interests of British industry and the unemployed, was a decision calculated to eradicate one of the principal causes of trade depression and unemployment.

This viewpoint of business circles was urged upon Churchill by his advisers; that it was shared by competent outside observers is proved by *The Economist*'s immediate reaction to the announcement, which I have already quoted. And it did have its bearing on the question of adjustment to parity. Looking back, it is possible to suggest that the case for a return to gold appeared so overwhelming that insufficient attention was given to the question, 4.86 or 4.40? The Bradbury Committee did, it is true, brush this issue aside, partly on grounds of prestige.[3] Nevertheless, the question whether Britain could stand the 4.86 rate was looked into, at length, before the decision was taken. Churchill's advisers in general argued that there was still appreciable disequilibrium between British and American prices. The Bradbury Committee itself advised that a fall in the price level 'of a significant, though not very large, amount' was necessary,[4] and Keynes's own estimate of a 10 per cent gap was put before Churchill before he took his decision.[5] It is possible to argue that Churchill was not advised of the

[1] The Gold and Silver Export Embargo Act was due to expire at the end of the year.

[2] cf. Clay, op. cit., pp. 141–2.

[3] To Montagu Norman no lower parity was acceptable, but he was willing to postpone return until 4.86 could be regarded as tenable (ibid., ch. iv). According to evidence given to the Macmillan Committee by the Federation of British Industries, the Federation had been told by the Treasury, apparently at an early stage in the Bradbury Committee's proceedings, that return at a 'devalued' rate was already ruled out of consideration (Committee on Finance and Industry, *Minutes of Evidence*, i, Q.3188).

[4] *Report*, para. 19, reprinted in T. E. G. Gregory, *Select Statutes, Documents, and Reports relating to British Banking, 1832–1928* (2 vols., 1929), ii, 376.

[5] Grigg, p. 182.

precariousness of all calculations of purchasing power parities; it was not until some time later that Gregory showed that quite a different answer to the sum resulted from choice of a more appropriate index number.[1] However that may be, it is certainly not possible to say that Churchill was not warned of appreciable disequilibrium.

Nor is it possible to justify Keynes's assertion[2] that there was 'a gamble on a rise in gold prices abroad'. His assertion may have been based on a careless reading of the Bradbury Committee's paragraph 19, but their paragraph 22 showed that they assumed no better than 'stability' in America.[3] And in Grigg's report of the arguments used at the famous dinner-party there is no mention of this among the points made by supporters of the gold policy. On the contrary, great stress was laid by Churchill's advisers on the risk that adjustment to the restored parity might be extremely painful.

Where I consider Churchill was ill-advised was in being led to suppose that the pre-1914 weapons of credit restriction were appropriate for bringing about the required adjustments. Keynes did make a point of this kind in his pamphlet,[4] but I should put it rather differently. In my view the ease of adjustments in Britain in the immediately pre-1914 period was based on the strength of London as an international lending centre, for this allowed London to shift much of the pain of adjustment on to other countries. Nothing like this was argued in 1925; I may perhaps be allowed to add that there had not been enough study of monetary history for people to appreciate the point.

I shall say no more about the arguments of 1925 but turn to the event. Churchill did decide to restore the gold standard, at the old parity of $4.86. By the time the Macmillan Committee reported in 1931 some of its members considered this act to have

[1] Keynes's charge that the experts had 'attended to index numbers of prices which were irrelevant or inappropriate' (*Economic Consequences of Mr. Churchill,* p. 10) was thus singularly inept. On the other hand, Keynes did get a result more credible, in the light of later events, than did Gregory (T. E. G. Gregory, *The First Year of the Gold Standard* (1926), pp. 39–54). In short, Keynes used the wrong index numbers, and Gregory the right, yet Keynes got the right result and Gregory the wrong. So much for Purchasing Power Parity as an aid to policy!

[2] op. cit., p. 12; and cf. his p. 27.

[3] Gregory, *Select Statutes, etc.,* ii, 376 and 377.

[4] ibid., pp. 11 ff.

been a mistake, while others did not;[1] all agreed that it had
'required a reduction of sterling prices'.[2] The disequilibrium
had been serious, perhaps of the order of 10 per cent: this was
the general view, people differing only on the question whether
the advantages of a gold standard policy had been worth the
agony. As Keynes had predicted, internal costs proved decidedly
resistant to any adjustment to the new parity, and the overvaluation persisted. The chronic difficulty of maintaining London's gold reserve and the international trade figures[3] support
the view that there was this persistent overvaluation through the
remainder of the 'twenties. There was certainly persistent
depression in the old export trades, and continuing unemployment. McKenna's forecast that it would be hell proved all too
correct; the hopes for an export revival to solve the unemployment problem proved illusory; and Keynes's criticism that 4.86
had posed too big an adjustment appeared to be all too well
justified.

Nevertheless, I venture to doubt whether a choice of 4.40 as
the 1925 parity, avoiding Keynes's 10 per cent adjustment,
would have made much difference in any but the very short run.
The initial strains were admittedly great, as most of Keynes's
opponents had expected. But from the end of 1926 onwards
international competition in the staple exports was gravely
affected by the French and Belgian currency stabilizations, both
at rates seriously undervaluing their currencies.[4] Now to anyone who reads the diary of Moreau, Governor of the Bank of
France at the time, it is crystal clear that the French deliberately
stabilized at a rate perpetuating the artificial advantage recently
enjoyed by French export industries.[5] And what happened to
the French franc had great influence on what was done about
the Belgian franc. Hence a lower level of the pound would have
meant an even lower level for the French and Belgian francs.

[1] *Report,* para. 242.
[2] ibid., para. 113.
[3] cf. below, p. 323.
[4] cf. M. Norman's Evidence to the Committee on Finance and Industry
(Macmillan Committee), especially QQ. 3355–62.
[5] E. Moreau, *Souvenirs d'un Gouverneur de la Banque de France* (Paris, 1954); pp. 177
and 182–3 are particularly relevant, and all Moreau's allusions to the subject show
that France was not willing to face any dislocation consequent upon removal of the
previous years' undervaluation of the franc.

Given the lack of international co-operation in these matters, this source of strain from 'exchange competition' in western Europe would have had to be faced by Britain whether the pound had been stabilized at one level or another. The trade statistics of various countries suggest that in fact the strain upon Britain came from Belgium rather than France. Between 1924 and 1927 Britain's share in world exports (by value) declined from 13 to 11 per cent; France's declined from 8 to 6·9, while Belgium's was maintained at 2·8 per cent. As sellers to Britain itself, France maintained her position with 5·2 per cent of Britain's imports, while Belgium's share in the market rose from 2·8 to 3·8 per cent.

The international trade figures of the period 1922–9 have a little further light to shed on the forces influencing international competition before and after Britain's return to gold.

The U.K. was obviously losing ground relatively to all the other countries listed; Belgium was gaining ground relatively to the U.S.A., the U.K., and France; but the most striking feature is the resurgence of Germany as a competitor both in the U.K. market and in world markets generally. In fact, what was to happen again a generation later was happening in a milder form in 1924–9: the reconstruction of the German economy after the stabilization of the mark was a principal source of strain in international competition and upon sterling in particular. It was this resurgence of Germany, coupled with the deliberate under-valuation of the Belgian and French francs, that created for Britain a second problem of adjustment, and it was this second problem rather than the original act of overvaluation of sterling that made life such a misery for British exporters.

It is, of course, possible to argue that the choice of a more tolerable parity in 1925 would have allowed a margin, in the shape of a favourable balance of trade, which would have allowed Britain to take the later strains without catastrophe. To argue thus, it is necessary to argue that these later strains might reasonably have been foreseen. It is not reasonable to argue so in relation to the French and Belgian stabilizations. But the prevailing mentality behind Britain's decision in 1925 was a desire 'to get back to 1913', and indeed a belief that such a return was possible. A thoughtful and discriminating view of

The Return to Gold, 1925

TABLE A. Value of Merchandise Exports
World Total, and for Selected Countries
(*In U.S.A. gold dollars*)

Year	World exports $ million	U.K.	U.S.A.	France	Belgium	Germany
1924	27,185	3,538	4,498	2,169	644	1,559
1927	31,378	3,451	4,759	2,164	740	2,435

Per cent of World Exports

Year		U.K.	U.S.A.	France	Belgium	Germany
1924	100	13·0	16·5	8·0	2·4	5·7
1927	100	11·0	15·2	6·9	2·4	7·8

Source: League of Nations, *Review of World Trade*, 1936; *Memorandum on International Trade and Balances of Payments 1913–27* and *1927–9*.

TABLE B. Value of United Kingdom Imports
Total, and for Selected Countries of Origin
(*£ million*)

Year	Total U.K. imports £ million	Country of origin			
		U.S.A.	France	Belgium	Germany
1913	768·7	141·7	46·4	23·4	80·4
1922	1,003·1	221·8	48·5	23·6	26·5
1924	1,277·4	241·2	66·6	36·4	36·9
1927	1,218·3	200·8	63·4	46·5	59·9
1929	1,220·8	196·0	56·5	44·0	68·8

Per cent of Total U.K. Imports

Year		U.S.A.	France	Belgium	Germany
1913	100	18·4	6·0	3·0	10·5
1922	100	22·1	4·8	2·4	2·6
1924	100	18·9	5·2	2·8	2·9
1927	100	16·5	5·2	3·8	4·9
1929	100	16·1	4·6	3·6	5·6

Source: *Annual Abstract of Statistics, U.K.*

'back to 1913' should have allowed for the possibility that Germany would win back something of her former trading strength. The superficiality of economic thought in high quarters passed over all such possibilities.

There is thus no doubt that, whatever the degree of blindness of responsible British authorities, the amount of adjustment required in the British economy was greater than had been foreseen. The later 'twenties did, however, show a quite considerable measure of adjustability in the British economy. Transfer of labour from one industry to another took place on a considerable scale. Although the volume of British exports still failed to reach the 1913 level, twelve out of the twenty groups into which the figures were divided showed that they had surpassed the 1913 level; these twelve included iron and steel and manufactures thereof.[1] By 1929 it was not fantastic to argue that the restoration of international currency stability had promoted the growth of world trade, that Britain had adjusted herself in part to the price disequilibrium created in 1925 even though that disequilibrium had been aggravated by the French and Belgian stabilizations, and that on a long view the 1925 action, taken by itself, had been worth while. There was still, of course, the major problem of excess capacity in certain of the old export industries, but the need for some fundamental reshaping of the British economy had been foreseen by Churchill's advisers in 1925 and had been represented by them, in my view correctly, as something that had to be faced anyway as industrialization proceeded elsewhere in the world.[2]

Then came the Wall Street slump. The immediate effect was to ease Britain's monetary problems. Very high rates of interest in America had been drawing short-term funds across the Atlantic, on an uncomfortable scale, and the easing of the tension in money markets brought a much-needed relief to the U.K. balance of payments at the end of 1929. The more fundamental effects of the slump came only in 1930, when it became

---

[1] See Macmillan Committee, *Report*, Addendum III (T. E. Gregory), p. 223, and G. W. Daniels, 'Recent Changes in the Overseas Trade of the United Kingdom', Transactions of the Manchester Statistical Society, November 1930.

[2] See the case put by Bradbury, as reported by Grigg, op. cit., p. 182. Sir Henry Clay, in his *Lord Norman*, which appeared after this paper was written, took substantially the same view.

clear that the movement was no mere Stock Exchange phenomenon. Precisely what these effects were on the British balance
of payments we cannot say, because it was not until Britain ran
into much more serious and more chronic difficulties that our
authorities ever produced usable balance of payments statistics.
But what evidence there is for the 1929–32 episode indicates
that the balance of payments for the U.K. itself stood up remarkably well to the crisis: the steep relative fall in the prices of
primary products, one of the extreme features of this slump, gave
appreciable compensation for the contraction of the world's
demand for U.K. products.[1] The balance of payments for the
sterling area as a whole must, however, have fared much worse;
the peculiar relief to Britain as an importer had its counterpart
in falling values of the exports of the Rest-of-the-Sterling-Area
not only to Britain itself but also to the non-sterling countries.
As the centre of the Sterling Area London therefore found that
the relief from the Wall Street crash all too soon gave way to
persistent weakness in the reserve position. Even so, 1930 was
survived, and at the beginning of May 1931 the Bank of England still felt strong enough to participate in a concerted international move to reduce interest rates. But that did prove the
last flicker of London's strength: the international liquidity
crisis, which was nothing to do with London's monetary policy,
was already bursting upon Central Europe and London's
financial involvement in Central Europe ensured a quick spread
of the crisis to London; and it was the development of this
movement that broke London's attempt to maintain the gold
standard. It is true that London's ability to withstand the crisis
was undermined by continuing (and justified) talk of the overvaluation of sterling; but it is very difficult to believe that

[1] A comparison of the 1930 with the 1929 figures shows that, despite a decline of
£182 million in visible exports, the net balance on income account deteriorated by
only £76 million and this was compensated to the extent of £11 million by a decline
in long-term lending. The figures for 1931 show the effect of the slump more fully,
but are distorted by the events (including anticipation of imports to avoid intended
import duties) of the latter half of the year. It seems likely that the continued heavy
decline in invisible net receipts had already created a net adverse balance on income account in the first half of 1931, though this balance could quite easily have
been compensated by the continued decline in long-term lending. All the available
figures are assembled in convenient form by T. C. Chang, *Cyclical Movements in the
Balance of Payments* (1951), table inset to face p. 144; and pt. ii of this book is the
best available discussion of these facts.

London would not have succumbed whether there had been overvaluation or not, especially when account is taken of the fact that there was an extreme American banking crisis just round the corner.

Thus, looking back I find it difficult to argue with any assurance that the 1931 collapse of the gold standard—and all that followed—was in any appreciable degree due to the overvaluation of sterling in 1925. If Churchill had accepted the 4.40 argument, we should still have had chronic depression in certain export trades, we should still have had the world slump and the international liquidity crisis, we should still have had the miseries of the 'thirties. It was basically the American trade cycle, and not British monetary policy, that made life so wretched for us.

My inclination is therefore to say that on the question of the valuation of sterling Churchill was fully advised, that the choice was made with substantial realization of the difficulties implied, and that the policy adopted was not substantially responsible for the major troubles of the next ten years. But that all refers to the *short-term* issue of the maladjustment in the international price situation. There was another issue, a long-term issue, that was not properly canvassed in 1925. This was the question whether London could, as a long-term policy, maintain a gold standard. (Keynes did just touch on it, but the question was generally neglected in controversy.) London's failure to maintain the gold standard in 1931 had no precedent before 1914 not because of the overvaluation but because of the fundamental change in London's position as an international financial centre. Before 1914 London had been able to survive the crises that followed each trade cycle explosion by pushing the main burden of adjustment on to other countries; since the first war it has not been strong enough to do this, and when a veritable cyclone came in 1931 it was inevitable that the international gold standard should break down. It was this long-term risk, rather than the short-term risk of maladjustment, that was not taken properly into account in 1925.

And the reason for this omission is quite simple. In the years between 1918 and 1925 people had too often said that London's financial strength before 1914 was due to the gold standard.

The Return to Gold, 1925

The truth was rather that the strength of the gold standard was due to London's international financial position. A little more systematic study of monetary history might have been useful in 1925, as well as now. I do not imply that a proper consideration of this point would have led to a different choice, nor that a different policy would have been better. The case for exchange stability for sterling in 1925 was very strong. But I do suggest that a fuller understanding of the past would have led to a proper appreciation of the long-term as well as the short-term risks, and more moderate hopes would at least have checked the revulsion against the gold standard, a revulsion that inhibited any reasonable degree of international monetary co-operation in the 'thirties.

Bibliography of Academic Writings
of T. S. Ashton

I. Books

1924 *Iron and Steel in the Industrial Revolution.* (Manchester. University of Manchester Publications. No. 164.) Second edition, 1951 (Manchester. University of Manchester Publications, Economic History Series, No. 2).

1929 (With J. Sykes) *The Coal Industry of the Eighteenth Century.* (Manchester. University of Manchester Publications. Economic History Series, No. 5.)

1934 *Economic and Social Investigations in Manchester, 1833–1933: A Centenary History of the Manchester Statistical Society* (London).

1939 *An Eighteenth-Century Industrialist: Peter Stubs of Warrington, 1756–1806.* (Manchester. University of Manchester Publications. No. 266.)

1948 *The Industrial Revolution, 1760–1830.* (The Home University Library, 204. London.)

1950 Editor, *Letters of a West African Trader, Edward Grace, 1767–70.* (Business Archives Council Publications, No. 1. London.)

1953 (joint editor with R. S. Sayers) *Papers in English Monetary History* (Oxford), including reprint of 'The Bill of Exchange and Private Banks in Lancashire, 1790–1830', from *Ec.H.R.*, xv, Nos. 1 and 2, 1945.

1955 *An Economic History of England: The Eighteenth Century.* (London.)

1959 *Economic Fluctuations in England, 1700–1800.* (Oxford: The Clarendon Press) (Based on the Ford Lectures for 1953.)

II. Articles and Lectures

1914 (With Professor S. J., later Sir Sydney, Chapman), 'The Size of Businesses, mainly in the Textile Industries.' (*Journ. Roy. Stat. Soc.* New ser., vol. lxxvii, 1913–14, pp. 469–549.)

1916 'The Relation between Unemployment and Sickness.' (*E.J.*, vol. 26, 1916, pp. 396–400.)

Bibliography of Academic Writings of T. S. Ashton

1920 'Early Price Associations in the British Iron Industry.' (*E.J.*, vol. 30, 1920, pp. 331–9.)

1924 'The Discoveries of the Darbys of Coalbrookdale.' (*Trans. Newcomen Soc.*, vol. v, 1924–5, pp. 9–14.)

1925 'The Records of a Pin Manufactory, 1814–22.' (*Economica*, vol. v, no. 15, 1925, pp. 281–92.)

1926 'The Growth of Textile Businesses in the Oldham District, 1884–1924.' (*Journ. Roy. Stat. Soc.* New ser., vol. lxxxix, pt. iii, 1926, pp. 567–83.)

1926 'The Domestic System in the Early Lancashire Tool Trade.' (*E.H.*, vol. i, 1926–9, pp. 131–40.)

1928 'The Coal Miners of the 18th Century.' (*E.H.*, vol. i, pp. 307–34.)

1929 (With Professor G. W. Daniels), 'The Records of a Derbyshire Colliery, 1763–1779.' (*Ec.H.R.*, vol. ii, 1929–30, pp. 124–9.)

1930 'Fluctuations in Savings Bank Deposits.' (*Trans. Manchester Stat. Soc.*, *1929–30*.)

1931 'The Origin of "The Manchester School".' (*M.S.*, vol. i, 1930–1, pp. 22–27.)

1932 'Population and Industry in Lancashire before 1921', in U.K., Board of Trade, 1932, *An Industrial Survey of the Lancashire Area (Excluding Merseyside) made for the Board of Trade by the University of Manchester*, Part ii, chap. i, pp. 47–70.

1934 'Studies in Bibliography. iii, The Industrial Revolution.' (*Ec.H.R.*, vol. v, 1934–5, pp. 104–19.) Subsequently published in pamphlet form by the Economic History Society.

1945 'The Bill of Exchange and Private Banks in Lancashire, 1790–1830.' (*Ec.H.R.*, vol. xv, 1945, nos. 1 and 2). Reprinted in T. S. Ashton and R. S. Sayers (ed.), *Papers in English Monetary History* (Oxford, 1953.)

1946 Inaugural Lecture, 'The Relation of Economic History to Economic Theory.' (*Economica*. New ser., vol. xiii, 1946, pp. 81–95.)

1948 'The Industrial Past.' (*In* Institute of Bankers, *The Industrial Future of Great Britain*, London, 1948.)

1948 'Some Statistics of the Industrial Revolution in Britain.' (*M.S.*, vol. xvi, 1948, pp. 214–24. Also printed in *Trans. Manch. Stat. Soc.*, 1947–8.)

1949 'Recent Trends in the Writing of Economic History in the United Kingdom.' (*J.E.H.*, vol. ix, 1949, pp. 263–6.)

1949 'The Standard of Life of the Workers in England, 1790–1830.'

(*J.E.H.*, vol. ix, 1949, Supplement, pp. 19–38.) Reprinted in F. A. Hayek (ed.), *Capitalism and the Historians* (London, 1954), pp. 127–59.

1951 'The Treatment of Capitalism by Historians', in Hayek, *Capitalism and the Historians*, pp. 33–63.

1955 *The Raleigh Lecture*, 'Changes in the Standard of Comfort in Eighteenth-Century England'. (*Proceedings of the British Academy*, vol. xli, 1955, pp. 171–87.)

1957 'A Note on George Unwin', in G. Unwin, *Industrial Organization in the Sixteenth and Seventeenth Centuries* (Oxford, 1904, reprinted London, 1957).

1958 Introduction to Paul Mantoux, *La Revolution Industrielle au XVIIIe Siecle* (First edition Paris, 1906, new edition Paris, 1958).

1958 'Business Hissory.' (*Business History*, vol. i, no. 1, Dec. 1958, pp. 1–2).

iii. Reviews

1924 J. Lord, *Capital and Steam Power, 1750–1800* (London, 1924), *E.J.*, vol. 34, 1924, pp. 617–20.

1926 H. Hamilton, *The English Brass and Copper Industries to 1800* (London, 1926), *E.J.*, vol. 36, 1926, pp. 495–7.

1928 W. A. Shaw, *Currency, Credit and the Exchanges (1924–26)* (London, 1927), *E.J.*, vol. 38, 1928, pp. 109–11.

1928 Rev. Walter Goodliffe, *Credit and Currency, National and International* (London, 1927), *E.J.*, vol. 38, 1928, pp. 111–12.

1930 G. C. Allen, *The Industrial Development of Birmingham and the Black Country, 1860–1927* (London, 1929), *E.J.*, vol. 40, 1930, pp. 269–71.

1930 L. C. A. Knowles and C. M. Knowles, *The Economic Development of the Overseas Empire*, vol. 2 (London, 1930), *E.J.*, vol. 40, 1930, pp. 475–7.

1930 A. Birnie, *An Economic History of Europe, 1760–1930* (London, 1930), *E.J.*, vol. 40, 1930, pp. 691–2.

1930 W. J. Warner, *The Wesleyan Movement in the Industrial Revolution* (London, 1930), *E.J.*, vol. 40, 1930, pp. 695–6.

1931 R. M. Haig, *The Public Finances of Post-War France* (New York, 1930), *M.S.*, vol. i, no. 2, 1930–1, pp. 46–48.

1931 I. Grubb, *Quakerism and Industry before 1800* (London, 1930), *Ec.H.R.*, vol. iii, 1931–2, pp. 170–1.

Bibliography of Academic Writings of T. S. Ashton

1931 J. L. and Barbara Hammond, *The Age of the Chartists: A Study in Discontent, 1832–54* (London, 1930), *E.J.*, vol. 41, 1931, pp. 126–8.

1931 E. Roll, *An Early Experiment in Industrial Organization: A History of the Firm of Boulton and Watt, 1775–1805* (London, 1930), *E.J.*, vol. 41, 1931, pp. 484–6.

1931 A. L. Dunham, *The Anglo-French Treaty of Commerce of 1860, and the Progress of the Industrial Revolution in France* (University of Michigan Press, 1930), *E.J.*, vol. 41, 1931, pp. 489–91.

1932 E. Lipson, *The Economic History of England, Vols. ii and iii, The Age of Mercantilism* (Edinburgh, 1931), *Economica*, vol. 12, no. 1, 1932, pp. 486–7.

1932 A. P. Wadsworth and Julia de L. Mann, *The Cotton Trade and Industrial Lancashire, 1600–1780* (Manchester, 1931), *M.S.*, vol. iii, no. 1, 1932, pp. 59–62.

1932 A. E. Feavearyear, *The Pound Sterling: A History of English Money* (Oxford, 1931), *E.J.*, vol. 42, 1932, pp. 81–83.

1932 N. S. B. Gras, *Industrial Evolution* (Oxford, 1930), *E.J.*, vol. 42, 1932, pp. 100–101.

1932 D. T. Jack, *Currency and Banking* (London, 1932), *E.J.*, vol. 42, 1932, p. 441.

1932 G. D. H. Cole, *British Trade and Industry, Past and Future* (London, 1932), *E.J.*, vol. 42, 1932, pp. 462–4.

1932 E. Roll, *An Early Experiment in Industrial Organization: A History of the Firm of Boulton and Watt, 1775–1805* (London, 1930), *Ec.H.R.*, vol. ix, 1932–4, pp. 120–1.

1933 Arthur Young, *Tours in England and Wales*, No. 14 in Series of Reprints of Scarce Tracts in Economics and Political Science. London School of Economics and Political Science (London, 1932), *Economica*, vol. 13, 1933, pp. 99–101.

1933 C. R. Fay, *The Corn Laws and Social England* (Cambridge, 1932), *E.J.*, vol. 43, 1933, pp. 477–9.

1933 P. B. Whale, *International Trade* (Home University Library, London, 1932), *E.J.*, vol. 43, 1933, pp. 498–9.

1933 J. W. Gough, *The Mines of Mendip* (Oxford, 1930), *Ec.H.R.*, vol. iv, 1932–4, pp. 363–4.

1934 D. Knoop and G. P. Jones, *The Mediaeval Mason. An Economic History of English Stone Building in the Later Middle Ages and Early Modern Times* (Manchester, 1933), *M.S.*, vol. v, no. 1, 1934, pp. 86–7.

1936 E. W. Gilboy, *Wages in Eighteenth-Century England* (Harvard 1934), *E.H.*, vol. iii, 1934–7, pp. 314–16.

Bibliography of Academic Writings of T. S. Ashton

1938 J. H. (later Sir John) Clapham, *An Economic History of Modern Britain, III. Machines and National Rivalries* (Cambridge, 1938), *M.S.*, vol. ix, 1938, pp. 110–13.

1938 R. S. Sayers, *Modern Banking* (Oxford, 1938), *M.S.*, vol. ix, 1938, pp. 186–8.

1939 D. H. MacGregor, *Public Aspects of Finance* (Oxford, 1938), *M.S.*, vol. x, 1939, pp. 87–90.

1940 Rhys Jenkins, *The Collected Papers of Rhys Jenkins* (printed for the Newcomen Society, Cambridge, 1936), *Ec.H.R.*, vol. x, 1940, pp. 178–9.

1940 H. W. Dickinson, *A Short History of the Steam Engine* (Cambridge, 1939), *Ec.H.R.*, vol. x, 1940, pp. 178–9.

1943 D. L. Burn, *The Economic History of Steelmaking, 1870–1939* (Cambridge, 1940, *Ec.H.R.*, vol. xiii, 1943, pp. 126–7.

1943 R. D. Best, *Brass Chandelier: A Biography of R. H. Best* of *Birmingham* (London, 1940), *Ec. H.R.*, vol. xiii, 1943, p. 138.

1944 G. M. Trevelyan, *English Social History* (London, 1944), *Ec. H.R.*, vol. xiv, 1944–5, pp. 191–3.

1945 Sir John Clapham, *The Bank of England: A History* (Cambridge, 1944, 2 vols.), *E.J.*, vol. 55, 1945, pp. 261–5.

1947 G. N. (later Sir George), Clark, *The Wealth of England from 1496 to 1760* (Home University Library, London, 1946), *Economica*, New ser., vol. 14, 1947, pp. 226–7.

1950 M. Morris, *From Cobbett to the Chartists: Extracts from Contemporary Sources* (London, 1948), *History*, vol. 35, 1950, pp. 163–4.

1950 R. W. Hidy, *The House of Baring in American Trade and Finance* (Harvard, 1949), *Ec.H.R.*, New ser., vol. 3, 1950, pp. 143–4.

1951 Sir William Ashley, *The Economic Organization of England* (3rd edition, with three supplementary chapters by G. C. Allen, London, 1949), *History*, vol. 36, 1951, pp. 278–9.

1951 *John Maynard Keynes, 1883–1946* (Cambridge, 1948), *History*, vol. 36, 1951, p. 279.

1951 *John Harold Clapham, 1873–1946* (Cambridge, 1948), *History*, vol. 36, 1951, p. 279.

1951 R. Pares, *A West-India Fortune* (London, 1950), *Ec.H.R.*, 2nd ser., vol. 4, 1951–2, pp. 123–4.

1951 (Review article) D. H. (later Sir Denis) Robertson, *A Study of Industrial Fluctuation* (London, 1915.) Series of Reprints of Scarce Works on Political Economy, No. 8. Reprinted by the London School of Economics and Political Science, London, 1948. Review entitled 'Industrial Fluctuation', *Economica*, New ser., vol. xviii, 1951, pp. 298–302.

1951 Charles Hadfield, *British Canals, an Illustrated History* (London, 1950), *E.J.*, vol. 61, 1951, pp. 409–10.
1955 (Review article). A. D. Gayer, W. W. Rostow, Anna J. Schwartz (with the assistance of Isaiah Frank), *The Growth and Fluctuation of the British Economy, 1790–1850* (Oxford, 1953, 2 vols.). Review entitled, 'Essays in Bibliography and Criticism, xxx, Economic Fluctuations, 1790–1850', *Ec.H.R.* 2nd ser., vol. vii, 1954–5, pp. 377–81.
1955 Edward Hughes, *North Country Life in the Eighteenth Century. The North-East, 1700–1750* (Oxford, 1952), *Eng. Hist. Rev.*, vol. lxx, 1955, pp. 455–7.
1957 Eli F. Hecksher, *An Economic History of Sweden* (Harvard, 1956), *The Scandinavian Econ. Hist. Rev.*, vol. v, 1957–8, pp. 82–85.

iv. Articles and Review Articles in *The Manchester Guardian*

1933 11 October: 'A Hundred Years of Service. Centenary of the Manchester Statistical Society.'
1935 19 June: 'Joint-Stock Banking in and around Manchester. A record of its first beginnings.'
1936 13 February: 'Banking. A Chapter of Social History.' (Review of W. F. Crick and J. E. Wadsworth, *A Hundred Years of Joint Stock Banking*.)
1936 24 February: 'Mr Keynes Bombards a Citadel.' (Review of J. M. Keynes, *The General Theory of Employment, Interest and Money*.)
1938 16 May (Civic Centenary Supplement): 'A Century of Commerce and Industry.'
1943 2 September: 'The Economist. The Centenary of a Great Weekly.' (Review of *The Economist, 1843–1943*. A Centenary Volume.)
1946 26 June: 'The Repeal of the Corn Laws.'
1951 25 May: 'The Founders of Owens College.'
1956 5 November: 'A. P. Wadsworth as an Economic Historian.' (Reprinted in *The Bedside Guardian* (6), 1957, pp. 247–9.)

Index

Index

Index

Index

Earle, Giles, M.P., 68, 79, 89–90
Earnings, of weavers, 89–93; of hewers, 227; *see also* Wages
Earthenware, 261, 277, 278; *see also* Potteries, Staffordshire
East Anglia, 134
East India Company, 82, 180; territories' trade with U.K., 256, 257; *see also* India bonds
East Indies, British, 244
Economist, The, 315, 319
Edinburgh 153
Edwards, Lewis, 45
Egmont, Earl of, 189–90, 193–4
Ekman, G., 62; furnace, 63
Elasticity, in agricultural demand, 128; in supply, 130
Elswick, 222
Elton, John, 30
Embezzlement, 89
Emigration of skilled men, 285, 287, 288, 289, 293–4
Enclosures, 98, 99, 100, 101, 125, 130, 146, 147, 148 n., 149; finance of, 176, 177; interest rates and, 194–5; Leicestershire, 100 n., 149, 194–5; Nottingham, 99, 102, 107; old, 132; parliamentary, 153, 154
Engineering, waterway, 1–22
Engineers, colliery, 221; evidence to Select Committee (1824), 288; London, 282; provincial, 282; textile, 283
'English principle' of yarn manufacture, 284
Entrepreneurs, and borrowing, 201; in coal industry, 227; in Swedish iron industry, 53, 54, 55, 56, 61, 64; in Wiltshire cloth industry, 87–8
Epidemics, 110, 113, 115, 118, 119, 121, 124
Erddig Park, 34
Esclusham, 34, 36, 37
Essex, 27, 128, 131, 142
Essones, 287
Eton, wheat prices at, 134, 135, 137, 141
Evan, Abraham, and William, 45
Evans & Co. of Derby, 196, 200–1
Eversley, D.E.C., cit., 98 n., 114 n., 116 n.
Exchange competition, 322
Exchange fluctuations, 318
Exchange, rates of, 159, 161, 166

Exchange rigidity, 315
Exchange stability, case for in 1925, 327; *see also* Currency stabilization
Exchanges, foreign, 173, 314, 318
Exchequer bills, *see* Bills
Exeter, 134 n., 137, 141, 202–3
Expectations, 204, 208, 209, 210
Export industries and markets, and the return to gold, 317–19, 321–3, 326
Exports, British, 177, 236–80, 324; coal, 71, 72; English to Ireland, 155; grain from England, 152 n.; overvaluation of sterling and, 321–2; world, 322–3
Eyles, John, 19 n., 20

Fairbairn, Peter, 283, 284; tow dressing machines, 285, 302
Fallow land, 130
Falmouth, 127
Famine, 138
Fatstock, 126; *see also* Cattle
Featherstonehaugh & Co., 223, 224
Federation of British Industries and return to gold, 315, 316; evidence to Macmillan Committee, 316 n., 319 n.; *see also* Businessmen
Felkin, William, 109
Fell, A., 27, 28, 29
Fell, Stephen, cit., 26
Fens, 150
Fenwick & Co., 226
Fiennes, Celia, cit., 107
Filkes, *see* Yerbury & Filkes
Fillmore, President, 256 n.
Finlay, Kirkman, 263
Flannels, 265 n., 266
Flax, 255, 283, 284
Fletcher, John, 11
Floating debt, *see* Bills, Government securities
Flour, 246, 248, 249
Fluctuations of trade, 243, 255, 279; *see also* Crises, Crisis
Fodder crops, 130, 131, 132
Food, riots, 11, 117, 153; shortages, 117; supplies, 109, 111; *see also* Prices
Foodstuffs, import from U.S.A., 279
Footrot, 134, 142, 143, 144
Foster, James, 219
Four per cent funds, 165; *see also* Government securities

339

Index

Index

Index

Melksham, 72, 73, 80, 84, 89, 94; *see also* Clothiers
Menai, Straits of, 21 n.
Mersey, R., 5, 14, 15, 19
Merthyr Canaid, 45
Merthyr Tydfil, 42, 43, 44, 45, 58
Merzagora, Defilipi & Co. of Arona, 295
Metal industries, 234
Middlesex, 184 n.
Middleton, Lord, 102
Milbanke, Sir Ralph, 225, 226
Milk prices, London, 145
Milling, roller, 30
Mines, *see* Collieries
Mines and Collieries Act (1872), 231
Mingay, G. E., cit., 150, 151
Money, demand for, 204; flexibility in supply, 179, 204; scarce in 1726, 68
Money market, 156-77, 179, 184, 195
Monkwearmouth, 220
Montargis, 286, 291
Moreau, E., 321
Mortgages, aristocratic borrowing on, 176; competition with other assets, 195; difficulties in borrowing on, 170, 175, 184; foreclosure prevented during Seven Years war, 183; lending on, 168, 186; loans on, 157; market, 176, 187
Mortgages, interest rates on, 164, 210; flexibility, 180; Hoare's bank, 163, 168, 173; importance of, 187, 193; variable, 187-90
Mortimer, Thomas, cit., 171, 207-8

Nantwich, 6
National debt, conversion operations, 180, 205-6; interest on, 180, 205-6; management of, 180; *see also* Bills, Government securities
Napped coatings, 266
Navigations, *see* Canal and river navigations
Navy bills, *see* Bills,
Near-money assets, 181
Netherhall furnace, 41
Netherlands investment in Swedish iron industry, 52; *see also* Dutch, Holland
Nevill, Captain, F., 7
New Orleans 249
New York, 249, 264 n.
Newark, 153, 155

Newcastle, balance of payments, 148; coal prices, 227; financial centre, 202; lead trade, 182 n., 200
Newcastle, Duke of, 103, 106, 167
Newcomen engine, 38
Newry, and canal, 6-11
Newspapers, provincial, 127
Niemeyer, Sir Otto, 317
Norfolk, 127, 131, 132, 135, 146 n., 147, 148
Norman, Montagu, 315, 319 n.
North, Lord, 172
North America, British, U.K. trade with, 244, 256, 257
Northamptonshire, 143
Northumberland, coalfield, 220, 221; rents, 133
Northwich, 17
Nottingham, baptisms, 98 n., 110, 121, 123, 124; birth rates, 117, 119, 120, 122, 124; births, 98 n., 110, 119, 121; burgesses, 99, 101-2; burials, 110, 114, 121, 123, 124; child burials, 114, 123; child death rates, 116, 120, 122, 124; child deaths, 98 n., 114, 115, 121, 124; Corporation, 99, 105, 106, 111, 113, 115, 117, 118, 120; death rates, 110, 115, 116, 117, 118, 119, 120, 121, 122, 124; deaths, 98, 110, 113, 114, 115, 117, 119, 121; enclosure, 99, 102, 107; General Hospital, 118 n., 119; immigration into, 100, 116, 122, 124; marriage rates, 116-17, 119, 122, 124; marriages, 98 n., 121, 123, 124; riot act read, 111, 120, steam factories, 116; town improvements, 99, 105; water supply, 106, 118, 120
Nottingham lace and lacemakers, 282, 289
Nottinghamshire, 186
Notes, discounting of, 157
Notes of hand, 68
Nystadt, Peace of, 131 n.

Oats, 129; prices, 133, 134, 135, 136, 138, 139, 140, 225; *see also under other grains*
Oatmeal, 135
Old Bersham Company, 34
Oldknow, Samuel, 196
Onions, Peter, 23
Openfield farming, 134, 148

Index

Index

Index

Parliament, 17–18; reported open, 18; shares, 16; survey of, 18–19
Schloss, D. F., cit., 215, 218
Schumpeter, Mrs. E. B. cit., 166
Scotland, 312; arable cultivation, 154; banking crisis (1761–2), 170; cattle, 142; grain production, 132; and London market, 128
Seedcake oil, 253
Severn valley, 127
Sheep, 141, 142, 143, 144, 146, 153
Sheffield, 56, 59, 60, 61, 63, 239, 273
Shepton Mallet, 93
Sherwin, John, 103
Shipbuilding, 234, 317
Shoddy-makers, 283
Shrewsbury, 43
Shropshire, 24, 35, 36, 42, 43, 44
Sigsworth, E. M., cit., 304
Silk industry, 253, 281–312; exports to U.S.A., 261, 276, 277; waste-silk, 284 285, 286, 306
Simple, William, 10
Skins, 253
Slump, of war of American independence, 120; after first world war, 317; Wall Street, 324–5; world, 326
Smallpox, 113, 115 n., 118 n., 121
Smith, Adam, 181
Smith, George (banker), 104
Smith, W. Hawkes, cit., 50
Smithfield, 144, 145, 146 n.
Smuggling, 242 n., 282
Snowden, Philip, 315 n.
Soil, and agriculture, 131, 132, 134, 149, 151, 154
Somerset, 126
Sorocold, George, 4
South Sea company, 180; stock, 189; 190
Spain, 58, 67, 160, 166–7
Sparke forge, 33
Spermaceti oil, 253
Spinning, in Nottingham, 112; in Wiltshire, 88, 90, 92, 93; machinery, 87
Spring-grown grains, 134
Stamp, Sir Josiah, 315–16
Staffordshire, 36, 130; coal industry, 215, 216, 231 n., export of products to U.S.A., 240 n., 278; see also Earthenware
Staves, British import of, 253

Steel, blister, 59; crucible, 59; shear, 59; Sheffield, 56, 59, 60, 61, 63; Swedish, 56, 59; unwrought, British exports of, 272–4; German products, 273; see also Iron, Iron and Steel industry
Steers, Thomas, and Douglas navigation, 6; Liverpool dock engineer, 6; Liverpool harbour improvements, 11; mayor of Liverpool, 9; Mersey and Irwell surveyed, 5; Newry canal, 8–9; 11; at Rotherhithe, 5; and Weaver navigation, 6
Stephens, W. B., cit., 3 n.
Sterling, 315, 321, 322, 325–6, 327
Stevenson, Mr., 27
Stock breeding, 151
Stock Exchange, 325
Stock feeding, 130
Stock jobbing, 204
Stockdale, James, cit., 27, 29, 30, 31, 33
Stocking frame, 184
Stocking manufacture, 111–12; cotton 264; woollen and worsted, 266, 267, 269
Stocks of grain, and prices, 140
Stout, William, 138, 185
Strutt, Jedediah, 111, 119, 184, 196–7
Strutts, the, 201
Stubs, Peter, 183
Subscription to the Circulation, 161
Suffolk, 126, 127, 128, 131; butter prices, 145
Sunderland, 224
Surrey, 48, 127, 149
Sussex, 138 n.
Swamp Mill, 292–3, 310
Sweden, iron industry: costs, 54, 57, 61–2, 63; Ekman furnace, 62, 63; entrepreneurial organization, 53, 54, 55, 56, 61, 64; exports, 56, 58, 59, 60; 'German process', 61; investment from abroad, 52; iron ore sources, 53, 61; 'Lancashire process', 62–4; markets retained, 64–5; output of works determined by charcoal supply, 54; output largely exported, 51; re-exports by Britain, 60, 63; restrictions, 56; Russian competition, 57, 58; U.S.A., importance of trade with, 58–9; 'Walloon process', 61
Switching of assets, by bank customers,

347

Index